THE GREENWOOD ENCYCLOPEDIA OF

ROCK HISTORY

The Greenwood Encyclopedia of Rock History

Volume 1
The Early Years, 1951–1959
Lisa Scrivani-Tidd

Volume 2
Folk, Pop, Mods, and Rockers, 1960–1966
Rhonda Markowitz

Volume 3
The Rise of Album Rock, 1967–1973
Chris Smith

Volume 4
From Arenas to the Underground, 1974–1980
Chris Smith with John Borgmeyer, Richard Skanse, and Rob Patterson

Volume 5
The Video Generation, 1981–1990
MaryAnn Janosik

Volume 6
The Grunge and Post-Grunge Years, 1991–2005
Bob Gulla

THE GREENWOOD ENCYCLOPEDIA OF
ROCK HISTORY

Folk, Pop, Mods, and Rockers,
1960–1966

RHONDA MARKOWITZ

GREENWOOD PRESS
Westport, Connecticut • London

Library of Congress Cataloging-in-Publication Data

The Greenwood encyclopedia of rock history.
    p.   cm.
    Includes bibliographical references and index.
    ISBN 0–313–32937–0 ((set) : alk. paper)—ISBN 0–313–32938–9 ((vol. 1) : alk. paper)—ISBN
0–313–32960–5 ((vol. 2) : alk. paper)—ISBN 0–313–32966–4 ((vol. 3) : alk. paper)—ISBN
0–313–33611–3 ((vol. 4) : alk. paper)—ISBN 0–313–32943–5 ((vol. 5) : alk. paper)—ISBN
0–313–32981–8 ((vol. 6) : alk. paper)   1. Rock music—History and criticism.
    ML3534.G754   2006
    781.66'09—dc22   2005023475

British Library Cataloguing in Publication Data is available.

This book is included in the *African American Experience* database from Greenwood Electronic
Media. For more information, visit www.africanamericanexperience.com.

Library of Congress Catalog Card Number: 2005023475
ISBN 0–313–32937–0 (set)
        0–313–32938–9 (vol. 1)
        0–313–32960–5 (vol. 2)
        0–313–32966–4 (vol. 3)
        0–313–33611–3 (vol. 4)
        0–313–32943–5 (vol. 5)
        0–313–32981–8 (vol. 6)

First published in 2006

Greenwood Press, 88 Post Road West, Westport, CT 06881
An imprint of Greenwood Publishing Group, Inc.
www.greenwood.com

Printed in the United States of America

The paper used in this book complies with the
Permanent Paper Standard issued by the National
Information Standards Organization (Z39.48–1984).

10 9 8 7 6 5 4 3 2 1

CONTENTS

 SET FOREWORD

Rock 'n' roll, man, it changed my life. It was like the Voice of America, the real America, coming to your home.

—Bruce Springsteen[1]

The term *rock 'n' roll* has a mysterious origin. Many have credited legendary disc jockey Alan Freed for coining the term. Some claim that it was actually a blues euphemism for sexual intercourse, while others even see the term rock as having gospel origin, with worshippers "rocking" with the Lord. In 1947, DeLuxe Records released "Good Rocking Tonight," a blues-inspired romp by Roy Brown, which touched off a number of R&B artists in the late-1940s providing their own take on "rocking." But many music historians point to the 1951 Chess single "Rocket 88" as the first rock record. Produced by Sam Phillips and performed by Jackie Brenston and Ike Turner's Kings of Rhythm (though released under the name Jackie Brenston & His Delta Cats), the record established the archetype of early rock and roll: "practically indecipherable lyrics about cars, booze, and women; [a] booting tenor sax, and a churning, beat-heavy rhythmic bottom."[2]

Although its true origins are debatable, what is certain is that rock 'n' roll grew into a musical form that, in many ways, defined American culture in the second half of the twentieth century. Today, however, "rock 'n' roll" is used with less and less frequency in reference to the musical genre. The phrase seems to linger as a quaint cliché co-opted by mass media—something that a *Top Gun* pilot once said in voicing high-speed, mid-air glee. Watching MTV these days, one would be hard-pressed to find a reference to "rock 'n' roll," but the term *rock* survives, though often modified by prefixes used to denote the growing hybridization of the genre: There is alternative rock, blues rock, chick rock, classic rock, folk rock, funk rock, garage rock, glam rock, grunge rock, hard rock, psychedelic rock, punk rock, roots rock, and countless other sub-genres of rock music. It seems that musicians found more and more ways to rock but, for some reason, stopped rolling—or to paraphrase Led Zeppelin's "Stairway to Heaven," the music world opted to rock, but not to roll.

Call it what you will, rock music has never existed within a vacuum; it has always reflected aspects of our society, whether it be the statement of youth culture or rebellion against adult society; an expression of love found, lost, or never had; the portrayal of gritty street life or the affirmation of traditional American values; the heady pondering of space-age metaphysics or the giddy nonsense of a one-hit wonder, rock music has been an enduring voice of the people for over five decades. *The Greenwood Encyclopedia of Rock History* records not only the countless manifestations of rock music in our society, but also the many ways in which rock music has shaped, and been shaped by, American culture.

Testifying to the enduring popularity of rock music are the many publications devoted to covering rock music. These range from countless single-volume record guides providing critics' subjective ratings to the multi-volume sets that lump all forms of popular music together, discussing the jazz-rock duo Steely Dan in the same breath as Stravinsky, or indie-rock group Pavement with Pavarotti. To be sure, such references have their value, but we felt that there was no authoritative work that gives rock music history the thorough, detailed examination that it merits. For this reason, our six-volume encyclopedia focuses closely on the rock music genre. While many different forms of rock music are examined, including the *influences* of related genres such as folk, jazz, soul, or hip-hop, we do not try to squeeze in discussions of other genres of music. For example, a volume includes the influences of country music on rock—such as folk rock or "alt.country"—but it does not examine country music itself. Thus, *rock music* is not treated here as synonymous with *popular music*, as our parents (or our parents' parents) might have done, equating whatever forms of music were on the charts, whatever the "young kids" were listening to, as basically all the same, with only a few differences, an outsiders' view of rock, one that viewed the genre fearfully and from a distance. Instead, we present a six-volume set—one that is both "meaty" and methodical—from the perspective of the rock music historians who provide narrative chapters on the many different stories during more than five decades of rock music history.

The Greenwood Encyclopedia of Rock History comprises six information-packed volumes covering the dizzying evolution of this exciting form of music. The volumes are divided by historical era: *Volume 1: The Early Years, 1951–1959*, spans from the year "Rocket 88" (arguably the first rock single) was released to the year of the infamous "Day the Music Died," the fatal airplane crash that took the lives of Buddy Holly, Ritchie Valens, and J. P. Richardson (a.k.a. The Big Bopper). *Volume 2: Folk, Pop, Mods, and Rockers, 1960–1966,* covers the period when the British Invasion irrevocably changed the world, while such American rock scenes as Motown and surf rock held their own. In *Volume 3: The Rise of Album Rock, 1967–1973*, Chris Smith chronicles the growing experimentation during the psychedelic era of rock, from *Sgt. Pepper* to *Dark Side of the Moon* and everything in between. In *Volume 4: From Arenas to the Underground, 1974–1980*, Smith et al., record how rock became big business while also spawning hybrid forms and underground movements. *Volume 5: The Video Generation, 1981–1990* starts with the year of MTV's debut and captures the era when video threatened to kill the radio star. Finally, in *Volume 6: The Grunge and Post-Grunge Years, 1991–2005*, Bob Gulla captures the many innovations of millennial rock music and culture. Within each volume, the narrative chapters are supplemented by a timeline, discography, bibliography, and a glossary of encyclopedia entries for quick reference.

We hope that librarians, researchers, and fans alike will find endless nuggets of information within this reference. And because we are talking about rock, we hope you will find that reading *The Greenwood Encyclopedia of Rock History* will be a whole lot of fun, too.

Rock on.

Rob Kirkpatrick
Greenwood Publishing Group

NOTES

1. Rock and Roll Hall of Fame and Museum home page, http://www.rockhall.com.
2. All Music Guide entry for Jackie Brenston, http://www.allmusic.com.

 **PREFACE**

I think the effects [of the 1960s] were very great, just on social terms. It's hard to remember just what that period was like, but I can assure you it was extremely different from now. There was attitude, things you take for granted now they wouldn't then: social values, the way people mix, racial segregation, sexual segregation and orientation, the opportunities people would or wouldn't have, class and money. And the list goes on.

—Mick Jagger[1]

I believe that the period 1960–1966 was, in a very real way, an early introduction to the twenty-first century. If Martin Luther King Jr., Malcolm X, or Berry Gordy had not existed, then where would Angela Davis, Tupac Shakur, Public Enemy, Russell Simmons, Diddy, or hip-hop have come from? Without Goldie and the Gingerbreads and Maureen Tucker, women musicians (in the Talking Heads, the Pretenders, Hole, Sonic Youth, and the White Stripes) would have had an even harder path. As Howlin' Wolf begat the Rolling Stones, so that group in turn fathered Aerosmith and many similar rock bands; without Bob Dylan, the road to protest music and/or lyrical self-determination would have been much longer. The events that took place during this time still shape and haunt us: the election and assassination of the first Roman Catholic president, the Vietnam War, the rise of the civil rights movement.

This is the period that saw the creation of women's liberation and the beginning of the free-your-mind-and-your-behind-will-follow concept. In 1964, visionary Marshall McLuhan's *Understanding Media* forecast the Internet and the idea of a "global village" where we would experience events on the other side of the Earth in real time: "Today, after more than a century of electric technology, we have extended our central nervous system itself in a global embrace, abolishing both space and time."[2]

When this series of volumes was proposed, this volume was the only one I wanted to write. Because I came of age during these years, I believe that almost everything now accepted as written in stone about rock and roll was first introduced here in a burst of pent-up youthful creativity still unmatched in quality and prolificness.

In talking to people younger than myself, I realized that many had heard of the Beatles and of the British invasion, but it meant very little to them. They might enjoy the music, but nothing can conjure up the context in which *we* first heard it—and context is all. They were not alive during the Eisenhower era and do not understand how gray the world appeared back in the 1950s; we did not know it ourselves until everything suddenly went into Technicolor overdrive. I was a "transistor sister" even before the Beatles, accompanied by a little radio both day and night (going to sleep with it inside the pillowcase, against parental edict). Too young to really appreciate Elvis, I was the perfect representative of Beatles demographics. I also believe that John Kennedy's assassination played a part; still sorrowing, we all needed to reaffirm life and the possibility of happiness, qualities offered in abundance by the lads from Liverpool.

When the Beatles came along, it was as if a broad highway of possibility had suddenly opened: a place to call home, where we might find a path of our own. Imagine the sense of freedom and potential belonging this offered, multiplied by the number of other kids growing up around the globe at this time, and you have a small idea of how this musical and cultural revolution affected the world. I hope that this book proves both edifying and enjoyable and causes the reader to seek out the music itself, for that is where the real story resides.

This volume's ten chapters cover the rise of the Beatles, the Rolling Stones, and other British artists, many inspired by American blues and rhythm and blues (R&B), as well as the artists who inspired the English, including those that recorded for Detroit's Motown label. It also examines how American pop music, previously ruled by songwriters, producers, and disc jockeys, responded to that "invasion"; the way folk music was revolutionized by Bob Dylan and his colleagues or competitors; the contribution of California's surf sound; the beginning of the "sex, drugs, and rock and roll" generation; and the manner in which popular media disseminated the new music.

Like the other volumes in *The Greenwood Encyclopedia of Rock History*, *Folk, Pop, Mods, and Rockers, 1960–1966* also includes an A-to-Z chapter that briefly defines the most important elements of this rock music era, including important performers, albums, managers, genres, and more. Other useful features of the book include a timeline of important events in rock music from 1960 through 1966, a discography of the top-selling recordings of the period, a discography of the most significant or influential albums of the period, and a resource guide to useful books, articles, Web sites, museums or special collections, and films. A comprehensive index provides access to the volume's contents.

NOTES

1. Mick Jagger as quoted in 1987 on the "Rolling Stones Way of Life, Part I: From WWII to the Sixties," http://www.timeisonourside.com/universe.html.

2. Marshall McLuhan, *Understanding Media: The Extensions of Man* (New York: McGraw-Hill, 1964), p. 3.

 # ACKNOWLEDGMENTS

I have been enormously fortunate in having friends and family who were un-stinting in their loving support, understanding, encouragement, ideas, advice, comfort, and/or nourishment of a material or spiritual nature during the writing of this volume. It would have been much more difficult without them, and I am truly grateful, as well as sincerely apologetic if anyone has somehow slipped through the net. I would like to thank Roz Black; Aaron and Bonnie Jaffe; Michael Shore; Dan Hedges; Danny Fields; Michael Musto; Philip Kamin; Yvonne Sewall-Ruskin, Jack Abbott, and the Max's Kansas City Project; Antone DeSantis and Holly Olchak; Claire O'Connor; Ed and Melani Rogers; Lenny Kaye; Steve Walter; Norena Barbella, Holly Cara Price, and "Little" Steven Van Zandt; Andrew Loog Oldham; Genya Ravan; Billy Altman; and Ken and Jane Dashow.

I have enormous respect for the musicians whose work has been inspiring. I have learned something of value from each one I ever admired, encountered, befriended, worked or lost patience with, loved or loathed.

Finally, I would like to dedicate this book to my late parents, Kate and Isadore (my dad could not foresee the future, or he might not have purchased those tickets to Shea Stadium); to the artists written about, especially the Beatles, for providing such wonderment, joy, and solace over the decades; and to anyone who was ever captivated by that *sound*, and became willing to follow wherever it might lead.

 **INTRODUCTION**

THE UNITED STATES AT THE BEGINNING OF THE '60s

As the calendar page flipped to January 1960, there was no outward indication that one of the most turbulent and divisive decades in American history had begun. Few paid much attention when the U.S. government announced in March that it was planning to send 3,500 troops to a tiny country in Indochina called Vietnam.

Although America was already involved in the cold war with the Soviet Union, it was also enjoying an unprecedented prosperity (excepting blacks, the poor, and the disenfranchised). There were a few rumblings of discontent: Some women who had worked during World War II were now bored as housewives; overstressed white-collar workers were using alcohol and tranquilizers to keep up with the demands placed upon them by bosses and wives; young men were subject to the draft; homosexuals and lesbians, banned from holding federal jobs by a 1953 presidential executive order, were kept under surveillance by the FBI and were subject to arrest, beatings, and worse. But those who were unhappy knew their place, and voices of dissent were not yet being heard. In a few short years, all that would change.

SUBURBIA AND THE BABY BOOM

World War II general and hero Dwight Eisenhower was serving his second term in the White House, and the world seemed a peaceful enough place, especially for those lucky citizens basking in postconflict prosperity. More than 75 million children, the so-called baby boom, were born between 1945 and 1964, and the eldest were already in or approaching adolescence in 1960. This bumper crop of infants contributed to an expanding consumer culture by creating a huge need for diapers, baby food, and schools. Furthermore, during the 1950s factory workers' paychecks had increased by a whopping 50 percent, making the so-called middle class a reality. In 1960, for the first time in U.S. history, a majority of high-school-age Americans actually graduated from high school. Veterans took advantage of the GI Bill to continue their education and secure low-interest mortgages.

The new found prosperity and the burgeoning families gave rise to the phenomenon of suburbia. Hordes of newly minted families fled rural outposts or cities. The latter population, intentionally or not, escaped their African American former neighbors, since the suburbs were mainly segregated communities. There was a concurrent boom in housing and related furnishings, in the building of highways and thoroughfares, and in automobiles. By 1960, some 30.5 percent of Americans, or 55 million of 180 million, lived in the suburbs.[1] This new lifestyle exacted a cost beyond the merely material: Surroundings were uniform, social life was homogenized, and conformity was encouraged, if not actually mandated. The men, many of whom had served in the military, were accustomed to regimentation. The transition from "soldier" to "company man" was relatively easy for such males, who were used to obeying orders. Their belief in authority and their pride in achieving material success left them poorly equipped to understand children who, in just a few years' time, would rebel against what they saw as a "plastic" society while protesting a war they felt was unjust.

Gender Roles

Women stayed home and raised children; men brought home the bacon. The new American middle class was a uniquely mid-twentieth-century innovation: Poorer females had always had to work outside the home, while their more affluent sisters ran households with the help of support staff. Now women, expected to make use of a new glut of laborsaving devices, were stranded in suburban split-level homes on their own. Husbands, with longer commutes, became almost absentee family members; wives, many of whom had been vital members of society while contributing to the war effort, were effectively isolated. After the upheaval of war, the suburban idyll seemed like a relief to many, but others were unhappy; women who had been forced out of jobs by returning soldiers saw their options shrink to wifedom and motherhood, period. These women were encouraged to believe that any discontent or career ambition was abnormal, and some were even given tranquilizers to help them cope.

Betty Friedan's protofeminist treatise *The Feminine Mystique*, published in 1963, helped identify this particular malaise. In the first chapter, "The Problem That Has No Name," Friedan wrote:

Millions of women lived their lives in the image of those pretty pictures of the American suburban housewife, kissing their husbands goodbye in front of the picture window, depositing their stationwagonsful of children at school, and smiling as they ran the new electric waxer over the spotless kitchen floor. . . . Words like "emancipation" and "career" sounded strange and embarrassing; no one had used them for years. . . . If a woman had a problem in the 1950s and 1960s, she knew that something must be wrong with her marriage, or with herself. Other women were satisfied with their lives, she thought. What kind of a woman was she if she did not feel this mysterious fulfillment waxing the kitchen floor? She was so ashamed to admit her dissatisfaction that she never knew how many other women shared it. If she tried to tell her husband, he didn't understand what she was talking about. She did not really understand it herself.[2]

These women's children, who would come of age in the '60s, sensed the unhappiness in their homes, and therefore many would eschew the conventional, exploring instead women's liberation, communal living, and "free love."

MEANWHILE, IN GREAT BRITAIN

In 1960, America's primary ally in World War II, England, was a quiet, civilized nation where men in quaint beaverskin hats stood watch over the palace of young Queen Elizabeth, who had just given birth to her third child. Earlier in the previous decade, around 1953, coffee bars had begun springing up in London's Soho district; despite the innocent-sounding name, these places were condemned as "dens of inquity" because they attracted existentialists and political activists, jazz players and their followers, and the earliest form of beatniks. They were usually furnished with espresso makers, little tables, a jukebox, and a central area for (illegal) dancing or small bands. Something of a nascent music scene was beginning to coalesce there.

While America was enjoying its post–World War II affluence, Britain had to struggle for the most minor luxuries. The country had sustained serious bomb damage during the Blitz, a fate the United States had escaped. Second, while America also had to deal with the rationing of food and other essentials during the war, this practice began in England in 1939 and did not end until 1954, nearly a full decade after the war's end (petrol—aka gasoline—was rationed for a year, from 1956 to 1957; coal, used for heating homes and other necessities, was also being rationed until that time).[3] In Great Britain, adults had been allowed a weekly allotment of three pints of milk, half a pound of sugar, three ounces of butter, one egg, four slices of bacon, three ounces of cheese, and two ounces of jam. Exotic imported foods such as bananas and oranges had disappeared, and chocolate and sweets were tightly controlled. The weedy, sunken-chested look of British rockers that affected a generation of American girls was a direct result of near starvation during their formative years. It was not until the 1970s that an American visitor would find much of what he or she was accustomed to at home over in England.

NOTES

1. Stanley K. Schultz, "American History 102: Civil War to the Present" (lecture, University of Wisconsin-Madison), http://us.history.wisc.edu/hist102/lectures/lecture24 .html.

2. Betty Friedan, "The Problem That Has No Name," *The Feminine Mystique*, as reproduced on H-Net: Humanities & Social Sciences Online, Michigan State University, http://www.h-net.org/~hst203/documents/friedan1.html.

3. Rationing was a system whereby a monthly booklet of coupons was issued to households; each coupon was redeemed on a strictly limited basis. In some cases, materials were not available at all, for example, silk, which was reserved for military use in parachutes and cord. In America during World War II, one pair of shoes was available to a family every three to four months; tennis shoes, or sneakers, were hard to find because they were rubber soled, and rubber was scarce during and after the war. Other clothes were also rationed, most severely in England: 66 points were supposed to last a year. A British newspaper produced this advice on how a woman might use them: 1 dress or dressing-gown or jacket (11); 2 pairs of shoes (10); 6 pairs of stockings (12); 1 nightdress, 1 lingerie set, 1 slip (13); 2 pairs of gloves (4); 1 jersey sweater, 1 cardigan (7); points held in reserve for an apron, scarf, or the like (8). More information on rationing is available at "WWII Ex-Raf Co. UK," http://www.worldwar2exraf.co.uk/ Online%20Museum/Museum%20Docs/clothing1.html.

TIMELINE: 1960–1966

1960

January 14:   Days after his twenty-fifth birthday, Elvis Presley is promoted to sergeant in the U.S. Army.

February 1:   Lunch-counter desegregation sit-ins begin in North Carolina and spread to other southern cities.

March 5:   Sgt. Elvis Presley is discharged.

April 17:   Eddie Cochran ("C'mon Everybody," "Summertime Blues"), age twenty-one, dies in a car crash in England; Gene Vincent, in the same car, is badly injured, as is Cochran's girlfriend, songwriter Sharon Sheeley.

April 20:   Elvis Presley arrives in Hollywood to begin filming *G.I. Blues*.

April 23:   Elvis Presley's "Stuck on You" hits No. 1 on the Cashbox Hot 100 singles chart and stays there until May 21.

May 7:   Sam Cooke's "(What a) Wonderful World" makes its debut on the singles chart (No. 70).

June 23:   Eddie Cochran's "Three Steps to Heaven" posthumously tops the British charts.

August 1:   The Beatles begin playing in the red-light district of Hamburg, Germany.

August 13:   Elvis Presley's "It's Now or Never" reaches No. 1.

September 10:   "The Twist" by Chubby Checker is No. 1.

September 26:   Presidential candidates John F. Kennedy and Richard Nixon participate in the first televised debates.

October 5:   Gerry and the Pacemakers make their first appearance at Liverpool's Cavern Club (as a supporting act).

October 19:   The Reverend Martin Luther King Jr. is jailed in Atlanta after a sit-in to desegregate lunch counters.

October 20:   Roy Orbison achieves his first No. 1 in England with "Only the Lonely."

November: Joan Baez, the sensation of the year's Newport Folk Festival, releases her eponymous first album.

November 1:   The Beatles return to Liverpool from Hamburg after their visas are revoked.

November 8:   John F. Kennedy is elected as both the youngest (at forty-three) and the first Roman Catholic president of the United States.

November 26:   Elvis Presley's "Are You Lonesome Tonight?" is No. 1.

Poet Allen Ginsberg takes psilocybin mushrooms under the supervision of Dr. Timothy Leary, phoning *On the Road* author Jack Kerouac (under the influence, he identifies himself to the operator as God) and actively promoting the use of psychedelic drugs.

December 17:   The Beatles play Liverpool's Casbah Club for the first time.

1961

January 20:   John F. Kennedy is inaugurated president; his inaugural address includes the memorable phrase "Ask not what your country can do for you; ask what you can do for your country."

January 28:   The Shirelles have a No. 1 hit with "Will You Love Me Tomorrow."

February 21:   The Beatles play their first "lunchtime" date at Liverpool's Cavern Club (12 noon–2 p.m.).

March 1:   President Kennedy issues an executive order to create the Peace Corps.

March 18:   Elvis Presley has another No. 1 with "Surrender."

March 21:   The Beatles play their first evening date at the Cavern Club.

April 12:   The Soviets launch Yuri Gagarin into outer space, the first man to breach the bonds of Earth.

April 22:   Del Shannon's "Runaway" begins a two-week run at the top of the charts.

May 5:   Alan Shepard becomes the first American to be sent into outer space, followed by Gus Grissom in July 21.

June 10:   Ricky Nelson's "Travelin' Man" hits No. 1.

July 14:   The Cavern Club holds a "welcome home" gig for the Beatles, returning from their second trip to Hamburg.

August: The three Wilson brothers (Brian, Dennis, and Carl), one cousin (Michael Love), and a schoolmate (Al Jardine) form the Beach Boys in Hawthorne, California.

August 15:   East Germany commences building the Berlin Wall.

October: Detroit's Motown Records, founded by Berry Gordy Jr., with the express idea of exposing R&B and pop to a broader white audience, has its first hit single with the Miracles' "Shop Around" (No. 1 R&B, No. 2 pop); it sells over a million copies.

October 14:   Ray Charles reaches No. 1 with "Hit the Road, Jack."

October 24:   President Kennedy dispatches military advisors and helicopters to Vietnam.

October 26:   Bob Dylan signs with Columbia Records.

October 28:   Brian Epstein is reportedly asked for the "My Bonnie" single by a customer in his North End Music Store in Liverpool; the customer accredits it to "the Beatles," although it is in fact by singer Tony Sheridan, backed by the Beatles.

November 4:   Bob Dylan plays Carnegie Chapter Hall.

November 9:   Brian Epstein sees his first Beatles performance at the Cavern Club during a lunchtime gig.

December 4:   The Marvelettes' "Please Mr. Postman" (on Tamla Records, owned by Berry Gordy) becomes Motown's first No. 1 pop single after a fourteen-week climb up the charts. The song is later covered by the Beatles.

1962

January 6:   Chubby Checker's "The Twist" re-enters the charts at No. 1 and stays there for four weeks.

January 15:   Motown signs the Supremes.

February 12:   John Glenn becomes the first American astronaut to orbit the Earth.

February 13:   Frank Sinatra forms Reprise Records, which will later release albums by, among others, the Beach Boys and the Kinks.

February 19:   Chuck Berry begins serving a twenty-month sentence for violating the Mann Act, the result of a 1959 conviction. Berry supposedly fired a fourteen-year-old hat-check girl at his St. Louis nightclub because he believed she was a prostitute, and she in turn accuses him of transporting her across state lines for immoral purposes. (In the words of the Beatles' John Lennon: "If you tried to give rock 'n' roll another name, you might call it 'Chuck Berry.'"[1])

March 19:	Bob Dylan releases his first, eponymous album.
April 10:	Former Beatle Stu Sutcliffe dies in Hamburg, Germany.
April 14:	Elvis Presley is No. 1 with "Good Luck Charm."
May 5–14:	"Soldier Boy" by the Shirelles is No. 1.
May 26–	
June 23:	Ray Charles' "I Can't Stop Loving You" is No. 1.
June 4:	The Beach Boys' first single, "409," backed with "Surfin' Safari," is released; after the A side flops, the latter song becomes a hit, peaking at No. 14 in October.
June 6:	The Beatles audition for producer George Martin.
July 12:	The Rolling Stones give their first public performance at the Marquee Club.
August 18:	Ringo Starr replaces Pete Best in the Beatles.
September 3–	
October 18:	"Sherry" by the Four Seasons is No. 1.
September 30:	James Meredith, defying fierce protests and escorted by federal marshalls, becomes the first African American student to attend the University of Mississippi.
October 5:	Parlophone releases the Beatles' first single, "Love Me Do"; Brian Epstein has been told that sales of 10,000 singles are required for a Top 20 hit, so he orders that amount for his North End Music Stores. The single reaches No. 17 on October 11.
October 20:	"The Monster Mash," by Bobby "Boris" Pickett, begins a three-week run at No. 1.
October 22:	President Kennedy announces that Russian missiles have been spotted in Cuba, precipitating the Cuban missile crisis; a nuclear war is narrowly averted.
November 3:	The Crystals' "He's a Rebel" (written by Gene Pitney) gives producer Phil Spector his first No. 1 single.
November 10–	
December 8:	The Four Seasons are again No. 1 with "Big Girls Don't Cry."
December 15:	Elvis Presley is No. 1 with "Return to Sender."

December 29: The Tornadoes' "Telstar" becomes the first British single to achieve an American No. 1, a position it maintains for three weeks.

1963

January 11: The Beatles' "Please Please Me" is released in England. The Whisky a Go Go, considered America's first discotheque, opens in Los Angeles.

January 14: The Rolling Stones (Brian Jones, Mick Jagger, Keith Richards, Ian Stewart, Bill Wyman, and Charlie Watts) first play together as a group at the Flamingo Club in the Soho section of London.

February 11: The Beatles record their first album, comprised of ten songs, in one day's work with producer George Martin.

February 22: The Beatles' "Please Please Me" reaches No. 1 in England, stays there for two weeks.

March 30: The Chiffons' "He's So Fine" begins a four-week run at No. 1.

April 28: Ambitious English teenager Andrew Loog Oldham sees the fledgling Rolling Stones at the Crawdaddy Club and signs the group to a management contract the following day.

May: Eric Clapton joins the Yardbirds; Harvard University dismisses Dr. Timothy Leary and Richard Alpert from teaching positions because of their experiments with LSD.

May 4–18: "Little" Peggy March holds the No. 1 singles slot with "I Will Follow Him."

May 27: *The Freewheelin' Bob Dylan*, the second album by the singer-songwriter, is released; it includes his song "Blowin' in the Wind."

June 12: Civil rights leader Medgar Evers is killed in the driveway of his home by a sniper.

July: Vee-Jay, an African American–owned label out of Chicago, releases the first Beatles album in the United States. Nobody notices.

July 27: Jan and Dean hit No. 1 with "Surf City."

August 3: The Beatles make their final appearance at Liverpool's Cavern Club.

August 3–24: "Little" Stevie Wonder has a month-long run at No. 1 with "Fingertips, Part 2."

August 28: The Reverend Martin Luther King Jr. (accompanied by Bob Dylan, Joan Baez, Peter, Paul and Mary, Mahalia Jackson, and

Harry Belafonte) delivers his "I Have a Dream" speech to an audience of 250,000 in Washington, D.C.

September 15: A church in Birmingham, Alabama, is bombed, killing four young African American girls.

October 12: The Ronettes reach No. 1 with "Be My Baby."

October 18: Chuck Berry's birthday present is his release from the Springfield, Missouri, Federal Medical Center.

October 26: "The Great March to Freedom," an album of speeches from Dr. Martin Luther King Jr., is released by (Berry) Gordy Records and reaches No. 41 on the Billboard charts.

November 4: The Beatles appear at the Royal Command performance in London, before an audience including the Queen Mother. John Lennon remarks before beginning "Twist and Shout": "Will the people in the cheaper seats clap their hands? And the rest of you, if you'll just rattle your jewelry."

November 22: President Kennedy is assassinated in Dallas, Texas. Lee Harvey Oswald is arrested for the murder of police officer J. D. Tippit and then charged with the Kennedy assassination.

November 24: As Lee Harvey Oswald is transported from prison, he is shot and killed by New Orleans nightclub owner, Jack Ruby. It is the first murder to be broadcast on live television.

November 29: "She Loves You" by the Beatles is released in England and immediately hits No. 1.

November 30–
December 28: The Singing Nun is No. 1 with "Dominique."

1964

January 1: *Top of the Pops* premieres on British TV (the show is still on the air as of 2004).

January 3: America's *Tonight Show with Jack Paar* becomes the first American television program to air footage of the Beatles.

January 3–4: The Rolling Stones begin recording their first album at London's Regent Sound; the group launches its first headlining English tour on January 6, supported by the Ronettes.

January 20: The album *Meet the Beatles!* is released by Capitol Records in America. On February 15, it hits No. 1 on *Billboard*'s album chart and remains there for eleven weeks.

January 25: The Beatles have their first U.S. No. 1 with "I Want to Hold Your Hand"; the single stays at the top of the charts until March 21, when it is replaced by "She Loves You." That single is No. 1 until April 4, when the Beatles again replace themselves with "Twist and Shout." The following week, the Beatles are No. 1 with "Can't Buy Me Love," which continues at the top of the charts until May 16. After a one-week break (Louis Armstrong with "Hello, Dolly!"), the Beatles again reach No. 1 on May 23 with "Love Me Do."

February 7: The Beatles land in New York City and the American version of Beatlemania is launched.

February 9: The first *Ed Sullivan Show* featuring the Beatles is aired; an estimated 73 million American homes tune in.

February 11: The Beatles give their first live performance in America at the Washington Coliseum in Washington, D.C.

February 12: The Beatles perform at Carnegie Hall in New York City, becoming the first pop group to play that venue.

March 2: Shooting begins in England on the Beatles' first feature film, *A Hard Day's Night*; it is completed in eight weeks.

March 16: The music trade magazine *Billboard* reports that the Beatles are responsible for 60 percent of all singles sales.

Disc jockey Alan Freed is charged with income tax evasion for his role in the "payola" scandal.

March 24: John Lennon's book *In His Own Write* is published.

March 31: The Beatles hold all five top positions on *Billboard's* Top Pop Singles chart with "Can't Buy Me Love," "Twist and Shout," "She Loves You," "I Want to Hold Your Hand," and "Please Please Me"—an accomplishment yet to be duplicated by any other artist. As of April 4, the Beatles have fourteen singles in *Billboard's* Hot 100.

April 17: The Rolling Stones issue their first, eponymous album in England.

May 2: The Beatles' *Second Album* hits No. 1 in its second week of American release, the fastest such rise to date.

May 18: Mods and rockers begin a series of clashes in Brighton and other English seaside resorts.

May 29: The Rolling Stones' first American album, *England's Newest Hitmakers!* is released; it will eventually reach No. 11.

June 1: The Rolling Stones arrive in New York City for the group's first American tour.

June 3: Beatles drummer Ringo Starr, afflicted with tonsillitis, collapses during a London photo shoot and is hospitalized. Brian Epstein and George Martin decide upon drummer Jimmy

	Nicol as a temporary replacement for the Beatles' world tour. The group, with Nicol, departs for the Far East the next day. Ringo rejoins the Beatles in Adelaide, Australia, on June 15.
June 10–11:	The Rolling Stones record in the United States for the first time, at Chicago's Chess Studios, where they finish their next single "It's All Over Now" and meet several of their rock and blues idols, including Muddy Waters and Chuck Berry.
June 16:	In New York City, Lenny Bruce goes on trial for obscenity.
July 4:	Independence Day sees a return of American supremacy to the record charts with the Beach Boys' first No. 1 hit, "I Get Around."
July 10:	*A Hard Day's Night* soundtrack is released in Britain. The album is the first to contain only compositions written by Lennon and McCartney.
July 25– August 8:	The Beatles are No. 1 with the single "A Hard Day's Night."
July 26:	*A Hard Day's Night* soundtrack, with a different track listing from the British version, is released in America.
August 8:	*Another Side of Bob Dylan* is released; it includes the songs "Chimes of Freedom," "All I Really Want to Do," "My Back Pages," and "It Ain't Me Babe."
August 11:	*A Hard Day's Night* opens in America.
September 5–19:	The Animals reach No. 1 with "House of the Rising Sun."
September 11:	The Beatles agree to play in Jacksonville, Florida, only if they are guaranteed that the audience will not be segregated by race.
September 16:	*Shindig* premieres on ABC-TV with the Rolling Stones, the Kinks, and the Byrds; the Stones' "Time Is On My Side" goes to No. 6 in the American Top 10.
September 17:	The Beach Boys make their first appearance on the *Ed Sullivan Show* and launch their American tour.
October:	The Kinks' first, eponymous album is released in America.
October 17:	Manfred Mann begins a two-week run at No. 1 with "Do Wah Diddy Diddy."
October 19:	Simon and Garfunkel release their first album, *Wednesday Morning 3 a.m.*; initially a flop, it will eventually rise to No. 30 in the wake of 1966's *The Sounds of Silence*. (By retaining his given surname, Garfunkel breaks the "ethnic" barrier in pop music.)

October 23:	The Rolling Stones arrive in New York for their second American tour; the next day, the group releases its second U.S. album, *12x5*.
October 24:	Dr. Martin Luther King Jr. is awarded the Nobel Peace Prize for his efforts to advance civil rights.
October 25:	The Rolling Stones make their first appearance on the *Ed Sullivan Show*.
December 4:	*Beatles for Sale* album is released in England.
December 11:	Sam Cooke is killed in Los Angeles.
December 15:	*Beatles '65* (the American counterpart to *Beatles for Sale*) is released and sells a million copies in one week.
December 19:	The Beatles hit No. 1 with "I Feel Fine," but are knocked out of the top perch the following week by the Supremes' "Come See about Me."
December 23:	The Beach Boys' Brian Wilson has his first public psychological breakdown on a plane from Los Angeles to Houston; he tells his group that he will no longer tour a few months later.

1965

January 2–16:	The Beatles' "I Feel Fine" returns to No. 1, but is replaced by Petula Clark's "Downtown" on January 23.
January 12:	NBC-TV debuts its rock music show *Hullabaloo*, which features comedian Woody Allen and a segment from London in which Beatles manager Brian Epstein introduces Gerry and the Pacemakers and the Zombies.
January 20:	Pioneering disc jockey Alan Freed dies of a heart attack.
February 6–20:	The Righteous Brothers hold down the No. 1 spot with "You've Lost That Lovin' Feeling."
February 13:	The Who's "I Can't Explain" is released in America, where it eventually reaches No. 97 on the Billboard charts. Also released on this date is *The Rolling Stones, Now!*, the band's third U.S. album.
February 21:	Malcolm X is assassinated in Harlem.
February 23:	The Beatles begin shooting *Help!*, their second feature film, in the Bahamas.
March 6–20:	The Beatles' "Eight Days a Week" is No. 1 for three weeks.
March 8:	Two United States Marine Corps Battalion teams land at Da Nang, the first ground troops to become involved in the Vietnam War.

March 18:	Rolling Stones Mick Jagger, Keith Richards, and Bill Wyman are fined five pounds for urinating on the wall of a London gas station after being refused entrance to an allegedly out-of-order lavatory; the incident inspires one Stone to pronounce, "We piss anywhere, man." *The Rolling Stones Now!* album reaches No. 5 on the U.S. charts; the single "The Last Time" is No. 9.
March 22:	Bob Dylan releases *Bringing It All Back Home*, the first true folk-rock album; songs include "Mr. Tambourine Man" and "Subterranean Homesick Blues."
March 25:	25,000 civil rights protestors, led by Dr. Martin Luther King Jr., arrive in Montgomery, Alabama, on a march from Selma.
April 3:	Herman's Hermits have their first American No. 1 with "Can't You Hear My Heartbeat."
April 10–17:	Freddie and the Dreamers are No. 1 for two weeks with "I'm Telling You Now."
April 24:	Wayne Fontana and the Mindbenders hit No. 1 with "Game of Love."
May 8–22:	Herman's Hermits hold down the No. 1 slot for three weeks with "Mrs. Brown, You've Got a Lovely Daughter."
May 10:	The Rolling Stones record several songs at Chicago's Chess Studios, where they also begin work on "(I Can't Get No) Satisfaction," to be released as a single on June 5.
May 14:	San Francisco radio station KYA presents the Rolling Stones, the Byrds, the Beau Brummels, and Paul Revere and the Raiders at the Civic Auditorium.
May 29:	The Beatles are No. 1 with "Ticket to Ride."
June 5:	The Supremes' "Back in My Arms Again" is No. 1.
June 7:	The Supreme Court rules in *Griswold vs. Connecticut* that a ban on the use of contraceptives is unconstitutional.
June 12:	The Beatles are named Members of the British Empire by Queen Elizabeth II, sparking protests from the English establishment.
	The Beach Boys take over the top singles spot in America with "Help Me, Rhonda."
July 3:	The Byrds' cover of Bob Dylan's "Mr. Tambourine Man" hits No. 1.
July 5:	The Beach Boys' *Summer Days (and Summer Nights!!)* album is released; "California Girls" becomes a No. 3 hit.

July 17– August 7:	The Rolling Stones have their first American No. 1 with "(I Can't Get No) Satisfaction."
August:	James Brown releases "Papa's Got a Brand New Bag."
August 6:	*Help!* soundtrack album is released.
	President Lyndon B. Johnson signs the Voting Rights Act into law, providing for federal registration of African American citizens.
August 11:	Race riots erupt in Watts, California, eventually resulting in dozens of deaths and the destruction of hundreds of businesses.
August 13:	San Francisco's first folk night club, the Matrix, opens at 3138 Fillmore in the Marina District; a new band called the Jefferson Airplane plays.
	The Beatles arrive in New York to begin their second North American tour.
August 15:	The Beatles play Shea Stadium for the first time; the appearance sets a world record for attendance (55,600) and is also the first time a pop group has performed in an open-air stadium. The box office takes in $304,000; the group receives a then-record $160,000.
August 28:	The Beatles smoke marijuana for the first time at the Hotel Delmonico in New York City. Their "dealer" is Bob Dylan, with an assist from journalist Al Aronowitz.
August 28– September 11:	The Beatles are back at No. 1 with "Help!"
August 30:	Bob Dylan releases the groundbreaking *Highway 61 Revisited*, which includes the landmark single "Like a Rolling Stone" (more than six minutes in length); it reaches No. 1 on September 18.
September 25:	The Beatles' cartoon show premieres on ABC-TV.
October 9–16:	The Beatles' "Yesterday" rules the singles chart.
October 13:	The Who records its first single, "My Generation," at London's Pye Studios, as well as the track "The Kids Are Alright."
October 16:	First Family Dog acid-rock dance is held in San Francisco.
November:	*Having a Rave Up With the Yardbirds* is released in America.
November 6–13:	The Rolling Stones are on top with "Get Off of My Cloud."

November 6:   The Byrds release "Turn! Turn! Turn!"; the single goes to No. 1 on December 4, staying there for three weeks.

December 3:   The Beatles' *Rubber Soul* is released in America.

December 25:   The Dave Clark Five has its first American No. 1 with "Over and Over"; the Rolling Stones' "As Tears Go By" enters the charts at No. 26.

1966

January 1–29:   "We Can Work It Out" by the Beatles is No. 1 for a month; it's supplanted by Simon and Garfunkel's "Sounds of Silence."

January 21:   First "Trips Festival" held in San Francisco at the Longshoreman's Hall; it lasts for three days and features, among other groups, Big Brother and the Holding Company.

February 4:   San Francisco promoter Bill Graham presents the Jefferson Airplane at the Fillmore Auditorium.

February 17:   Nancy Sinatra's "These Boots Are Made for Walkin'" has been British No. 1 for four weeks.

February 28:   Liverpool's Cavern Club closes.

March 3:   Neil Young, Stephen Stills, and Richie Furay form Buffalo Springfield in Los Angeles.

March 4:   John Lennon muses on the popularity of the Beatles relative to Christianity in an interview given to Maureen Cleave for London's *Evening Standard*; when reprinted in America's *Datebook* magazine on July 29, his comments create an uproar and a strong Bible Belt backlash against the group.

March 5:   The Kinks' *Dedicated Follower of Fashion* is released in England, where it rises to No. 1.

               The Walker Brothers release "The Sun Ain't Gonna Shine Anymore," which also eventually tops the British charts.

March 5–26:   Sgt. Barry Sadler's "Ballad of the Green Berets" is No. 1 for four weeks, replaced by the Rolling Stones' "19th Nervous Breakdown" on April 2.

March 25:   The Beatles' famous "butcher block" photos are taken in London for the original cover of their *Yesterday and Today* album; it is immediately pulled from the market after horrified response, and a new cover substituted.

March 30:   Riots break out during the Rolling Stones' concert at the Paris Olympia; their compilation album *Big Hits (High Tide and Green Grass)* reaches No. 3 on American charts.

April:	*The Who Sings My Generation* album is released in the United States.
April 9:	"Daydream" by the Lovin' Spoonful is No. 1.
April 12:	Jan Berry, of Jan and Dean, suffers massive injuries in a Los Angeles car crash and is paralyzed for more than a year.
April 23:	Manfred Mann releases "Pretty Flamingo" in England, where it rises to No. 1.
	The Rolling Stones release *Aftermath*, which becomes No. 1 in America.
May 1:	The Beatles play their last official concert in England (not counting an impromptu 1970 session on the roof of Apple Records, seen in the film *Let It Be*) at a London party for *New Musical Express* poll winners. Other artists on the bill include the Rolling Stones, the Who, the Yardbirds, the Walker Brothers, and Dusty Springfield.
May 7–28:	"Monday, Monday" by the Mamas and the Papas is No. 1 for three weeks.
May 10:	Bob Dylan begins his second British tour in Bristol, "going electric" during the latter half of his show.
May 15:	Major antiwar protest takes place in Washington, D.C.
May 16:	The Beach Boys release their seminal *Pet Sounds* album, which will help inspire the Beatles to write *Sgt. Pepper*.
	Bob Dylan releases rock and roll's first double album, *Blonde on Blonde*; it peaks at No. 9 on the *Billboard* charts.
May 20:	The Who's Pete Townshend and Keith Moon have a fight on-stage in London, and Moon threatens to leave the group.
May 27:	Andy Warhol presents the Velvet Underground and Nico at the Fillmore Auditorium in San Francisco; the Mothers of Invention are also on the bill.
	During a performance at London's Royal Albert Hall, Bob Dylan is jeered with a shout of "Judas!" from the audience.
June 4:	Wayne Fontana and the Mindbenders have their second (and last) No. 1 with "A Groovy Kind of Love."
June 11:	The Rolling Stones have another American No. 1 with "Paint It, Black."
June 24:	In San Francisco, Lenny Bruce and the Mothers of Invention appear at the Fillmore, while a radio-sponsored show at the Cow Palace headlines the Beach Boys, along with Jefferson Airplane, the Lovin' Spoonful, Chad and Jeremy, Percy Sledge, the Byrds, and Sir Douglas Quintet.

June 25– July 2:	The Beatles' "Paperback Writer" is No. 1 for two weeks; the two-sided single is backed with "Rain," which introduces guitar feedback as an intentional component.
	Paul Revere and the Raiders' "Hungry" makes its chart debut at No. 69.
June 30:	The Beatles become the first musical group to appear at Tokyo's Nippon Budokan Hall.
July 4:	The Beatles, on tour in the Philippines, misunderstand an invitation to visit the Marcos family as being optional; the group's failure to show up is perceived as an insult to the president and his wife. The following day, a mob attacks the group and its entourage at Manila airport. Manager Brian Epstein, road manager Mal Evans, and chauffeur Alf Bicknell are all beaten as the band escapes.
July 23:	The Troggs achieve their sole American No. 1 with "Wild Thing."
July 29:	Bob Dylan suffers unconfirmed injuries (rumored to be a broken neck) in a motorcycle crash in upstate New York and effects a temporary retreat from the public eye.
July 30:	"They're Coming to Take Me Away, Ha-Haaa!" by Napoleon XIV is No. 1 (the flip side is the same track played backwards); after mental health professionals complain about light-hearted treatment of insanity, radio unofficially bans single.
August 3:	Lenny Bruce, forty, is found dead of a drug overdose at his Los Angeles home. His friend Phil Spector pays for the funeral.
August 11:	John Lennon holds a Chicago press conference to apologize for "Beatles versus Christianity" remarks.
August 29:	The Beatles' final public concert appearance takes place at Candlestick Park in San Francisco. Opening acts include the Ronettes and the Cyrkle (whose hit "Red Rubber Ball" was written by Paul Simon).
September 12:	*The Monkees* premieres on NBC-TV; the series runs through 1968.
September 14:	Beatle George Harrison travels to India for six weeks to study sitar-playing under master Ravi Shankar.
September 17:	The Beatles' "Yellow Submarine" is knocked from the No. 1 spot by the Supremes' "You Can't Hurry Love."
October 6:	California bans LSD; San Francisco's Haight-Ashbury district holds a "Love Pageant" rally.

October 22:	The Byrds release "Mr. Spaceman," and Gene Clark leaves the group.
October 29:	? and the Mysterians' "96 Tears" is removed from No. 1 by the Monkees' first chart-topper, "Last Train to Clarksville."
	NOW (National Organization for Women) holds its first National Conference in Washington, D.C., declaring its purpose to fight for women's equal rights and pay, an end to sexual harassment, and the legalization of abortion.
November 8:	Ronald Reagan defeats California's incumbent governor Edmund G. Brown by almost a million votes.
November 9:	In London, John Lennon meets Japanese-American conceptual artist Yoko Ono for the first time, an event that some believe paves the way for the Beatles' eventual break-up.
November 19:	The Beach Boys are No. 1 with "Good Vibrations."
December 10:	The Rolling Stones release their first live album, *Got LIVE If You Want It!*, which eventually reaches No. 6 in the United States.
December 20:	Otis Redding plays the Fillmore Auditorium in San Francisco.
December 23:	The last episode of *Ready, Steady, Go!* is seen in England; the next-to-last show, on December 16, features the first TV appearance of the Jimi Hendrix Experience.
December 24–31:	The year ends with the Monkees' "I'm a Believer" at No. 1.

NOTE

1. *Quotes, The Official Site of Chuck Berry*, http://www.chuckberry.com/about/quotes.html; and *Berry, Chuck, MusicWeb Encyclopaedia of Popular Music*, http://www.musicweb-international.com/encyclopaedia/b/B105.HTM, as well as various other sources.

EARLY IDOLS

In America in 1960, the television set had replaced the radio as a source of family information and entertainment. The prime-time lineup included *The Many Loves of Dobie Gillis*, with a resident comical "beatnik," Maynard G. Krebs; *Ozzie and Harriet*, which starred an amiable former bandleader, his wife, and their two adorably crew-cut boys, David and little Ricky; *Lassie*, a series about a brave, intelligent collie dog that saved its young master from danger like clockwork; the self-explanatory *Shirley Temple's Storybook*; and the *Ed Sullivan Show*, a variety hour on Sunday evenings hosted by a strangely stiff newspaper columnist. There were just three networks: ABC, CBS, and NBC.

Radio, however, was still an important source of information, news, and entertainment, and it had just shrunk, with the help of Japanese transistors, to portable size. Radio serials like *The Shadow* and *The Lone Ranger* had vanished; similar family fare had been adapted to the new medium of TV. But the hit parade remained, in various permutations, in its role as an ongoing soundtrack to American life. The music being played at this time reflected the sunny innocence of the period's television fare: TV's own Ricky Nelson, the sweet harmonies of the Everly Brothers, the soundtrack to *South Pacific*, the folkie chords of the Kingston Trio, the warbling of Connie Francis and Brenda Lee, and, of course, Elvis Presley, freshly out of the army and musically tamer than before. His label, RCA Victor, became the first to announce that it would release all pop singles in stereophonic (stereo) and monaural (mono) sound simultaneously.

DISC JOCKEYS

The men (they were always men in those days) who played these records on the air were called "disc jockeys" (abbreviated to deejays or DJs), and they, or their program directors, could create stars overnight if and when certain singles received airplay. But how exactly were these stars anointed? Was it an unerring sense of what the marketplace might want, or could there be another compelling reason?

Alan Freed and the Payola Scandal

In February 1960, the payola scandal broke. "Payola" was a contraction of the words "pay" and "Victrola" (a trademarked name for an early form of record player) and meant cash or gifts to ensure radio airplay. The investigation had been sparked by a similar look into how TV game shows were being "fixed," and also at the urging of the American Society of Composers, Authors, and Publishers (ASCAP), which had noticed that songs licensed by the rival Broadcast Music Incorporated (BMI) seemed to have a stranglehold on the charts. Many of these songs were rock and roll, a format ASCAP did not favor; it argued that demand for this music was created through constant airplay by DJs on the take. House Oversight Subcommittee chairman Oren Harris convened hearings, prior to which the Federal Trade Commission filed complaints against a number of record manufacturers and distributors, many of which immediately folded.

The entertainment trade publication *Billboard* noted that payola did not begin with rock and roll: the practice had been rampant during vaudeville in the Roaring Twenties, and in the big-band era as well. But now it appeared that an attack was being mounted on rock itself. The committee declared that it would look into which DJs had taken gifts or cash, and panicked record companies fell all over themselves to testify just who had been given what. Some twenty-five DJs were caught up in the scandal, most notably Dick Clark and Cleveland's Alan Freed. Clark played ball, testifying that he had relinquished any related outside interests, which he insisted were merely "tax advantages" in the first place. He was a most fortunate man in that area: his $125 investment in Jamie Records (which had also spent $15,000 on payola, none of which Clark would admit to accepting) yielded a profit of $11,900, and of the 163 songs to which Clark held the rights, 143 had been given as no-strings-attached gifts. Somehow, despite the committee's obvious disbelief in such largesse, Clark escaped with only the proverbial slap on the wrist. Chairman Harris even referred to him as "a fine young man."[1]

Alan Freed was less lucky. Freed is the man many have credited with coining the term "rock and roll" to describe the rhythm and blues (R&B) he played in 1951 during his *Moondog Rock 'n' Roll Party* show on Cleveland's WJW. The following year, a Freed-sponsored Coronation Ball, considered the nation's first rock concert, was canceled when almost 20,000 fans, nearly all of whom were African American, tried to get into a venue that would hold only half that number. When Freed went on to a bigger market in New York's WINS, his audience grew to include fellow Caucasians. He continued to promote rock music through appearances in film, TV, and the all-star shows he produced at New York's Paramount Theatre, which were aired across the country on CBS Radio. In 1957, Freed landed his own nationally televised show on ABC, which was cancelled after an installment in which Frankie Lymon of the Teenagers danced with a white girl, infuriating the network's southern affiliates. In 1958, Freed produced a show at the Boston Arena that resulted in his being charged with incitement to riot. Even though the charge was later dismissed, WINS refused to renew his contract, which forced Freed into bankruptcy.

In 1959, under pressure from the payola hearings, Freed's then employers at WABC Radio demanded that he sign a statement denying any involvement; he refused to do so "on principle" and was promptly fired. On February 8, 1960, a New York grand jury began looking into the recording industry, and various parties were indicted for receiving "illegal gratuities." Freed was subpoenaed by the Oversight Committee but refused to testify, despite being offered immunity. Such things as the writing credit he received on Chuck Berry's hit "Maybelline" also aroused suspicion; one wonders which lyrics or music Freed actually contributed. The more he played such songs on the air, the more money he would make as one of the "authors." Freed managed to find a few other jobs, but they did not last very long. In December 1962, he entered a guilty plea to commercial bribery and was fined $300 and given a six-month suspended sentence. His career was finished, but the Internal Revenue Service was not through with Freed yet; he was charged with income tax evasion in 1964. By the following year, Freed—forty-three, bitter, and penniless—died, partially because of cirrhosis of the liver caused by heavy drinking. In 1986, he was inducted into the Rock and Roll Hall of Fame.

The overall power of the DJ first faded when free-form FM radio came into being in the late '60s and then was eroded further when national "consultants" and chains began gobbling up independent stations in the '90s. Playlists were no longer set by idiosyncratic individuals who really loved the music they spun, but by faceless corporate "suits" working to a mysterious formula. In its heyday, AM radio was something of a battlefield in which personalities vied for attention. Carroll James, a DJ at WWDC in Washington, D.C., took credit for being the first to play the Beatles upon request from a local fan (see Chapter 4); he claimed that the response was so strong that it forced Capitol to release the first U.S. single weeks ahead of schedule.

Other Significant DJs

Murray "the K"

In major markets like New York, the advent of the Beatles had DJs vying for supremacy, and Murray the K (for Kaufman) of WINS trumped them all by showing up at the group's hotel with the Ronettes, who had met the band during an earlier European tour. Kaufman was the brashest of a loud lot, but he amused the Beatles for a while: Ringo Starr thought that he was "the hippest, swingingest guy I ever met," and, as Paul McCartney explained, "he always brings the best birds [girls]."[2] Kaufman even became George Harrison's hotel roommate during the band's first stay, a coup to outrank all others; he took them out clubbing to the Peppermint Lounge and tagged along on the train ride from New York to Washington, D.C., all of which can be seen in *The Beatles: The First U.S. Visit* documentary.

Kaufman was a star. He could play a record, and within a week, it would become a monster hit in the rest of the nation. He was credited with "breaking" Bobby Darin, Stevie Wonder, the Supremes, the Ronettes, and even Bob Dylan. In those days, New York's three major stations (WMCA, WINS, and WABC) captured 50 percent of all listeners during prime time. Kaufman hosted "Swingin' Soiree" shows at the Brooklyn Fox or Paramount Theatres, coaxing artists to play for scale, six shows a day. By 1965, his Easter extravaganza grossed $298,000, while the competition could only pull in a quarter of that amount. Realizing his power, Kaufman began demanding the rights to include singles in later anthology albums if he was going to play them. He put out more than twenty such compilations, which sold 6 million copies overall. Back then, nobody screamed "conflict of interest"; it was just the way business was done. Kaufman played approximately 150 new singles every week, refusing to conform to a playlist handed down from above. He later toured with the Beatles, made TV specials, and wrote a book.

But Kaufman's day in the sun was ending. A "format designer" named Bill Drake had signed a contract with the chain that owned the FM station where Kaufman had landed in the latter part of the '60s that allowed Drake to impose his dictates anywhere. Kaufman, handed a memo telling him what he could and could not play, suffered a heart attack that very evening. He later bounced from station to station in smaller markets, but he had offended too many people to ever make a comeback. Even the Fab Four had washed their collective hands of the man who had loved boasting that he was the "Fifth Beatle"; as former roommate Harrison cryptically stated, "Murray's already taken all he's going to get."[3] When Kaufman died of cancer in 1982, only a handful of mourners attended his memorial service.

Wolfman Jack

Growing up in Brooklyn, young Robert Weston Smith enjoyed listening to Alan Freed so much that he began hanging around the Paramount Theatre, hoping to meet his hero; the aspiring DJ received his first break by becoming a "gofer" ("go for this, go for that") at the venue. A high-school dropout, Smith supported himself as a door-to-door salesman while attending broadcasting school at night; his aptitude for the form resulted in an A average, and he graduated at the head of his class.

The Wolfman's original *nom de radio* was Daddy Jules, in honor of the black DJs who had influenced him growing up, but because of that monicker, his growly voice, and his fondness for R&B, his first broadcasting gig in Newport News, Virginia, (and the dance club he had opened there) incited the ire of the local chapter of the Ku Klux Klan, which burned a cross on his lawn. Smith beat a retreat to Shreveport, Louisiana, where, in 1962, he became "Big Smith with the Records," a suitably innocuous title. But he was already thinking ahead, creating the Wolfman character in his mind before emigrating to Mexico's powerful XERF-AM. Until his arrival, the station had mostly blanketed North American airwaves with American evangelists looking to expand their followings, but it was Wolfman Jack who found the most devoted flock.

Wolfman Jack, 1966. Courtesy of Photofest.

In 1965, Smith began to really become prominent when he moved to XERB-AM, another Mexican station; there he drew so much attention with his crazy antics, inimitable voice, and hot playlist that national magazines and major newspapers wrote stories about him. The R&B records he exposed to his vast audience influenced many up-and-coming musicians, some of whom—including Todd Rundgren—paid him tribute in song. Wolfman Jack revealed the face behind the voice in George Lucas's seminal 1973 film *American Graffiti* and went on to even greater fame as a frequent host of the NBC-TV music series *Midnight Special*, which began an eight-year run in 1973. He died in 1995 at age fifty-seven.

MUSIC AT THE BEGINNING OF THE '60s

The Last of the Leather-Jacket Rebels

The current music scene continues to reflect the past in that many of the most influential artists never really hit the charts, or if they do, they do not stay there very long. These artists may not come to the attention of the mainstream while doing their best work, but the few who hear them are inspired to create enduring music of their own. One such progenitor was the rebel memorialized by this plaque set on the grounds of St. Martin's Hospital, in Bath, England: "Singer Eddie Cochran aged 21 was killed as the result of a taxi crash at Chippenham,

Wiltshire, after leaving the Bristol Hippodrome. He was returning to America to headline on the *Ed Sullivan* TV show. Eddie left behind a number of classic recordings on various labels. Three Steps to Heaven."

Cochran died a long way from home on April 17, 1960. Born in Minnesota in 1938, he had a brief career, with only one major hit in the United States and one chart-topper in England, yet he is now considered one of the greatest influences in rock. Cochran started playing as a rockabilly artist at fifteen and began moving toward harder rock and away from country in the mid-'50s. He somewhat resembled a bantam James Dean, and those photogenic looks—and his phenomenal rock energy, fondly remembered by Rolling Stones manager Andrew Loog Oldham, among others—led to Cochran's first big break, performing "Twenty Flight Rock" in the 1956 comedy *The Girl Can't Help It*. (The following year, Paul McCartney played this song as his "audition" upon meeting John Lennon, whereupon he was taken into the latter's skiffle group, then called the Quarrymen.) In 1958, Cochran released "Summertime Blues," which during the ensuing decades has been covered by dozens of artists, perhaps most famously by the Who on the album *Live at Leeds*. The central riff—E, A, B, E—is one of the easiest for guitar novices to master, and therefore has been copied innumerable times. When Cochran appeared in the 1958 film *Go Johnny Go*, he was effortlessly able to communicate teenage angst with his timeless "C'mon Everybody."

British impresario Larry Parnes brought Cochran and Gene Vincent over to England, where they were wildly popular with "teddy boys" and "rockers"—teenagers given to leather jackets and ducktail hairstyles; their opposites, known as "mods" (see Chapter 5), would not begin to emerge until around 1964. Cochran planned to take a short break to record back in the United States and was scheduled to return to England later that year. The taxi carrying him and Vincent away from their final gig veered off the road; although he was in the backseat, Cochran was thrown clear of the wreck and died a few hours later in the hospital. His girlfriend Sharon Sheeley (co-writer of Cochran's posthumous hit "Something Else," later covered by the notorious Sex Pistols) was badly injured, while Vincent suffered a broken collarbone. Cochran's next release, the eerily titled "Three Steps to Heaven," topped the British charts after his death, but failed to make a dent in his homeland. All these years later, England still appreciates Cochran more than his homeland ever did: The British label Rockstar Records has released collections of Cochran's demos, outtakes, and unreleased songs, while repackaged versions of his slim "official" catalogue continue to sell well. There are annual UK conventions dedicated to Cochran, where devotees who were not even born when he was alive gather to worship the man and his legacy.

Gene Vincent was entirely different. Whereas Cochran was basically sunny, Vincent was tormented, not least because he had been partially crippled by a 1955 motorcycle accident. Vincent's slow and sexually insinuating "Be-Bop-A-Lula," released the following year, briefly gave him a run on the American

Gene Vincent and His Blue Caps, 1960. Courtesy of Photofest.

charts, but he was too inarticulate and menacing to be readily marketed as a "new" Elvis Presley. His next record, "Race with the Devil," flopped in the United States, but did catch on in England. Vincent also appeared in *The Girl Can't Help It*, yet even that appearance did nothing to slow his commercial free fall. There were personnel problems with his group, the Blue Caps, and Vincent's emerging alcoholism began to make him a liability in the view of promoters. Worse, his leg was constantly reinjured, which forced him to wear a brace. Vincent was pretty much washed up in America when he relocated to England in the late '50s; even though he survived the crash that took Cochran's life, his career never regained momentum. Nonetheless, Vincent kept touring throughout the following decade, and when a comeback album failed to catch on, he returned to churning out the old hits with a backup band. Redundant as far as the new breed of the day was concerned, Vincent was bitter and bloated from drink when he died of a bleeding ulcer in October 1971. Now he is revered as one of rock's founding fathers, a bit too late for him to enjoy the status and rewards that title might confer.

Clean-Cut Idols in Great Britain and the United States

British Rockers of the Era

British promoters like Parnes and TV producer Jack Good were building up their own stables of homegrown pretty-boy singers with catchy new names to compete with imports from the United States. While most of these acts went unnoticed in America at the time, they were influential by their mere existence; they encouraged British youngsters to believe that the United States did not have a monopoly on music. Cliff Richard, the biggest of the bunch, was supposedly England's answer to Elvis. Before being steered into bland middle-of-the-road (MOR) pop, Richard did rock—as evidenced by his late-'50s single "Move It"—and he and his group the Shadows were wildly important to British teens. Like John Lennon, Richard was intrigued by Elvis Presley; and like Lennon, Richard formed his own "skiffle" group (for more on this genre, see Chapter 4), the Drifters. The band played around the English countryside before landing at Soho's famous 2i's coffee bar. The 1959 British movie *Expresso Bongo*, which starred Richard, uses a similar setting to launch his character's music career; this "cinematic pop landmark, brilliantly evoking the rapacious world of Tin Pan Alley . . . remains one of the most revealing and humorous films ever made on the music business."[4]

Cliff Richard performing on British television, 1967. Courtesy of Photofest.

Jack Good, who ran the TV show *Oh Boy!*, took over after hearing Richard's audition disc of "Move It." The Drifters changed their name to the Shadows to avoid confusion with the African American singing group and underwent some personnel shifts, and Richard was given the full star buildup, including slots on Good's show. In what was now practically a guarantee of success, he was denounced for his Elvis-like hip swivels and "crude exhibitionism."[5] Richard scored forty-three UK Top 20 hits between 1958 and 1969, but he was mostly a nonentity in America, entering the Top 40 only a few times (with "Living Doll" in 1959, "It's All in the Game" in 1963, and "Devil Woman" in 1976). However, in England Richard remains an institution. He is one of Great Britain's most popular entertainers ever, outlasting every musical trend of the past four decades, and is also now a sir, having been knighted in May 1995 for services to popular music.

Adam Faith, another of Good's projects, was launched in 1959 with a single clumsily titled "What Do You Want If You Don't Want Money?" He had a No. 1 hit with this, as well as with his subsequent single "Poor Me." Faith branched out into acting, which served him well after his pop career ended around 1963 (he is most convincing in the rock-related films *Stardust* and *That'll Be the Day*). He also produced, managed, and promoted other artists and later made fortunes from property and in the stock market. That led to a newspaper column that promised to make his readers millionaires and a celebrity financial consultancy that collapsed when one of Faith's financiers was convicted of fraud. That did not stop him from creating a British TV network called the Money Channel, devoted to all things financial; a year after it began, it was over. Faith died of a heart attack in 2003, at age sixty-two.

Parnes, for his part, had Tommy Steele, Billy Fury, Marty Wilde, Johnny Gentle, Vince Eager, and the quite credible Georgie Fame, a keyboard player and singer whose blend of jazz and R&B gave him three No. 1 UK singles. Fame was actually a real musician, whereas the others were primarily prefabricated frontmen. Fame's influences included Fats Domino, Jerry Lee Lewis, Booker T. and the MGs, and Jamaican ska and bluebeat, which genre he helped popularize. During a residency by his group the Blue Flames at a West End jazz club called the Flamingo, Fame discovered the Hammond B-3 organ via listening to records lent by visiting American servicemen; in 1962, he became one of the few British musicians playing the instrument. One of the most popular live acts in town, Fame was signed the following year and in 1964 released the album *Rhythm and Blues at the Flamingo*. In early 1965, he had a No. 1 British hit with "Yeh Yeh," which just missed entering the U.S. Top 20. Fame continues to work as a musician to this day.

American Idols

Meanwhile, in the United States, Frankie Avalon (born Francis Avallone) from Philadelphia had passed his musical commercial peak in 1959 after "Venus," but managed to reinvent himself as a romantic lead in teen exploitation flicks, often appearing opposite former *Mickey Mouse Club* TV star Annette Funicello; the series of early and mid-'60s "beach" movies they costarred in are now considered camp classics.

Another Italian American, Fabian (born Fabiano Forte Bonaparte, he went by an abbreviated version of his first name) was discovered in 1957 by two local Philadelphia talent scouts who hoped to create a tamer version of Elvis. A few *Bandstand* appearances later, Fabian was a teen sensation and had a Top 40 single in 1959 with "I'm a Man," composed by Doc Pomus and Mort Shuman, who also wrote "Turn Me Loose" and "Hound Dog Man," the theme from the singer's movie debut. By the time the '60s rolled around, Fabian was an idol past his sell-by date, so he began concentrating on film for as long as the audience would have him. He had little choice: during the height of the payola scandal, Fabian confessed that a great deal of electronic tinkering had gone into making his voice recordable. He had been selected for stardom by managers who decided that he had a marketable pretty face and thereafter would do whatever was necessary to cover up any related musical failings. This pattern would be repeated with the 1990s boy-band boom, and will no doubt stay in the playbook in one form or another until teenage hormones cease to exist.

The Descendants of Doo-wop

In the United States, the genre known as "doo-wop" after the vocal rhythm riffs supplied by backup singers was mutating from its basically black origins to the Italian American domain as the original street-corner feel was burnished to a higher sheen in the recording studio. Dion DiMucci, who went by his first name only, left his group the Belmonts in 1960 after they had racked up nine hits in the preceding two years, including "Teenager in Love," written by Doc Pomus. Keeping to that profitable theme, Dion's first solo hit was titled "Lonely Teenager," but the following year, he delivered two tunes destined to become rock classics, "Runaround Sue" and "The Wanderer"—the former song castigated the titular character for the type of behavior that, when practiced by a male, was celebrated in the latter. (The double standard was still alive and well, although when the birth-control pill was introduced in 1960, it would have far-reaching implications.) Dion was a front-runner in many ways, including his heroin addiction, which began in 1960. By 1963, he had seven hits in the charts, but by the following year he dropped out of music in an effort to kick his habit. He did not return to the charts until 1968, with the emotional "Abraham, Martin, and John"; his career underwent various ups and downs, but he continued to perform and was rewarded by election to the Rock and Roll Hall of Fame in 1989.

Another East Coast Italian American who made a major impact on the charts in these early days was Frankie Valli, lead singer of the Four Seasons. His soaring falsetto was all over the radio with hits like "Sherry," "Big Girls Don't Cry," and "Dawn." He went on to a solo career before reuniting with the group in the 1980s. The Four Seasons were inducted into the Rock and Roll Hall of Fame in 1990, and for the rest of that decade the group toured the well-paying "oldies" circuit.

Jay and the Americans was a decidedly non-Italian entry in the school of doo-wop. The New York–based group was fortunate enough to fall under the auspices of the hit songwriting team Jerry Leiber and Mike Stoller, who signed the group to a contract. The original singer, John "Jay" Traynor, left around 1963; it was the second lead singer, David Black (né Blatt), who actually sang on the hits after being brought into the existing framework. Black, who had previously fronted an all-Jewish group from Brooklyn's Tilden High School, obligingly also changed his first name to Jay, while two other members of the group changed their surnames to disguise their ethnic origins. In 1963, the Drifters (one of Lieber and Stoller's mainstay vocal groups) cut the Barry Mann–Cynthia Weil song "Only in America"; when the label decided against releasing it as recorded, Jay and the Americans stepped into the breach and scored their first chart hit. They went on to have a string of smashes, including "Come a Little Bit Closer" (which led to their inclusion

The Four Seasons (left to right) Frankie Valli, Tommy DeVito, Bob Gaudio, and Nick Massi, 1962. Courtesy of Photofest.

on the Beatles' first tour of America in 1964), "Let's Lock the Door," and the semioperatic "Cara Mia." Jay Black stayed on as lead singer well into the '80s, doing the time-honored "oldies" routine, while two members of the re-vamped backup group (Walter Becker and Donald Fagen) left in the 70s and went on to form Steely Dan.

AIP AND THE RISE OF THE TEENSPLOITATION FLICK

The baby-boom generation was starting to hit critical mass, with time on its hands and money to spend. By 1964, this group represented about 40 percent of the population; almost half of the United States was under nineteen years of age. Furthermore, the "teenager" concept was something entirely new. The transition from child to grownup had been simple in the past: one minute, un-der the age of consent; the next, burdened with the responsibilities of adult-hood. In all recorded history, there had never been such an affluent leisure class as that represented by adolescents during this period. Previously, as soon as a child was able to work—whether on the family farm, in a factory, or worse, on the streets—he had done so. Education was reserved for the wealthy. Now there were millions of thirteen- to nineteen-year-olds, some with part-time jobs outside of school, others collecting sizable weekly allowances from doting parents.

Outside of music moguls, most of the ruling culture disdained the idea of catering to adolescents. But other savvy entrepreneurs spotted a bulging demo-graphic all too willing to be relieved of its cash. Samuel Arkoff of American International Pictures (AIP) was one of the godfathers of the teen exploitation flick, and he made a mint with his low-budget/low-concept movies. When Arkoff launched AIP in 1954, the major film studios were hurting; TV had taken a major part of their market away. It was Arkoff's partner, Jim Nicholson, who realized that there was a fortune to be made by marketing directly to teens. The price of a movie ticket then was around fifty cents; popcorn cost twenty cents, and a soft drink added another dime to the tab. A young couple could easily go on a date for just a few dollars; even adjusted for inflation, movies were considerably less expensive than they are now.

AIP began with cheap sci-fi flicks (the company made its name with the sensationally titled *I Was a Teenage Werewolf*, starring Michael Landon, later of the TV series *Bonanza* and *Little House on the Prairie*) and moved into various related areas, such as horror (most notably in a series that began in 1960, based on the work of Edgar Allan Poe) and "juvenile-delinquent"-themed movies. These early films played on teens' anxieties about fitting in and their suppressed desire to rebel against parental or institutional authority. The monster genre was a canny nod to the physical turmoil suffered by young people in a society that then, as now, condemned their sexuality: what better way to absolve responsibility for raging hormones than to blame the moon for turning you into a wolf? Then AIP hit box-office gold with the studio's "beach-party" series, which began with the titular *Beach Party* and moved on to *Muscle Beach Party*, *Bikini Beach*, *Pajama Party* (all released in 1964), and *Beach Blanket Bingo* and *How to Stuff a Wild Bikini* (both 1965).

According to at least one pundit, the subtext of this group of movies

Frankie Avalon in *Beach Party*, 1963. Courtesy of Photofest.

(which usually featured Frankie Avalon and former Mouseketeer Annette Funicello as chaste young lovers) is that of reassurance. There is no cold war, no blacks, no drugs, no sex. It is always summer vacation, so there is no school and no work either. Even though the stars themselves were well into adulthood, they were portraying youngsters who had yet to enter, or even decide upon, a profession. The beach became an expanded version of the backyard, where America's (white) teenagers could have good clean fun while consuming products such as soft drinks, beach gear, and surfboards, all the while safely flirting under the watchful eye of adults. Any excess (i.e., sexual) energy could be worked off by dancing during the musical numbers. Everything here exists in a pristine bubble; "the beach seems to be providing the setting not for an endless party, but for a last desperate party before the horrors of the real world engulf it."[6]

TEMPLATES FOR REBELLION

Marlon Brando and James Dean

While the teen exploitation films ranged from completely absurd (the aforementioned *Teenage Werewolf*) and inanely innocent to subtly subversive (*Blackboard Jungle*), the most influential movies were *The Wild Ones* with Marlon Brando (1953) and *Rebel without a Cause* (1955), starring James Dean. It is hard to say whether Dean would have wound up like Brando, an overweight parody of his former self, if he had not died from crashing his Porsche in September 1955 after just three films (*Rebel* was sandwiched between *East of Eden* and *Giant*). But since he left the world at twenty-four, he would always remain young, beautiful, and mysterious. "How bigger than life, defining our behavior, up there on the screen were Elvis and Jimmy Dean," Andrew Loog Oldham, the Rolling Stones' manager, would later muse. "American cinema gave us hope and attitude."[7] Dean's inarticulate rage and brooding self-pity resonated with this young audience, who saw their own confusion reflected back to them. Although he was physically somewhat slight, Dean's attractiveness was amplified by his ambiguous, tortured sexuality.

Annette Funicello in *Beach Blanket Bingo*, 1965. Courtesy of Photofest.

Brando, on the other hand, was a macho, sleekly muscled stud as the leader of a motorcycle gang in *The Wild Ones*; his insinuating sexuality burned a hole in the screen. His surly response to a local who wanted to know what he was rebelling against ("Whaddaya got?" he drawled) became a classic catchphrase.

Elvis Presley before and after the Army

None of this was lost on Elvis Presley, the biggest rock and roll star the world had ever seen. In one of the first cases of commercial crossover, Presley (who did, in fact, have serious acting aspirations) made his first film, *Love Me Tender*, in 1956 and what many consider his finest as an actor, *King Creole*, two years later. *Loving You* (1957) was, in retrospect, more revealing than most such "backstage" looks at how a star was constructed. But then Presley received his call-up notice and dutifully entered the army in March 1958 for a two-year hitch. It was a turning point for him on many levels.

His beloved mother died while he was on leave, and Presley was unable to make it to her bedside before she passed away, which sent him into a tailspin of grief from which he never fully recovered. Then he was shipped overseas to Germany to serve out his tour of duty. This was a major culture shock for the southern boy, who promptly sought permission to live off base and imported as many family and friends as possible. Finally, this was where he met fifteen-year-old army brat Priscilla Beaulieu, who became his wife and the mother of his only child, Lisa Marie. All of these events conspired to tame the wild hillbilly cat who had scandalized the nation with his pelvic swivels and R&B-tinged howls. He was now a clean-cut all-American boy, as if the requisite army crewcut had had a Samsonesque effect and sheared his potency as well: "They not only shaved his hair off, but I think they shaved between his legs, too," John Lennon of the Beatles observed. "It was like something happened to him psychologically."[8] Many years later, after Presley succumbed to decades of drug use, poor diet, and heartbreak, Lennon (who had idolized the man called the King) was asked to comment on his passing. He responded that in his opinion, "Elvis really died the day he joined the army. That's when they killed him, and the rest was a living death."[9]

It is true that the promise Presley showed in his early black-and-white films seemed to dissipate almost entirely once he began making what he himself disparagingly called "travelogues"; from 1960 to 1966, he made no fewer than eighteen films, most of which had preposterous plots and increasingly scarce musical high points. It is generally agreed that although his prearmy films were the best of his career, Presley did not start out badly here with 1960's *G.I. Blues* (which yielded a new cover of Carl Perkins's "Blue Suede Shoes," the song "Wooden Heart," and the title track), and 1961's *Blue Hawaii* was a huge success, with highlights like his gorgeous rendition of "I Can't Help Falling in Love with You"; the film also created an association between Presley and the fiftieth state that continued through other movies and a later live broadcast from the area. The No. 2 hit "Return to Sender" was included on the soundtrack of 1962's *Girls! Girls! Girls!*, and 1964's *Roustabout* had a good midtempo version of the Coasters' Leiber and Stoller number "Little Egypt."

The brightest moment of all came with 1964's *Viva Las Vegas*, where Presley costarred with the fiery singer, dancer, and actress Ann-Margret; their chemistry turned what was nominally a piece of fluff into something tougher and livelier, and Elvis rose to the challenge by recording a rousing version of Ray Charles's "What'd I Say," along with the still-exciting title track, written by the team of Doc Pomus and Mort Shuman. As time went on, though, Presley became more comfortably numb, uncomplainingly cutting silly songs such as "(There's) No Room to Rhumba in a Sportscar" (from 1963's *Fun in Acapulco*),

Elvis Presley in *Blue Hawaii*, 1961. Courtesy of Photofest.

"Do the Clam" (1965's *Girl Happy*), or the cringeworthy "Queenie Wahini's Papaya" (*Paradise, Hawaiian Style*, 1966).

Still, most fans were happy to consume anything he did. The movies continued to rake in money at the box office, no matter how absurd they were: while it was one thing to accept the premise that Elvis was a GI who could sing, it was quite another to believe him as the scion of a pineapple-growing empire, a fledgling boxer, a tuna fisherman, a bush or airline pilot, a trapeze performer suffering from vertigo, a singing rodeo cowboy, a singing auto racer, a singer on a Mississippi riverboat, and so on. If ever there were a case of a star popular enough to simply sit and read the phone book while still drawing a wildly enthusiastic audience, it was Presley, but ironically, it only served to his creative detriment.

Elvis and "the Colonel"

Some have wondered why Presley allowed himself to be so badly, baldly exploited, and the answer is the Colonel. Presley's manager Tom Parker was not a colonel, nor was he even really Tom Parker. He was born Andreas van Kuijk in Breda, the Netherlands, and slipped into the United States at an unspecified time and place. He was not a citizen and for some unknown reason (perhaps having to do with an unsolved murder in his homeland) never applied to be naturalized. This is why Presley never toured or appeared anywhere outside the continental United States, except his posting to Germany (even Parker could not control the army) and his concerts from Hawaii, where no passport was required. Parker would never allow his meal ticket out of the immediate vicinity if he could help it.

Even Hollywood moguls were mystified by Parker's insistence on "the formula": as he saw it, the movies promoted the soundtracks, the single promoted the film. In fact, it was one of the earliest examples of what is now known as synergy. "I think Parker is more interested in selling records than he is [in] building a motion picture career for Presley and making fortunes out of his picture reruns," one executive wrote to another. "It's a helluva way for a partner to act. Too bad."[10]

Furthermore, once *Blue Hawaii*, the first of Presley's bikini flicks, easily recouped its cost of $2 million, the star was effectively trapped. There was no reason to stretch or try something new. Despite the fact that Presley had shown distinct dramatic talent in *King Creole*, producer Hal Wallis did not believe that he could carry a film without musical numbers, and Parker shared this opinion. "They'll never win any Academy Awards," Parker said of the films as early as 1960. "All they're good for is to make money."[11]

Yet some think that there is a case to be made that Hollywood helped keep Presley's career intact during a time when his recording career might have taken a nosedive, even though the *Roustabout* soundtrack did manage to best the Beatles saleswise. One critic pointed out that because Presley did not write his own material, his label would have not known what to do with him during the tumultuous times just ahead. "By dumb luck, the movie years had the effect of preserving Elvis . . . when the time was right and people were ready to see him in concert, he was . . . ready to pounce. . . . Inadvertently, Parker's decisions in the early and mid-'60s gave us the great Elvis music of the very late '60s and early '70s."[12] After Presley was found dead at age forty-two in 1977 (some felt that it was one of the most drawn-out suicides in history), Parker proclaimed: "Elvis didn't die. The body did. It don't mean a damned thing. It's just like when he was away in the army. . . . This changes nothing."[13]

Naturally, other would-be managers and wannabe stars were hoping to grab a piece of the action once Presley was taken off the market by his enlisted status. In those days, as now, no one could ensure that a career would last past a few token hits. Even one smash single was enough to put quite a bit of money in the bank (at least for the label and manager), and possibly even launch a film career à la Elvis. It was no surprise that hopefuls began to flood the market. Of these, Ricky Nelson was in a class by himself.

RICKY NELSON

The handsome-verging-on-pretty Nelson was the son of beloved radio and TV icons Ozzie and Harriet Nelson. As Presley himself once declared, "If James Dean sang, he would sound just like Rick Nelson." Carl Perkins, an early Sun Records labelmate of Presley's and a great inspiration to the Beatles, said: "I only know two cats in this business that really had it all; Elvis was one of those guys, the other was Ricky Nelson. There was a difference. . . . Elvis moved. Ricky never had to; he stood flat-footed and captivated his audience with his good looks. We grew up with him; those who didn't missed something.

History books are gonna have to say that he played a big role in rock 'n' roll music, and he did it his way."[14]

Nelson was underestimated, not least because "we grew up with him"; the cute kid brother on TV could not possibly rock. First seen in 1952, aged twelve, on his parents' ABC sitcom, by sixteen he was a full-fledged star with a Top 10 single ("A Teenager's Romance," backed with a cover of Fats Domino's "I'm Walkin'"). Little Ricky may have pulled strings to get recorded in the first place—his father Ozzie had been a bandleader, and the kid was starring on a highly rated television show that could promote every single—but, as was noted during his 1987 induction into the Rock and Roll Hall of Fame, "Nelson was the real thing: a gentle-voiced singer/guitarist with an instinctive feel for the country-rooted side of rockabilly. And he had exquisite taste in musicians, utiliz-

Ricky Nelson, 1963. Courtesy of the Kobol Collection.

ing guitarist James Burton (formerly a Dale Hawkins sideman, later an Elvis Presley accompanist) as his secret weapon in the studio."[15] Nelson had thirty-three Top 40 hits in a seven-year period (he dropped the "y" from his first name after he turned twenty-one). If Bill Haley had been something of a stealth missile for the mainstreaming of rock music, Nelson was even more so—he helped rock become acceptable by playing it on his family's TV show weekly and being sweet faced, clean-cut, and adorable. From outward appearances, Rick Nelson was a rock star one could take home to mother—while hoping that she would keep her hands to herself.

GENE PITNEY AND THE BOBBYS (VEE, RYDELL, VINTON, AND DARIN)

Gene Pitney got his start in the music business around 1960 through writing songs at the Brill Building alongside the great teams of the day; his "He's a Rebel" was a huge hit for the Crystals under the production of Phil Spector (see Chapter 3). Pitney, who began studying guitar while still in high school, was in a band when he was spotted by "the proverbial fat man with a cigar [who] came and said, 'Do you want to make a record?'"[16] Pitney then wrote "Rubber Ball," a No. 1 hit for Bobby Vee, and "Hello Mary Lou," which Ricky Nelson put on the B side of his "Travelin' Man." It hit the Top 10 and became one of Nelson's best-loved songs. Pitney had his first hit on his own in 1961 with "(I Wanna) Love My Life Away"; unusually for the time, he produced it himself, pioneering such techniques as multitracking vocals and overdubbing the instruments, all of which—except bass—he also played. Pitney was best known for a melodramatic delivery of pained ballads such as "It Hurts to Be in Love" and "Town Without Pity" (1964). His 1965 single "Last Two People on Earth" actually used the outbreak of nuclear war as the backdrop for its star-crossed lovers.

Yet Pitney never got caught up in fame or showbiz lunacy, despite befriending the young Rolling Stones (after meeting the band on a 1963 tour of England, he recorded the Jagger-Richards composition "That Girl Belongs to Yesterday," making it their first American chart appearance when it hit No. 49 in 1964) and recording with country hell-raiser George Jones. He married and stayed wed, settling down in Connecticut where he was raised; he still tours six months a year and keeps the music industry at a safe distance. Of his 2002 induction into the Rock and Roll Hall of Fame, he mused: "It's a nice thing, but there's a lotta screwballs there. It was a zoo. That was the last time I saw [Phil] Spector. He was like being directed by someone behind him, who was kind of aiming him in the right direction. I just left it alone."[17]

Pitney, as level-headed as he was clean-cut, was clearly no one's pop puppet. The same could not be said of acts like Bobby Vee (né Velline), who got his big break upon the much-lamented death of Buddy Holly. Vee and his group, the Shadows, were booked to play the Winter Dance Party in his hometown of Fargo, North Dakota, after a plane carrying the scheduled acts (Holly, the Big Bopper, and Ritchie Valens) went down in an Iowa cornfield. Vee landed a recording contract, and although his first few singles went nowhere, he somehow managed to hook up with the hit-making songwriters of the Brill Building. "Devil or Angel" crashed the Top 10 in 1960, followed by "Rubber Ball," written by Pitney, later that year; in 1961, Vee had his biggest single, "Take Good Care of My Baby," which spent three weeks at No. 1. "The Night Has a Thousand Eyes" also charted the following year, but Vee was eclipsed by the UK torrent of talent, even though he gamely tried to get on the bandwagon by recording *Bobby Vee Sings the New Sound From England!* By the late '60s, he was on the oldies circuit.

A similar Bobby (born Ridarelli, renamed Rydell) came out of Philadelphia, where he had been drumming behind Rocco and the Saints; Frankie Avalon was the trumpet player. He was good-looking enough to be signed to a local label and turned into a teen idol at seventeen with the 1959 single "Kissin' Time"; the following year, he was performing at New York's Copacabana. Rydell segued into acting and achieved immortality of a sort by playing the character Hugo Peabody in the 1962 camp classic *Bye Bye Birdie*, the film adaptation of a hit musical loosely based on Presley's induction into the army; the movie also featured a radiant young Ann-Margret.

Bobby Vinton was nowhere near being a rocker, but young people did buy his pop music in the '60s, even though it was a throwback to the prerock era—sentimental songs like "Roses Are Red (My Love)," "Blue on Blue," "Blue

Velvet" (which David Lynch used to memorable effect in his film of the same title), and "There! I've Said It Again," which was knocked off the top of the charts by the Beatles' "I Want to Hold Your Hand." "Mr. Lonely," in 1964, was Vinton's last No. 1 single.

There was also a Bobby who had no resemblance whatsoever to the others: Darin. Born Walden Robert Cassotto in the Bronx, he first came on the scene in the late '50s with "Splish Splash," "Dream Lover," and the No. 1 single "Mack the Knife"; "Beyond the Sea" was a Top 10 hit in 1960. Even though Darin was originally marketed as a teen idol (he was married to another "good-girl" screen icon, Sandra Dee), he was altogether much more complicated. He never stuck to one style, although he could easily have had a long career as a Sinatra-esque crooner; instead, he darted between rock, standards, folk, and Vegas. Darin was socially conscious enough to attend a 1965 civil rights march through Alabama and tasteful enough to cut songs by the Stones, Dylan, the Lovin' Spoonful's John Sebastian, and Tim Hardin (resulting in a Top 10 hit with his 1966 cover of "If I Were a Carpenter"). Darin even employed Roger McGuinn, who later led the Byrds, in the folk-rock segment of

Bobby Darin, as seen on *The Bob Hope Show*, 1960. Courtesy of Photofest.

his nightclub act. Darin was born with a rheumatic heart, and died during open-heart surgery before reaching forty. Whether he was actually a rocker or not seemed to have been decided when he was inducted into the Rock and Roll Hall of Fame in 1990.

DEL SHANNON

Del Shannon was nobody's idea of a pretty boy. He wrote his own material, teaching himself to play guitar when he was fourteen and honing his skills during a stint in the army, stationed overseas in Germany. When he returned home to Michigan, he began playing with a club band while working as a carpet salesman during the day. It took two years for him to be discovered by a local DJ

Del Shannon, 1962. Courtesy of Photofest.

who had connections to a Detroit label, but once he was signed, he had a No. 1 hit on his hands. Shannon's 1961 debut single, "Runaway," employed minor chords (presaging the British invasion, in the opinion of some critics) and a naggingly insistent organ riff to great effect. The follow-up, "Hats Off to Larry," reached the Top Ten. In 1964, Shannon recorded "Keep Searchin' (We'll Follow the Sun)," which would become one of his most popular songs, and the following year Peter & Gordon (who had their first hit with a Lennon-McCartney number because Peter's sister was McCartney's girlfriend) entered the Top 10 with their cover of Shannon's "I Go to Pieces." In turn, Shannon was the first American artist to cover the Beatles; huge in England, he first heard the band during a UK tour and cut "From Me to You" in 1963. Yet despite similarities to the sound coming out of England and a later association with Rolling Stones manager Andrew Loog Oldham, Shannon's recording career slumped around 1965. He was plagued with personal issues, including a tendency toward depression and a resultant overindulgence in alcohol.

Shannon managed to get free of alcohol, but not his other problems. Although he continued to work, both on his own music and producing other artists, Shannon's demon caught up with him in 1990. Shannon, 55 when he died of a self-inflicted rifle wound shortly after he began taking a controversial antidepressant, was inducted into the Rock and Roll Hall of Fame in 1999.

NOTES

1. D. K. Peneny, *History of Rock and Roll*, http://www.history-of-rock.com/payola.htm.

2. Al Aronowitz, *Bob Dylan and the Beatles: Volume One of the Best of the Blacklisted Journalist* (New York: 1st Books Library, 2003), pp. 140, 149.

3. Ibid., p. 167.

4. *Lyrics Vault Hall of Fame: Cliff Richard*, http://www.lyricsvault.net/halloffame/Cliff_Richard.html.

5. Ibid.

6. Gary Morris, "Beyond the Beach: AIP's Beach Party Movies," *Bright Lights Film Journal*, no. 21 (May 1998), http://www.brightlightsfilm.com/21/21_beach.html.

7. Harvey Kubernik, "The Backpages Interview: Andrew Loog Oldham," *Rock's Backpages* (January 2001), http://www.andrewloogoldham.com/reviews/rocksbpgs.html.

8. John Lennon (1975) quoted in the Beatles, *The Beatles Anthology* (San Francisco: Chronicle Books LLC, 2000), p. 192.

9. Ibid.

10. Charles Einfeld, Twentieth Century Fox vice president of advertising and publicity, writing to producer David Weisbart, in Alanna Nash, *The Colonel: The Extraordinary Story of Colonel Tom Parker and Elvis Presley* (New York: Simon & Schuster, 2003), p. 196.

11. Ibid., p. 201.

12. Music journalist Michael Streissguth, quoted ibid., p. 211.

13. Parker quoted ibid., p. 312.

14. Carl Perkins quoted on Rick/Ricky Nelson's Official Web site, http://www.ricknelson.com.

15. Ibid.

16. Gene Pitney quoted in Alexis Petridis, "Life After Tulsa," *London Guardian* (May 14, 2003), http://www.guardian.co.uk/arts/critic/feature/0,1169,955783,00.html.

17. Ibid.

"THE SOUND OF YOUNG AMERICA"

BERRY GORDY AND MOTOWN

It is not coincidental that Berry Gordy labored on an automobile factory production line before founding Motown, the most successful black-owned label of all time. He named the label after a contraction of the slang term for Detroit, "Motor City," using "town" to represent the small-village feel of his childhood. Because Gordy understood the process of assembling a product step by step, he missed nothing when he was constructing his records and artists' careers: his instincts were aligned with those of old-school Hollywood moguls when it came to the business of star-making. Gordy had a charm school on the premises to teach deportment and manners; exceptional choreographers; the best available studio players; and his own unerring eye and ear. He created a model of black capitalism and creativity, assembling some of the greatest talent ever gathered under one roof, at a time when African Americans were called "Negroes" or "colored" in polite company and were still not allowed to share drinking fountains, swimming pools, or other public facilities with Caucasian citizens. As Smokey Robinson pointed out, "Motown was the first bridge between white and black music. It was one of the great barrier breakers. . . . Berry told us we were going to make music for everybody. I hear it on the radio now, almost as much as I did then—and it still holds up."[1] One of Motown's bold slogans was "The Sound of Young America," and that prediction came true: after Gordy's revolution, African American music would never be ghettoized again.

Gordy (actually Gordy Jr.) was born seventh of an eventual eight children, the son of a plastering contractor in Detroit's inner city. He was a boxer, served in the army, where he obtained his GED, and managed a record store financed by his family, which failed. Gordy landed his first break when Jackie Wilson's label bought one of his songs, "Reet Petite," which gave Wilson a 1957 hit. That was the year Gordy spotted Smokey Robinson and the Miracles and began recording that group. After Robinson sang to Gordy the song that would become Motown's first single, "Bad Girl," Gordy recalled: "All I could think about was how happy I was that I had met this young genius. . . . I felt honored."[2] In 1958, he produced records for Eddie Holland and his brother Brian, who became the nucleus of Holland-Dozier-Holland, one of the most staggeringly successful songwriting teams in popular music. (After Gordy signed a group once known as the Four Aims, rechristened the Four Tops, Holland-Dozier-Holland took them in hand and came up with 1964's "Baby I Need Your Loving," the first in a long string of hits.)

Gordy redoubled his songwriting efforts, leasing a song he had produced and co-written with Janie Bradford—"Money (That's What I Want)," sung by Barrett Strong—to his sisters Anna and Gwen, who had a small label distributed by Chess out of Chicago. (Strong never again came close to the success of "Money," which reached No. 2 R&B and grazed the pop Top 20, but he was an important associate of Gordy's and did work on other historic records, including collaborations on Marvin Gaye's "I Heard It through the Grapevine," The Temptations' "Papa Was a Rolling Stone" and "Ball of Confusion," and Edwin Starr's "War.") When "Money" did well, Gordy was able once more to turn to his family and receive an $800 loan to launch Tamla in January 1959; the name was inspired by "Tammy," Debbie Reynolds's then-current hit song. Tamla, later joined by Motown and other imprints, operated out of a house at 2648 West Grand Boulevard that Gordy grandly called "Hitsville U.S.A."

Gordy developed a mantra for himself: "Create, Make, Sell." The first part had to do with writing, producing, and recording; the second, with the actual manufacturing process; and the third is self-explanatory. His motto later became "Create, Sell, Collect"—that is, get paid, which evolved into "Pay (the bills), Save, Reinvest (back into the business)." He insisted upon an in-house finishing school, where the rough diamonds he had taken off the tough streets of Detroit would be polished, learning how to comport themselves both onstage and off. The artist development crew (most notably Cholly Atkins, choreographer, Harvey Fuqua, show coordinator, and Maurice King, bandleader and vocal coach) handled everything from staging, dance moves, and costumes to stage patter and musical arrangements. Motown even had a quality-control program, complete with weekly evaluations, the same as in the auto plants. Yet Gordy also managed to foster a working environment that encouraged artistic endeavor: "Hitsville had an atmosphere that allowed people to experiment creatively and gave them the courage not to be afraid to make mistakes."[3]

Now that Detroit finally had a strong indie label, all the local talent began beating a path to Gordy's door. He auditioned a group called the Primettes in 1960; he liked the young women, but advised them to finish high school. Gordy did, however, sign a girl named Mary Wells, found by producer Robert

Bateman; he also acquired the contract of a young Marvin Gaye and discovered a group called the Distants, which he renamed the Temptations. Bateman also brought the Marvelettes to Motown in 1961 after spotting them at a high-school talent show; he and Brian Holland produced their first single, "Please Mr. Postman," which gave Gordy his first No. 1 pop hit.

The Supremes

When the Primettes graduated and returned to Motown in 1961, Gordy signed them and rechristened the group the Supremes. If the Beatles were the

The Supremes (left to right) Diana Ross, Mary Wilson, and Florence Ballard. Courtesy of Photofest.

original "boy band," the Supremes were the ultimate "girl group," a trio of African American women so sleekly groomed and elegantly gowned, so upbeat and smiling that racism did not even seem to enter the gleaming picture. Gordy realized that this group could deliver standards and Broadway show tunes, the key to vaulting his performers out of chitlin-circuit venues into top nightclubs. As with the Beatles-Stones "rivalry" touted at that time, the Supremes were considered lightweight, suitable for white consumption, whereas Martha and the Vandellas were thought to be more authentically "black."

Believing the Supremes to be unique, Gordy made the group a top priority, even though it took three long years to get their first hit, "Where Did Our Love Go?" Once the floodgates were open, the Supremes ran up a string of No. 1 singles during 1964 and 1965: "Baby Love," "Stop! In the Name of Love," "Come See about Me," and "Back in My Arms Again," all written by Holland-Dozier-Holland and fraught with tension created by Diana Ross's cooing vocals against a thunderous backdrop courtesy of Motown's house band, the Funk Brothers. It was a cinch to get the Supremes booked on *Ed Sullivan* and then into New York's Copacabana, the country's premiere nightclub; every other top venue in the nation began clamoring for the act—and the other Motown artists, as well.

Stevie Wonder

Gordy's knack for finding new names for his stable continued unabated when one of the Miracles brought him a blind eleven-year-old, Steveland Judkins; declaring the child a "wonder," Gordy decided that henceforth he would be known as Little Stevie Wonder. A live recording of this prodigy at Chicago's Regal Theatre, called "Fingertips, Part 2," made it to No. 1 on the pop singles chart in 1963; the subsequent record, *12 Year Old Genius*, gave Motown its first No. 1 pop album.

Wonder had been brought to Gordy in 1961 by Ronnie White of the Miracles; born premature, he had been put in an incubator, where an excess of oxygen had probably caused his blindness. It did not stop him one bit: the child sang in his church's choir and had learned piano, harmonica, and drums by age nine. He adored Ray Charles, another blind African American genius, and his first Motown album (in 1962) was titled *A Tribute to Uncle Ray*.

While Wonder's youth and disability would instantly grab the attention of any reviewer or audience, that was never Gordy's first consideration. Mable John, the elder sister of R&B singer Little Willie John, was the first female singer Gordy ever signed; she pointed out that his "plan was for each artist to be an artist, not a gimmick . . . if you're a good artist, you don't even need a [current] record to work, once you became established . . . many of the original Motown artists don't have recording contracts at this time. But they work, because number one, the way he groomed the artists, they could work anywhere and anytime. And that is the greatest foundation you can have."[4]

The Funk Brothers

In addition to all these artists and producers (at this point, only Robinson was allowed to produce his own work), Gordy made sure that the backing players were the hottest around. The core of this handpicked team, known as the Funk Brothers, was composed of the astonishing James Jamerson (inducted into the Rock and Roll Hall of Fame in 2000) on bass, drummer Benny Benjamin (although he later became a heroin addict, it still took two men to replace him after he died of a stroke), guitarist Robert White, and Earl Van Dyke on keyboards.

They recorded in the basement of Hitsville, a dimly lit room they dubbed "the Snakepit." While other players were added or subtracted as the occasion demanded, these four were the original basis for the Motown Sound. The Funk Brothers have been credited with playing on more No. 1 singles than the Beach Boys, the Rolling Stones, Elvis, and the Beatles combined, making them the greatest hit machine that popular music has ever had.[5] A sampling of the singles on which the group played during this period includes the Supremes' 1964 hits "Baby Love" and "Where Did Our Love Go?" plus "Stop! In the Name of Love" (1965) and "You Keep Me Hanging On" (1966); Martha and the Vandellas' "Heat Wave" (1963) and "Dancing in the Street" (1964); The Miracles' "Shop Around" (1961), "Ooh Baby Baby" (1965), and "Going to a Go-Go" (1966); the Temptations' "The Way You Do the Things You Do" (1964) and "Ain't Too Proud to Beg" and "Get Ready" (both in 1966); Marvin Gaye's "Wonderful One" (1964) and "How Sweet It Is to Be Loved By You" (1965); and Mary Wells's "My Guy" (1964).

According to drummer Steve Jordan (who once anchored David Letterman's *Late Night* band), interviewed in the documentary about the Funk Brothers, *Standing in the Shadows of Motown*: "When these cats cut tracks—and really, no offense to any of the great artists who sang on them—[the cartoon character] Deputy Dawg could've sung on them, and they would've been a hit." The film's co-producer, Allan Slutsky, adds: "When you think [about] Motown, it's the story of the incredible studio band with a revolving set of vocalists. They were the continuity. They were the reason Motown sounded the way it sounded."[6] Gordy realized this, calling the Funk Brothers "the greatest house band that anyone would ever want";[7] each was paid between $25,000 and $50,000 annually in the early '60s, when that kind of salary really meant something (the buying power of $1 then is equivalent to about $6 in 2004 terms).[8]

Motown eventually moved to Los Angeles, in part because of Gordy's desire to conquer films; inevitably, some of the magic and family feel of the original operation was lost in translation. There were problems with artists who felt that they had been financially kept in the dark, if not actually ripped off, or somehow ignored and neglected in favor of others. Then the company was sold. But, as Brenda Holloway somewhat wistfully pointed out, "Motown was an era, an epoch, something that will never happen again. It was a once-in-a-lifetime

Sam Cooke, 1964. Courtesy of the Library of Congress.

thing, as the Beatles were."[9] In 1990, Berry Gordy was inducted into the Rock and Roll Hall of Fame.

SAM COOKE

For all his accomplishments, Gordy was not the first African American to own his own label: that honor belonged to singer-songwriter Sam Cooke, who already had his own publishing company and formed SAR in 1960. He was also the first black singer who refused to perform unless a concert was integrated. Whereas Gordy ensured that Motown and its artists stayed upbeat and nonpolitical (he admitted to becoming "scared" when Marvin Gaye declared that he wanted to do a protest album),[10] Cooke spent time with Malcolm X and the boxer Cassius Clay, who renamed himself Muhammad Ali upon converting to Islam. After hearing Bob Dylan's "Blowin' in the Wind," Cooke wrote what he called his own "civil rights" song, "A Change Is Gonna Come" (1965). Among his other best-known songs were "You Send Me" (1957); "Chain Gang" (1960); "Cupid" (1961); and "Twistin' the Night Away," "Havin' a Party," and "Bring It on Home to Me" (all in 1962).

Cooke's career started in gospel music in 1950 when he joined the Soul Stirrers on traditional songs such as "Touch the Hem of His Garment," "Nearer to Thee," and "That's Heaven to Me" (many of his performances from this period are included on the album *The Original Soul Stirrers Featuring Sam Cooke*). But because it was considered an honor and privilege to sing for the glory of the Lord, the religious community castigated Cooke when his singing turned secular in nature in 1956 with the pop single "Lovable," recorded under the name Dale Cooke in an effort to avoid recognition. His ambition drove him to reach the widest audience possible, while his handsome face and silky voice could drive even the most devout ladies into frenzy. As Aretha Franklin once admitted, "I just loved him. That man could mess up a whole roomful of women."[11]

Cooke got off the road for a while in 1964, but was still working hard at home in Los Angeles, preparing a live album recorded at New York's Copacabana (which would go to No. 1 upon its release the following year), screen-testing for a possible film career, and finishing off the next single, "Shake." But Cooke was unhappy with his manager, Allen Klein, hinting to a friend that he had discovered "something" and was planning to part ways. On the evening of December 10, Cooke (who was in the habit of carrying thousands of dollars in cash on his person, a great sum of money in those days) was having dinner with friends in Hollywood. Someone he knew arrived with a Eurasian woman named Lisa Boyer; she and Cooke left together and wound up at a motel nearby, where Cooke signed his real name in the register. The story becomes somewhat murky after that. Bertha Franklin, the motel manager, told police that sometime in the early hours of the morning, a half-clad man (Cooke) had begun pounding on her door, shouting that "his girl" was in there with her. He broke the door down and attacked Franklin, who fought back, shooting him three times with a gun she owned. Even after she shot him in the heart, Franklin claimed, Cooke kept coming, so she beat him on the head with a stick.

The autopsy found an elevated level of alcohol in Cooke's blood, and the coroner described his killing as a "justifiable homicide." Franklin, who received $30,000 from Cooke's estate for the battery he had allegedly committed, died eighteen months after his death. No one ever investigated further, since Cooke's widow, Barbara, did not want her children put through more pain. (She had now wed singer Bobby Womack; they divorced six years later.) Cooke's legacy, however, lives on despite the shadowy circumstances of his demise; as the Rolling Stones' Keith Richards once put it, "Sam Cooke is somebody other singers have to measure themselves against, and most of them go back to pumping gas."[12] After the loss of Cooke, there was a huge vacuum in the African American heartthrob department, which was ably filled by two very disparate Motown-affiliated singer-songwriters: William "Smokey" Robinson and Marvin Gaye.

SMOKEY ROBINSON

The majority of singles on John Lennon's portable jukebox were by the Miracles, headed by Smokey Robinson. Robinson was a good-looking, green-eyed, fair-complected man with an outwardly amiable manner, blessed with a pure and soaring falsetto and extraordinary lyrical talent. Bob Dylan, no slouch in the songwriting department himself, once called Robinson "America's greatest living poet."[13] Robinson was second only to friend and mentor Gordy in the public's association with Motown: he was a bandleader (of the Miracles), songwriter, in-house producer, and talent scout. He helped put Motown/Tamla on the map in 1961 when the Miracles' "Shop Around," their first hit, went to No. 2 pop, No. 1 R&B, and sold more than a million copies. Diana Ross came to Motown in part because she was Robinson's neighbor. In all, he was responsible

Smokey Robinson and the Miracles (left to right), Pete Moore, Smokey Robinson, Ronnie White, and Bobby Rogers, 1961. Courtesy of Photofest.

for more than two dozen Top 40 hits with the Miracles and on his own, writing and/or producing "You Beat Me to the Punch," "Two Lovers," and "My Guy" for Mary Wells; "Get Ready," "The Way You Do the Things You Do," and "My Girl" for the Temptations; "Don't Mess with Bill" and "The Hunter Gets Captured by the Game" for the Marvelettes; and "Ain't That Peculiar" and "I'll Be Doggone" for Marvin Gaye.

Robinson began singing and writing material when he was still in high school in the mid-1950s, with a group called the Five Chimes. Several personnel shuffles later, with the addition of Claudette Rogers (whom Robinson would wed, precipitating her retirement), the Matadors, as they were now called, auditioned for Jackie Wilson's manager. Although he passed, Gordy was interested, but suggested that the Matadors was not the right name for a group that had a woman involved. Names were written down and tossed into a hat; Smokey's favorite, the Miracles, was pulled. Berry produced the group's first single, "Got a Job" (as a then-popular "answer" song, this time to the Silhouettes' previous hit "Get a Job") for a New York label, which was released on Robinson's eighteenth birthday in 1958. That failed to chart; the follow-up "Bad Girl" (co-written by Gordy and Robinson), issued on Gordy's own Tamla/Motown, reached a dismal No. 93. But with "Shop Around," the third try was the charm. In 1962, the group had its first No. 1 with "You've Really

Got a Hold on Me" (later covered by the Beatles), going on to cut "Mickey's Monkey" (Top 10 in 1962), 1965's "The Tracks of My Tears" and "Ooo Baby Baby," and "Going to a Go-Go" (1966), all co-written by Robinson and sung in his caress of a voice.

Robinson was raised without much in the way of material riches, but was surrounded by soul: "From the time I can remember, I always heard music in my house. The first voices that I ever remember hearing were Sarah Vaughan, Billy Eckstine, Woody Herman, Count Basie, Duke Ellington; I grew up listening to those people and my mom also played gospel music. She played the Five Blind Boys . . . the Soul Stirrers and people like that. So I had all kinds of music coming at me at all times. . . . I have been influenced by all of those people, by jazz and by symphony and opera and blues and gospel. . . . I cannot imagine a world without music." He added that having such a grounding was an immeasurable help in his career:

> If music is going to be your life, you better know who preceded you, what they did, what their music was like and how it influenced their generations. If you don't know that, and you're trying to make music your life, then you're incomplete. You're just a pass-through. There's a lot of pass-throughers in show business; they have one hit record, and next day you don't know where they are. If you want to be a pass-through, then fine— you don't have to know any music history, you don't have to know who influenced you, you don't have to know anything about your predecessors or anything like that, but if you're really a music person, you're going to know that kind of stuff.[14]

In 1972, Robinson left the group to pursue a solo career, which has been somewhat spottier than his track record with Motown would suggest. Looking back, Robinson seemed to acknowledge that fact: "Motown was a once in a lifetime event; it had never happened like that before that time, nor do I think it will ever happen like that again."[15] Yet Robinson's position in the pop pantheon is assured; as one British critic points out: "In the list of the hundred best songs of the 1960s, at least ten written by Smokey Robinson would have to be included. . . . For anybody who has heard the songs a few times, the titles by themselves conjure a mood, a few intricately-rhyming lines, even a place where a vocal group comes in to harmonize. . . . Smokey's style can establish innocence and devotion better than any other singer—and those are two of the most common and important moods in popular music."[16]

MARVIN GAYE

Pop music will always celebrate romance, yet underneath the prettification, there is often raw sex appeal. That quality—along with style, charisma, and

Marvin Gaye, 1961. Courtesy of Photofest.

visionary songwriting skills—was abundant in the person of Marvin Gaye. His is a tragic story, beginning with much promise and ending in the most sordid manner possible when he was shot to death by his own father one day short of his forty-fifth birthday. As Gaye's biographer (the book is aptly titled *Divided Soul*) once put it, "His biography and discography are twin reflections of the same duality: the artistic and personal struggle to heal the split between head and heart, flesh and spirit, ego and God. . . . His legacy as artistic rebel and sensual romanticist is secure. His songs are loved the world over, sung and resung by younger generations who feel the sincerity of his struggle and the joy of his spirit."[17]

Gaye was the second of three children born to a California minister who belonged to a strict, conservative Christian sect that observed no holidays; little Marvin was singing in the church choir when he was only three. Music became an escape from his miserable home life, which included beatings doled out on an almost daily basis by Marvin Gay Sr. (the singer added the "e" professionally after enduring years of teasing about the homosexual implications of his surname). Marvin senior was a deeply troubled man, a cross-dresser devoted to a faith that undoubtedly condemned such activities.

Gaye got out of his father's house as soon as possible, joining an R&B vocal group called the Rainbows with Don Covay and Billy Stewart and later switching to the Marquees in 1957; they recorded for Chess under the auspices of Bo Diddley. The following year, Gaye joined a doo-wop outfit, the Moonglows, run by producer-singer Harvey Fuqua, and when Fuqua moved to Detroit, Gaye went along. Harvey hooked up with Berry Gordy at Motown, where Gaye became a session drummer and vocalist before catching the eye of Gordy's sister Anna. After they wed in 1961, he was offered a solo contract. Gaye envisioned himself a crooner in the mold of Nat "King" Cole or Frank Sinatra; he wanted to sit center stage sipping a martini while interpreting classic ballads. That was not quite how Gordy pictured it, even though he indulged his new brother-in-law for a while. The following year, Gaye complied with Gordy's wishes, writing his first R&B hit in "Stubborn Kind of Fellow," which, according to Gordy and others, was all too apt an autobiographical description. In July 1963, Gaye had a Top 10 smash with "Pride and Joy."

Gaye continued his behind-the-scenes work, too, co-writing "Dancing in the Streets" for Martha Reeves and the Vandellas (who had done backup vocals on "Stubborn") and drumming on some early Stevie Wonder albums. By 1965, he was moving toward a smoother singing style, notching consecutive hits with "How Sweet It Is to Be Loved by You," which reached No. 6 pop in 1965, "I'll Be Doggone," and "Ain't That Peculiar." Gaye's biggest hit, 1968's "I Heard It through the Grapevine," went to No. 1 R&B, No. 2 pop, and sold 4 million copies, giving Motown its greatest '60s chart success. As the company's top-selling male vocalist, Gaye was teamed with Motown "queen" Mary Wells; once she left the company, he was thrown together with Kim Weston. Only when Gaye was matched with Tammi Terrell did the duets really take off, with "Ain't No Mountain High Enough" and "You're All I Need to Get By." Tragically, Terrell developed a brain tumor and collapsed in Gaye's arms onstage in 1967; her death three years later sent Gaye into a sorrowful seclusion. He later remarked that he felt that he had somehow died along with her.

THE FOUR TOPS AND THE TEMPTATIONS

A happier tale is that of the Four Tops. Lead vocalist Levi Stubbs, first tenor Abdul "Duke" Fakir, second tenor Lawrence Payton, and baritone Renaldo "Obie" Benson, who had gotten together soon after graduating from high school, arrived at Motown in 1963 with ten years of performing and recording experience. Between 1965 and 1967, the group cut some of Motown's most memorable tracks with the help of the Holland-Dozier-Holland team: "Reach Out, I'll Be There," "Standing in the Shadows of Love," "I Can't Help Myself (Sugar Pie Honey Bunch)," and "Baby I Need Your Loving." They stayed together without a change of personnel for some four decades, a staggering achievement in pop music, and were inducted into the Rock and Roll Hall of Fame in 1990.

The Temptations were a merger between two vocal groups: a trio from Alabama named the Primes (which provided Eddie Kendricks, high tenor, and Paul Williams, baritone) and a quintet called the Distants (Otis Williams, middle tenor, Melvin Franklin, bass, and Elbridge Bryant). The Temptations were Gordy's first signing to his label, but by 1963, they had still had no hits. Then gospel-influenced tenor David Ruffin replaced Bryant to complete the lineup of what the group liked to call "five lead vocalists." In early 1964, their version of Smokey Robinson's "The Way You Do the Things You Do" landed in the Top 20. From that year until 1968, when Ruffin left to go solo, the Temptations had a string of hits such as "My Girl," "Ain't Too Proud to Beg," "Beauty's Only Skin Deep," "(I Know) I'm Losing You," and "I Wish It Would Rain." The group, in various incarnations, continued to perform well for Motown and racked up many more hits in the 1970s and beyond. It was inducted into the Rock and Roll Hall of Fame in 1989.

The Temptations, 1963. Courtesy of Photofest.

The one and only Ray Charles, 1961. Courtesy of Photofest.

OTHER AFRICAN AMERICAN PERFORMERS

Ray Charles

Meanwhile, there were plenty of African Americans who achieved success on the charts outside of Motown, including the pioneers Ray Charles and James Brown. Charles has been credited with breaking down the barriers between gospel and secular to create soul. During the Depression, his family was mired deep in poverty in the segregated South. "Even compared to other blacks," Charles once wrote, "we were on the bottom of the ladder looking up. Nothing below us except the ground."[18] However, a local café owner encouraged Charles's interest in the piano while Ray was still a toddler. At five, Charles saw his brother drown in a tub his mother used for laundry, and two years later, he lost his sight entirely (while some reports cite glaucoma as a cause, Charles himself said that there had been no official diagnosis). Orphaned as a teen, he studied musical composition and learned how to read and write music in Braille while mastering instruments, including piano and saxophone, during the nine years he spent at the School for the Deaf and the Blind in St. Augustine, Florida.

At seventeen, he moved to Seattle, choosing a state as far as possible from his original home, and there he met and befriended Quincy Jones. Charles signed with Atlantic in 1952 just as that label was getting off the ground. There he recorded the classic "What'd I Say" (No. 1 R&B, No. 6 pop in 1959) and a string of No. 1 pop hits, beginning with his 1960 cover of Hoagy Carmichael's "Georgia on My Mind" (since named the official state song). That was followed by "Hit the Road Jack" (No. 1, 1961) and "Unchain My Heart" (No. 9, 1962). After Charles moved to ABC-Paramount in 1962, he accomplished the highly unlikely feat of topping the *Billboard* charts for fourteen weeks with the album *Modern Sounds in Country and Western Music*, proving that no genre was off limits. In 1962, he once again perched at the top of the pop charts with "I Can't Stop Loving You" and reached No. 7 with the standard "You Are My Sunshine" (No. 1 R&B). At the beginning of 1966, Charles had a No. 6 hit on the Pop Singles chart with "Crying Time"; by the end of that year, he may have been shedding real tears when he was arrested for possession of heroin and marijuana. Given a five-year suspended sentence, Charles made the most of it by kicking the drug habit that had plagued him since his teen years. In 2004, at seventy-three, Ray Charles died of complications from liver disease.

JERRY WEXLER (B. 1918) AND THE STAX STORY

During his time at Atlantic, Ray Charles was fortunate enough to work with Jerry Wexler, Ahmet Ertegun's second-in-command and an integral part of the R&B story. Wexler began his music business career as a song plugger for BMI and then a reporter at *Billboard*, where he famously changed the term "race records" to "rhythm and blues" (R&B); those connections immeasurably helped Atlantic during its formative years after Wexler came on board as an executive. He began producing by default ("No one really knew how to make a record when I started. You simply went into the studio, turned on the mike and said play").[19]

Wexler discovered Stax Records while he was in Memphis plugging some Atlantic releases to local DJ Dewey Phillips (who had had a big hand in making Elvis Presley known). Stax had an amazing house band in Booker T. and the MGs, studio space already set up, and an owner eager for wider distribution. Wexler took that infrastructure and brought in Sam and Dave, whom he had signed out of Florida, and Wilson Pickett, who had big hits with songs like "In the Midnight Hour" (1965), "634-5789," "Mustang Sally," and "Land of 1,000 Dances" (all in 1966), but also helped to destroy the relationship between the Stax and Atlantic labels when he could not get along with the local musicians. Wexler hit gold a second time when he uncovered a similar scene at the FAME Studios in Muscle Shoals, Alabama: extraordinary house writers and musicians working at a studio already in progress. With Percy Sledge, Wexler cut the immortal "When a Man Loves a Woman" there. The producer was inducted into the Rock and Roll Hall of Fame in 1987.

James Brown and the Famous Flames during a live performance in 1964. Courtesy of the Library of Congress.

James Brown

James Brown was born in 1928 in South Carolina, although he prefers to shave five years off his age and give his birthplace as Georgia in his "official" biographies. Brown's two main nicknames—"the Godfather of Soul" and "the Hardest-Working Man in Show Business"—are well earned, considering the powerhouse he was back in the 1960s. "I'll Go Crazy" and "Think" made dents in the segregated charts of 1960, and in 1963, Brown finally cracked the pop Top 20 with "Prisoner of Love." That same year, he financed the recording of his epochal *Live at the Apollo* album, about which the *Encyclopedia of Popular Music* says: "Raw, alive and uninhibited, this shattering collection confirmed Brown as the voice of black America—every track on the album is a breathtaking event. More than 30 years on, with all the advances in recording technology, this album stands as one of the greatest live productions of all time."[20]

To watch Brown utterly destroy the audience on *The T.A.M.I. Show* in 1965—and to then see the tentative Rolling Stones, on the same bill, fail to even touch his explosive star quality—is highly instructive. "Papa's Got a Brand New Bag" (1965) and "I Got You (I Feel Good)" the following year made the white public even more aware of Brown, who has continued to make records and news, with sad reports of erratic behavior, a bizarre personal life, and troubles with the law. Artists as widely varied as Public Enemy, George Michael, and Sinead O'Connor have all taken something from James Brown, and as long as there is such a thing as popular music, he will undoubtedly continue to exert a powerful influence.

Percy Sledge

Sledge wrote only one song, his biggest hit—the immortal No. 1 churchified smash "When a Man Loves a Woman"—but wound up giving all his royalties to two musicians who had written a demo the song was based upon. Sledge felt that it was their idea originally, and he had "plenty of money" at the time. He has continued working, particularly overseas, although on a much slower track; remarkably, Sledge holds no bitterness, especially since he was inducted into the Rock and Roll Hall of Fame in 2005. He also cherishes his memories of being mentored by the likes of Otis Redding.

Otis Redding

Redding was the giant of soul, "Mr. Excitement," the one who was going to cross over big-time. He worked at Stax, writing almost all his own material, often in collaboration with Booker T. and the MGs; his first hit was "These Arms of Mine" in 1962, the same year Booker T. and the MGs had their first smash with the instrumental "Green Onions." In 1965 and 1966, Redding had huge R&B hits with "Mr. Pitiful," "I Can't Turn You Loose," a cover of the Rolling Stones' "Satisfaction" (the band returned the favor by covering Redding's "Pain in My Heart" and "That's How Strong My Love Is"), and "Respect," which Aretha Franklin later covered and made her signature song. Additionally, his 1965 hit "I've Been Loving You Too Long" was selected by the Library of Congress for the 2003 National Recording Registry; criteria for inclusion are that a recording must be

Otis Redding performing at the Monterey Pop Festival, 1967. Courtesy of Photofest.

"culturally, historically or aesthetically important, and/or inform or reflect life in the United States."[21] Redding was rightly worshipped in England, where he appeared on *Ready, Steady, Go!* in 1966, the same year he covered the Beatles' "Day Tripper." In fact, during the Stax-Volt tour of Europe the following spring, the Fab Four themselves reportedly met the MGs right off the plane. When Redding played the Whisky a Go Go in Los Angeles in 1966, a who's who of rock royalty was there, from the Mamas and the Papas to the Smothers Brothers and Bob Dylan. According to Redding's (Caucasian) manager Phil Walden, Dylan gave the singer a prerelease copy of his "Just Like a Woman," saying that it had been inspired by him. "Otis' appraisal of it was that it had too damn many words."[22] According to Walden, it was Rolling Stones manager Andrew Loog Oldham who helped arrange for Redding to appear on the bill at the 1967 Monterey Pop Festival, which served the purpose of exposing him to the crossover audience he had been hoping to reach.

Redding was ahead of his time in many ways; he had spoken to colleagues like James Brown and Solomon Burke about forming an organization to improve working conditions and health benefits for soul performers, and he had already set up a talent management agency and a demo studio at his "Big O" ranch, planning to create his own version of Stax-Volt. He influenced artists from Bob Marley to Janis Joplin and was always interested in expanding his creative horizons. Redding's sense of exploration and his color blindness, his personal warmth and emotional generosity toward others, might have made him as big a mogul as Berry Gordy ever was. Redding had supposedly been trying to fill the void left by the death of Sam Cooke; to date, no one has been able to fill the hole created by his own early demise at age twenty-six in a 1967 plane crash.

NOTES

1. "100 Greatest Moments in Rock," *Entertainment Weekly*, http://www.ew.com/ew/fab400/music100/5-7.html.

2. Berry Gordy, *To Be Loved* (New York: Warner Books, 1995), p. 117.

3. Ibid., p. 174.

4. Mable John quoted in Susan Whitall and Dave Marsh, *Women of Motown: An Oral History (For the Record)* (New York: Quill/HarperCollins, 1998), p. 39.

5. Claim of "more No. 1 singles" made in film quoted by, among other sources, Alex Abramovich, "Hit Man: Learn To Love the Tyrant Who Made Motown," *Slate* (Tuesday, January 14, 2003), http://slate.msn.com/id/2076709/.

6. Allan Slutsky quoted in Steve Jones, "Motown's Funk Brothers Cast Long 'Shadows,'" *USA Today* (November 28, 2002), http://www.usatoday.com/life/music/news/2002-11-28-funk-brothers_x.htm.

7. Gordy, *To Be Loved*, p. 129.

8. Inflation calculation, U.S. Department of Labor, Bureau of Labor Statistics, "Consumer Price Index Home Page," http://www.bls.gov/cpi/.

9. Brenda Holloway quoted in Susan Whitall and Dave Marsh, *Women of Motown: An Oral History* (New York: Avon Books, 1998), p.83.

10. Gordy, *To Be Loved*, p. 313.

11. Quoted by Pamela Des Barres, *Rock Babylon: Dark Moments in Music Babylon* (New York: St. Martin's Press, 1996), p. 96.

12. Keith Richards, quoted ibid., p. 91.

13. Bob Dylan quote reproduced on "Smokey Robinson," BBC, http://www.bbc.co .uk/music/profiles/smokeyrobinson.shtml.

14. Interview with Smokey Robinson, The Experience Music Project Web site, http://www.emplive.com/explore/int_feature3.asp?pg=1.

15. Ibid.

16. Charlie Gillett, "The Miracle of Smokey Robinson," *Record Mirror* (September 25, 1971), accessible at: http://www.rocksbackpages.com/writers/gillett.html.

17. David Ritz (author of *Divided Soul*, a biography of Marvin Gaye), compact disc liner notes for *The Very Best of Marvin Gaye*, Motown, 2001; also available from "Marvin Gaye Biography," http://www.sing365.com/music/lyric.nsf/Marvin-Gaye-Biography/ 2479E1513170C15348256BD400117645.

18. Charles and David Ritz, *Brother Ray: Ray Charles' Own Story* (New York: Da Capo Press/Perseus, 2003), pp. 3–4; also quoted on "Ray Charles Dead at 73," CNN .com, http://edition.cnn.com/2004/SHOWBIZ/Music/06/10/obit.charles/.

19. Jerry Wexler quoted on Rock and Roll Hall of Fame, http://www.rockhall .com/hof/inductee.asp?id=209.

20. "Soul Deep: Biographies," BBC, http://www.bbc.co.uk/music/static/p/biographies .pdf.

21. National Recording Registry, http://www.loc.gov/rr/record/nrpb/nrpb-nrr.html.

22. Phil Walden quoted in Carol Cooper, liner notes for *The Definitive Otis Redding*, Rhino Records, 1993; also quoted on "Carol Cooper on the Web," http://carolcooper .org/music/redding-93.php.

SVENGALIS AND SONGBIRDS

One of the revolutions started by the Beatles was due to the songwriting partnership of John Lennon and Paul McCartney: superior pop tunesmiths, when they began writing from personal experience, they changed the rules of the game. Before this self-contained unit came along, singers were interpreters of someone else's words and emotions; their relationship to their producers was much like that of actors and directors. Songs were like orphans, sent into the world to be adopted by others. Producers shifted group personnel from one outfit to another without regard to an artist's creative needs or organic growth. This made life simpler for label executives, managers, and producers; if a singer or musician created any trouble, he or she was easily replaced, or the entire project was discarded. (The resurgence of "boy bands" several decades later, from Menudo to *NSYNC, testifies to the ongoing efficiency of this process.) As producer/impresario Lou Adler notes, "In the U.S. from 1961 to 1964, there weren't any bands; we had a vocalist or vocalists and we used a studio rhythm section."[1] After hearing the Beatles' confessional lyrics, coupled with the heartfelt delivery of the authors and the telepathic communication achieved after disparate individuals bond within a band, listeners began to demand more from rock and pop music. The audience now wanted a glimpse into the artists' hearts and minds, to know that what they were hearing was authentic and not a confection churned out by middle-aged hacks working with pop puppets.

SVENGALIS

Phil Spector

Of the many producers who made their mark on the pre-Beatles landscape, none was more influential than Phil Spector, who made a point of befriending the Beatles, the very harbingers of his career doom. At the dawn of 2004, Phil Spector had been out of the headlines for decades when he made the front pages again, for a startling reason: he was facing Los Angeles murder charges and a trial for the gunshot death of a C-level actress, Lana Clarkson. Yet in the '60s, Spector's "little symphonies for the kids" had ruled the airwaves, making him the "first tycoon of teen," in the memorable catchphrase coined by author Tom Wolfe. At twenty-five, Spector was a millionaire, although warning signs of trouble were already evident; when asked why he did certain things, he would wearily respond: "I'm paying a doctor six hundred dollars a week to find out."[2]

Merv Griffin and Phil Spector, 1966. Courtesy of Photofest.

Despite ongoing mental and emotional problems, Spector was talented and/or energetic enough to attract powerful mentors, studious enough to absorb every bit of useful information, clever enough to combine these disparate influences into something wholly his own, commanding and forceful enough to make others do his bidding, and hugely prolific when all these factors came together. Between 1961 and 1966, Spector's famous "Wall of Sound" (once described as "a musical mind-slam; it overloaded the auditory nerves with such sweepingly complex arrangements and such a barrage of instruments that it rendered the individual parts of the whole unrecognizable"[3]) made him the most successful record producer in the world, with almost two dozen Top 40 hits by such artists as the Ronettes, the Crystals, and the Righteous Brothers.

Before Spector, the role of the producer was publicly unknown; listeners simply assumed, if they gave the matter any thought at all, that records somehow made themselves. When Spector stood behind the console, he flipped the script on the Wizard of Oz: "Pay all of your attention to the man behind the curtain." His artists (excepting Veronica "Ronnie" Bennett, whom he became obsessed with, wed, and lost) were mere voices, pawns, interchangeable tools; all that mattered was the auteur's vision. "Phil Spector was the first one to go into the studio with one song, and if it needed two sessions to do the rhythm section, that's the way it happened," as his arranger Jack Nitzsche re-called. "Producers these days seem more like PR people or business people. Maybe they like the records, but Phil loved the records. He was really the artist."[4]

Despite his insecurities, Spector always had an unshakable vision and total belief in his professional abilities. "People made fun of me, the little kid who was making rock 'n' roll records. But I knew. I would try to tell all the groups, we're doing something very important. Trust me. And it was very hard because these people didn't have that sense of destiny. They didn't know they were pro-ducing art that would change the world. I knew. . . . I think when Thomas Jef-ferson wrote the Declaration of Independence he was thinking, people will remember this. Gershwin may have said to himself, I'm not sure about this American in Paris, but I think he said, this is something special. I think Irving Berlin had an ego. I think he wanted to be number one. And so did I."[5]

Spector paraphrased the inscription on his father's gravestone—"To Know Him Is to Love Him"—for his first No. 1 hit in 1958, recorded by a trio called the Teddy Bears (the other Bears were Marshall Leib, a nineteen-year-old col-lege student, and Annette Kleinbard, a sixteen-year-old still at Fairfax High School in California). To book a session at Gold Star Studios in Hollywood cost fifteen dollars an hour, plus six dollars for a reel of blank tape. Spector felt that he would need forty dollars; he borrowed money from his mother, Harvey Goldstein, a classmate of Lieb's who wanted to sing bass, and Kleinbard, a glee-club singer who kicked in ten dollars to be included.

The studio owners and recording engineers, Stan Ross and Dave Gold, taught Spector just about everything they knew: how to record drums, how to arrange, how to mix down a record. Gold Star pioneered one of the most important innovations in twentieth-century music, the concept of the studio itself as an instrument: its acoustical wall coating made it the perfect echo chamber. Spector played rhythm guitar, Leib played piano, and Kleinbard took lead vocals, which were overdubbed—layering track upon track to make the three-piece sound much larger. Spector later would raise this technique to an art form. The recording was released on a local independent label, in whose of-fices Spector spent the summer after graduation working and learning the ropes. The A side of the single, "Don't You Worry My Little Pet," did all right in the Los Angeles area, but the big break came later that year when a DJ in Fargo, North Dakota, flipped the record to play the B side; an order soon ar-rived for 18,000 copies, and within a week, the song was on the national charts and the Teddy Bears had an invitation to appear on *American Bandstand*. The song went on to sell more than a million copies, snaring Spector his first No. 1.

Unhappy with the label's inability or refusal to spend money promoting the record, Spector chose another imprint to release the follow-up Teddy Bears al-bum; he was clearly in control of this group, installed as producer while still a teenager himself. He had already grasped the fact that he would eventually need his own label and total control, including financial. During the recording of the Teddy Bears album, Spector had the good fortune to meet and impress a

LIEBER AND STOLLER

Jerry Lieber and Mike Stoller (both born in 1933) were a top songwriting team who had hit the big time with the Coasters and the Drifters (their songs include "Kansas City," "Hound Dog," "Love Potion #9," "Poison Ivy," "Stand by Me," "On Broadway," and many others). When Spector arrived in New York in mid-1960, he began by playing guitar on these artists' records, carefully noting the string arrangements and Latin rhythms the songwriters employed. He also paid attention to the ways in which the team put deals together with writers, publishers, and labels, and the talent currently available—writers such as Ellie Greenwich and Jeff Barry. Spector was no slouch as a writer himself, partnering with Lieber on "Spanish Harlem," which became a 1961 hit for Drifters singer Ben E. King.

Hollywood power broker named Lester Sill (then the partner of Lee Hazlewood, who would go on to write "These Boots Are Made for Walkin'" for Nancy Sinatra). Hazlewood was then producing Duane Eddy, for whom he had developed an echo-laden guitar sound. When Hazlewood, who had his own studio in Phoenix, took Spector under his wing by demonstrating experiments with echo and "bouncing" sound (doubling-down tracks on three-track tape), the fledgling duly absorbed it all. Hungry to learn more, Spector asked his new mentor Sill to send him to New York, where he understudied with Jerry Lieber and Mike Stoller.

At the close of 1960, Spector returned west, going back to work under Lester Sill with his first "girl group," the Paris Sisters; of the five singles he made with them, "I Love How You Love Me" went into the Top 10 in late 1961. Spector and Sill formed their own label around this time, Philles (Phil/Les), backed by money from Johnny Mathis's manager, and had a smash with the Crystals' "Uptown." Within months, Spector had bought out his partner to establish total control and began churning out hit after hit at the tiny Gold Star Studios at Hollywood's Santa Monica Boulevard and Vine Street, the same place he had cut the Teddy Bears' records: "He's a Rebel," "He's Sure the Boy I Love," "(Today I Met) the Boy I'm Gonna Marry," and dozens more; a Spector discography fills volumes on its own.

A brief scan of his biggest hits is an amazing chunk of rock history and sonic glory: "Da Doo Ron Ron" and "Then He Kissed Me" (the Crystals); "Be My Baby," "Baby, I Love You," and "Walking in the Rain" (the Ronettes); "You've Lost That Lovin' Feelin'," "Unchained Melody," and "Ebb Tide" (the Righteous Brothers); and "River Deep, Mountain High" (Ike and Tina Turner). That last record bombed after its release, astounding both the artists and Spector himself, and the flop effectively put paid to his career for quite a while. Ironically, it is now considered one of his finest productions, if not a magnificent capper to his most prolific period.

The Ronettes

The Ronettes were Spector's most profound production on a personal level; not only did he finally discover the perfect voice to center his Wall of Sound, he fell in love with its owner, Ronnie Bennett. From 1963 to 1965, Spector produced some of the most spectacular girl-group singles ever recorded for the Ronettes, including the immortal "Be My Baby," and—all in 1964—"Baby I Love You," "(The Best Part of) Breaking Up," and "Walking in the Rain." By 1965, it was all over for the group, torn apart by internal jealousies and Spector's possessiveness, which led him to withhold singles for fear that Ronnie's success would lead to his abandonment.

The three girls—Veronica, or Ronnie as she was known to everyone; her sister Estelle; and their cousin Nedra Talley—grew up in Harlem, and started out in 1960 by singing at bar mitzvahs and sock hops. After meeting a struggling talent agent, the group landed its first recording session (as Ronnie and the Relatives) in June 1961, where four tracks were cut; two were used for a single released that August, which flopped. Undeterred, the girls made themselves up to look older to sneak into the then-hot disco, midtown Manhattan's Peppermint Lounge; and, mistaken for a group of dancers that had not shown up for work, the trio got the job. The girls' exotic good looks (attributed by Ronnie to Cherokee Indian, African, and Caucasian ancestry) did not hurt. After dancing at the opening of a Miami branch of the club, the group, now being called the Ronettes, received an offer from disc jockey Murray the K (see Chapter 1) to dance and sing backup during his popular variety shows at the Fox Theatre in Brooklyn. Ronnie recalls that for $2.50, a fan could see performances by "the Shangri-Las, Marvin Gaye, the Miracles, the Supremes, Martha and the Vandellas . . . the Temptations, the Searchers, Jay and the Americans,"[6] and more on the same bill—plus a movie. But the girls still wanted their own fame, which prompted Estelle to make a cold call to Phil Spector. She was actually put through to the man who was then, Ronnie says, "already a legend."[7] The group auditioned, Spector saw and heard Ronnie, and after extricating the group from its original contract, he signed the group in March 1963.

Spector immediately set about collaborating with skilled songwriters Ellie Greenwich and Jeff Barry on what would become the Ronettes' first major hit, "Be My Baby," which hit No. 2 on the pop charts almost immediately after its release that spring. "It just oozes sex, that record," Billy Joel wrote, "Ronnie's voice, I mean, it sounds almost lubricated. It's got a smell to it, like sweat and garlic. There's an urgency about that voice, a sexuality that screams *street* . . . Ronnie's voice is like the neon glow that hits the streets under the elevated tracks on a hot summer night . . . [she] can wring more emotion out of one long phrase than most other singers can from a whole song."[8]

In autumn 1963, the Ronettes were touring with Dick Clark's Caravan of Stars when Spector pulled Ronnie off the road and replaced her with her cousin Elaine, in order to record "Baby I Love You." The switch was a trick Spector would employ again when the Beatles asked the Ronettes to open for their second American tour in 1966, since by that time the producer was so infatuated with Ronnie that he was determined not to expose her to temptation. In 1964, Ronnie had a flirtation with John Lennon (as did her sister Estelle with George Harrison) when the Ronettes met the Beatles during a tour of

England, where the girls were supporting the fledging Rolling Stones on the latter group's first headlining tour. Ronnie became concerned because the Rolling Stones seemed to give her group the cold shoulder; when she asked their manager Andrew Loog Oldham why the Londoners seemed so standoff-ish, he informed her that Spector had sent a telegram specifically threatening the young men with "dire consequences" if they spoke to the girls at any time.[9] In February 1964, John Lennon invited the Ronettes to fly home to America on the same plane as the Beatles; the latter group was about to embark on its historic first tour of the United States. Spector would not allow it, and flew with the Beatles himself instead.

Spector would say later that the trip "was a lot of fun. It was probably the only time I flew that I wasn't afraid, because I knew that they weren't goin' to get killed in a plane. They were terribly frightened of America. They even said, 'You go first' [getting off the plane]. Cause the whole thing about Kennedy scared them very, very much. They really thought it would be possible for somebody to be there and want to kill them."[10] Instead, the Beatles uninten-tionally helped to kill off Spector's career, along with all the other behind-the-scenes writers and producers that propped up interchangeable singers and groups. As for Ronnie Bennett, she wed—then divorced—Spector, and spent decades trying to revive her once soaring career.

The Brill Building Songwriters and Their Descendants

Tin Pan Alley, the home of America's top popular songwriters, had origi-nally been located in New York's West Twenties, but later migrated just north of Times Square, settling in some anonymous office towers. Among these was 1619 Broadway, aka the Brill Building, named after two brothers who had a clothing store at street level (which, since 1972, has been occupied by the famed Colony Music Shop). The Brill was completed in 1931, with art deco flourishes to prove it; after the Depression set in, the only people willing to rent space turned out to be music publishers. One after another flocked in, and by 1962 there were no fewer than 165 such businesses there. Not only publishers, but demo (demonstration record) studios, duplication offices, arrangers and copyists able to knock off instrumentation lead sheets, managers, radio promo-tion men, record companies, and more songwriters, musicians, and singers available for hire in that one area than almost anywhere else in the city, in-cluding the team of Burt Bacharach and Hal David, occupied offices there.

Yet the business was even more concentrated at another nearby address, ac-cording to Al Kooper (who, before going on to play with Bob Dylan, was a songwriter for hire): "The 'actual' Brill Building was the last bastion of Tin Pan Alley and was widely regarded as an old man's building. Other than Lieber, Stoller, Bacharach, Barry and Greenwich, everything else took place at 1650 Broadway. . . . The education I received in that building for seven years far outweighs any university matriculation. . . . Dylan and the Beatles began the destruction of 1650. The new hip area became Greenwich Village in down-town Manhattan [see Chapter 8]. But from 1958 to 1965, all the great music that came out of New York City was primarily conceived at 1650."[11] The Brill Building was more a state of mind than an actual address. As Genya Ravan (then the lead singer of Goldie and the Gingerbreads) cautions, though: "Whenever you hear a hit from the 1960s you can never be sure who really wrote it." From her late-night perch at a restaurant called Ham 'n Eggs directly across from the Brill Building, she witnessed drug addicts selling songs to "pro-ducers and publishers right there on the sidewalk . . . anyone who bought a nodding junkie's song would claim the credit for writing it."[12] That under-handed commerce might explain the lack of a follow-up in some cases, but there were plenty of songwriters who churned out hit after hit without having to resort to assistance from the pavement brigade.

Burt Bacharach and Hal David

Burt Bacharach began his career in the 1940s by playing piano with jazz bands; he later became a pianist and arranger for nightclub acts, including a 1950s stint with Marlene Dietrich. After Bacharach met lyricist Hal David, whose Famous Music office in the Brill Building was down the hall from his own, the pair began producing a stream of pop hits in 1957 (although Bacharach actually wrote "Baby, It's You" for the Shirelles, later covered by the Beatles, with Hal's brother Mack). In 1964, Bacharach and David ruled the British charts—an unusual reversal of fortune for Americans at the time—with Cilla Black, Dusty Springfield, and Sandie Shaw ("Anyone Who Had a Heart," "I Just Don't Know What to Do with Myself," and "Always Something There to Remind Me," respectively). However, the team's longest-lived, most commercially rewarding collaboration was with Dionne Warwick, who scored more than a dozen hit singles from 1962 to 1968, crossing over on the R&B and pop charts beginning with "Don't Make Me Over," then with "Anyone Who Had a Heart," "Walk On By," "You'll Never Get to Heaven (If You Break My Heart)," "I Say a Little Prayer," "A House Is Not a Home," "I'll Never Fall in Love Again," "Trains and Boats and Planes" (also a hit in the United Kingdom for Billy J. Kramer and the Dakotas), "Do You Know the Way to San Jose?" "Message to Michael," and "Alfie," the theme of the film that launched Michael Caine's long career. Warwick also cut "What's New Pussycat?" from the 1965 Woody Allen–Peter Sellers sex comedy with that ti-tle, even though it will forever be associated with Tom Jones, who had the big-ger hit. Bacharach and David were often dismissed as pop hacks, but it is a fact that the impeccable Walker Brothers had a hit in 1965 with "Make It Easy on Yourself," while both Manfred Mann and Arthur Lee and Love (one of the hardest-rocking acts of the psychedelic era) covered the team's "Little Red Book." Bacharach later collaborated with Elvis Costello and, in deference to his role as a penultimate '60s icon, appeared as himself in the first two *Austin Powers* films.

Ellie Greenwich and Jeff Barry

One day, so the story goes, young singer-songwriter Ellie Greenwich was auditioning in one demo studio when she was overheard by Lieber and Stoller, who mistook her for Carole King; they snapped her up as a staff writer upon realizing her availability. She wrote "Why Do Lovers Break Each Other's Hearts" with another staffer, Tony Powers, which became a hit for Bob B. Soxx and the Blue Jeans, but after she married Jeff Barry (whom she had known for a few years), they became an exclusive writing team. Barry had already written "Tell Laura I Love Her," but their combined talents formed a hit machine: "Baby, I Love You" and "Be My Baby" for the Ronettes, "Da Doo Ron Ron" and "Then He Kissed Me" for the Crystals, and "River Deep, Mountain High" for Ike and Tina Turner. In 1964, Lieber and Stoller installed the newlywed pair at the equally new Red Bird label, where fifteen of the first twenty releases charted. Barry and Greenwich left the label in 1966 with a discovery named Neil Diamond, whom they then managed and produced, but when their marriage ended, the songwriting partnership did likewise. Greenwich later went on to write a musical about her Brill Building days titled *Leader of the Pack*, which had a trial run at the Bottom Line Cabaret and moved to Broadway in 1985.

Carole King and Gerry Goffin

Aldon signed a group of young, hungry writers, including lyricist Gerry Goffin and melodist Carole King, already married, who were hired on the recommendation of their high-school friend, Neil Sedaka. They had a No. 1 hit in 1961 with their first Aldon song, "Will You Love Me Tomorrow," as recorded by the Shirelles. Ironically, the very British invasion bands who eventually put Goffin and King out of business as a songwriting team had nothing but the utmost admiration for them; Paul McCartney reportedly said that he wished he could write as well, and as proof the Beatles recorded the pair's "Chains," previously a hit for the Cookies. The partnership was also responsible for, among other influential tunes, "Up on the Roof" (the Drifters), "One Fine Day" (the Chiffons), "I'm Into Something Good" (Herman's Hermits), "Don't Bring Me Down" (the Animals), and "Goin' Back" (the Byrds).[13] They were inducted into the Rock and Roll Hall of Fame in 1990.

Cynthia Weil and Barry Mann

Aldon also employed Barry Mann (a lyricist who had already had some success with "I Love How You Love Me," recorded by Phil Spector with the Paris Sisters) and Cynthia Weil (melodies), who would eventually wed. They had at least fifty chart hits during their tenure, including "Uptown" and "He's Sure the Boy I Love," both with the Crystals under Spector's production, along with the Ronettes' "Walking in the Rain" and "You Baby," "Only in America" for Jay and the Americans, "We Gotta Get out of This Place" by the Animals, the towering "You've Lost That Lovin' Feelin'" with the Righteous Brothers, and

Don Kirshner, Carole King, and Gerry Goffin, c. 1964. Courtesy of Photofest.

still more for Paul Revere and the Raiders. In early 2004, Mann and Weil put together an off-Broadway revue titled *They Wrote That?* in which they played and sang their hits while sharing anecdotes about the Brill Building days. They received good reviews and are still married.

Doc Pomus and Mort Shuman

Another of Aldon's prize teams was lyricist Doc Pomus and composer Mort Shuman, who together wrote more than 500 tunes between 1958 and 1965. Pomus, whose real name was Jerome Felder, suffered polio as a child and used crutches (and later, after a bad fall, a wheelchair) to get around. His career began in the mid-'40s when he had an R&B song recorded by Big Joe Turner. Shuman was an alumnus of the classical New York Conservatory and another R&B devotee. Among their first hits at Aldon around 1959 were "A Teenager in Love" for Dion and the Belmonts, the Mystics' "Hushabye," and Fabian's "I'm a Tiger." In 1963, Bobby Darin had a smash with "Can't Get Used to Losing You," originally recorded by Andy Williams. But the team really scored with the Drifters, including 1961's "Sweets for My Sweet," which also became a hit for the Searchers in 1964, "This Magic Moment" (1964, credited solely to Pomus), and "Save the Last Dance for Me" (also 1964), and Elvis Presley, who recorded almost two dozen Shuman-Pomus compositions, including "Surrender" (1960),

"(Marie's the Name) His Latest Flame" and "Little Sister" (1961), "Suspicion" (1962), and "Viva Las Vegas" (1964).

In 1964, perhaps seeing the writing on the wall, Shuman and Pomus went to England, where Shuman began collaborating with others, writing "Little Children" for Billy J. Kramer and the Dakotas part of Beatles manager Brian Epstein's stable, as well as other songs for Cilla Black, the Hollies, the Small Faces, and Freddy and the Dreamers. In 1992, Doc Pomus was posthumously inducted into the Rock and Roll Hall of Fame.

Don Kirshner and Aldon Music

Don Kirshner, who was the famously wooden host of a television program in the '70s, was the king of this little colony. He had gotten his start as a songwriter in the late 1950s, meeting and befriending a kid who would become Bobby Darin, and he also hired another friend to sing on commercial jingles, a young girl then named Concetta Franconero, later known as Connie Francis. At twenty-one, Kirshner met Al Nevins, a former composer and recording artist, and convinced him that they should go into business together, producing records aimed directly at the teen market. They formed Aldon Music in 1958, setting up shop in 1650 Broadway, across the street from 1619; soon afterward, Neil Sedaka and Howard Greenfield literally walked in off the street to pitch them some tunes. Kirshner took a couple over to his friend Connie, who by now had cracked the Top 40, and she cut "Stupid Cupid"; it reached No. 17. Before the year was out, Francis (and Aldon) had two more charting songs with the new songwriting team.

Most of Aldon's writers, who made millions for record labels with their labors, worked in small cubicles equipped with pianos. They churned out songs that they would play for each other to critique, and they were usually paid less than $150 a week, with Kirshner always having final approval. As he envisioned his operation, so it became: literally a pop music factory.

In 1962, Kirshner started his own record label, Dimension, and put Goffin and King at the helm. In its first year, Dimension released thirteen records, ten of which were hits. One was for Little Eva, a short-lived dance craze called "The Loco-Motion"; Little Eva had been King's baby-sitter. The following year, Kirshner sold his entire operation to Columbia–Screen Gems for $2 million plus stock; he also took the title of executive vice president to oversee all of the parent company's publishing and recording. Nevins was named a consultant, and while the writers should have been in for a big payday, they saw little of this windfall.

Kirshner had little time to enjoy his fiefdom, which now included Colpix, a label that primarily featured TV and movie actors; by 1964, the Beatles had arrived, and his type of prefabricated music was now seen as manufactured, which of course it was, and therefore undesirable. As more and more groups and artists began to write their own material, expressing their own feelings instead of words put in their mouths by slick professionals, the Brill Building era drew to a close. Kirshner rallied with the Monkees (their "Pleasant Valley

Sunday," which hit No. 3 in 1967, was a Goffin-King collaboration), but it was pretty much a last hurrah. Goffin and King divorced, and the latter went on to a hugely successful solo career as a performer starting in 1970.

Tommy Boyce and Bobby Hart: The Men behind the Monkees

The prolific team of Tommy Boyce and Bobby Hart reportedly wrote some 300 songs and sold more than 42 million records. Tommy Boyce first tasted success via Curtis Lee, with whom he wrote "Pretty Little Angel Eyes" in 1961. Boyce and his new songwriting partner, Bobby Hart, then scored with "Lazy Elsie Molly," by Chubby Checker, and Jay and the Americans' No. 3 hit, "Come a Little Bit Closer," in 1964. The team was selected by Bert Schneider and Bob Rafelson two years later to write and record the music for the pilot of *The Monkees*; when Don Kirshner was brought in to oversee the music, he felt that Boyce and Hart did not have enough experience to act as producers. Then as one producer after another was jettisoned or left, he finally gave in to their repeated assurances that they were up to the job. Boyce and Hart wound up recording the backing tracks and vocals for the first album, and the Monkees were brought in for lead vocals. "Last Train to Clarksville," the first Monkees hit, went to No. 1 that autumn, helped immeasurably by the weekly TV show.

SONGBIRDS

Girl Groups

Goldie and the Gingerbreads

If a woman instrumentalist (such as the White Stripes' drummer Meg White or Sonic Youth's Kim Gordon) is now considered unremarkable, credit Goldie and the Gingerbreads, Maureen Tucker of the Velvet Underground (see Chapter 8), and, later, studio session bassist Carol Kaye. These women were pioneers to later female rockers, such as the Runaways with Joan Jett, Talking Heads' Tina Weymouth, the Pretenders' Chrissie Hynde, the Bangles and Go-Gos, P. J. Harvey, Sleater-Kinney, and Courtney Love's mixed-gender Hole.

Goldie and the Gingerbreads created a sensation around 1964 at New York's Peppermint Lounge as the first all-female rock group playing their own instruments. Atlantic's Ahmet Ertegun signed the Gingerbreads: singer Goldie Zelkowitz, Carol MacDonald on guitar, keyboard player Margo Crocitto (later Lewis), and drummer Ginger Bianco. Their live show then caught the attention of the visiting Animals (whose lead singer, Eric Burdon, remarked: "There was so much feeling in Goldie's voice that I was stunned to find such a 'black' sound could be produced by a group of white girls")[14] and Mike Jeffries (whose surname is sometimes also spelled "Jeffreys"), the group's manager. The Gingerbreads accepted Jeffries's offer of management and moved to England, where Keith Richards booked it as the opening act for a Rolling Stones tour of the United Kingdom. Animal Alan Price produced the Gingerbreads' single, "Can't You Hear My Heart Beat" (later covered by Herman's Hermits)—a hit in England, but not in America. The Gingerbreads later toured with the Kinks, the Yardbirds during the Jeff Beck period, and the Hollies and made a cameo appearance on a poster in the swinging London film *Blow Up*. But the appeal that knocked out the British rockers never quite translated to the band's homeland. Goldie later changed her name to Genya Ravan and became the first female rock producer, working with Cheetah Chrome and the Dead Boys and also fronting a group called Ten Wheel Drive.

The Crystals

Goldie and the Gingerbreads aside, most girl groups consisted of singers backed by studio musicians and were usually teenagers (or sounded as if they could be) from an urban environment. The focus was fixed on the lead; backup singers were interchangeable. In fact, the lead was also replaceable, since all these groups were creations of producers and songwriters. Yet the singer had to vocally project enough to somehow grab the listener through a tinny car radio or a small transistor, be she heartbreakingly vulnerable or sassily seductive. As pop critic Greil Marcus put it, "It sounds insufferably sexist, and the soul of the records bears out that it was. The oppression of the process [was] the source of much of the acute pain and desire these discs convey so powerfully."[15]

The most obvious example of this Svengali-esque method was Phil Spector's manipulation of the Crystals, originally a quintet: Barbara Alston, Dee Dee Kennibrew, Mary Thomas, Patricia Wright, and Myrna Gerrard, all of whom began by singing in church. The group was organized while the girls were still in high school. They managed to land a job recording demos (unknowns singing or playing on a recording to demonstrate a song's possibilities for a name artist) for the publisher Hill and Range, which brought them to the Brill Building. While rehearsing, the group was overheard by Spector, who was just starting his Philles label. Gerrard had left, replaced by LaLa Brooks as lead. Spector liked their sound, but preferred Alston's voice to Brooks's and pushed the former to the front. In September 1961, this revamped lineup put "There's No Other like My Baby" on the charts; it eventually hit No. 20 nationally.

The follow-up, "Uptown," was written by the team of Mann and Weil; its subject, thwarted romance in the ghetto, was unusually topical for its era, and the single reached No. 13 early in 1962. All seemed to be going ahead full steam until Spector made the mistake later that year of forcing the group to record a bizarre number written by Goffin and King, "He Hit Me (and It Felt like a Kiss)"; the song was supposedly inspired by a story told by the couple's baby-sitter, Eva Boyd, who was rechristened "Little Eva" before she sang their composition "The Loco-Motion." Quite rightly, the Crystals disliked the single's theme (which involved accepting physical abuse from a boyfriend), and radio stations also avoided it like the plague.

For his next foray, Spector decided that since he had now appropriated the Crystals' name and created their sound, he could make anyone into the "Crystals," so he selected Darlene Love to sing lead on the classic "He's a Rebel" and its follow-up, "He's Sure the Boy I Love." By early 1963, the "original" Crystals were back in the studio with Spector to cut "Da Doo Ron Ron," this time with LaLa back in the lead singer slot—although it was originally recorded by Love, Spector had erased her vocals. That single hit No. 3 in the United States and No. 5 in the United Kingdom; the next, "And Then He Kissed Me," did equally well. But Spector was already beginning to lose interest in the group: he had discovered Ronnie Bennett and the Ronettes, and the Crystals suffered accordingly. He used the group to settle one of his personal vendettas, making them sing backup for his own recitation of lyrics on "(Let's Dance) the Screw," a flip of the bird at his estranged partner Lester Sill. Their contract required Spector to pay Sill part of the profits from the next Crystals single, so this was a clever out: the single was unreleasable, but Spector had met the legal requirements. That was in 1964; by the following year, the Crystals bought out their contract and headed to another label, where they had no further hits. By 1966, when the group finally disbanded, the only girl groups enjoying any real success were coming out of Motown.

Darlene Love, the other participant in this drama, was chosen for a group called the Blossoms around 1958 after singing at a choir friend's wedding; it happened to be attended by the other Blossoms, who were looking to replace a pregnant founder. As a quartet, the group backed other artists, including Bobby "Monster Mash" Pickett and Bobby "Rockin' Robin" Day. Lester Sill introduced Love to Spector, who needed a voice to front his next single, "He's a Rebel," which he planned to release under the Crystals' banner for name recognition value. Love, who was being paid triple scale for the session, did not mind. Under Spector's aegis, she later cut "Zip-A-Dee-Doo-Dah," credited to Bob B. Soxx and the Bluejeans, and six singles under her own name, the biggest of which was "Wait Till My Bobby Gets Home," which made No. 26 in 1963. She also sang the heartrending "Christmas (Baby Please Come Home)" on Spector's Christmas album. After Spector had gotten all he needed out of her, Love went back to the Blossoms, and the group became regulars on *Shindig*; they also toured with Elvis Presley in the early '70s.

The Shangri-Las

The Shangri-Las, a white group, sounded like the trashiest of street-corner teen molls on their first record, 1965's "Leader of the Pack," complete with vroom-vroom motorcycle effects. In a Greek-chorus type of call-and-response, the singer announces to the querying backups that she has fallen for the local Marlon Brando wannabe because he is, you know, like, really sensitive; then he smashes his bike and dies. This was an immortal example of the "death-rock" (actually pop) genre, discussed further in Chapter 9. The flexible lineup of

Mary-Ann and Marge Ganser and Betty and/or Mary Weiss (depending on individual moods, including those of George "Shadow" Morton, their Spector-esque producer) was the aural equivalent of those girls who hung out by the local pizza place with teased beehive hairdos, Cleopatra eye makeup, and sullen expressions. The Shangri-Las and Morton were also responsible for "Give Him a Great Big Kiss" ("Mm-WAH!"), "(Remember) Walking in the Sand," and "I Can Never Go Home Anymore" (after the singer leaves with her boyfriend, her mother dies of a broken heart)—each one a campy classic.

The Shirelles

Rock critic and author Greil Marcus calls the Shirelles, with lead singer Shirley Owens, "the real class of the girl groups" on the basis of their Goffin-King hit "Will You Love Me Tomorrow"; he also believes that their 1960 version of "Tonight's the Night" is "perhaps the sexiest [record] ever made."[16] What is certain is that the Shirelles became the first all-female group of the rock era to hit No. 1 with "Tomorrow" when it was released in late 1960. That helped drive a chart-topping rerelease of the group's 1959 single "Dedicated to the One I Love" (in itself a cover of the "5" Royales original; a 1967 version by the Mamas and the Papas that hewed closely to the Shirelles' take went to No. 2).

The Shirelles originally came together in 1958 in Passaic, New Jersey, made up of four high-school friends, including namesake Shirley Owens (later Alston). The girls entered a school talent show with a song they had written, "I Met Him on a Sunday," and drew the attention of a classmate's mother, who had a small label and became their manager. A song co-written by that manager, "Soldier Boy," was their second pop No. 1 in 1962. They also had a Top 10 hit (both pop and R&B) with "Baby, It's You" (one of the earliest Bacharach-David compositions) and did it again the following year with "Foolish Little Girl," but by then their chart reign was over. The British invasion groups that helped bury the Shirelles' career were, ironically, among their biggest admirers: John Lennon called them his favorite group (the Beatles covered "Boys"), and "Sha La La" became a hit for Manfred Mann. The Shirelles, or various combinations thereof, found work on the oldies circuit and in 1996 were inducted into the Rock and Roll Hall of Fame.

The Chiffons

The Chiffons, featuring fourteen-year-old lead singer Judy Craig, were formed at a Bronx high school in 1960, where the girls met manager Ronnie Mack at an after-school center. It would be two more years, during which Mack convinced them to take on a new co-lead singer (Sylvia Peterson), before he returned with "He's So Fine," a song of his that the former Tokens had expressed interest in recording. The producers needed a group to voice it, and the nearest to hand happened to be the Chiffons. It was recorded in December 1962; by March 1963, it was No. 1 on both the pop and R&B charts. Shortly afterward, Mack died from Hodgkin's disease.

The Chiffons' second single flopped, but the third—"One Fine Day," written by Gerry Goffin and Carole King, who also played piano on the track—went to No. 5 pop and No. 6 R&B. A few more singles charted erratically, partially because the group did not do much touring due to their age and gender, but it was still chosen to open for the Beatles' first U.S. concert on February 11, 1964, at Washington Memorial Coliseum, and the Stones' first American tour that summer. (Ironically, "He's So Fine" created trouble for George Harrison seven years later when he was accused of lifting its "doo-lang" backup for his "My Sweet Lord." Although the former Beatle claimed that any resemblance was purely coincidental, after years in court he was ordered to pay more than half a million dollars in damages to Mack's estate.) In June 1966, the Chiffons had their final Top 10 record with "Sweet Talkin' Guy."

The Dixie Cups

The Dixie Cups had a smash in 1964 with their wishful "Chapel of Love," which Phil Spector, Jeff Barry, and Ellie Greenwich had originally written as a possibility for the Ronettes, Darlene Love, or the Crystals. Signed to Lieber and Stoller's Red Bird label, the Dixie Cups also charted later that same year with "People Say" and, in 1965, "Iko Iko," a New Orleans standard based on an Indian chant first recorded in the 1940s. The trio (sisters Barbara Ann and Rosa Lee Hawkins with cousin Joan Marie Johnson) hailed from a New Orleans housing project and would have been stuck with the infelicitous name Little Miss and the Muffets had wiser heads not prevailed; fortunately, the Dixie Cup company did not sue for copyright infringement. After the hits dried up, the Hawkins sisters moved back home, where they began modeling careers; they later resumed touring with Dale Mickle, who replaced Johnson.[17]

Martha and the Vandellas

As Motown recording artists, Martha and the Vandellas cut several extraordinary songs, starting in 1963 with "Come and Get These Memories"—the first song written by the unstoppable team of Brian Holland, Lamont Dozier, and Eddie Holland. Later that year, they gave Reeves "(Love Is Like a) Heat Wave," in which her urgency makes it sound as if she is singing for her life.

In 1961, Detroit-raised Martha Reeves was working as an unpaid secretary in Hitsville's Artists and Repertoire (A&R) department after winning a local talent competition; she seized any chance to perform backup vocal duties, most notably on Marvin Gaye's "Hitchhike" and "Pride and Joy." The Vandellas (originally Rosalind Ashford and Annette Sterling) were named after Van Dyke Street, a thoroughfare near Reeves's home, and singer Della Reese (who later starred on the '90s TV series *Touched by an Angel*).

The Velvelettes' Betty Kelly replaced a pregnant Sterling on 1964's "Dancing in the Streets," which the Rock and Roll Hall of Fame declared "perhaps the definitive Motown anthem"; it has since been covered by others, including Mick Jagger and David Bowie for 1985's LiveAid. In 1965, Reeves's distinctive wail propelled "Nowhere to Run" into the Top 10, followed by "My Baby Loves Me" and "I'm Ready for Love" in 1966 and "Jimmy Mack," which inexplicably sat in the vaults for two years prior to its 1967 release. Martha and the Vandellas charted twenty-four R&B hits for Motown and became one of the company's most successful touring acts, trumped only by Diana Ross and the Supremes, with whom they competed for resources and attention. When Motown moved west in 1971, Martha and the Vandellas left the company, and Reeves tackled a solo career; the trio regrouped by the end of the '70s and continues to perform. Martha and the Vandellas was inducted into the Rock and Roll Hall of Fame in 1995.[18]

American Solo Artists

Mary Wells

Mary Wells was, at one point, the Queen of Motown. "Nothing was easy for her," as her former publicist once put it: after her father abandoned the family, Wells was still a child when she was stricken with spinal meningitis, which caused temporary paralysis and a permanent loss of some hearing and sight. Singing since age ten, she came to Berry Gordy seven years later with a song she had written for Jackie Wilson. Instead, Gordy had Wells record "Bye Bye Baby," and it became Motown's first chart hit in 1961. Gordy saw to it that Wells received some of Smokey Robinson's prettiest compositions, including "Two Lovers," "You Beat Me to the Punch," and "The One Who Really Loves You," all of which reached the Top 10. "My Guy" hit No. 1 in mid-1964, during the height of Beatlemania; it was Motown's first chart-topper. In fact, the Beatles declared Wells their favorite American singer and invited her to join them on a British tour. But "My Guy" was her last major hit; at twenty-one, Wells left Motown under a legal cloud of recriminations (she had been underage when she signed her contract) and signed with Twentieth Century Fox, which reportedly gave her a huge advance and promises of film stardom through its movie division; certainly, the latter never materialized. She died in 1992.

Motown's Mary Wells, 1965. Courtesy of Photofest.

Carla Thomas

Known as the "Queen of Memphis Soul," Thomas was the daughter of Rufus "Walking the Dog" Thomas, and their duet on 1960's "'Cause I Love You" launched her career at age eighteen; her "Gee Whiz (Look at His Eyes)" made the Top 10 on both the R&B and pop charts the following year. Thomas really hit her stride in 1966 with "B-A-B-Y," and the following year, her duet, "Tramp," with Otis Redding hit No. 2 on the Black charts and No. 26 on the Pop charts.

Aretha Franklin

Aretha Franklin was "discovered" by legendary Columbia Records A&B man John Hammond—the word is in quotes simply because a talent such as hers would have had to be found sooner or later. Hammond said later that he "wasted no time. I . . . knew she would be a star."[19] Furthermore, he had heard that Sam Cooke was determined to sign Franklin for RCA Victor. After Hammond nabbed her, and she signed her contract with Columbia in 1960, he planned to keep Franklin rooted in gospel while recording material that would attract

"Queen of Soul" Aretha Franklin, 1964. Courtesy of Photofest.

a jazz audience. His interest did not lie in R&B, which is where she eventually found her strongest suit. Upon Hammond's return from a vacation the following year, he was chagrined to find that the label had shifted assignments: he would work only on Franklin's albums, while someone else took responsibility for her singles. "I watched her go from one producer to another while these lavish single records did little to increase her sales and nothing to enhance her career," he lamented.[20] When her five-year contract was up, Hammond was actually relieved to see Franklin go to Atlantic, where he was sure that Jerry Wexler would know how to best utilize her talents. His instincts, as usual, were infallible: Franklin was an instant hit.

Connie Francis

Connie Francis was one of the world's most popular female singers from the late 1950s through approximately 1964 (in 2000, VH-1 cited Francis as the female singer who had appeared on the Hot 100 chart the second-most times in history: Aretha Franklin came in first, with seventy-seven times, while Francis and Dionne Warwick tied at fifty-six). Her biggest hit, "Where the Boys Are" (she also starred in the 1960 movie with the same title), was No. 1 in fifteen countries. She made a series of Annette Funicello–type girl-looks-for-boy

Connie Francis, 1965. Courtesy of Photofest.

Nancy Sinatra and boots, 1966. © Central Press/Getty Images.

movies up through 1965, when the British invasion pushed her aside. Francis still recorded forty-four albums during the '60s, which might have had something to do with the fact that she was addicted to pills—both uppers and downers. She was also thwarted in romance: her abiding love was fellow singer Bobby Darin, but her controlling stage father kept them from marrying.

Lesley Gore

Lesley Gore was a genuine teenager, just seventeen in 1963 when she landed her first No. 1 with "It's My Party." Her next hit, that same year, was an answer song to the first, "Judy's Turn to Cry," and then she really scored with "You Don't Own Me," in 1964. During the next three years, she had four Top 20 hits ("That's the Way Boys Are" and "Maybe I Know" in 1964) and made appearances in several films (most notably *The T.A.M.I. Show*) and various TV shows, but her career peaked early.

Nancy Sinatra

Nancy Sinatra was the daughter of an icon named Frank Sinatra, but she was also the frosted-blonde sex kitten who made the sassy "These Boots Are Made for Walkin'" a massive hit in 1966. She followed it up with "Summer Wine," "Sugar Town," and "Somethin' Stupid" (a duet with her father), making a total of ten Top 40 hits in just three years. Her movie appearances include *Get Yourself a College Girl* and *For Those Who Think Young* (both in 1964), singing in the memorably titled 1966 opus *The Ghost in the Invisible Bikini*, alongside Peter Fonda in *The Wild Angels*, and a costarring role opposite Elvis Presley in *Speedway* (1968). With her miniskirts, boots, and mass of hair, Sinatra was considered quite a fashion influence.

Jackie DeShannon

Jackie DeShannon was one of the first successful female singer-songwriters. Her first hit was the Sonny Bono and Jack Nitzsche composition "Needles and Pins" (also covered by the Searchers) in 1963; the following year, she was one of the opening acts on the Beatles' first U.S. tour with her self-penned hit "When You Walk in the Room" (later recorded by the Searchers, Del Shannon, the Ventures, and Jim Croce and also performed live by Bruce Springsteen); the Byrds covered her "Don't Doubt Yourself Babe" on their auspicious debut album. DeShannon had a Top 10 hit in 1965 with "What the World Needs Now Is Love"—ironically, written by Bacharach and David; she did not see that height again until 1969, with "Put a Little Love in Your Heart." DeShannon recorded thirty-eight albums and penned at least 600 songs, many of which have been covered by others, and she has also collaborated with Van Morrison, Randy Newman, and Jimmy Page. During the '60s, she appeared on various TV shows, including *Ed Sullivan*, *Shindig*, *Shivaree*, *Where the Action Is!*, and *Hullabaloo*, as well as in the films *Surf Party*, paired with Bobby Vinton (1964; she sang "Glory Wave"), *Intimacy* (1964), and *C'mon, Let's Live a Little* (1967).

Dionne Warwick

Dionne Warwick may have become the butt of late-night comics' jokes for touting the Psychic Friends telephone service, but in the '60s her velvety voice was inescapable. On her 1963 debut, the nation's collective ear was soothed by her rendition of the Bacharach-David song "Don't Make Me Over"; the following year, she had her first Top 10 hit with "Anyone Who Had a Heart." The hit-making troika was unstoppable during the years 1963 through 1966, when Warwick had a dozen consecutive Top 100 singles.

Wanda Jackson

Wanda Jackson has been credited with being America's first female rock singer (in 1956) and was dubbed the "Queen of Rockabilly" after her 1960 Top 40 hit, "Having a Party." In the late '50s, she shared tour dates with Elvis Presley, who became a friend (but not a boyfriend, since her dad was on the road with her as chaperone). In 1966, Jackson hit the Top 20 with "The Box It Came In" and "Tears Will Be the Chaser for Your Wine." She toured regularly and was twice nominated for a Grammy; however, after being "born again," she recorded strictly Christian music, and her career became confined to that particular market.

British Solo Artists

Dusty Springfield

Mary Isabel Catherine Bernadette O'Brien, aka Dusty Springfield, was one of the most soulful singers ever to hit the charts; listeners so often mistook her for a soul sister that the British press tastelessly dubbed her the "white Negress." As Elton John said when he inducted her into the Rock and Roll Hall of Fame in 1999, less than two weeks after her death, she was "a songwriter's singer. I think she's the greatest white singer there ever has been."[21] She also created an iconic visage (and a role model for countless drag queens) with a piled-up blonde "beehive" hairdo and layers of black eye makeup. Springfield started out with the Lana Sisters and later joined her brother Tom and another male singer, Tim Field, in the folk-styled Springfields before striking out on her own. She was an instant smash with "I Only Want to Be with You."

In December 1964, Springfield created a furor when she was told to leave South Africa after playing only five of seven contracted concerts because of her refusal to sing before segregated audiences. Government officials were quoted in local papers: "She was on two occasions warned through her manager to observe our South African way of life in regard to entertainment. . . . She chose to defy the Government and was accordingly allowed to remain in the country for a limited time only." Springfield retorted: "I just think that anybody, if they want to buy a ticket, should be allowed to. I was determined not to play to segregated audiences."[22] Ringo Starr, among others, came to her support in the press.

Springfield walked it as she talked it: a great supporter of American black music, she hosted Martha Reeves and the Vandellas, Stevie Wonder, and other artists on a Motown-themed episode of *Ready, Steady, Go!* (see Chapter 6). The London-born Springfield's hits included "You Don't Have to Say You Love Me," "Wishin' and Hopin'," "Stay Awhile," and "I Just Don't Know What to Do with Myself"; she died of breast cancer at age fifty-nine in 1999.

Marianne Faithfull

What suited Marianne Faithfull to the purposes of the mid-'60s marketplace was, in the words of author Nik Cohn, her "perfect face. She looked incredibly virginal, incredibly sexual . . . she didn't naturally belong in pop; she was high above it." Andrew Loog Oldham, manager of the Rolling Stones, met Faithfull at a London party: "In another century you'd have set sail for her—in 1964 you recorded her."[23] He ordered his fledgling team to write a song to help make Faithfull a star. Mick Jagger and Keith Richards came up with the wistful "As Tears Go By," and Oldham, aided by the tremulous singer's gorgeous blonde innocence, did the rest, making it a U.S./UK pop hit in 1965. Faithfull had more success in England than in America that year with "This Little Bird" and "Come and Stay with Me"; she soon left her husband and small son to become Jagger's consort. In this role, Faithfull and Anita Pallenberg, first as the girlfriend of guitarist Brian Jones and then the common-law wife of guitarist/songwriter Keith Richards, exerted a strong influence over what their men wore, read, thought, and wrote about, and they were considered icons of style and desirability in their own right.

Petula Clark

Petula Clark burst on the American consciousness with her 1964 No. 1 hit "Downtown" (for which she also won a Grammy), becoming the first British female singer to top the U.S. charts. But she had been entertaining for years: as the British version of Shirley Temple during World War II, a young Clark kept up the troops' morale via the radio and in concert. Popular enough to be asked to perform at a national victory celebration in Trafalgar Square, Clark made her first film appearance in 1944. She even appeared on television in its '40s infancy, becoming a regular guest on variety shows and eventually hosting several series of her own. After marrying a Frenchman, Clark began a reconfigured career as a chanteuse, singing in her husband's native tongue and going on to record in German, Italian, and other languages, becoming a European superstar. After her first U.S. smash, she followed up with 1965's "I Know a Place" (according to the lyrics, it sounded much like the Cavern Club, which saw the rise of the Beatles) and won another Grammy.

Marianne Faithfull, 1966. Courtesy of Photofest.

NOTES

1. Lou Adler quoted in Andrew Loog Oldham, *2Stoned* (London: Vintage/Random House 2003), p. 150.

2. Tom Wolfe, "The First Tycoon of Teen," in *Meaty Beaty Big & Bouncy! Classic Rock & Pop Writing from Elvis to Oasis*, ed. Dylan Jones (London: Hodder & Staughton, 1996), p. 43.

3. Mary Elizabeth Williams, "Top of the Pops: How Phil Spector Invented Teen Lust and Torment," *Salon* (November 10, 1998), http://www.salon.com/bc/1998/11/cov_10bc.html.

4. Jack Nitzsche quoted by Harvey Kubernik, "Legendary Music Arranger and Composer Jack Nitzsche Dies," *Goldmine* (June 17, 1988), available at: "The Sorcerer's Apprentice, Jack Nitzsche's Magical Musical World," http://www.spectropop.com/JackNitzsche/lovingmemory.htm.

5. Phil Spector to Mick Brown in "Pop's Lost Genius," *The London Daily Telegraph*, February 4, 2003.

6. Ronnie Spector with Vince Waldron, *Be My Baby: How I Survived Mascara, Miniskirts and Madness or My Life as a Fabulous Ronette* (New York: Harmony Books, 1990), p. 37.

7. Ibid., p. 39.

8. Ibid., Billy Joel's introduction, p. xiv.

9. Ibid., p. 74.

10. Phil Spector quoted by Jann Wenner, "Phil Spector Sounds Off," *Rolling Stone* 45 (November 1, 1969).

11. Quoted in Oldham, *2Stoned*, p. 2.

12. Genya Ravan, *Lollipop Lounge: Memoirs of a Rock and Roll Refugee* (New York: Billboard Books, 2004), p. 73.

13. Rock and Roll Hall of Fame, http://www.rockhall.com/hof/inductee.asp?id=110.

14. Eric Burdon quoted on "Goldie & the Gingerbreads," http://www.genyaravan .com/goldie.html.

15. Greil Marcus, "How The Other Half Lives: The Best of Girl Group Rock," *Let It Rock* (May 1974).

16. Ibid.

17. "History of Rock," http://www.history-of-rock.com/dixie_cups.htm; and Charlotte Dillon, "The Dixie Cups," America Online, http://aolsvc.musicsearch.aol.com/artistbio.adp?artist_id=17053.

18. Bill Dahl, "Martha Reeves & The Vandellas," Motown Historical Museum, http://motownmuseum.com/mtmpages/pop/vanpop.html.

19. John Hammond with Irving Townsend, *John Hammond on Record* (New York: Summit Books, 1977), p. 348.

20. Ibid.

21. Elton John quoted by Rhonda Markowitz, "One Hall of a Night: The Rock and Roll Hall of Fame Convenes in New York City to Induct its Newest Members," People.com (posted March 16, 1999; article now discontinued).

22. Dusty Springfield quoted in "Dusty—'There Were Threats'," *Record Mirror* (December 26, 1964), http://www.isd.net/mbayly/article3.htm.

23. Cohn and Oldham quotes from Oldham, *2Stoned*, pp. 104–105.

FROM LIVERPOOL TO LONDON AND BEYOND: THE BEATLES AND THE ROLLING STONES

> Part of what America loved so much about The Beatles was that they appeared not as gods but as mortals whom the gods had blessed, which was vastly more inspirational. You could—maybe—do what they did. You could try.
>
> —Dave Marsh[1]

England was still suffering deprivation, and rebuilding after the Great War had been ploddingly slow. There had been a postwar baby boom in the United Kingdom, as in the United States, so there were thousands of these new creatures called "teenagers" just waiting for something, anything, to happen. But what ever happened in England? Everything, from blue jeans to movies to rock and roll, always originated in and was done best by America.

AMERICAN BLUES INFLUENCES

It would be almost impossible to overstate how influential and important American blues and R&B were in sparking the British invasion. Neglected and overlooked in their homeland save for a relatively small audience, African American blues artists were all but worshipped by just about every aspiring English musician, including the Beatles, who appropriated their falsetto "Whoo!" from Little Richard, an artist who had toured with the Beatles early on. The group also cut cover versions of songs by Arthur Alexander ("Anna"), the Cookies ("Chains"), the Shirelles ("Boys," "Baby, It's You"), the Marvelettes ("Please

Mr. Postman"), the Miracles ("You Really Got a Hold on Me"), Barrett Strong ("Money"), and the towering Chuck Berry ("Roll over Beethoven"). The Beatles studied these records the way others would eventually dissect theirs.

The Rolling Stones, the Yardbirds, the Who, and other such bands were even more purist than the Beatles in their approach. At least in the beginning, they disdained pop music; these skinny white English boys aspired to be authentic bluesmen. The Who promoted their music as "maximum R&B"; the Animals, from gritty Newcastle, definitely took their cue from American soul, as did Irish powerhouse Van Morrison, who fronted Them, and the astonishingly young Stevie Winwood of the Spencer Davis Group. The Rolling Stones, who took their name from a Muddy Waters tune, may have been the biggest fans of all.

The Original African American Inspirations: Muddy Waters, Howlin' Wolf, and Jimmy Reed

McKinley Morganfield, aka Muddy Waters, was born in the Mississippi Delta, raised on a plantation, and discovered in 1941 by famed musicologist Alan Lomax, who was making tapes of indigenous American musicians for the Library of Congress. But Waters still had to make his own way up to Chicago, where he obtained a day job delivering Venetian blinds while playing his bottleneck-slide guitar around clubs at night. In 1947, Waters accompanied Sunnyland Slim into the studio, where the pair cut 78 rpm singles for the Aristocrat label. It was not until the following year that Waters caught fire with his "I Can't Be Satisfied," such a big local hit that he was hard pressed to find a copy in the stores, and "I Feel Like Going Home," a national R&B breakout. Waters put together a band that included Little Walter (who would himself revolutionize the role the harmonica played in urban blues); the group recorded "Rollin' Stone," from which a British blues combo and a youth culture magazine would take their names, in 1950 for Chess Records.

Four years later, with a different lineup that included the songwriter/bassist Willie Dixon ("I'm Your Hootchie-Cootchie Man," "I'm Ready"), Waters was appearing regularly on the (segregated) R&B charts. There was friendly competition with Bo Diddley, whose driving "hambone" beat anchored the Rolling Stones as much as their admiration of Chuck Berry, whom Waters had recommended to Chess. Waters made his first trip to England in 1958. His 1962 hit "You Need Love" was later covered by Led Zeppelin; two years after he cut that single, when the Rolling Stones paid their first trembling visit to the legendary Chess Studios to record, they were astonished to find their idol up on a ladder painting the walls and offering to help carry in their equipment. Waters reportedly said later on that the Stones "stole my music but they gave me my name,"[2] meaning that their allegiance helped put him over to the wider white audience that had been ignorant of his importance.

Harmonica player Howlin' Wolf (real name Chester Arthur Burnett) was a giant of a man, well over six feet tall and 300 pounds in his prime; his classic "Smokestack Lightnin'" hit the R&B charts in 1958, and in 1960 he and his invaluable guitarist, Hubert Sumlin, were teamed with Willie Dixon. This unbeatable combination produced such standards as "I Ain't Superstitious," "The Red Rooster" (covered by the Rolling Stones and a No. 1 hit for them in England), "Back Door Man" (covered by the Doors), and "Spoonful" (covered by Cream). When the Stones arrived in America in 1965 and appeared on *Shindig*, their one demand was that Howlin' Wolf be their special guest. As the band sat at his feet, Wolf made his network television bow to an audience of millions; years later, he continued to express his gratitude to the group for their devotion. Wolf was inducted into the Rock and Roll Hall of Fame in 1991. A life-size statue of him stands in a Chicago park, and his face has been featured on a U.S. postage stamp.

Jimmy Reed's was a tragic story, all the more so because his music was so readily accessible. His best-known songs ("Bright Lights, Big City," "Ain't That Lovin' You Baby," "Honest I Do," and "Big Boss Man") made him the first Chicago electric bluesman to break through to the pop market. Reed's tunes, conveyed by slurred vocals, boogified rhythm guitar, and harmonica, had a simplicity of construction that would inspire generations of musicians first to imitation, then to innovation.

Born in 1925 on a Mississippi plantation, Reed was fifteen when his friend Eddie Taylor taught him the basics of guitar and mouth harp. He left school in 1939 and did some farming in the area, but moved to Chicago in 1943 in hopes of finding work; instead, he was drafted into the navy the following year. Upon his 1944 release, he played the blues at night while working in a meatpacking plant during the day. Reed was rejected by Chess (he was brought to the then-fledgling label by his drummer, Albert King, who went on to become a guitar-playing legend after switching instruments), but was picked up by Vee-Jay in 1953. It was at that label that Reed and his old friend Taylor were reunited, and their partnership soon yielded a Top 5 R&B hit in 1955 with "You Don't Have to Go." Reed's career soon took off; his 1961 live album was recorded at Carnegie Hall. But he was burdened not only with illiteracy (his wife sat beside him in the studio, prompting him on lyrics) but also with severe alcoholism, compounded by long-undiagnosed epilepsy; his "fits" were originally thought to be delirium tremors brought on by drinking. Despite these problems, as well as drunken acting out that made him professionally unreliable and personally unpopular, from 1955 through 1966 Reed managed to place eleven songs on the *Billboard* Hot 100 pop charts and also had fourteen R&B hits, besting even B. B. King. He was finally properly diagnosed and quit drinking, but it was too little, too late; he died in 1976 while attempting to make a comeback. Reed was inducted into the Rock and Roll Hall of Fame in 1991.

White Boy Bluesmen

Paul Butterfield

American blues harmonica player Paul Butterfield made his name as one of the first white artists to create an indelible style; the power with which his band (which included early guitar god Mike Bloomfield) put over electrified Chicago blues opened the field to those who preferred the urban style to the earlier, acoustic fieldhand version, and also helped convince other white players that skin color alone did not disqualify them from attempting the genre.

"Butter," as he was nicknamed by friends and fans, grew up in a racially integrated area on Chicago's South Side, home to some of the nation's most talented blues artists, and began hitting the clubs in 1957 at age fifteen. He dropped out of college to pursue playing music full-time, winning black musicians' respect while drawing a white audience. Elektra's A&R man Paul Rothschild signed the Butterfield Blues Band in 1965, although it took two tries to complete a debut album. Before its release, the band (already booked to play the 1965 Newport Folk Festival) was spotted by Bob Dylan, who had it back him on his famous "plugged" performance, his first public foray into electric folk rock. When the Butterfield Blues Band's first album came out later that year, it was an instant sensation.

Mike Bloomfield

Mike Bloomfield grew up on Chicago's North Side and received his first guitar at his bar mitzvah; he and some of his equally precocious friends would visit the South Side via their families' domestic help, where amused R&B musicians would allow the kid to sit in. Bloomfield grew so proficient that he wound up doing session work, where he was discovered and signed by John Hammond, but the label had no idea how to market a white American blues player. In 1965, Bloomfield hooked up with Butterfield; at just about the same time, Dylan selected the guitarist to play on his landmark *Highway 61 Revisited* album. Like George Harrison, Bloomfield became intrigued by Indian music; the obsession surfaced on the next Butterfield Band album, *East-West* (1966), a groundbreaking meld of blues, psychedelic rock, and raga-influenced guitar solos. The blues alone were no longer enough for Bloomfield, who departed the popular Butterfield outfit to form the Electric Flag. His later career trajectory was derailed by alcoholism and an addiction to heroin; in 1981, the thirty-seven-year-old guitarist was discovered in his car, dead of an overdose.

EARLY BRITISH BLUES MUSICIANS

Even before Butterfield and Bloomfield picked up their instruments for the first time, Alexis Korner and John Mayall were working blues musicians, forming the very epicenter of London's nascent R&B scene.

Alexis Korner

A teenaged Alexis Korner arrived in London just in time for the Blitz after a youth spent in France and North Africa. He had a vivid memory of hearing a blues record during that period, and from that point on his path was set. He began playing piano and guitar after the war and experimented with an electrified sound as early as 1947. Korner returned to acoustic when he joined the Chris Barber Jazz Band two years later, which then merged with the larger Ken Collyer Jazz Band. It was then that Korner met guitarist/harmonica player Cyril Davies, a kindred spirit; by 1954, the pair was making a name for itself on the London nightery circuit as an electric blues duo. They opened the London Blues and Barrelhouse club, inviting visiting American bluesmen to drop by, which made the club a must for anyone who loved the music.

Korner and Davies formed Blues Incorporated in 1962, with a large rotating cast of players; among those who passed through the ranks were drummer Charlie Watts, later to become the backbone of the Rolling Stones, and Jack Bruce, who became the bass of Cream. The pair also opened another club, which drew Brian Jones, Mick Jagger, and Keith Richards, as well as "sixth Stone" Ian Stewart, Manfred Mann (and Paul Jones, the vocalist for his group), and Steve Marriot, who later joined the Small Faces and headed Humble Pie. All of these fledgling blues players took turns onstage and followed Korner and Davies to the residency Blues Incorporated soon established at London's Marquee Club. By the end of 1962, the group had released its debut album, a live recording of R&B From the Marquee (the first full-length album ever made by a British blues band). But already there was creative dissension between the partners: Davies left, objecting to Korner's insistence on adding horns to the mix. In 1963, the British invasion was under way, leaving Korner's traditional sound in the dust. Almost all of his "children" went on to fame and fortune, while Korner was considered washed-up before he was forty.

John Mayall

John Mayall was the musical equivalent of a bridesmaid, never the bride; he could also be likened to the talented director whose actor protégés steal all the thunder. The Bluesbreakers, which he was inspired to form after seeing Korner and Davies, helped launch the careers of (among others) Mick Taylor, Eric Clapton, and three members of Fleetwood Mac: Peter Green, John McVie, and Mick Fleetwood. Yet Mayall himself, while a capable enough player, lacked the essential charisma and songwriting talent that might have made him a star. His specialty was Chicago electric blues, and within the context of the Bluesbreakers (more of a concept than an actual band, with members entering and departing as if through a revolving door), he helped put British blues players onto the worldwide stage.

Mayall, the son of a part-time jazz player, was influenced by Louis Armstrong and Django Reinhardt in his youth; as he would recall, "It was a lot harder in those days to follow your musical bent because LPs hadn't been invented yet; you just persevered, sending off to vintage jazz shops and people who collected and exchanged 78s."[3] When he finished his army service, he attended art school and put together a group called the Powerhouse Four; when he spotted Korner and Davies doing their electrified act, Mayall promptly developed a band he called the Blues Syndicate and befriended Korner.

He had managed a few flop singles and a debut album by 1964, but Mayall's reputation among musicians was solid: one of the first people Bob Dylan wanted to meet when he came to London was, by Mayall's admission, himself. "I went over to the Savoy Hotel, which was a total circus. He had a suite of rooms, and all these Americans and Donovan was up there. . . . After he left London to go up to Birmingham or some place like that, he had a limo and I travelled up with him and Joan Baez in the back seat while Pennebaker was doing his film *Dont Look Back* . . . he was so surrounded by his entourage that it was hard to get more than five minutes with him. Total frenzy. This was London—he was thrilled to be here, and he wanted to see and do it all."[4]

Mayall's Bluesbreakers was the band Clapton joined when he left the Yardbirds, disdaining the pop leanings of the latter for the strictures of the former; in 1966, the group's eponymous first album with Clapton not only established him as a guitar hero, but was even a commercial hit, entering the British Top 10. Yet almost as quickly as he came, Clapton went, going on to form Cream with Jack Bruce and Ginger Baker. Mayall replaced Clapton with guitarist Peter Green, but within months he, too, had left to create Fleetwood Mac. Mayall, with his unerring ear for talent, chose Mick Taylor (then just nineteen) to take Green's place. He stayed for two years before switching to the Rolling Stones in 1969, around which time Mayall moved to Los Angeles. He made a decent living playing live, cut several albums, none of which sold exceptionally well, and enjoyed his new life in a warmer climate.

THE BEATLES

"As a cultural phenomenon, as musicians, to the way they changed people's dress . . . [and] outlook on life, I don't think there's been any entertainers since that have had that kind of an impact. . . . As much as the R&B people, and the gospel people, and spiritual music, and the country-western people influenced them, I think the Beatles were the bar. And they set the bar, and nobody's quite been able to jump beyond it," according to Larry Kane, author of *Ticket to Ride* and the only U.S. journalist who toured with the group on its first visit to America.[5] As another writer phrased it, referencing a famous movie: "Everything [that went] before was Kansas, in black-and-white. The Beatles were, musically, a Technicolor Oz."[6] Steven Van Zandt adds: "There were no bands before The Beatles. There were hundreds minutes later, but before them there were only singing groups and individual rock and rollers and it was all pop."[7]

Rock critic Dave Marsh wrote: "Nobody ever captured in words what The Beatles wrought, and nobody's going to. Their achievement—their conscious, deliberate achievement; what they wanted to do and what they pulled off—can be reduced to a cliché or a slogan, but it can't be summarized. . . . The Beatles came . . . and you realized what was possible—in this music, in your life . . . they never doubted that people, just by being people, could shape a better world. . . . They were the American dream incarnated, with long hair, no collars, and an extremely healthy disrespect for all authority, and they didn't need to grimace like John Wayne to prove it—this freedom actually made them look and sound happy."[8]

Beginnings in Liverpool

In order to understand something of the Beatles' impact, it is instructive to look back at the group's hometown. The port city of Liverpool is far down the scale in national importance compared with the glittering capital, although the populace of any port city is more sophisticated than one inland. In 1961, crime was on the rise, due to the decline of the shipping industry and a related rise in unemployment. Nonetheless, there was a thriving music scene in town, although the idea of anyone from London (never mind Merseyside, as locals called the area) even daring to challenge the American superstars at their own game was as ludicrous as a trip to the moon. There were, of course, British stars like Cliff Richard and the Shadows, and—less glamorous, perhaps, but even more important—Lonnie Donegan, whose 1956 single "Rock Island Line" popularized the funky DIY (do it yourself) music known as "skiffle."

Skiffle was a throwback to making music on whatever happened to be available: no need to know notes or how to write music, or even how to play. The form did not require expensive instruments; all a group needed was a tea chest (wooden box), a bass (which might be a string attached to a pole), and perhaps a cheap acoustic guitar. Skiffle was, in effect, a forerunner to punk. "Until skiffle, popular music was made by 'musicians'—people who had real instruments, like the trumpet and clarinet, which cost money, were hard to play, required learning. Skiffle was primitive music, played on primitive instruments. It encouraged anyone to have a go. . . . Music became democratic, open to all."[9] It was not dissimilar to the way punk, rap, sampling, and home-recording/mixing technology would revolutionize music-making decades down the line.

Beatles founder John Lennon was sixteen, and his Quarrymen skiffle group had just finished playing a 1957 church fete when their mutual school friend Ivan Vaughn introduced a fifteen-year-old Paul McCartney. McCartney impressed the older lad by writing out the lyrics to Eddie Cochran's "Twenty Flight Rock" and Gene Vincent's "Be-Bop-A-Lula"; to cap it off, he took Lennon's guitar, retuned it from banjo chords, and played some Little Richard songs, including "Long Tall Sally" and "Tutti Frutti." As Lennon recalled: "Paul could obviously play the guitar. I half thought to myself, he's as good as me. I'd been kingpin up till then. Now I thought, if I take him on, what will happen. It went through my head that I'd have to keep him in line, if I let him join. But he was good, so he was worth having. He also looked like Elvis. I dug him."[10] The next week, McCartney was in the group. In contrast to Lennon's aggression and sometimes overt cruelty, McCartney developed a sunny charm and polite demeanor that would later make him the diplomat of the group.

George Harrison was the youngest Beatle and the only one brought up in a two-parent household, albeit a working-class one. He was the only child in his family to make it as far as grammar school, but failed every class except art and was working as an electrician's apprentice when the Beatles began. His older sister Louise had married an American and moved to the United States, so George was the only member of the group to have visited overseas before the band's triumphant 1964 arrival.

Ringo Starr (born Richard Starkey) was the oldest member. He was the sickly child of a single working mother, and his appendix burst when he was six, forcing him into hospital for a year of stomach operations. At thirteen, after his mother remarried, Richie developed pleurisy, which led to a two-year confinement in a sanitorium. As a result, he never finished school and had enormous difficulty reading and writing. However, Richie's stepfather, who later arranged a pipefitting apprenticeship for the lad, also gave him his first drum kit, purchased on credit.[11]

The Beatles backstage, before Ringo Starr replaced Pete Best. (Left to right) George Harrison, Paul McCartney, John Lennon, and Pete Best. Courtesy of Photofest.

In 1959, Mona Best (the mother of Pete Best, the Beatles' original drummer) opened a coffeehouse called the Casbah Club in the cellar of the family home as a space for local youngsters to congregate. On August 29 of that year, the Quarrymen, with Lennon and McCartney, became the club's opening act when the originally scheduled group failed to appear. The club attracted the cream of the burgeoning Liverpool scene—including the area's top act, Rory Storm and the Hurricanes, which employed Ringo Starr on drums.

In 1960, the Silver Beatles, as they were then called, were composed of Lennon, McCartney, and Harrison on guitars, Lennon's art-school friend Stu Sutcliffe on bass, and drummer Tommy Moore, with a de facto manager in Allan Williams, who owned Liverpool nightclubs like the Blue Angel and the Jacaranda. That summer, Williams arranged an audition for the band with powerful London impresario Larry Parnes, who ran the careers of big stars like Tommy Steele, Billy Fury, and Georgie Fame. Parnes hired the group to back his latest find, Johnny Gentle, on a short tour of Scotland. While they were off in the hinterlands, Williams booked them for a lengthy stint in Hamburg, Germany's second-largest city. When the drummer's girlfriend heard the news, she was unhappy; Moore then departed, and Pete Best was in, almost by default.

HE GAVE AWAY THE BEATLES

Williams parted ways with the band after a dispute over an unpaid commission from the last Hamburg tour, telling Brian Epstein: "Brian, don't touch 'em with a fucking bargepole."[12] Paul McCartney later gave him credit: "When we started off we had a manager in Liverpool called Allan Williams. He was a great guy, a really good motivator and very good for us at the time."[13] Williams later wrote the aptly titled *The Man Who Gave the Beatles Away*, which served as the basis for a play; he released a compact disc discussing his former charges, and still occasionally appears at Beatles conventions or as a guide on Liverpool tours to supplement his old-age pension.

At this point, around 1961–1962, the Beatles were performing covers of songs like Chuck Berry's 1956 "Too Much Monkey Business," "I Got to Find My Baby" (1960), and "I'm Talking about You" (1962, immediately adopted by the group); Phil Spector's Teddy Bears number "To Know Him Is to Love Him" (with the gender changed); a novelty tune called "Your Feet's Too Big" (popularized by Fats Waller around 1939 and recorded again by Chubby Checker in 1961); Carl Perkins's 1957 "Your True Love" and "Everybody's Trying to Be My Baby" (recorded in 1958, and both sung by Harrison), along with "Honey Don't" (1956, sung by Lennon until 1963, when Starr took over); the Hank Williams compositions "Hey Good Lookin'" (1951) and "You Win Again" (1951); Ray Charles's "Hallelujah, I Love Her So" (1956) and "I Got a Woman"; the Jerry Lieber, Mike Stoller, and Doc Pomus "Young Blood" (originally cut by the Coasters in 1957); the Shirelles' "Baby It's You" (recorded in 1961 and co-written by Burt Bacharach); "Don't Ever Change" (written by Carole King and Gerry Goffin and cut by the Crickets in 1962, it was promptly taken on); Lieber and Stoller's "Hound Dog" (recorded by Elvis Presley in

1956); and Buddy Holly's "Words of Love" (1957). In other words, the typical Beatles set list was a smorgasbord of country, R&B, and Brill Building pop.

They were also performing some originals: a McCartney song called "Tip of My Tongue" (later rejected by George Martin); "Hold Me Tight" (written by McCartney, it was left off the *Please Please Me* album but later rerecorded for *Meet the Beatles*); McCartney's "Like Dreamers Do" (included at an audition for the Decca label on New Year's Day 1962); a Lennon number, "Hello Little Girl" (which the group used on auditions for Decca and Parlophone); his "The One after 909" (which eventually showed up on the 1970 *Let It Be* album); and the Lennon-McCartney "P.S. I Love You" (played for the Parlophone audition and released as the B side of the band's first British single, "Love Me Do"). At this point, the band had made just one recording, which was never released: a 1958 acetate of an original McCartney-Harrison composition called "In Spite of All the Danger," backed with Holly's "That'll Be the Day."

The Young Beatles in Germany

While home had helped toughen the young Beatles ("The musical groups rose above . . . street battles and seemed to accept, almost as commonplace, that physical altercation were part and parcel of Liverpool life"),[14] Hamburg was the crucible in which the band was forged. The five-piece group played in sleazy bars like the Kaiserkeller and Indra in the Grosse Freiheit district, located on a street off the notorious Reeperbahn; the main artery of St. Pauli was a "jungle of neon and sex."[15] The Beatles learned to ply their trade during gigs that lasted up to seven hours. The emcee would scream at them, "Make show!" and they did: at one point, a drunken Lennon took the stage while wearing a toilet seat around his neck and chanting "Sieg Heil!" Their quarters consisted of a miserable little room backstage at a rundown cinema, the Bambi Kino, furnished with two single beds and an ancient couch; the urinals were where the band shaved and washed in cold water. Their weekly salary was fifteen pounds apiece (about forty dollars then).

Lack of money notwithstanding, the Beatles could have invented the mantra "sex, drugs, and rock and roll" during these days and nights: George Harrison lost his virginity there, and the group managed the grueling stretches of "make show" by getting trashed on beer and taking "slimming" pills, also known as, speed. But Hamburg was also where the group made its first professional recording, as backup for fellow Brit Tony Sheridan on his rock version of "My Bonnie." Sheridan later explained that the song was "selected because the lyrics were easily understood by the German audience and the tune was recognizable. Our goal was to sell some records, but it was a joke, really."[16] It was an inauspicious beginning, but at least they had made a record.

The Beatles were sent back to England after being rebuffed for a raise by their promoter, Bruno Koschmider. They were now playing at the Kaiserkeller (the first venue, the Indra, had been closed down after noise complaints), but were still stuck in the dire quarters they had had for four months. They received an offer from the rival Top Ten Club and agreed to go there after their contract lapsed; however, Koschmider got wind of their plans and reported Harrison to the police for being underage (he was, in fact, seventeen). The group decided to continue as a quartet. After McCartney and Best went to the Bambi Kino to retrieve their belongings, they attached condoms to the wall and lit them to see by; spotting the scorch marks left behind, Koschmider pounced. The pair was arrested and accused of trying to start a fire at the club, thrown in cells, then escorted to the airport by police and deported. Bassist Stuart Sutcliffe, Lennon's closest friend, stayed behind with newfound love Astrid Kirchherr and died of a cerebral hemorrhage soon afterwards, aged twenty-one. Persistent rumors blamed his demise on a head injury he once sustained in a street brawl either with or alongside Lennon. Lennon, said Best, was "absolutely shattered" and "wept like a child" upon learning of Sutcliffe's death.[17]

Brian Epstein

Back in Liverpool, the Beatles set up residency in an underground club aptly called the Cavern, and although they had had a falling out with Mona Best, she was still looking out for them. According to her son Pete, "A lot of people have claimed they introduced The Beatles to the Cavern. But the manager Ray McFall has now said Mrs. Best persuaded him he was missing out if he didn't book this band."[18] At lunchtime, scores of secretaries and schoolkids packed the sweaty space to rock with these homegrown heroes, who still wore the black leather gear they had purchased in Hamburg, ate sandwiches, and smoked onstage while joking with the crowd. It was all very informal.

This audience, and the Beatles themselves, usually bought their music at the Whitechapel branch of Liverpool's North End Music Stores (NEMS), where the owner's son, Brian Epstein, was in charge of the store and paid close attention to running the record department. Epstein prided himself on keeping the customers satisfied by stocking hard-to-find records, even if he carried only a few of each, and his buying power afforded a certain clout with record labels. Legend has it that a client named Raymond Jones kept asking for Tony Sheridan's "My Bonnie" single, specifying he wanted it only because the Beatles were on the record (Alistair Taylor, Epstein's assistant, says that it was he who placed the first order—a box of twenty-five singles—having made up the name of this alleged customer). Epstein supposedly first thought that the Beatles were a German band and became intrigued when he discovered that they were actually locals. Pete Best, among others, thinks that that is untrue: "It seems almost impossible that Brian had no knowledge of us. The Cavern was only a short walk away from Whitechapel [where NEMS was located] and we were appearing several times a week. Since the start of *Mersey Beat* [a local pop newspaper] we had been splashed across its pages. Perhaps Brian never read the magazine himself, even though he wrote for it and sold it in his shop."[19] Bill Harry, *Mersey Beat*'s publisher, agrees: by the time Epstein walked into the Cavern on November 9, 1961, "he was very familiar with the Beatles and they were aware of him."[20] That would hardly be surprising: The first issue, which Epstein reordered when it sold out, contained a mock bio of the Beatles written by Lennon, while the cover of the second issue (NEMS had bought 144 copies) announced details of the Beatles' Hamburg recording session.

After catching the rough but riveting Beatles during a lunchtime gig at the Cavern, Epstein reportedly asked Mona Best if she managed the band; she explained that her interests lay with the Casbah and, naturally, her son. "So when Epstein asked if she minded if he became The Beatles' manager, she said no, not at all," according to Pete Best. "She just wanted what was best for the band and said: 'Make sure you do right by them.' "[21] She later explained, "He was also young and certainly seemed to be the type of person who could do something for the Beatles. I had tried to help them as much as I could along the way and perhaps now he might be able to push them along further."[22]

Epstein was taken by the group's raw charisma and also allegedly drawn to John Lennon, whose faux-punk attitude epitomized "rough trade" (a phrase used to describe gay hustlers with a street-tough aura). That was the genteel sales-man's secret vice: Epstein was a closeted Jewish homosexual in an era when Jews were viewed with suspicion, and gay people who acted on their desires could be sent to jail. "I'm sure Brian was in love with John," Paul McCartney says. "We were all in love with John, but Brian was gay so that added an edge."[23]

On December 3, 1961, the group met with Epstein in his shop to talk business. They met again three days later, when Epstein laid out his terms: 25 percent of the group's gross on a weekly basis, for which consideration he would ensure that they would never play for less than fifteen pounds (excepting lunchtime at the Cavern: he said he would have their five-pound fee doubled). He also promised to get the band a recording contract with a major label. The Beatles would have signed then and there, except that Epstein had no contract at hand; he felt that the standard artist-management deal of the era was unfair, and he wanted to have it modified into something more balanced. An adapted contract was signed by all four Beatles and countersigned by Alistair Taylor on January 24, 1962, but Epstein did not put pen to paper that day; it is thought that he wanted to prove himself to the Beatles before holding them legal hostage, and in fact he did not sign the contract until that October.

Epstein began shopping the group to every possible outlet, with discouraging results; upon each return from London by train, once or twice a week, he was invariably met at Liverpool's Lime Street Station by the boys, who would cho-rus, "Have they signed us yet, Bri?"[24] The inexperienced Epstein attempted every conceivable avenue: in January 1962, he submitted a completed three-page "Application for an Audition by Variety Department" to the BBC's Man-chester headquarters and was rewarded the following month when the band was selected to play before a producer of teen radio shows. It passed the test and wound up performing three cover songs on the show in March. Then the Beatles went back to Hamburg, this time for seven weeks in the Star Club, the city's newest rock venue: seven days a week, four hours onstage one night, three the next, in a one-hour-on, one-hour-off rotation. (Two weeks of this engagement were shared with the group's early hero Gene Vincent.)

Meanwhile, back in London, Epstein was putting in a last-ditch effort, appealing to anyone he could corral. Dick Rowe, a Decca A&R executive, famously dismissed him with "We don't like your boys' sound. Groups are out; four-piece groups with guitarists are particularly finished," and added insult to injury by saying, "The boys won't go, Mr. Epstein; we know these things. You have a good record business in Liverpool; stick to that."[25] When McCartney later commented that Rowe must have been kicking himself over the group's success, Lennon retorted that he hoped the man kicked himself to death.[26] Again, conflicting stories abound: Roy Moseley, a well-placed British writer and manager of the day, claims that it was not, in fact, Rowe who turned down the Beatles, but former Shadows drummer Tony Meehan, then working in A&R and production at the label.[27] Others confirm that the decision was Rowe's to make, and he chose to sign Brian Poole and the Tremeloes instead. In any case, Rowe—unhappy over becoming the laughingstock of the music industry—later signed the Rolling Stones after the Beatles recommended the band.

Epstein finally paid a visit to an acquaintance who happened to be the general manager of the HMV Record Shop in Oxford Street, and asked him to listen to the Beatles' demo tape. The music was not to the man's taste, but he was impressed enough to call in another employee who might know someone to approach at EMI—even though Epstein and the Beatles had already been turned down by the label, a fact that he wisely kept to himself. Epstein was referred to yet another man who had offices on the fourth floor at HMV and was in charge of EMI's music publishing, and this person suggested that Epstein talk to George Martin. Epstein had never heard of Martin, but discovered that he was the head of Parlophone, a label within EMI that had a virtually bare roster in the area of pop music. An introductory call was made, and Martin agreed to see Epstein the following morning.

George Martin

George Martin, thirty-six at the time, was best known for his work with the *Goon Show* team of Spike Milligan and Peter Sellers; the Beatles were big fans of this absurdist humor (which would later also exert an influence over the British comedy troupe Monty Python, whose movie *Life of Brian* was financed by George Harrison's Handmade Films). At this point, Epstein was so discouraged that he dithered over whether to keep the appointment with Martin or give up and go home. He rang his brother Clive back in Liverpool, who urged him to stay. When the two men met the next morning, Martin was impressed with Epstein's demeanor and style, but felt that the group's demo tape was second-rate. "In defense of all those people who turned it down," as he told the British music paper *Melody Maker* in 1971, "it was a pretty lousy tape, recorded in a back room, very badly balanced, not very good songs, and a rather raw group. But I wanted something, and I thought they were interesting enough to bring down for a test . . . they came to London and I spent an after-noon with them . . . in Abbey Road [EMI's recording studio]. I liked them, I liked them as people apart from anything else, and I was convinced that we had the makings of a hit group but I didn't know what to do with them in terms of material."[28]

If anyone deserves the title of "fifth Beatle" after the actual group members and Brian Epstein, it must be Martin, who oversaw the band's studio work throughout its recording career. His creative partnership and ability to trans-late the group's artistic whims while maintaining a semblance of order were es-sential to the innovation that helped set the Beatles apart from the pack. As Beatles biographer Philip Norman states, Martin's contribution "cannot be over-emphasized. First of all, he signed them. Second, he did not cheat them. Third, he did not adulterate them. . . . Martin happened to be of the rare breed who are content to use their talents in improving other people's work. . . . He took the raw songs; he shaped and pruned and polished them and, with scarcely believable altruism, asked nothing for himself but his EMI salary and the satisfaction of seeing the songs come out right."[29]

During his incredible early run of success with the Beatles, Martin was paid a staff producer's salary of 3,000 pounds annually (about $7,000). Shockingly, Parlophone declined to give him either a raise or even a small producer's roy-alty (then standard in the business) when it came time to renegotiate his con-tract. The shortsightedness of the parent company was made even more glaringly apparent when Martin received a memo informing him that he did not qualify for a 1964 Christmas bonus after his productions had dominated the No. 1 spot on the charts for thirty-seven out of the previous fifty-two weeks: "She Loves You" had sold 1.3 million copies (a million in the United States), and "I Want to Hold Your Hand" had sold 1.25 million. The latter sin-gle became the fastest-breaking record that EMI's American subsidiary Capitol had ever released.[30] In the United States, the single sold 250,000 copies in three days (at that time, a hit record might peak at around 200,000); by Janu-ary 10, sales had passed 1 million, and three days later, 10,000 copies an hour were being sold in New York City alone.[31] A month later, it had sold 2 million copies in America. Likewise, the group's debut album *Meet the Beatles* became the fastest-selling album in U.S. history when it was released in January 1964, shooting into the *Billboard* charts at No. 1 and staying there for eleven weeks;[32] by March, it had sold 3 million copies.

Martin would have to strike out on his own to earn his proper due, which he did in 1965 by forming a production company named Associated Independent Recording (AIR); he continued to produce the Beatles, who remained under contract to EMI. "I always thought that if you were artistic and did the right thing people would give you a fair deal. I realised that . . . you had to be cunning and nasty and sly as well. I learned a basic truth then."[33]

Martin had the rare gift of perfect pitch and taught himself to play piano by ear; at seventeen, he joined the Fleet Air Arm, where he was trained as an observer, passing along information he considered important. His army service provided funding to attend the London Guildhall School of Music, where he studied composition, conducting, orchestration, and theory. Paul McCartney believed that his military training also gave Martin the skills to deal with the Beatles in the studio: "I think it is an incredible stroke of fate that he had that experience. That's what a producer does. He doesn't write the songs or play them—he doesn't fly the plane—but he is in charge. And that, tied in with his music, made him the perfect producer for the Beatles. . . . He accommodated us. I think a lesser producer might not have done."[34]

Martin joined Parlophone in 1950, and after the label's head of A&R retired, the twenty-nine-year-old became the youngest boss of an EMI label. In 1960, Martin was on the lookout for a pop group similar to Cliff Richard and the Shadows. After he decided upon the Beatles, Martin produced their first album in just one day (in the succinct summation of Beatles historian Mark Lewisohn, "There can scarcely have been 585 more productive minutes in the history of recorded music").[35] One important judgment call Martin made right away was to include Lennon's raw one-off take of "Twist and Shout"; another producer might have opted for a more conservative sound on a group's debut.

Indeed, Martin's experience of communicating directly with his low-level charges during his early days at the label gave him the impetus to work with, rather than at, the Beatles; he educated them, which gave the composers an entirely new mind-set, allowing them to conceive more complicated material such as "Yesterday" (for which Martin wrote the string quartet accompaniment) and "Strawberry Fields Forever" (where his experience in backward tapes and layered musical effects came into play). It was Martin who composed the harpsichord break for "In My Life" and the French horn bit on "For No One." He gave the Beatles freedom and shaped their sound, and they in turn rose to the occasion. Other artists soon began to view the recording studio as another instrument, something that might not have occurred to them without the groundbreaking work George Martin did with the Beatles.[36]

The Music of the Beatles

Musically, the group set out its personalities from the very start. Lennon was drawn to the rough rockers, while McCartney had more melodic (some would say corny) sensibilities, as evidenced by his cover of "Till There Was You" on the debut album. As a songwriting partnership, the pair was beautifully matched: Lennon toughened McCartney's style, while McCartney helped smooth away Lennon's harder edges. There would be a track or two on each album thrown in as a sort of sop to George Harrison (a talented songwriter in his own right, but so overshadowed by the main team that on his first post-Beatles foray, nothing less than a triple album of long-stored compositions would suffice), and to Ringo Starr, whose genial amiability and lack of "real" singing voice gave him an everyman, lucky-bloke image. This division of labor gave the band an aura of all-for-one comradeship that has been a model for rock groups ever since. As David Crosby of the Byrds (a group that more than once was called "the American Beatles") notes: "The band format, their instruments, the band as attempt at democracy or a kind of family . . . we learned all of that from The Beatles. . . . They set the bar."[37]

"The form [sound] of the Beatles contained the forms of rock & roll itself," according to rock critic Greil Marcus.[38] He believed that the novelty of the band's sound was tempered by echoes of recognition, since it combined the harmonies of '50s vocal groups with rockabilly "flash," the unique personal qualities of individual rock stars with the inventiveness of Brill Building pop songwriting. The Beatles were avid students of rock, R&B, country, and pop; they had studied and absorbed all relevant history up to that point and had mastered and reinvented the sounds they loved through nonstop listening, writing, and playing.

Indeed, much of the Beatles' early music took its primary components from what had gone before. Both Lennon and McCartney adapted Little Richard's falsetto to thrilling effect (the "whoo"s in "She Loves You" always sent the audience into paroxysms of delighted screaming). The Beatles' harmonies, often three-part, may have been inspired by the Everly Brothers, but were exceptional for their tightness, layering, and blend of voices, especially given the fact that none of the Beatles were blood relations (as opposed to, say, the Everlys or the Beach Boys). Additionally, the songwriting takes the standard pop form and gives it a unique twist: in "She Loves You," the singer is not talking about his own love interest, but is telling another male about confidences shared by the other man's girlfriend ("She says you hurt her so") and advising that he "should be glad" to have her. The singer is not an ex-lover of the woman in question; he is a friend and only interested in seeing this potential couple happy together. The song remains unusual for these lyrical qualities, as well as the energy and style with which it was delivered; only a handful of others have attempted to remake it, and of those, several were comedians trying to cash in on the group's overwhelming impact.

Most of all, as Marcus says, the music was delivered with unparalleled grace, enthusiasm, and a raw physicality. "The beat, first of all, was not big, it was enormous. . . . At the same time, there was a lightness to almost every tune, a floating quality, a kind of lyrical attack that shaped but did not lessen the rhythmic power of the numbers . . . the use of rock group dynamics [was] so fluid and intelligent that for years they made nearly everything else on the radio sound faintly stupid." He adds that the "lovely, naked emotion" of these early records, rare in white singers, mixed with the steely determination to make it that lent spine to the band's explosive exuberance, simply "blew away all that stood before them . . . [and kept] virtually every promise rock & roll ever made."[39]

To Americans, the group appeared exotic rather than familiar: "The Merseyside moptops were the divine Other: different, hence better," they seemed "almost otherworldly, as if they had just beamed down from some distant and far happier planet."[40] They entranced everyone, including other musicians who had never before considered the options they represented. "They were our heroes," Crosby says. "They were absolutely what we thought we wanted to do. We listened to every note they played, and savored it, and rubbed it on our foreheads, and were duly affected by it. . . . [A friend] walked in one afternoon with that first Beatles album, *Meet the Beatles*. He put it on, and I just didn't know what to think. It absolutely floored me—'Those are folk-music changes, but it's got rock and roll backbeat. You can't do that, but they did!'"[41]

There was also a Beatle to suit all tastes: acerbic John, brooding George, charming Paul, or lost-puppy Ringo (who was the most popular band member in the United States). At first, especially when the group seemed like just another teen craze, they were deemed harmless—although some stuffy types still hated the haircuts—especially after the Rolling Stones came along to offer a scruffier, surlier counterpoint. The irony lay in the fact that the Stones came from middle-class backgrounds, whereas the Beatles originated in a much tougher milieu. As Marcus points out, "The Beatles opened up the turf the Stones took as their own. There was no possibility of a Left until the Beatles created the Center."[42]

The "Professional" Beatles

In June 1962, the group had its audition at Abbey Road; two months later, Pete Best was sacked and replaced by Ringo Starr. Speculation over the reasons for Best's dismissal varies: he had a sullen personality, was too forceful, or was too good-looking, which created jealousy among the other Beatles (his mother thought that, and some fans agreed). Best claims that Epstein had once propositioned him with a "very gentle approach," but did not seem to resent being refused.[43] Epstein told Best that the other band members, and especially George Martin, thought that his skills were not up to par. "I didn't like his drumming, it wasn't solid and he didn't bind the group together," Martin explained to the British music paper *Melody Maker* in 1971. "I said to Brian that I didn't want to use him on the records, although he could do what he liked with him outside the studio . . . there was no reason why I shouldn't use a session drummer. No one was going to know. This was obviously the trigger, because the boys had been thinking of getting rid of him anyway, but they wanted someone to do the dirty work for them."[44]

Whether Epstein's backing of the Beatles stemmed from an infatuation with the unattainable Lennon, a desire to vicariously enjoy attention he had been denied in his unsuccessful try at acting, or some other reason, the fact remains that he was fiercely devoted to the Beatles and, in their own fashion, they to him. Without Epstein's guidance, the group's disparate personalities would not have jelled for long. It was his judgment that set the lads on course for "the top-permost of the poppermost," as Lennon liked to joke. If he had not insisted on taking them out of their scruffy leathers, and they had not agreed, they would not have taken the world by storm. "We liked the leather and the jeans," Lennon later said, "but we wanted a good suit, even to wear off stage. 'Yeah man, all right, I'll wear a suit—I'll wear a bloody *balloon* if somebody's going to pay me; I'm not in love with leather *that* much!' "[45] The group now cut a professional appearance in matching, custom-made, velvet-collared jackets, narrow trousers, and Cuban-heeled boots crafted by a theatrical shoemaker, all paid for by their manager.

Epstein made the Beatles behave professionally as well; no longer would they indulge in cursing, smoking, eating, or drinking onstage. A teenage girl who worked for their first fan club was astonished when she saw the new, improved Beatles: "Suddenly they looked steam-cleaned, from their skin and shiny hair to their fingernails and their clothes."[46] Epstein instructed the group members to bow deeply at the end of each song, which would make them appear humble and help win over many adults who were otherwise horrified by the hairstyles.

When the Beatles were given their Member of the British Empire awards in 1965 while Epstein was denied (a slight that he correctly attributed to the fact that he was a Jewish homosexual), one member of the band, in a statement variously credited to Harrison or McCartney, generously said that the acronym for the honor, MBE, actually translated to "Mr. Brian Epstein." Yet they could also be cruel and abrupt with him, as George Martin remembered for *Melody Maker*: "The boys were downstairs and I was talking to them through an intercom. Brian picked up the mike and said, 'Why don't you do such-and-such' and John said 'Brian, you look after your money,

⊚ THE ORIGINS OF THE MOPTOP

George Harrison was the first to try out the moptop in Hamburg, after a trip to the swimming baths; the band's friends Astrid Kirchherr and Klaus Voorman told the youngest Beatle that he looked good with his hair flopped over his face, and to let it dry that way. Harrison found it a real effort to get his thick hair slicked into "rocker" style, because it naturally wanted to fall forward; he used to grease it back with Vaseline. A short while later, Lennon and McCartney were on a quick Paris holiday when they asked their friend Jürgen to cut their hair in a similar style to his own, flattened down with "fringe"—the British word for what Americans call "bangs." "When we got back to Liverpool, it was all, 'Eh, your hair's gone funny.'—'No, this is the new style.' We tried to change it back, but it wouldn't go, it kept flapping forward. And that just caught on," McCartney reminisced.[47]

It is comical in retrospect to realize that those famous bowl cuts, actually quite short on the sides and back by current standards, were considered revolutionary—even dirty—by virtue of length alone. Literally tons of Beatles wigs, cheap synthetic concoctions that bore no resemblance to the real thing, were sold as gag gifts. The irritation of many parents when their children adopted the hairstyle was soothed by the idea that the Beatles were the musical equivalent of the hula hoop, a previous fad that also sold like wildfire before vanishing.

and we'll look after our music.' Brian flushed to the roots of his hair and never said any more. He was obviously very hurt by that."[48]

As Andrew Loog Oldham, once an Epstein employee and later the manager/provocateur behind the Rolling Stones, summed up: "Brian was a passionate man who would not take a 'no' on behalf of his lads and that is how we got to hear The Beatles. End of story."[49] He was so protective of his charges that he once followed a DJ up a 200-foot lighting scaffold to ensure that the latter was not taping the show in progress. One reason that there is so little footage of the Beatles performing live during their heyday is that Epstein would not allow them to take the stage until all filming news crews were ejected; and since early tape recorders were much bulkier, heavier, and less technologically advanced, any bootleg recordings that do exist tend to be of very poor quality.

The Right Sort of Attention

Thanks to Epstein's machinations, the Beatles were finally receiving the right sort of attention. Summoned to a royal command performance in London on November 4, 1963, Lennon introduced "Twist and Shout" by instructing the audience: "Those of you in the cheap seats clap your hands; all the others, rattle your jewelry."[50] (Lennon had originally planned to use an obscene description before "jewelry," which Epstein—for once successful in reining him in—had argued would be inappropriate.) The queen's sister, Princess Margaret, the Queen Mother, and the rest in attendance were amused rather than appalled by Lennon's cheek. The next day, British newspapers coined the phrase "Beatlemania" to describe hysteria sparked by the band.

The music critic of the prestigious *London Times* wrote a column raving about the Beatles' use of "Aeolian cadences," "submediant switches," and "melismas with altered vowels" that must have amused the group members, none of whom could actually read music.[51] That critic also pointed out that "The virtue of the Beatles' repertory is that, apparently, they do it themselves; three of the four are composers, they are versatile instrumentalists. . . . one wonder[s] with interest what the Beatles, and particularly Lennon and McCartney, will do next, and if America will spoil them or hold on to them, and if their next record will wear as well as the others. They have brought a distinctive and exhilarating flavour into a genre of music that was in danger of ceasing to be music at all."[52]

The Beatles Come to America, 1964

Even as his "boys" were creating a sensation in the United Kingdom, Epstein had his eyes on the bigger prize, America, but he felt that he would have to wait until the Beatles were too huge to deny. Fate decreed that in the spring of 1963, a New York agent named Sid Bernstein, working with cabaret acts at the time, began studying the music business at the New School. Instructed by his teacher to read the British papers daily, Bernstein noticed the Beatles story as it began to unfold: a *London Times* article of October 28, 1963, was headlined "Disorder in Rush for Beatles Tickets" and noted that "thousands [of fans in Newcastle upon Tyne] broke ranks and surged forward," requiring forty police officers to spend three-quarters of an hour to restore order. On November 25, two days after the Kennedy assassination, the same paper ran a story stating that dozens of fans had been injured in a crush of more than 12,000 Liverpudlians waiting to buy tickets for a one-night stand the following month; the mile-long queue, which had started forming at 10 p.m. the previous night, had been patrolled by more than 100 police on both foot and horseback.

Bernstein could practically smell the success across the Atlantic. Without having heard a single note, he tracked down Epstein's home phone number and tried to book the band. Epstein declined, citing the fact that they did not yet have an American label, audience, or radio airplay. Undeterred, Bernstein discovered the price Epstein had set for the group (then the American equivalent of $2,000), and offered him $6,500 for two shows in one day. At which venue? Epstein wondered. Carnegie Hall, Bernstein replied. Even Epstein had heard of Carnegie Hall, the world's preeminent home of classical music. No pop or rock group had ever played there. Epstein once more said that they had no airplay, crucial for breaking an artist; Bernstein responded that they might, if the date was set far enough in the future. The men agreed upon February 1964 in a "verbal handshake" over the phone, with the out that if the Beatles' records had not achieved any airplay by then, the date could be canceled.

Meanwhile, Capitol Records, EMI's American arm, had turned the Beatles down four times, but Vee-Jay, a small African American label out of Chicago that was having success with the Four Seasons, was interested in trying out one single. Calvin Carter, Vee-Jay's A&R man in charge of acquisitions, remembered: "[An EMI affiliate] had a #1 record and they asked us if we wanted it. . . . It was 'I Remember You,' by Frank Ifield. We took the record, and as a throw in, they had a group and asked us if we would take them, too. The group turned out to be the Beatles, and we got a five-year contract on the Beatles as a pickup on the Frank Ifield contract."[53] A few weeks after this deal was signed, the Beatles recorded "Love Me Do," which cracked the British Top 30. The next single, "Please Please Me," backed with "Ask Me Why," made the Top 5 in England in February 1963, and Vee-Jay decided to release it in America.

As Beatles historian Bruce Spizer relates, DJ Dick Biondi of Chicago's WLS "played 'Please Please Me' right out of the box because he was good friends with Vee-Jay Records. Chicago was the only city that had significant air play. It was a top 40 hit, but ignored everywhere else. Sold about 5,000 copies."[54] When Vee-Jay ran into some financial problems, it granted a release to Frank Ifield, but not the Beatles, who had not sold very well for the company. Carter remembers having the first Beatles album in his desk drawer for several months, which is where it stayed until 1964.

EMI handed the second single ("She Loves You," backed with "I'll Get You") over to an even smaller label named Swan, best known for having Freddy

Cannon ("Tallahassee Lassie"). This also failed to chart when it was first released in September 1963, yet is now acknowledged as one of the Beatles' crowning early achievements, a record so magical and so unique that other artists shy away from even attempting to cover it. "Nothing that came before hints at this kind of power," one critic marvelled. "At two minutes and eighteen seconds, it packs twice the number of ideas into even less space than usual, and blasts the future of rock wide open . . . it's like a whole new world opening—the music defines ecstasy."[55]

George Harrison, Ringo Starr, Paul McCartney, and John Lennon taking a break from recording outside EMI's Abbey Road Studio, c. 1963. Courtesy of Photofest.

In late 1963, Capitol Records launched the largest promotional campaign in music history, reportedly spending $50,000 just in the New York City area. The day after Christmas, when children would presumably still have gift money in their pockets, the company released "I Want to Hold Your Hand," backed with "I Saw Her Standing There"—but the second song was already held by Vee-Jay, since it was on the album it had contracted from EMI. The single hit the No. 1 spot on all American reporting charts in January 1964. Now Vee-Jay rereleased "Please Please Me" and "From Me to You" and put out its own version of the first album, *Introducing the Beatles* (the company had removed "Please Please Me" and "Ask Me Why," replacing these with "Love Me Do" and "P.S. I Love You"). Capitol went berserk, and two weeks into January hit Vee-Jay with injunctions forbidding the release of any Beatles product. The legal wrangling had just begun in earnest, and there was a confusing flurry of competing releases on all three labels until the two independents (which had had the honor, and attendant profit, of releasing the first Beatles singles in America) were crushed under the onslaught. Capitol had no intention of letting its belated investment go awry now.

Epstein made a trip to New York that November with the aim of getting his band national television exposure. Again, according to the "official" tale, fate decreed that Ed Sullivan, the host of America's biggest variety show, had passed through Heathrow Airport several months earlier, just in time to witness a miniriot caused by fans of the Beatles, then returning from a Scandinavian tour. Sullivan's newspaperman instincts and the group's British success resulted in the group being booked for three successive Sundays: February 9, 16, and 23, 1964. Epstein had to subsidize the big break out of his own pocket because Sullivan's show paid only $10,000 for all three appearances. He did, however, demand—and receive—top billing for the group.

It may well be that Sullivan spotted the fury at the airport. However, it is a fact that the news department of his network had already gotten wind of what was going on. A report that originally aired on November 22 (the morning of John Kennedy's assassination) was revived several weeks later, after news anchor Walter Cronkite decreed that America was in need of some happy news. Viewers of the CBS *Evening News* on December 10, 1963, saw a package that began with the sound of "She Loves You" up full, and then-unfamiliar scenes of four grinning musicians with cutaways to screaming girls. That, and the reporter's voice-over, told the tale:

> This is Beatleland, formerly known as Britain, where an epidemic called Beatlemania has seized the teenage population, especially female.... These four boys from Liverpool with their dishmop hairstyles are Britain's latest musical and, in fact, sociological phenomenon. They have introduced what their press agents call the "Mersey Sound," after the River Mersey on which Liverpool stands. Musicologists say it is no different than any other rock & roll, except maybe louder....

And besides being merely the latest objects of adolescent adulation, and culturally the modern manifestation of compulsive tribal singing and dancing, the Beatles are said by sociologists to have a deeper meaning. Some say they are the authentic voice of the proletariat; some say they are the authentic heart of Britain. . . . Some say the Beatles represent the authentic British youth, or British youth as they would like to be: self-confident, natural, direct. . . . They symbolize the 20th century non-hero, as they make non-music [and] wear non-haircuts. . . .

Yeah, yeah, yeah: the fan mail keeps rolling in, and so does the money.[56]

A fifteen-year-old girl in Silver Spring, Maryland, saw this report and wrote to Carroll James, a disc jockey at radio station WWDC in nearby Washington, D.C., asking why Americans could not have music like the Beatles. The enterprising DJ found a stewardess willing to bring over a copy of "I Want to Hold Your Hand" from England, which the station began playing hourly. The overwhelming response forced Capitol to rush-release the single, which was No. 1 the following month.[57] Now the label changed its corporate mind and developed a big-deal sales plan to push the band; Epstein was able to secure a commitment for $20,000 in advertising (more than $123,000 in 2004 dollars, adjusted for inflation;[58] by some accounts, this original amount later more than doubled), along with an ambitious 5 million badges proclaiming, "The Beatles Are Coming."

With this newfound muscle behind him, Epstein was ensconced in the most posh hotel he could find (the Regency) when the *New Yorker* magazine came to call. In an article published on December 28, 1963, he rhapsodized: "They are the most worshipped, the most idolized boys in the country. They have tremendous style and a great effervescence which communicates itself in an extraordinary way. . . . I think that America is ready for the Beatles. When they come, they will hit this country for six."[59] He was absolutely correct. The *Ed Sullivan Show*'s theater had a capacity of 700; before the group's February 9 appearance, the show received an astonishing 600,000 ticket requests.

The Beatles may have been thrilled to finally arrive in America, but America's teenagers were even more excited to welcome them. Anywhere from 3,000 to 5,000 (accounts vary) were on hand when they touched down in New York, and another 4,000 were in Miami to greet the jet that brought them to another *Sullivan* appearance. All were screaming their heads off, primed by breathless radio reports on stations such as New York's WMCA, which gave blow-by-blow accounts in which no detail was too trivial to remain untouched by that special magic: "It is now 6:30 a.m., Beatle time. They left London thirty minutes ago. They're out over the Atlantic Ocean, headed for New York. The temperature is 32 Beatle degrees."[60]

The band members, coming off a French tour that had presented them with rather diffident audiences, were floored by the hysterical reception. "They told

The Beatles appear on the *Ed Sullivan Show*, 1964. Courtesy of the Library of Congress.

us it would be fab," George Harrison wrote in his column for Britain's *Daily Express* about the group's February 7 touchdown at New York's John F. Kennedy International Airport. "But this was ridiculous! We have seen some mobs of fans in our time but somehow we weren't prepared for what was waiting for us. 'There won't be many there,' said Ringo. 'The airport's too far out from the city.' Was he wrong!"[61] (Starr was, in fact, correct in his geographic supposition; it is something of a mystery how so many youngsters managed to be there that day. The fans in question were far too young to drive, and even the most indulgent parents might have balked at taking them: it was a Friday, so both school and work were in session. Stories unsubstantiated by hard evidence indicate that adolescents cutting classes to congregate at the hotel in advance of the band's arrival were given free round-trip transport to the airport, courtesy of chartered buses hired by the record label.) McCartney said, "There were millions of kids at the airport, which nobody had expected. . . . We thought, 'Wow! God, we have really made it.' I remember, for instance, the great moment of getting into the limo and putting on the radio, and hearing a running commentary on *us*: 'They have just left the airport' . . . It was like a dream. The greatest fantasy ever."[62]

The popular supposition is that the United States was still in mourning for the recently assassinated John F. Kennedy, and therefore, the Beatles were a timely tonic with their joyous sound, irreverent attitude, and semiexotic Liverpudlian origins and accents. Also, as one British psychiatrist bluntly noted, "Beatlemania would not have taken on the magnitude it has if there had not been the need to release sexual urges. These urges exist within us and they demand to be taken notice of"[63]—certainly during adolescence, a state that millions of baby boomers were currently enduring or about to enter.

But the simple truth is that the Beatles would have been a hit no matter when they appeared, simply because they were overwhelmingly irresistible. Filmmaker Albert Maysles, whose documentary on the band's first visit is an invaluable historical reference, says that the group remained down-to-earth and unchanged under the unprecedented barrage of publicity, an undeniable part of their charm. Then British prime minister Sir Alec Douglas-Home understood this, telling an annual conference of the Young Conservatives: "The Beatles are now my secret weapon. If any country is in deficit with us I only have to say the Beatles are coming. Let me tell you why they have had such a success in the United States—it is because they are a band of very natural, very funny young men."[64] He was quite right: the Beatles were already spinning income for their home country at the rate of half a million British pounds a month, at a time when the pound was worth almost two American dollars.

The cynical media, expecting a group of manufactured pop flashes in the pan, were stunned by the group's first U.S. press conference, at New York's John F. Kennedy International Airport (the former Idlewild Airport had just been renamed in honor of the slain president). Accustomed to docile celebrities prepped by handlers and stumped by innocuous questions, the press found the Beatles a delightfully disarming surprise. "Sing for us," one reporter demanded. The group immediately chorused "No!" in unison with Lennon adding that they would need to be paid first. The rest of the brief encounter saw the Beatles employ their quick wit to charm and spar with the flummoxed reporters. "Being cheeky chappies saved our arses on many occasions," Ringo Starr observed. "These reporters, being New Yorkers, yelled at us, but we just yelled back. . . . Up until then, pop groups had been milk and honey with the press: 'No, I don't smoke,' that kind of thing. And here *we* were, smoking and drinking and shouting at *them*. That's what endeared us to them."[65]

The establishment's reviews of the *Sullivan* show were mixed, often downright condescending. Yet an estimated 73 million viewers were tuned in, among them countless teenagers who had a very different perception; they all decided then and there that being a Beatle, or something as close to it as possible, was life's only worthwhile goal. "I remember thinking, 'This can be done. I can do that,'" singer Billy Joel said.[66] And, as Bruce Springsteen guitarist Steve Van Zandt states, "This was the main event of my life. It was certainly the major event for many others, whether or not they knew it at the time. For me, it was no less dramatic than aliens landing on the planet."[67] During the week of April 4, 1964 (two months after that first *Sullivan* appearance), the Beatles held down the entire Top 5 on *Billboard*'s singles chart, a feat that had never been achieved before, nor repeated since.

The Maysles film depicts a Beatles show at the Washington Coliseum, sandwiched between the New York and Miami appearances on *Sullivan*, that is laughable in its primitivity. Starr actually tries to turn his entire drum kit (up on a small platform) himself, before someone lends him a hand; there are no monitors for the musicians to hear themselves, and since they are playing on a small stage in the center of the venue, every few songs they have to physically reposition their microphones, and Ringo's kit, to face another segment of the audience. There are a few policemen nearby, but security is otherwise nonexistent; the stage is only a few feet above the audience, and if it were not for a well-behaved crowd, the band could easily have been torn to pieces before anyone could prevent it. This was before one of the members said he enjoyed "jelly babies," an English confection considerably softer than American jellybeans, which the U.S. audience began hurling at high velocity toward the stage. It is something of a miracle that none of the Beatles lost an eye during that period.

A Hard Day's Night

Despite the loyal enthusiasm shown by local fans everytime the band returned to Liverpool, the Beatles moved to London to begin production on their first feature film, *A Hard Day's Night*. The film, which commenced shooting in March 1964 and was in theaters three months later, was budgeted at around half a million dollars and was shot in black and white to save money; the filmmakers were prepared to cash in on this new craze, but were also hedging their bets. The director was Richard "Dick" Lester, whose previous credits included *The Running Jumping and Standing Still Film* (1959) with Peter Sellers and Spike Milligan, the *Goon Show* comedy team that George Martin had recorded and the Beatles admired. He had about six and a half weeks to bring it in on budget (and did so well that he would later be tapped for the group's lesser follow-up, *Help!*, shot in color in London and various far-flung locales). Alun Owen, born in Wales but raised in Liverpool, wrote the script, with ad-libs courtesy of the group; it was nominated for an Academy Award, as was George Martin's adapted score, and went on to earn well over $18,500,000 in American theatrical gross and rentals alone.[68]

Not once did anyone in the film ever mention the name of the featured group: the assumption was that if one did not know whom one was watching, one had been living under a rock for the last year. Eventually, as critic Roger Ebert would say of this cheaply and hastily produced ninety minutes of celluloid: "It was so joyous and original that even the early reviews acknowledged it as something special. After more than three decades, it has not aged and is not dated; it stands outside its time, its genre and even rock. It is one of the great life-affirming landmarks of the movies . . . filled with the exhilaration of four musicians who were having fun and creating at the top of their form and knew it. . . . Today when we watch TV and see quick cutting, hand-held cameras, interviews conducted on the run with moving targets, quickly intercut snatches of dialogue, music under documentary action and all the other trademarks of the modern style, we are looking at the children of *A Hard Day's Night*."[69] Even the staid *New York Times* raved, "This is going to surprise you—it may knock you right out of your chair—but the new film with those incredible chaps, the Beatles, is a whale of a comedy. I wouldn't believe it either, if I hadn't seen it with my own astonished eyes, which have long since become accustomed to seeing disasters happen when newly fledged pop-singing sensations are hastily rushed to the screen. But this . . . has so much good humor going for it that it is awfully hard to resist . . . it is much more sophisticated in theme and technique than its seemingly frivolous matter promises."[70]

In August 1965, the Beatles arrived in New York to play an unprecedented date at Shea Stadium in Flushing, Queens, near the recently opened World's Fair. When Sid Bernstein, the man who had originally brought the group to America, proposed the idea to Brian Epstein, the manager was at first unsure whether his boys could fill such an enormous venue: over 55,000 seats, with the highest-priced ticket set at $5.65. A confident Bernstein offered to pay $10 for any unsold seat; the Beatles would receive $100,000 against 50 percent of the gross receipts for an evening's work. Epstein came back the next day with a request for 60 percent, and the deal was set. Within three weeks of mentioning the show to a fan, Bernstein had received three duffle bags of mail requesting tickets—all achieved via word-of-mouth. It was a complete, historic sell-out.

On August 15, 1965, the band departed Manhattan by helicopter, which landed at the World's Fair site, and were taken into the venue by a Wells Fargo armored truck

THE "TEMPORARY BEATLE"

In June 1964, Ringo Starr (whose history of susceptibility to ailments dated back to a childhood often spent in hospital) collapsed during a photo session. As Starr was being treated for tonsilitis and pharyngitis, Brian Epstein and George Martin had an emergency meeting at which it was decided to hire a temporary replacement, which upset George Harrison so much that he threatened to leave until the drummer could rejoin the group. He was persuaded to stay on while Martin rustled up one Jimmy Nicol, who knew the band's material from playing on a low-budget Beatles covers album. Nicol sat in with the group for a quick session at Abbey Road to ascertain that he was up to the job, then was told to get ready to leave for Denmark immediately.

Nicol's first appearance with the Beatles took place on June 4, 1964, at the Tivoli Gardens in Copenhagen; the band had decided to delete Ringo's spotlight number, "I Wanna Be Your Man." It had all happened so quickly that there was no time to get Nicol a suit to match the others; he had to wear Starr's, for which his legs were too long. After Starr was discharged from the hospital, he caught up with the group in Melbourne, Australia, in mid-June, where a photo session caught all five together.

Nicol was promptly sent packing now that the rightful owner of the drum kit was back in place, and while he had only kind words to say about the other musicians, he noted that he could not help but feel "like an intruder . . . they have their own atmosphere, their own sense of humour. It's a little clique and outsiders just can't break in."[71] Taken to the airport personally by Epstein, Nicol received a payment of 500 pounds and, classily, a watch inscribed "From the Beatles and Brian Epstein to Jimmy—with appreciation and gratitude." Unfortunately for Nicol, his ascent was brief. A single later released by his band did not chart, and he bounced around the globe for a while, never again attaining anything near the notoriety of his short stint as the "Temporary Beatle."

(they departed the same way). Murray the K emceed the show, while the honor of introducing the Beatles was reserved for Ed Sullivan. The fans' reaction was so overwhelming that all Brian Epstein could say, over and over, was: "I hope we can get them out of here. I hope we get out of here alive."[72] It was the first time that an open-air sports arena had been utilized for a musical event, and was such a radically new idea that the group had to play through an inadequate public address system meant for announcements, instead of via powerful amplifiers. The screaming of hysterical fans effectively drowned out the band anyway. While Ringo Starr pointed out, "I never felt people came to *hear* our show—I felt they came to *see* us,"[73] McCartney disagreed; he noted that his future wife Linda, who was in the audience, had been annoyed by all the noise, as "she genuinely wanted to hear the show. That wasn't the deal, though. Not then."[74]

The highlight of the Beatles' tour, besides playing Shea Stadium for the first time (they would repeat the feat in August 1966), was finally meeting Elvis Presley at his mansion in Los Angeles. McCartney recalled: "We were all major fans, so it was hero worship of a high degree. . . . I think the success of our career started to push him out a little, which we were very sad about, because we wanted to co-exist with him. He was our greatest idol, but the styles were changing in favour of us." Starr added, "The saddest part is that, years and years later, we found out that he tried to have us banished from America. . . . That's very sad to me, that he felt so threatened."[75]

The hazards of live performance were becoming increasingly evident. At a Chicago date in September 1964, a raw beefsteak hit McCartney onstage; it splattered his jacket, but otherwise caused no harm. Fans were being trampled and injured at concerts, crashing through plate-glass walls at the group's hotel, and posing a very real threat to the Beatles' lives above and beyond simply trying to tear the group apart. In Houston in 1965, admirers crawled over the wings of the group's just-landed aircraft as they held lit cigarettes, totally oblivious to the idea that the plane, themselves, and their idols could become a fireball with just one misplaced spark. "The police had no control," press officer Tony Barrow would complain.[76]

On August 21, 1965, smoke began pouring from the right engine of the Electra plane that was transporting the band from Minneapolis to the next date in Portland. Journalist Larry Kane had to prevent a panicked John Lennon from opening the rear emergency door midflight. The pilot managed to land, assisted by firefighters and a runway blanketed in foam. Almost exactly eight months later, one of the two Electras used to fly the Beatles crashed in Ardmore, Oklahoma, killing five members of the crew (including three who had flown with the group during its tour) and seventy-eight soldiers.

It is little wonder, then, that the Beatles were sick of touring. When they were not bored, they were in fear for their lives, unable to hear themselves play, torn from family and friends at home, and prevented from enjoying the fruits of their labors, as well as having to endure the frustration of creating music in the studio that was impossible to duplicate in a live setting at that time. At the beginning of 1966, Brian Epstein was compelled to deny reports of a breakup, but the truth was that the group was rapidly approaching its end as a performing entity. If the band had not already been itching to get off the road, the events leading up to its next and final tour of America would have sealed the deal, most notably the furor created by John Lennon's comments on Christianity.

"We're More Popular Than Jesus"

In March 1966, John Lennon gave an interview to his friend Maureen Cleave at the London *Evening Standard* that included a few offhand remarks about religion: "Christianity will go. It will vanish and shrink . . . we're [the Beatles] more popular than Jesus now; I don't know which will go first—rock 'n' roll or Christianity. Jesus was all right but his disciples were thick and ordinary. It's them twisting it that ruins it for me."[77]

In England, people took Lennon's comments with a grain of salt. However, when they were picked up and reprinted in America by Danny Fields (then the editor of teen favorite *Datebook* magazine), the story exploded. Radio stations across the country, especially in the South and the Midwest, banned the Beatles' records, there were bonfires of Beatle albums and memorabilia, and death threats against Lennon and the group poured in. The Ku Klux Klan hosted events in America's so-called Bible Belt at which the Beatles were burned in effigy and the group's albums were nailed to flaming crosses. Cleave tried to explain: "I was astonished that John Lennon's quotation was taken out of context from my article and misinterpreted in that way. I don't think for one moment that he intended to be flippant or irreverent, and he certainly wasn't comparing the Beatles to Jesus Christ. He was simply observing that, to many, the Beatles were better known. He was deploring, rather than approving this. Sectors of the American public were given the wrong impression, and it was totally absurd."[78]

Lennon was forced to hold an August 11 press conference in Chicago as the Beatles were preparing to tour the United States: "I'm not saying that we're better or greater, or comparing us with Jesus Christ as a person or God as a thing or whatever it is. I wasn't saying whatever they're saying [I said]. . . . I never meant it to be a lousy anti-religious thing. I apologize if that will make you happy. I still don't know quite what I've done. I've tried to tell you what I did do but if you want me to apologize, if that will make you happy, then OK, I'm sorry."[79]

The Vatican, which had denounced Lennon ("Some subjects must not be dealt with lightly . . . even in the world of beatniks"),[80] accepted this semiapology, but others did not. The reaction was spreading worldwide, and it gave those who had always disliked the group justification for any attack they chose to mount. Beatles records were banned in Spain, Holland, and South Africa, where the broadcasting corporation declared, "The Beatles' arrogance has passed the ultimate limit of decency."[81] The ban on Lennon in that country lasted for years, long after the group had broken up and South Africans could hear solo work by McCartney and Harrison.

The Impact of Drugs on the Beatles' Music

The Beatles' music can be divided into two categories: before and after their discovery of marijuana and psychedelic drugs. Albums made before these experiences evidence standard inspirations: for example, the album *Beatles for Sale/Beatles '65* (see How the Beatles' Albums Differed in America) contains covers of Carl Perkins's "Honey Don't" and "Everybody's Trying to Be My Baby" (country), Chuck Berry's "Rock and Roll Music," and a medley of Lieber and Stoller's "Kansas City" with Little Richard's "Hey, Hey, Hey, Hey" (R&B), as well as Buddy Holly's "Words of Love" (pop).

While the group had had plenty of experience with alcohol and amphetamines during its Hamburg sojourn, the psychedelics were not there to blot out reality or lend extra energy, but to trigger internal journeys and expand consciousness. "Once pot was established as part of the curriculum," as Paul McCartney noted, "you started to get a bit more surreal material coming from us, a bit more abstract stuff."[82] According to several sources, Bob Dylan was the party responsible for introducing the Beatles to marijuana in August 1964, although a woman named Cherri Gilham insists that she witnessed John Lennon smoke his first joint in London around March of that year, and reports that he vomited afterwards.[83] McCartney, on the other hand, took to marijuana so enthusiastically that he wrote the exuberant love song "Got to Get You into My Life," included on 1966's *Revolver*, specifically about marijuana; he later explained, "It's actually an ode to pot, like someone else might write an ode to chocolate or a good claret."[84]

At some point in the spring of 1965, Lennon, Harrison, and their wives were "dosed" with LSD by a dentist "friend"; while the women and Harrison did not much enjoy the trip, Lennon was enamored of the drug after recovering from his initial fright, and McCartney was later convinced to try it.

Rubber Soul, released in 1966, is the first indication that something has changed, from the distorted cover photograph to the music within. Fans have now begun to realize that the main singer (except Starr) is also the songwriter, even though all original compositions not by Harrison are still credited to "Lennon-McCartney." The group is still purveying love songs, but more social commentary and offbeat revelation are creeping in (in the form of Lennon's "Nowhere Man" and "Norwegian Wood," the latter song featuring one of rock music's first multicultural explorations with a sitar). This album, while not exactly a concept record, is carefully constructed, with one song flowing into the next: taking the tunes out of context, as is done on various compilation records, destroys the conscious planning that went into each Beatles album from this point on.

In May 1966, the Beatles released a double A-side single, "Rain," backed with "Paperback Writer." The former track was recorded at 42 cps, rather than the usual 50, giving it a psychedelic sound; the latter experimented with using a loudspeaker as a microphone on McCartney's bass. The previous month, after their first vacation in five years, the Beatles had begun work on *Revolver*, which was released on August 8. It was a quantum leap for the band's use of the studio as another instrument: the psychedelic "Tomorrow Never Knows" routed Lennon's voice through a Leslie organ speaker to create a whirling effect, accompanied by reverse-playing tapes and tape loops (achieved by removing the erase head of the tape machine, then recording many times over the same piece of tape). Harrison's "Love You Too" is even more emphatic in its use of the sitar than "Norwegian Wood" had been; a few months before *Revolver* was released, the Rolling Stones had issued a sitar-propelled single, "Paint It, Black," which annoyed John Lennon ("I would like to just *list* what we did and what the Stones did two months after, on every fuckin' album and every fuckin' thing we did").[85]

Indeed, the Beatles and producer George Martin were such innovators that musicians and fans are still debating which of their accomplishments were the most historically significant. The following are only a few that took place during this time period: The group had pioneered four-track recording with "I Want to Hold Your Hand," making overdubbing (the process of adding new sounds to already-recorded tracks) standard in the industry. "I Feel Fine" opens with the first purposely recorded feedback (the sound created when a guitar is held against an amplifier). The Beatles also helped popularize double-tracking, which involved recording a second performance and layering it on top of the original, and constantly employed other unique studio techniques. For instance, George Martin's piano on "In My Life" was recorded at half-speed, then played back at double-speed, since he had trouble finding the right tempo; the result sounds like a baroque instrument. "Eight Days a Week" was the first pop single to have a faded-up intro, while "Yesterday" was the first to use a string quartet. In addition, the Beatles revolutionized the now-defunct 45 rpm single: normally, the A side was promoted as the hit and the B side was a lesser track. The quality of the group's records was such that those distinctions were soon erased, and all their singles were considered double A sides.

In June 1966, the Beatles' good-boy image was tarnished when *Yesterday And Today* was released with a cover photograph depicting the quartet wearing bloodied butcher smocks, covered in slabs of meat and decapitated baby dolls, and grinning widely. It was thought to be the group's protest against Capitol Records' "butchering" of the band's British releases. The response was immediate and furious, and thousands of albums were pulled and hastily re-covered with a more acceptable photograph. In a letter dated June 14, 1966, Capitol asked reviewers to return the record they had been sent, with a statement by label president Alan W. Livingston: "The original cover, created in England,

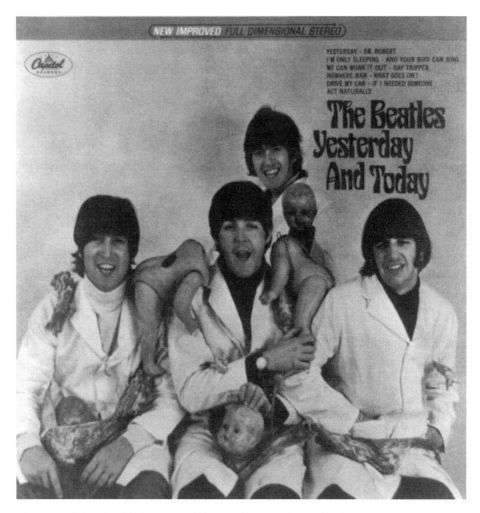

The original "butcher-block" cover of the Beatles' *Yesterday And Today*, 1966. Courtesy of the Library of Congress.

was intended as 'pop art' satire. However . . . in the United States . . . [it has been] subject to misinterpretation . . . to avoid any possible controversy or undeserved harm to the Beatles' image or reputation, Capitol has chosen to withdraw the LP and substitute a more generally acceptable design."[86] The subtle implication would seem to be that the English audience was more sophisticated than the Americans. As many as 750,000 of the original sleeves went back into record stores five days later with a new cover (of the Beatles posing with a steamer trunk) pasted over the old one. The "butcher" covers became instant collectors' items, and many fans fruitlessly steamed and peeled the later covers in hopes of finding one. Original album covers, if they are in mint condition, now fetch a stunningly high price.

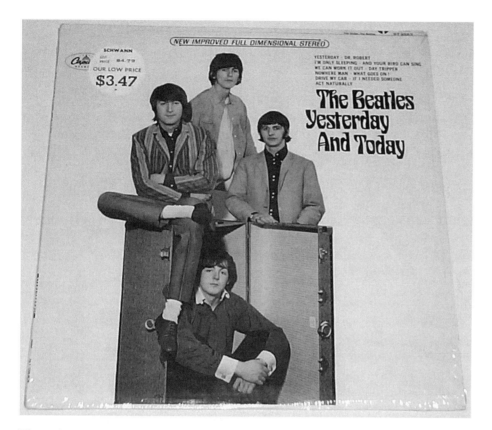

The replacement cover of the Beatles' *Yesterday And Today*, 1966. Courtesy of the Library of Congress.

How the Beatles' Albums Differed in America

Starting in 1964, Capitol stretched the first three original Beatles albums into four releases; in the thirty-month period between January 1964 and June 1966, the Beatles' U.S. label (and United Artists, for the film soundtracks) released nearly twice as many Beatles albums in America as EMI Parlophone had overseas. This feat was accomplished by several methods: including fewer songs per album (typically ten or eleven, as opposed to fourteen on the British versions), adding stand-alone singles to the lineup (usually not included on UK albums), and padding the soundtracks for *A Hard Day's Night* and *Help!* with instrumental versions of Beatles songs. "We used to say, 'Why can't we put fourteen [tracks] out in America?' Because we would sequence the albums—how we thought they should sound—and we put a lot of work into the sequencing, too," John Lennon complained. "It used to drive us crackers."[87] Ringo Starr added, "America had that crazy way of only putting ten tracks [on a record] and they always ended up with extras. And then suddenly we'd have some new album in America."[88]

The first Beatles album released in America by Capitol was actually the second British album, originally titled *With the Beatles*. Renamed *Meet the Beatles!*, the "new" version deleted five R&B covers (Chuck Berry's "Roll over Beethoven," the Miracles' "You Really Got a Hold on Me," the Donays' "Devil in His [now 'Her'] Heart," Barrett Strong's "Money," and the Marvelettes' "Please Mister Postman"), since it was supposedly thought that these would sound old to Americans more familiar with the originals than the British audience. Instead, the album included the single "I Want to Hold Your Hand," along with its British ("This Boy") and American ("I Saw Her Standing There") B sides. Three months later, to create the misnamed *Second Album*, those cover versions were lumped with "She Loves You" (the single, initially refused by Capitol and released on the tiny Swan label, was now topping the charts), three B sides ("Thank You Girl," off "From Me to You"; "You Can't Do That," from the newest single, "Can't Buy Me Love"; and "I'll Get You," the flip side of "She Loves You"), and two newly recorded tracks: a cover of "Long Tall Sally" and the original song "I Call Your Name," then being considered for the *Hard Day's Night* soundtrack. That album, which came out in June 1964, had eight actual Beatles numbers—seven from the film, but taken out of order as compared to the movie, and "I'll Cry Instead"; the rest were instrumental covers of the same movie songs. In contrast, the British soundtrack had five other Beatles songs, none of which came from the film.

Something New, released in July 1964, was even more of a hodgepodge, containing four songs originally recorded for *A Hard Day's Night* ("Tell Me Why," "And I Love Her," "If I Fell," and "I'm Happy Just to Dance with You"); the film's title song and "I Should Have Known Better" were not included, because these were the respective A and B sides of the new American single. Capitol threw in five tracks from the British album, plus two covers culled from a UK extended-play album, "Slow Down" and "Matchbox" (which were released as a U.S. single a month later), along with the German version of "I Want to Hold Your Hand," originally recorded for the market that helped shape the band in its Hamburg days, but left out "Sie Liebt Dich" ("She Loves You"), previously released by Swan.

In November, Capitol put out a barrel-scraping double album, *The Beatles' Story*, that ran less than an hour, consisting of interviews with the group, larded with bits of song. The following month saw the release of *Beatles '65*, which had actually been recorded the previous October. It had just eight of fourteen songs from the British *Beatles for Sale* album, which had come out in England less than two weeks before. To make up the difference, Capitol tossed in "I'll Be Back" (left over from *A Hard Day's Night*) and the A and B sides of the then-current single, "I Feel Fine" and "She's a Woman." In March 1965, Capitol released *The Early Beatles*, a repackaging of *Please Please Me*, the first British album, on which the United States had originally passed; the company deleted "Misery" and "There's a Place," as well as "I Saw Her Standing There," which had been included on *Meet the Beatles*.

For the June 1965 *Beatles VI* album (the band had only released four full albums at this point), Capitol recommandeered songs saved from *Beatles for Sale* ("Eight Days a Week" and "I Don't Want to Spoil the Party," released four months before as a U.S. single, the "Kansas City/Hey-Hey-Hey-Hey" medley, "Words of Love," "What You're Doing," and "Every Little Thing"), added three from the yet-to-be-released UK version of *Help!* ("You Like Me Too Much," "Tell Me What You See," and "Dizzy Miss Lizzy") and one B side ("Yes It Is," from the American single "Ticket to Ride"), and filled the whole mess out with another leftover, "Bad Boy."

Two months later, United Artists released the soundtrack to *Help!*, which included the film's songs in their correct order, along with six instrumentals by the George Martin Orchestra, but deleted seven new Beatles songs that appeared on the British version. A couple of those turned up later on *Rubber Soul* ("I've Just Seen a Face" and "It's Only Love") in December 1965, which was released in tandem by Capitol and EMI, although the versions were not identical: the American version deleted four tracks ("Drive My Car," "If I Needed Someone," "Nowhere Man," and "What Goes On") with the idea of holding them as potential singles; in fact, the latter two did come out as a U.S. single two months later.

In early 1966, Capitol was faced with a dilemma: previously, it had released these reconfigured Beatles albums at least four or five times a year. Now that the Beatles were spending more time and effort crafting their work in the studio, the American label would not have any new product to sell until at least the second quarter, an unthinkable eight whole months without fresh material. To resolve the shortage, Capitol took six tracks it had withheld from the last two albums, along with both sides of the previous single ("We Can Work It Out" and "Day Tripper"); since a mere eight songs was not enough to sell an album even by the label's low standards, it also cannibalized three finished songs from the work-in-progress *Revolver* ("Doctor Robert," "And Your Bird Can Sing," and "I'm Only Sleeping") to complete the *Yesterday and Today* album released in June 1966.

The Beatles were appalled. Their U.S. label was no longer content just to mess with the group's previous records and milk its audience for all it could get; now it was "stealing" from an album that had not even been finished, at a time when the band was conceiving its records as holistic works of art. Several weeks later, *Revolver* was released in America minus the tracks pulled for *Yesterday And Today*; after that, all American releases (singles and albums) were identical to those in England. Nonetheless, Capitol continues to exploit its back catalogue as it sees fit: for Christmas 2004, the label put out a boxed compact disc set of the "first four" Beatles albums, as originally released. Executives defended the decision by declaring that Americans would want to hear the records as they had first been experienced; British Beatles historian Martin Lewis complained that that was the same as "saying, 'I remember first seeing the Mona Lisa with five inches of grime on it—so I'd like to see it that way again.' "[89]

No More Tours

On August 11, 1966, the Beatles embarked on what would be their final tour of America in support of *Revolver*. The band was still shaken after a July riot in Manila spurred by an inadvertent snub of President Ferdinand and Imelda Marcos (Brian Epstein and other members of their entourage were kicked and beaten at the airport). The group again performed at Shea Stadium, but this time the audience numbered "only" 44,600 fans (11,000 fewer than in 1965). On August 29, 1966, the Beatles played their last-ever public concert (not counting the impromptu London rooftop concert seen in the film *Let It Be*) at San Francisco's Candlestick Park. After the tour ended and Lennon had returned to England from a stint in Spain filming his first and only dramatic role in Richard Lester's *How I Won the War*, he met Japanese artist Yoko Ono at London's Indica Gallery in the autumn; their resultant romance would break up his marriage to his first wife, Cynthia, and start the first fissures in the world's most popular rock band.

In November, the Beatles began recording a stand-alone single, which would not be included on their eagerly anticipated next album: the rather spooky "Strawberry Fields Forever," another psychedelic-influenced Lennon track with variable-speed recording effects, backed with the more cheerful "Penny Lane," McCartney's somewhat surreal memories of the good old days back in Liverpool. That deceptively simple-sounding single employed keyboard, percussion effects, including conga drums, piano through a Vox guitar amplifier with added reverberation, harmonium, flutes, trumpets, oboes, and (last but not least) a double bass.

The group was about to begin work on an album inspired by the Beach Boys' magnificent *Pet Sounds*, in which the members would take on new "identities" as "Sgt. Pepper's Lonely Hearts Club Band." That album would astonish the world when it was released the following year, just before what became known as "the Summer of Love." It was now amply clear that (given the constraints of then-modern technology, which would not allow for live reproduction of their studio experiments, not to mention the hysteria still engendered by live performance) the Beatles were no longer a touring band, although diehard fans long continued to cling to hope. It was even worse for Brian Epstein, a victim of success beyond anyone's wildest dreams. There was no question of the Beatles firing him; there was simply nothing left for him to do. His job had entailed getting the band a recording contract and bookings, and now all that was behind them. While the group as a unit would barely last out the tumultuous decade it kick-started, the musical and sociological revolution the Beatles had aided and abetted would have repercussions long into the future.

OTHER BRITISH ROCK PERFORMERS

Billy J. Kramer

Lennon and McCartney also launched the career of another of Epstein's protégés, Billy J. Kramer, with several lightweight songs. "Do You Want to Know a Secret," a No. 2 UK chart hit in 1963, was followed by the discarded "Bad to Me," which went into the U.S. Top 10 the following year. Kramer was also the beneficiary of "I'll Keep You Satisfied," "From a Window" (both Top 30), and "I'll Be on My Way," all in 1964, but his biggest hit in the United States was the non-Beatles ballad "Little Children," which reached No. 6 that year. Backed by his band, the Dakotas, Kramer performed on the landmark 1964 *T.A.M.I. Show* and had his final chart showing (a paltry No. 47) with the Bacharach and David "Trains and Boats and Planes" the following year. After Epstein and the Beatles lost interest, Kramer eked out a living for decades on the oldies circuit and appearing at Beatles-related events.

Gerry and the Pacemakers

Gerry Marsden and the Pacemakers, formed in the late '50s, worked the same Hamburg-Liverpool axis as their Beatles contemporaries and, for a while, enjoyed almost parallel popularity. After Epstein took over their management, Gerry and the Pacemakers had three consecutive No. 1 British hits in one heady year (1963) with "How Do You Do It," "I Like It," and a remake of the pop standard "You'll Never Walk Alone." Marsden was also a talented song-writer in his own right, penning "Don't Let the Sun Catch You Cryin'" and "Ferry Cross the Mersey," which benefited from string arrangements by producer George Martin (before he ever worked in such a capacity for his most eminent clients). The Pacemakers had a slightly longer life in America, since their songs came out stateside months after the initial British release. After the group faded in 1965, Marsden worked for many years in children's pantomime and cabaret, and in the '80s revived both "Walk Alone" and "Ferry," when they once more topped the UK charts.

The Dave Clark Five

As 1964 drew to a close, Epstein could feel proud of what he had accomplished, but the enormous success of the Beatles had also driven other musicians and managers to attempt to get in on the action. The biggest challenger to the Beatles, at least for a short time, was the Dave Clark Five (DC5), which reached the Top 10 eight times between 1964 and 1967 with songs like "Glad All Over" (which kicked "I Want to Hold Your Hand" out of a six-week run at the top of the UK charts), "Bits and Pieces," "Can't You See That She's Mine," "Catch Us If You Can," "Because" (a ballad departure from the group's usual hard-thumping sound), and "Over and Over," the only track to hit No. 1 in America. The DC5 made more appearances on *Ed Sullivan* than any other British act, performed twelve sold-out shows at Carnegie Hall during a three-day period, and was both managed and produced by Clark himself. An extremely savvy businessman, he owned the master recordings and negotiated highly lucrative royalty rates for them—a real anomaly at that time.

Clark (formerly a drama student and film stuntman) taught himself how to play the drums with an eye toward raising money for his North London football club, the Tottenham Hotspurs. After he formed the band in 1962 and it quickly caught on with the locals, the DC5 cut a cover of the Contours' "Do You Love Me," which was beaten out for chart position by a different group's version. Clark quickly determined that writing original material was the road to success, and with the group's next single ("Glad All Over," which was co-authored with singer Mike Smith), the DC5 was on that road. Magazines and DJs on both sides of the Atlantic tried to create a feud between the DC5 and the Beatles, as they later did with the latter group and the Rolling Stones, although all these bands were clearly quite different from the start. By 1967, the DC5's popularity in America had come to an end. The Dave Clark Five was not as serious a threat to the Liverpudlians' supremacy as another London band would prove to be: the anti-Beatles, the Rolling Stones.

THE ROLLING STONES, "THE WORLD'S GREATEST ROCK AND ROLL BAND"

> The Beatles want to hold your hand, but the Stones want to burn your town.
> —Tom Wolfe, 1965

Origins

On July 12, 1962, the Rolling Stones gave their first public performance at London's Marquee Club. This particular lineup included singer Mick Jagger, guitarists Keith Richards and Brian Jones, bassist Dick Taylor, and drummer Mick Avory, who later joined the Kinks. Jagger's original group, which included Taylor, was called Little Boy Blue and the Blue Boys, while Brian Jones was playing with Alexis Korner's Blues Incorporated, with which Jagger and Richards began to jam. A year later, Bill Wyman replaced Dick Taylor (a friend of both Jagger and Richards), Charlie Watts replaced Mick Avory, and stalwart Ian Stewart, the lantern-jawed piano player whose job with a chemical company had kept the band together, was relegated to a road manager/recording-only position because his looks did not fit with the image the group's manager wanted it to project.

In May 1962, Jones placed an ad in a musicians' paper looking for other members; Ian Stewart was the first to audition, astonishing Keith Richards with his mastery of boogie-woogie piano. But the group could not afford a rhythm section, and so they each played with other bands; Jagger, however, never went anywhere without Richards, not even when he began fronting Alexis Korner's Blues Incorporated. By the time the first lineup played at the Marquee, they were already controversial: some blues purists hated Richards's affinity for Chuck Berry–style R&B, while other listeners began buzzing about the energy of the band. The group lived rough in various miserable flats around London, starving while obsessively studying their heroes, taking apart the tracks and trying to duplicate the sound they loved. As far as Richards was concerned, the group was formed purely to spread the gospel: "We wanted to sell records for Jimmy Reed and Muddy Waters and John Lee Hooker and Howlin' Wolf. We were missionaries, disciples. . . . 'If we can turn people on to that, then that's enough' . . . There was no thought of rock 'n' roll stardom."[90]

Muddy Waters and Otis Spann. © Terry Cryer/Corbis.

Bill Perks, who changed his name to Wyman for the stage, joined the group as bass player in December 1962; the oldest of the band, he got the job in part because he had two enormous Vox amplifiers. At the beginning of January 1963, drummer Charlie Watts came on board. Within a few months, the band had regular dates almost every night of the week. Soon a Russian émigré impresario named Giorgio Gomelsky set up an ongoing Thursday night set for the Rollin' Stones (as they were then billed) at the Manor House pub; the group members were now earning eight British pounds a week, equivalent to the pay of an ordinary working stiff, to do what they loved. Within a few weeks, Gomelsky had booked the group into the back room of a venue he promoted, the Station Hotel in Richmond (a suburb of London), on a Sunday night, which became a regular event—a "residency." Along with the Sunday afternoon shows the Stones were performing in Soho, the group began attracting a following: by March 1963, there were 300 fans packed into the small back room. Gomelsky renamed the club the Crawdaddy, after the Stones' customary final number, Bo Diddley's "Doin' the Crawdaddy." On April 21, the band had a very special group of guests drop by: the Beatles, riding the top of the charts with their third single ("From Me to You") and fresh from the TV show *Thank Your Lucky Stars*, which was filmed nearby. The two bands became friends, so much so that Lennon and McCartney gifted the Stones, who were still only doing cover versions of others' material, with what would become their second single and first hit (No. 9 on the British charts), "I Wanna Be Your Man."

Andrew Loog Oldham

By now, Andrew Loog Oldham was managing the group. Oldham had hustled his way into jobs with fashion designer Mary Quant (see Chapter 5) and Brian Epstein, resigning from NEMS when he found that he would not be entrusted with press agentry for Epstein's treasured Beatles. After joining forces with a financial backer named Eric Easton, Oldham glimpsed rock and roll future during his first Richmond visit to hear the Stones. As one observer said of that defining moment: "He looked at Mick like Sylvester looks at Tweetie Pie" (referring to the Warner Brothers' cartoon characters, Sylvester the cat and Tweetie Pie the bird).[91] While Giorgio Gomelsky was out of the country on other business, Oldham promptly signed the Stones to a management contract; Brian Jones covertly arranged for an extra five pounds a week as the "leader," a side deal that, when discovered, widened the schism already growing between him and the Jagger-Richards unit. Richards was told to drop the "s" from his surname, which he did; Ian Stewart was jettisoned from public sight, but still arranged for the group to be recorded by his friend Glyn Johns, who would later become invaluable to the Stones in the studio. For years, before signing with Allen Klein for representation, the Stones put ultimate faith in this brash upstart Oldham (who referred to himself as "ALO"); as he once succinctly explained the attraction, "I told the Stones who they were and they became it."[92]

Oldham, wasting no time, invited Dick Rowe from Decca—the man who had famously turned down the Beatles—to see "his" Rolling Stones play at the Crawdaddy. Mindful of his laughingstock reputation and also keeping in mind that none other than George Harrison had also recommended this group of shaggy malcontents, Rowe signed the Rolling Stones in May 1963. Two months later, the band made its first television appearance with a cover of Chuck Berry's "Come On" on *Thank Your Lucky Stars*. At the time, the Stones were neatly turned out in matching outfits, a tactic that Oldham, recognizing the market value of an anti-Beatles, soon discarded. On the first British tour, in the summer of 1963, the Stones were billed with heroes such as Bo Diddley, Little Richard, and the Everly Brothers. "What an education," Richards later reflected. "Like going to rock 'n' roll university . . . working with these guys every night . . . learning shit it would take you years to pick up."[93] They were earning forty-two pounds a night. This was where Jagger and Richards discovered Jones's side deal, which they considered an unforgivable betrayal. By September, the group was voted sixth-best British group in a poll by the influential music paper *Melody Maker*; in the end-of-year stakes, they finished in the same slot.

Oldham was impatient with his charges; once more glimpsing the future, this time from chats with Lennon and McCartney, he sequestered Jagger and Richards in one room of their flat and told them not to emerge until they had written a song. They came up with "As Tears Go By," which Oldham matched to Marianne Faithfull. Another early composition, "That Girl Belongs to Yesterday," became a Top 10 hit for Gene Pitney, although some lesser numbers were covered by other artists and disappeared without a trace. Although Lennon and McCartney switched roles with ease, in this new songwriting team it was Jagger who came up with the lyrics, Richards the melody.

In January 1964, the Stones began recording their first album in London's Regent Sound studios and also took on another British tour—this time with the Ronettes (Phil Spector warned Oldham to keep the Stones away from the act, particularly his obsession, Ronnie Bennett; it is possible that his threats were ignored), the Swinging Blue Jeans, and Freddie and the Dreamers. The group's first extended-play single was released, with covers of Chuck Berry's "Bye Bye Johnny," Berry Gordy's "Money," "Poison Ivy" by Jerry Lieber and Mike Stoller, and "You Better Move On," by Arthur Alexander; it reached No. 15 within three weeks.[94] By the end of the month, the Stones were back in the studio to make another try at their version of Buddy Holly's "Not Fade Away"; Phil Spector guested on maracas, and Graham Nash and Allan Clarke of the Hollies (named after Buddy) took on backing vocals. When the single came out the next month, it reached No. 3.

Then the Stones were off on their third British tour, rapidly followed by their fourth, in April 1964, just as the first eponymous album was released. It went directly into the No. 1 slot, with advance orders for 100,000 copies; in its first week at retail, *The Rolling Stones* moved an additional 110,000 units. In this day of multiplatinum recordings that enter the charts at No. 1, then vanish, this achievement may sound commonplace, but this took place in England, a much smaller place than America; rock and roll was still relatively young, and this particular album heralded the arrival of a new kind of rock.

As the Stones' inner circle continued to fracture (Brian Jones, unable to write songs and bedevilled by demons even he did not fully understand, was becoming more ostracized for his erratic behavior, which included missing various shows), the group set out for its first tour of America. When they landed in New York on June 1, 1964, they were not met at the airport by thousands of screaming girls, as their benefactors the Beatles had been, and the tour, as it wended its way through the heartland, was mostly disappointing. The group was threatened by yahoos and police officers alike (a cop pulled a gun on Richards backstage when he refused to pour his Coke down the toilet; there was an antialcohol law in effect, and the Stones had a bottle of whiskey in their dressing room), played next to a tank of trained seals to an audience of a few hundred in a San Antonio venue meant to hold 20,000, and were repeatedly insulted by Dean Martin during their appearance on *The Hollywood Palace* TV show. The highlight of the trip was the group's visit to its shrine, Chess Studios in Chicago, where it recorded "It's All Over Now" and Willie Dixon complimented Jagger on his vocals. Back in New York, the Stones played Carnegie Hall, and Jagger and Richards slept at Phil Spector's office, also making a trip out to Long Island to visit Spector and his wife Ronnie at home.

Like Brian Epstein, his former mentor and management rival, Oldham had world-empire dreams; in 1965, he established Immediate, England's first pop independent record label. Before it folded four years later, Immediate put out discs by (among others) the Small Faces, Fleetwood Mac, Eric Clapton, Jimmy Page, John Mayall, Jeff Beck, and Humble Pie. Furthermore, during this time, the Andrew Loog Oldham Orchestra recorded several worthy albums: *16 Hip Hits* (1964, featuring Mick Jagger and John Paul Jones and Jimmy Page, both later of Led Zeppelin), *East Meets West* (in the same year, a tribute to the Beach Boys and the Four Seasons), and *The Rolling Stones Songbook* (released in 1966).

Another Oldham innovation was the way in which he put Jagger and Richards forward as a team. The lead-singer/guitarist interplay that came about as a result is now a mainstay of rock, for example, Aerosmith's Steven Tyler and Joe Perry, Jon Bon Jovi and Richie Sambora, Axl Rose and Slash, or Bruce Springsteen and Steve Van Zandt, to name only a few. The Beatles had the line of three in front, with Starr in the back; Harrison and McCartney would harmonize, or McCartney and Lennon would share a mike. But the Stones were the first to present this particular configuration, which is now considered almost de rigueur for rock bands.

According to Oldham, it was the Stones' sojourn to their shrine—America and, in particular, Chess Records—that allowed the group to get in touch with its original inspirations and end up with its "very first international anthem," the classic single "Satisfaction," which was included on the *Out of Our Heads* album, released in July 1965. Keith Richards has long told a story about how he woke up in the middle of the night in a Florida motel room, recorded that insistent riff for about a minute, and fell back asleep; the next morning, he rediscovered his signature lick preceding hours of snoring on the tape. Mick Jagger sat down by the motel pool and immediately got to work on the verse. The group cut a nonstarter at Chess, then redid it at Los Angeles's RCA studios soon afterwards. That version, nailed in one take, was released at the end of May 1965, and as Anthony DeCurtis put it thirty-four years later in *Rolling Stone*, that summer "on the radio, in the streets, in the car, at the beach—it sometimes seemed that there was only one song and that was 'Satisfaction.'"[95] The Rolling Stones, with their first No. 1, were no longer standing in the shadow of the Beatles. Yet even as the group reached its initial moment of satisfaction, it found itself in competition with America's own Bob Dylan, whose "Like a Rolling Stone" (which had nothing to do with the British band) came out on June 1, 1965. Critics noted that its very length—more than twice that of the average single—and vitriolic topic, not to mention the snarling vocal, had knocked pop music sideways. The Stones, and everyone else, now had a new benchmark to contend with.

While *Out of Our Heads* still had a strongly bluesy feel, *December's Children (and Everybody's)*, released at the end of 1965, has the wholly original-sounding "Get off of My Cloud," a complaint about everybody and everything that was bringing the singer down; it is instantly identifiable as by the Rolling Stones while still marking a radical departure from previous covers of others' material.

The Rolling Stones performing on the *Ed Sullivan Show*, 1965. (Left to right) Bill Wyman, Brian Jones, Mick Jagger, Charlie Watts, and Keith Richards. Courtesy of Photofest.

In April 1966, the group released its first compilation album, *Big Hits: High Tide and Green Grass*. In July came the American version of *Aftermath*, the first Stones album to consist entirely of original material (much like the Beatles, the Rolling Stones suffered from their U.S. label tinkering with the order and contents of early albums). The Europeans did not get "Paint It, Black," but both releases included the delicate, dulcimer-filigreed "Lady Jane," a reimagining of a courtly romance, whereas the modern-day relationship songs "Stupid Girl" and "Under My Thumb" led to accusations of misogyny (even though John Lennon sang in *Rubber Soul*'s "Run for Your Life" that he would rather see his girlfriend dead than with another man, the Beatles were still considered good boys to the Stones' bad, and were not criticized). Then there was the salacious closing number, "Going Home," a boundary-busting eleven and a half minutes of grunting and verbal ejaculations from Jagger that built to a tense peak, then slowly uncoiled—the sonic equivalent of a sexual climax.

The Stones closed out 1966 with *Got LIVE If You Want It!*, which included "19th Nervous Breakdown," with its references to pill-popping and debutantes falling from grace, and the ominous-sounding new single "Have You Seen Your Mother, Baby, Standing in the Shadows?" The picture sleeve on the 45 rpm single depicted the group done up in 1940s-style full drag—granny wigs, lipstick and all; the band also made a short promotional film in the same outfits (one of the first music videos). While such behavior does not seem particularly outrageous now, this occurred six years before David Bowie's gender-bending appearance in a frock on the cover of his *Hunky Dory* album. Older people were shocked and affronted; naturally, that reaction delighted anyone who loved the Stones for their rebellious attitude.

The Stones would roll on to decades of fame and fortune, but as the years went by, close associates found that surviving in the band's wake was not a given. In 1967, the group ditched both manager Oldham (who later underwent shock treatment) and guitarist/founder Jones, who soon after his dismissal drowned under mysterious circumstances in the swimming pool of his home, previously owned by *Winnie the Pooh* author A. A. Milne.

NOTES

1. Dave Marsh, "How the Beatles Changed America," *Mojo*, September 2004, pp. 59–60.

2. Muddy Waters as quoted on MusicWeb Encyclopaedia of Popular Music, http://www.musicwebinternational.com/encyclopaedia/w/W27.HTM, as well as "Muddy Waters, Famous Quotes and Quotations," Music With Ease, http://www.music-with-ease.com/muddy-waters-quotes.html.

3. John Mayall quoted in Mat Snow, "John Mayall: This Is Where I Came In," *Q Magazine*, August 1990; also available at: Rock's Back Pages, http://www.rocksbackpages.com/article.html?ArticleID=1857.

4. Ibid.

5. Larry Kane quoted in Stephanie Snipes, "Encounter Sparks a Musical Revolution," CNN.com, July 5, 2004, http://www.cnn.com/2004/WORLD/europe/07/02/beatles/.

6. Richard Corliss, "That Old Feeling: Meet the Beatles," *Time*, February 7, 2004, http://www.time.com/time/columnist/corliss/article/0,9565,588789,00.html.

7. Steven Van Zandt, "From E Street to the Disciples of Soul," Little Steven Online, http://www.littlesteven.com/essays-meaculpa2.html.

8. Marsh, *Mojo*, September 2004, p. 60.

9. Hunter Davies, *The Quarrymen* (New York: Omnibus Press, 2001), p. 35.

10. Davies, *The Quarrymen*, p. 59.

11. The biographical information is adapted from Mark Hertsgaard, *A Day in the Life: The Music and Artistry of the Beatles* (New York: Delta, 1995), pp. 14–18.

12. Mark Lewisohn and George Martin, *The Complete Beatles Chronicle* (New York: Harmony Books, 1992), p. 35.

13. Paul McCartney in the Beatles, *The Beatles Anthology* (San Francisco: Chronicle Books LLC, 2000), p. 41.

14. "The Bootle Group Presents: Taming Liverpool's Crime in the 1960s: Success or Failure?" The Liverpool Project: History, Music and Crime in Liverpool 1960–1969, http://www.stthomasu.ca/~pmccorm/liverpoolcrime.html.

15. Pete Best and Patrick Doncaster, *Beatle! The Pete Best Story* (London: Plexus Publishing Ltd., 1985), p. 33.

16. Tony Sheridan quoted by Richard E. Altman, Autograph Collector Online, http://www.autographcollector.com/acm0803/beatles.htm.

17. Best and Doncaster, *Beatle!*, p. 150.

18. Elizabeth Sanderson, "Pregnant By Her Son's Best Friend; It Was At Mona Best's

Club, the Casbah, That the Boys First Played As the Beatles," *The London Mail on Sunday*, August 18, 2002, no page available.

19. Best and Doncaster, *Beatle!*, p. 125.

20. Bill Harry, *Encyclopedia of Beatles People* (Dorset, England: Blandford, 1997); also available at: Beatles64, http://www.beatles64.co.uk/eppy.htm.

21. Sanderson, *The London Mail on Sunday*, August 18, 2002.

22. Paul McCartney in the Beatles, *Anthology*, p. 266.

23. Ray Coleman, *The Man Who Made the Beatles: An Intimate Biography of Brian Epstein* (New York: McGraw-Hill, 1989), p. 103.

24. Ibid., p. 98.

25. Beatles, *Anthology*, p. 103.

26. As told by Alistair Taylor, *With The Beatles* (London: John Blake Publishing Ltd., 2003), pp. 43–44.

27. Philip Norman, "In My Life > George Martin > The Melody Maker Interview, 1971," About The Beatles: The Complete Guide to The Beatles, http://aboutthebeatles.com/biography_georgemartin_mminterview.html.

28. Ibid.

29. Philip Norman, *Shout! The Beatles in Their Generation* (New York: Simon and Schuster, 1981), pp. 257–258.

30. Steve Chapple, *Rock 'N' Roll is Here to Pay: The History and Politics of the Music Industry* (Chicago: Nelson-Hall Publishers, 1977), p. 70; also available at: BeatleMoney, http://www.beatlemoney.com/beatles6063records.htm.

31. Lewisohn and Martin, *Beatles Chronicle*, p. 136.

32. George Martin quoted in Mark Espiner, "The Guardian Profile: George Martin—'Sounds and Vision,'" *London Guardian*, June 30, 2001, http://www.guardian.co.uk/Archive/Article/0,4273,4212909,00.html.

33. Paul McCartney quoted in ibid.

34. Lewisohn and Martin, *Beatles Chronicle*,' p. 99.

35. After the Beatles' breakup, Ringo Starr tapped George Martin for his *Sentimental Journey* album, and McCartney employed him for his *Live and Let Die* James Bond soundtrack. When EMI began to reissue Beatles material, as well as previously unheard tapes, Martin worked on *Live at the Hollywood Bowl* and *Rock and Roll Music*. In the mid-1990s, he went back to the vaults to dig out and prepare unreleased Beatles tracks for the *Anthology* series; the first volume entered the U.S. album charts at No. 1 in December 1995. The following year, Martin was knighted by the queen and received a Lifetime Achievement Award at the Grammys. In 1999, Martin was inducted into the Rock and Roll Hall of Fame, alongside Paul McCartney (the latter as a solo artist). He resigned from record production that same year with *In My Life*, a collection of Beatles covers recorded by artists such as Jeff Beck, Celine Dion, and Phil Collins. His retirement was a forced one; as Martin confessed, "Music and recording have been a passion, but the irony is, I'm going deaf. And of course it is my own doing, it's years and years of listening to music at much too high a level. I didn't know that at the time." He now wears hearing aids in both ears. Of his work with the Beatles, he has said: "It was a group of five people with one of them in the control room most of the time. Sometimes he was the one playing the instruments and they were in the control room. . . . They were the geniuses. I was the guy who helped fix it." (All quotes are from an interview with Espiner, *Guardian*, June 30, 2001.)

36. David Crosby quoted in Larry Kane, *Ticket to Ride: Inside the Beatles' 1964 Tour that Changed the World* (Philadelphia: Running Press/Perseus, 2003), p. 226.

37. Greil Marcus, "The Beatles," in *The Rolling Stone Illustrated History of Rock & Roll*, edited by Anthony DeCurtis and James Henke with Holly George-Warren, p. 178 (New York: Rolling Stone Press/Random House, 1992).

38. Ibid.

39. Ibid.

40. Kurt Loder, "The Beatles: Irrepressible and Irresistible, They Were—and Remain—the World's Most Astonishing Rock 'n' Roll Band," *Time*, June 8, 1998, http://www.time.com/time/time100/artists/profile/beatles.html.

41. Steve Silberman, contributing editor at *Wired* magazine, "An Egg Thief in Cyberspace: An Interview with David Crosby, 1995," reproduced at the Crosby/Silberman page of the Crosby, Stills, and Nash fan Web site, http://www.levity.com/digaland/crosby95.html.

42. Marcus, *Rolling Stone Illustrated History*, p. 178.

43. Best and Doncaster, *Beatle!*, p. 136.

44. "George Martin," About the Beatles, http://aboutthebeatles.com/biography_georgemartin_mminterview.html.

45. Best and Doncaster, *Beatle!*, p. 72.

46. Coleman, *Man Who Made the Beatles*, p. 102.

47. Paul McCartney, Beatles, *Anthology*, p. 64.

48. "In My Life: George Martin, The Melody Maker Interview, 1971," About the Beatles, http://aboutthebeatles.com/biography_georgemartin_mminterview.html.

49. Harvey Kubernik, "Rock's Backpages Interview with Andrew Loog Oldham," http://www.andrewloogoldham.com/reviews/rocksbpgs.html.

50. As reported by Guardian Unlimited Special Reports, "Key Dates," Guardian Newspapers Limited, http://www.guardian.co.uk/thebeatles/page/0,11302,607848,00.html.

51. William Mann, "What Songs the Beatles Sang . . . ," *London Times*, December 23, 1963; available at: http://jolomo.net/music/william_mann.html. "Aoelian" is the mode from which minor scales in music are drawn; a "cadence" is the progression of one chord to another in forming the end of a phrase. The "submediant" is the sixth degree of the scale and also refers to a relationship of musical keys; a modulation (change of key) to the submediant can induce relaxation in the listener. Finally, according to *The American Heritage Dictionary of the English Language* (4th ed., 2000), a "melisma" is "a passage of several notes sung to one syllable of text, as in Gregorian chant."

52. Mann, "What Songs," *London Times*.

53. Dave Dermon III, "The Beatles on Vee Jay Records," http://www.dermon.com/Beatles/Veejay.htm.

54. Bruce Spizer, "The Beatles Are Coming!," *CBS News*, http://www.cbsnews.com/stories/2004/02/04/earlyshow/leisure/books/main597992.shtml.

55. Tim Riley, *Tell Me Why: The Beatles Album by Album, Song by Song, The Sixties and After* (Cambridge, MA: Da Capo Press/Perseus, 2002), pp. 66–67.

56. Alexander Kendrick, "Beatleland," *CBS News*, December 1963, http://www.cbsnews.com/htdocs/videoplayer/newVid/framesource2.html?clip=/media/2004/02/06/video598543.wmv&sec=207&vidId=207&title=CBS$@$News$@$Beatleland$@$1963&hitboxMLC=entertainment.

57. Spizer, "Beatles Are Coming!," *CBS News*.

58. Inflation calculator supplied by the Consumer Price Index for the U.S. Department of Labor, Bureau of Labor Statistics, http://data.bls.gov/cgi-bin/cpicalc.pl.

59. Brian Epstein's *New Yorker* interview from Ray Coleman, *The Man Who Made the Beatles* (New York: McGraw-Hill, 1989), pp. 204–205.

60. Andy Davis, *The Beatles Files* (London: Metro/Salamander Books, 2000), p. 39.

61. Ibid.

62. Paul McCartney quote in the Beatles, *Anthology*, p. 116.

63. Davis, *Beatles Files*, p. 7.

64. As reported in the *London Times*, February 17, 1964, Web site no longer available.

65. Ringo Starr quote in the Beatles, *Anthology*, p. 120.

66. "Beatles' *Ed Sullivan* Appearance Rated Rock's Top TV Moment," *CNN.com*, July 25, 2000, http://archives.cnn.com/2000/SHOWBIZ/TV/07/25/tv.rocks.ap/.

67. Steven Van Zandt quoted in the article Larry McShane, "Beatlemania Strong 40 Years After Sullivan," *Yahoo! Music*, February 6, 2004, http://music.yahoo.com/read/news/12174263.

68. Figures courtesy of Bruce Nash, "The Numbers Box Office Data, Movie Stars, Idle Speculation," http://www.the-numbers.com/movies/1964/0HRDD.html; and Brandon Gray, http://www.boxofficemojo.com/genres/chart/?id=popstardebuts.htm.

69. From the review dated October 27, 1996 at Roger Ebert, "Great Movies," http://rogerebert.suntimes.com/apps/pbcs.dll/article?AID=/19961027/REVIEWS08/40 1010326/1023.

70. Bosley Crowther, review of *Award Day's Night*, *New York Times*, August 12, 1964.

71. Quoted in Bill Harry, *The Ultimate Beatles Encyclopedia* (New York: Hyperion, 1992), p. 484.

72. Brian Epstein quoted by Sid Bernstein as told to Arthur Aaron, *"It's Sid Bernstein Calling . . ."* (New York: Jonathan David Publishers Inc., 2002), p. 189.

73. Ringo Starr quoted in the Beatles, *Anthology*, p. 86.

74. Paul McCartney quoted in ibid., p. 187.

75. Ringo Starr quoted in ibid., p. 192.

76. Larry Kane, *Ticket to Ride: Inside the Beatles' 1964 Tour that Changed the World* (Philadelphia: Running Press/Perseus, 2003), p. 226.

77. "John Lennon," Wikiquote, http://en.wikiquote.org/wiki/John_Lennon.

78. Maureen Cleave in David Pritchard and Alan Lysaght, *The Beatles: An Oral History* (New York: Hyperion, 1998), p. 218.

79. Sourced from Ray Coleman, "Lennon," Dark Side of Beatlemania, http://www.beatlesagain.com/bapology.html.

80. "Today in Odd History: John Lennon Proclaims Beatles 'More Popular than Jesus' (March 4, 1966)," News of the Odd, http://www.newsoftheodd.com/article1012.html; also on the John Whelan, "Beatles Timeline" http://beatles.ncf.ca/timeline.html; and "Historical the Beatles 1965–1966," http://www.av-groups.com/1965-1966.htm.

81. Ibid.

82. Paul McCartney in Barry Miles, *Many Years from Now* (New York: Henry Holt and Company, 1997), p. 185.

83. Cherri Gilham, "Joint Accounts," *London Observer*, September 10, 2000, http://observer.guardian.co.uk/print/0,3858,4061575-102280,00.html.

84. Paul McCartney in Miles, *Many Years*, p. 185.

85. John Lennon interviewed by Jann Wenner, "Lennon Remembers," *Rolling Stone*, November 1971, January 21–February 4, 1971, as reproduced in *Rolling Stone*, no. 641, October 15, 1992, p. 48.

86. Excerpted from the Capitol Records letter as reproduced in its entirety on the Web site, "History of the Beatles Year by Year 1966," http://www.beatles.ws/bcvrltr.htm.

87. John Lennon quoted in the Beatles, *Anthology*, p. 205.

88. Ringo Starr quoted by Steve Knopper, "Ringo Talks Beatles CDs," *Rolling Stone*, November 8, 2004, http://www.rollingstone.com/news/story/_/id/6597905/thebeatles?pageid=rs.Artistcage&pageregion=triple3.

89. Martin Lewis quote, ibid.

90. Chris Salewicz, *Mick & Keith* (London: Orion, 2002), p. 30.

91. Ibid., quote from jazz singer and author George Melly, p. 58.

92. Kubernik, "Andrew Loog Oldham," http://www.andrewloogoldham.com/reviews/rocksbpgs.html.

93. Salewicz, *Mick & Keith*, p. 67.

94. The now-extinct EP, or "extended-play" format, usually contained four tracks, as opposed to two tracks, on a single.

95. Anthony Decurtis, *Rolling Stone*, 1998.

OTHER BRITISH INVADERS

Once the Beatles had achieved success in America, hordes of British musicians sought fame and fortune in the former colonies. Some made lasting impressions; others' fortunes were fleeting.

This period also marked the first time that fashion became an important statement aligned with and driven by the current music and musicians, unless we were to count a brief 1940s flirtation with "zoot suits." What someone wore, from hair on down to shoes, was an external proclamation of musical preferences, and therefore one's personal philosophy. In mid-April 1966, *Time* magazine declared in a cover story that London was the "swinging" epicenter of hipness. While this pronouncement was actually well after the fact, as was usually the case for mass media, the publicity helped focus the attention of American youth on their highly style-conscious English peers, who were already influenced by rock and pop music in their choices of hairstyles and clothing. It was not long before U.S. stores were stocking their version of "mod" fashion, and hair salons had to learn about new cuts and techniques in order to stay in business. Outstanding innovators in these areas will be covered in the latter half of this chapter, after a look at some of the other trend-setting British musicians of the era.

THE MUSICIANS

The Who: "Maximum R&B"

This explosive quartet was known as the Detours when it formed in 1961 around the nucleus of bassist John Entwistle and singer Roger Daltrey;

guitarist/songwriter Pete Townshend joined six months later. It was not until 1964 that a then seventeen-year-old Keith Moon signed up, and as Townshend recalled, "When we found Keith, it was a complete turning point. Before then we had just been fooling around."[1] Now it was the Who (having considered but discarded the Hair), but called the High Numbers for the group's first single, "I'm the Face" (to be "a face" was a high accolade inside the mod movement; a "number" was a mod who wore the then-popular T-shirt with a numerical figure printed on the front).

The Who's attention-grabbing stage act consisted of Daltrey's dancing and screaming, Moon's flailing, almost hysterical thrashing, and Townshend's leaping like a madman, power-chording as if his life depended on the volume of his guitar, while a stolid Entwistle anchored the group. The band was all energy, rage, and stylish fury, and its fortunes changed when Kit Lambert, the son of a famous composer named Constant Lambert, noticed the crowd of mods mobbing its show at London's Railway Hotel. He and his partner Chris Stamp (the brother of actor Terence Stamp) had been thinking about making a film about a group, and this one seemed to have attracted the interest of the fashionable set.

After catching the Who's performance, in which a frustrated Townshend smashed his guitar to bits after a low ceiling broke its weakened neck (he had been jabbing it into the amps "to get banging noises"), the pair became its managers. Lambert and Stamp had to teach themselves about the music business, with a few misses. But in one clever move, Lambert booked the Who into South London's Marquee Club for a residency on Tuesday nights, a notoriously dead evening, and packed the place with the group's mod followers, which allowed the band a chance to build its fan base.

Townshend's impromptu instrument bashing had become such a crowd favorite that soon no performance seemed complete without an amp-piercing, wood-splintering finale, and Lambert and Stamp's investment began to grow fairly costly. Townshend explained his initial foray into performance art: "There were a couple of people from art school I knew at the front of the stage and they were laughing their heads off. So I just got really angry and got what was left of the guitar and smashed it to smithereens."[2] A week later, Townshend realized that the audience expected a repeat performance, which he declined to provide; however, after the show was over and the house emptied, Moon went back onstage and trashed his drum kit as a sympathy gesture. The following week, both Moon and Townshend gave the crowd what it wanted, and by the end of 1965, despite having several hits, the group was in the red by roughly 60,000 pounds (well over $100,000 at the exchange rate for that time).

Lambert's secretary played a Who demo record for the wife of Kinks producer Shel Talmy, who—deeming the group "loud, raw, funky and super-ballsy"[3]—took it under his wing, which helped secure a recording contract. Stamp was pressuring pirate radio station Caroline to push the stalled single

"I Can't Explain" when the Who landed a booking on *Ready, Steady, Go!*, the most influential of British TV shows devoted to pop and rock music (see Chapter 6). A bit more than a month later, the group took over a vacated slot on British TV's *Top of the Pops*, and its first single subsequently went to No. 8.

Then the band released its debut album, *My Generation*, reportedly completed in just seven hours (a remarkable feat by any standard, especially given how strong the record still sounds); it is probably not insignificant that pep pills (speed) were the mods' drug of choice. The title track was released as a single at the end of October, sold 300,000 copies and made it to No. 2 in the United Kingdom. Daltrey's famous stutter on it was the result of his struggle to read Townshend's scribbled lyrics during the recording. However, it sounded to a gleeful mod audience as if the singer was tongue-tied from the effect of too many pills, and the implied curse word only dawned upon the band later on. Townshend was left to face down the line about dying before he got old with each successive birthday. The album itself reached No. 5 in England and inspired everyone from American garage-rock bands to mod revivalists such as the Jam and Oasis. "Heard today, it sounds like a revolution," writes the British music magazine *Mojo*. "The energy and unstable power of this music is surely one of the era's finest achievements. It's sometimes called the first punk album, which isn't so far-fetched."[4] In December 1965, the time of its release, reviewer John Emery observed in *Beat Instrumental*: "They haven't copied anyone. . . . Without a doubt they are in a class of their own."[5] The Who's instrumentalists would be highly influential for succeeding musical generations. Drummer Keith Moon's innovation and energy, whether pill provided or natural, were revelatory, his solos a jaw-dropping hurricane of sound and fury. "He did revolutionize rock drumming because everything was going on at once," as Jimmy Page recalled. "He was the lead instrumentalist, really."[6] Moon could be utterly charming, but he was also the original rock maniac; for any outrageous act committed by a rock and roller from then on, "Moon the Loon" did it first—and better. He may not have actually invented trashing hotel rooms, but he certainly raised it to an art form. Meanwhile, Townshend's guitar-destruction act may have inspired a quick flurry of imitators (including Jimi Hendrix, who upped the ante with flame), but it was his "windmill" strumming style—a stiff-armed, 360-degree attack upon the strings—and song structures that would last long beyond the Who's performing lifetime. John Entwistle's expressionless appearance belied the fluidity of his bass runs.

The group was also quick to capitalize on visual iconography, which promoted brand identification long before such ideas were commonplace. A black-and-white photo of Townshend in full "windmill" was used on a poster staking the band's claim to "Maximum R&B"; the "h" in Who ended in the shape of an arrow. Keith Moon took to wearing a much-copied bull's-eye-target shirt, while Townshend adopted a blazer made out of the British Union Jack flag—an act almost as confrontational as that of the hippies who would use the American flag to patch their jeans in a few years' time.

The Who, during their 1966 German/Swiss tour (left to right), Keith Moon, Roger Daltrey, John Entwistle, and Pete Townshend. Keystone/Getty Images.

The problem with the Who, always, was interpersonal friction. Four very distinct, powerful personalities, they were constantly at each other's throats. Long before drugs came along to widen the fissures, Daltrey and Townshend were given to punch-ups onstage and in the studio; it did not help matters when Lambert recognized Townshend's importance as the songwriter and took him into his own swank flat as a roommate, while Daltrey wound up spending a homeless nine months living in the band's van. Yet it was he who had been the one to "bang on the bloody door" and get Townshend out of bed to make the gigs in the first place. It was Daltrey who drove to the shows, picked up the other members in the van, wrote the set list, and stayed positive when the others lagged behind, and it was Daltrey who co-wrote "Anyway, Anyhow, Anywhere" with Townshend, which became a No. 10 hit in 1965, yet his name was left off the lucrative credits. In the autumn of 1965, Daltrey beat Keith Moon within an inch of his life after the drummer's intake of pills and alcohol resulted in a miserable show; Moon being Moon, it would not be the last time he was incapacitated. In May of the following year, Townshend was the beater and Moon again the beatee, this time onstage; the drummer sustained a black eye and took stitches in his leg after being hit by Daltrey's mike stand. Moon began looking elsewhere for employment; in the words of co-manager Chris Stamp, "He always thought he was going to be The Beach Boys' drummer, The Beatles' drummer, the Stones' drummer."[7] None of these jobs came to pass, although after the Yardbirds had their own physical altercations in 1966, Moon was invited to play on Jeff Beck's "Bolero" single (backed by Jimmy Page on rhythm guitar and John Paul Jones on bass—two-quarters of the later supergroup Led Zeppelin, which name was suggested by Moon, according to Page). Moon's side session infuriated Townshend, and he returned to the fold soon after.

On the group's sophomore effort, titled *A Quick One* in England and *Happy Jack* in the United States, Shel Talmy was replaced as producer by Lambert after a dispute over money. Since each member was contractually obligated to write two songs for the record, the result was a rather disjointed affair that nonetheless yielded Entwistle's theme song "Boris the Spider," a nine-minute-long epic of Townshend's concerning adultery titled "A Quick One, While He's Away," and Moon's over-the-top noisefest, "Cobwebs and Strange." "Happy Jack" replaced a cover of Martha and the Vandellas' "Heat Wave" on the American version. The Who, however, were just getting started.

The Kinks

The Kinks were the foremost band that sounded ineffably British. Their music carried only the barest trace of American blues, despite the fact that they actually did start out with the idea of "updating . . . Muddy Waters and Chuck Berry, Howlin' Wolf and all these people."[8] The group, consisting of frontman/songwriter Ray Davies, his younger brother Dave on guitar, Pete Quaife on bass and Mick Avory behind the drum kit, was straight out of modern-day London—although Ray Davies, the walking contradiction, was a young man nostalgic for a long-gone Victorian/Edwardian era. Davies even admitted, "I didn't want to sound American. I was very conscious of sounding English."[9] The songs he penned ranged from the acerbic 1966 attack on hypocritical toffs, "A Well Respected Man," to the ragingly randy, including the protometal hit "You Really Got Me," which shot into America's Top 10 upon its 1964 release and inspired Pete Townshend (who had just played a gig with the Beatles and the Kinks) to write "I Can't Explain," the Who's first hit. The follow-up, a stomping "All Day and All of the Night," made it into 1965's Top 10, rapidly chased by a ballad ("Set Me Free") and the classic "Tired of Waiting for You."

Davies had a sharp eye and a sharper tongue: 1966's "Sunny Afternoon" sounded blissful on the surface, but a closer listen to the lyrics—sung in an appropriate upper-class drawl—revealed a wastrel aristocrat complaining about his dreary lot in life. In "Dedicated Follower of Fashion," Davies skewered the self-conscious mod version of what would now be deemed a metrosexual, if not something decidedly more effeminate. Davies's withering lyrics were the result of talent and discipline, but also his self-perceived outsider status, a condition that has given impetus to the greatest rock and roll. When Davies is not slicing others down to size, he often cuts a solitary figure himself. The wistful "Waterloo Sunset" is not about the singer's own romance; he is alone, visualizing (or spying upon) young lovers Terry and Julie from within the safe confines of his flat.[10] Even the mates who remain after his girl has gone in "See My Friends" are geographically (and by inference emotionally) distant, while in another song, Davies states the obvious: "I'm Not Like Everybody Else."

The Kinks have been somewhat underrated next to their showier compatriots; perhaps this was due to the fact that the group was (in the words of rock critic Greil Marcus) "a classy little outfit, neurotic, long on intelligence and short on raunch."[11] A case could also be made for the destructiveness of sibling rivalry. The Kinks benefited enormously from Dave Davies's ur-garage-rock sensibilities, yet as brothers dating back to Cain and Abel (or Don and Phil Everly, or the Beach Boys' Wilson clan) would attest, it is not always easy getting along, especially within the confines of a pop group. The Davies brothers literally came to blows, frequently onstage, as the Kinks continually broke up and reformed in different configurations over the years.

Yet it was Dave Davies whose guitar innovations gave the Kinks a brutal power that contrasted with his elder brother's often more wistful moments, and he had almost died to get them. At fifteen, he fed his small amplifier into a larger one; the resultant electrical shock knocked him across the room and blew out all the lights in the family home. Undaunted, Dave went right back to work, finally slashing the speaker cone with a razor blade, which gave his guitar a distinctive crackly tone.

There was also a mysterious ban from the American Federation of Musicians that kept the group out of the United States during its heyday, while other British bands were scoring successes stateside. Ray Davies was a newlywed and the father of an infant when the group's first U.S. tour began in late 1964, and he was woefully unprepared for the task at hand, "I didn't want to be away from my wife and child. . . . the agency we were with had done some dodgy deals with some of the promoters. We'd get people coming into the dressing room shouting, 'We don't want you to go on tonight!' with 5,000 kids waiting, so they wouldn't have to pay us. And [the managers] had stayed in England. We were just thrown on the road, into the lion's den. . . . America terrified me. A few years earlier [sic] they'd shot a President, and there were guns everywhere. . . . We were not connecting. . . . But, you know, we didn't get diplomatic training in N10 [his London postal code]. And all I wanted to do was go home."[12]

That attitude played out in minor and major scuffles. When the group appeared on the U.S. TV show Hullabaloo, it was instructed to dance to someone else's novelty hit. When the camera panned to Ray Davies and Mick Avory, they were swaying cheek-to-cheek like lovers, a very British bit of humor that proved horrifying to Americans. At another television program in Los Angeles, a physical altercation with a union official ensued when the band refused to sign contracts being shoved at them. The man reportedly raged at Davies: "You're gonna find out just how powerful America is, you limey bastard!"[13] After the group returned to England, the American Federation of Musicians ban suddenly went into effect. "They never said exactly why," Ray reminisced. "That's what cost us the top spot . . . it cost us a lot of our youth. Our prime . . . by then people like Jimi Hendrix and the Who were coming back [from the U.S. as] megastars."[14]

Most of the Kinks' early recordings have held up beautifully over the decades and remain textbook examples of economically observational songcraft. Ray Davies is in no small part responsible for rock's evolution from a raucous burst of teenage hormones into wider social commentary; his work can stand alongside that of any other great composer, inside or out of rock, without need of apology. The Kinks were inducted into the Rock and Roll Hall of Fame in 1990.

Herman's Hermits

Herman's Hermits were clearly not profound, aimed at the younger end of the audience and offering innocuously melodic pop, but they were wildly successful commercially with at least fifteen Top 20 singles between 1964 and 1970. The group started out as the Heartbeats in Manchester (also home to the Hollies and the Mindbenders); the group changed its name to its more distinctive one after a sixteen-year-old former child actor, Peter Noone, joined as lead singer in 1963. The photogenic Noone was a nonthreatening charmer, the perfect front person for such a group. After the band's managers invited producer Mickie Most to catch a show, he signed the Hermits to a label and took the reins for the band's first single, a Carole King and Gerry Goffin tidbit called "I'm into Something Good," which rapidly eclipsed an earlier version by the all-female American group Goldie and the Gingerbreads. Most, like many pop Svengalis of the day, was not about to take a chance on the untested Hermits to make a hit record, and so the bouncy number was played by studio musicians such as guitarist Jimmy Page and bassist John Paul Jones, later of Led Zeppelin; it went to No. 13 in the United States (and No. 1 in England) in the summer of 1964. That was followed in 1965 by "Can't You Hear My Heartbeat," which rose to No. 2.

The group's first two albums, both released that year, landed at No. 2, while a third "best" compilation made a quite respectable showing at No. 5. Then the band really had an anomaly on its collective hands with the 1965 music-hall-style throwback "Mrs. Brown, You've Got a Lovely Daughter," which hit No. 1 in America, although it was never released as a single back home; it eventually sold an astounding 14 million copies. Most, to build on that success, had the group (or, more accurately, Noone) record a real turn-of-the-century tune, "I'm Henry the Eighth, I Am," which also landed at the top spot in the American charts that year. In 1965, the Hermits made the charts twice more with the No. 5 "Silhouettes" (a remake of a 1957 hit for the Rays and the Diamonds that had been co-written by Four Seasons producer Bob Crewe) and a cover of Sam Cooke's "(What a) Wonderful World" (No. 4). The group scored again in 1966 with a cover of the Kinks' "Dandy" (No. 5), "Leaning on the Lamp Post" (No. 9), "Listen People" (No. 3), "This Door Swings Both Ways" (No. 12), and "Must to Avoid" (No. 9). That was the same year, however, that the Monkees were cobbled together for the lower age range of the teen spectrum, which marked the beginning of the Hermits' decline.

The Animals

In the summer of 1964, "House of the Rising Sun" (a doleful six-minute song about a brothel, with melodic roots in seventeenth-century British folk music) raced to the top of the charts in both England and America, thanks in no small part to a brooding guitar intro and the menacing delivery of singer Eric Burdon, whom most listeners believed was black. The Animals, fierce blues acolytes (they backed Sonny Boy Williamson on their first, little-heard 1963 album), had formed in Newcastle upon Tyne the previous year and were booked in London by Crawdaddy Club impresario Giorgio Gomelsky. Producer Mickie Most signed the group and then secured a label contract, resulting in "Baby Let Me Take You Home," which grazed the British Top 20 early in 1964. The next single was "House of the Rising Sun," and the band was on its way, recording one classic after another: "Don't Let Me Be Misunderstood," "We Gotta Get out of This Place" (both Top 15 in 1965), "Don't Bring Me Down," and "It's My Life" in 1966. However, the group was already splintering: keyboardist Alan Price got out right after "Place" because he had been feuding with Burdon over the band's direction and/or was refusing to share royalties accrued for his arranging credit on the single. After "Life," Most was jettisoned, and as "Don't Bring Me Down" was climbing the charts, all the original members save Burdon had already moved on.

The Yardbirds

In 1963, a London group called the Metropolitan Blues Quartet metamorphosed into the Yardbirds; the lineup consisted of singer Keith Relf, Anthony Topham on lead guitar, Chris Dreja on rhythm, bassist Paul Samwell-Smith, and drummer Jim McCarty. Topham was soon gone, replaced by Relf's art-school classmate Eric Clapton. The band took over the Rolling Stones' residency at Giorgio Gomelsky's Crawdaddy Club, and the promoter became their manager. By 1964, the group's jam-improvisational take on the blues, which it was calling "rave-ups," was attracting R&B fans, not least for Clapton's stunning guitar runs. The Yardbirds' first two singles did not fare very well, but the third—a pop-rock number, "For Your Love," which featured odd tempos and eerie harmonies—reached No. 6 on the American charts in 1964. The band's turning away from strict blues, though, disenchanted Clapton, who left the next year to join John Mayall's Bluesbreakers. Jeff Beck took his spot after the group had approached session guitarist Jimmy Page. Beck used the platform for intriguing experimentation—scraping his guitar's strings as if it were a percussion instrument, employing amplifier distortion to create a droning, Middle Eastern effect, and imitating a sitar with fuzzbox on his first single with the group, 1965's "Heart Full of Soul." It went into the Top 10 while other rock guitarists watched and listened in awe. Beck would prove to be one of the most influential players of the British invasion; he was quite conspicuous on that year's Bo Diddley remake of "I'm a Man," backed with "Still I'm Sad," which also charted in America. The next single, "Shapes of Things," was one of rock's first full-fledged forays into psychedelia, bolstered by the buzzy follow-up "Over Under Sideways Down." After bassist Samwell-Smith left the group midway through 1966, Jimmy Page took his place; it was not long before the band realized that Page was far more useful on guitar, alongside Beck, and switched Chris Dreja over to bass duties. The guitar dream team only appeared together on one single, 1966's "Happenings Ten Years Time Ago," which struggled to reach No. 30; later that year, an "exhausted" Beck took his leave, and the group—which had replaced Gomelsky as producer with the ubiquitous Mickie Most, a mismatch of monumental proportions—began its slow slide downward.

Spencer Davis Group Featuring Stevie Winwood

Stevie Winwood first blazed onto the scene in 1965 with the Spencer Davis Group; two years earlier, Stevie and his brother Muff had decided to pursue music full-time and hooked up with guitarist Davis. Stevie's sizzling vocals and pumping organ on 1966's "Keep On Runnin'" and the following year's "Gimme Some Lovin'" (since used on innumerable film soundtracks) and "I'm a Man" helped propel these singles to chart success. Winwood's mature sound belied the fact that he was just seventeen, although he had been performing with his father and brother since age eight. By 1967, Winwood was out of the group and on to greener pastures, first with Traffic, then in Blind Faith with Eric Clapton, and later in a solo career.

Van Morrison and Them

Them formed in Belfast in 1963, fronted by the then teenage Celtic mystic-cum-soul shouter Van Morrison. Signed to a recording contract soon after arriving in London, Them succeeded with its second single, "Baby Please Don't Go," which peaked at No. 10 in England and stayed on the charts for nine weeks. It was the flip side, though, that would become an all-time rock classic: Morrison's "Gloria," covered by everyone from the Doors to Patti Smith and beyond. Them's next single, "Here Comes the Night," reached No. 24 in the United States in 1965, followed by "Mystic Eyes" (No. 33). After the band split up in 1966, Morrison went on to an eccentric but successful solo career; he may be most widely known for his constantly played hit "Brown-Eyed Girl," which enjoyed a revival after its use in the film *Pretty Woman*, but the albums *Astral Weeks*, *Moondance*, and *Tupelo Honey* are the ones that consistently show up on rock critics' best-ever lists.

The Zombies

Those who have heard the wonderfully ethereal Top 10 singles "She's Not There" (1964) and "Tell Her No" (1965) would agree with the late rock critic Lester Bangs that it amounted "almost to tragedy" that the Zombies were not able to maintain their success, but the group "was apparently cursed by [its] own musical adventurousness";[15] when it veered away from pop jewels like these with a string of more experimental singles, the mass audience was not interested, even though a handful of cognoscenti did appreciate the band's later efforts.

Manfred Mann

Manfred Mann has had other lineups, most notably the one that scored a hit with a cover of Bruce Springsteen's first single "Blinded by the Light," but here the original is meant, with Paul Jones singing lead (1963–1966). That period not only coincides with this volume's time frame, but was also the group's finest hour; Jones was able to deliver a real R&B shading to these tracks, proving that even seminonsensical lyrics ("Do Wah Diddy Diddy") were no bar to great rock.

Keyboardist Manfred Mann was an émigré from South Africa (the United Kingdom was then offering a one-year grace period in work permits for citizens of the former British commonwealth) when he began playing at London jazz clubs around 1961. He hooked up with drummer Mike Hugg and was looking for a vocalist who would help them land more work when Jones turned up at a Carnaby Street audition the following year. The band began getting regular gigs at the Marquee and the Crawdaddy Club (homes to the Who and the Stones, respectively) and was picked up by a publicist who became their manager. "Diddy" (the original was cut by the Exciters, a girl group produced by Lieber and Stoller) was the group's fifth single and its first U.S. hit, nabbing the No. 1 spot on both sides of the Atlantic in the summer of 1964. Yet the band preferred to keep its focus on England and Europe, not the much larger American commercial market, which naturally led to a lower profile in the United States, although Mann was one of the first artists to cover Bob Dylan, including "With God on Our Side" and "Just like a Woman" (the group later had an unlikely smash hit with Dylan's "Quinn the Eskimo" after Jones's departure).

Mann's version of "My Little Red Book" (later a hit for the psychedelic-soul group Love) was chosen for the soundtrack of the 1965 film *What's New Pussycat?*, but all the attention went to the title track, sung by Welshman Tom Jones. Paul Jones handed in his notice around 1965 and continued to sing with the group until Mann could find a replacement, but the keyboardist wanted to take his band in a more jazz-oriented direction, and it floundered during the rest of the British invasion. Jones went on to star in a little-seen film about the power of pop music called *Privilege* and a rather bland solo career—remarkable given what he had been able to accomplish during his time with Manfred Mann.

The Moody Blues

This Birmingham-based group, formed in 1964, had one memorable hit with "Go Now," sung by guitarist Denny Laine. The song spent a week at No. 1 at the beginning of 1965 and was the last Top 10 hit for the Moody Blues until 1972's "Nights in White Satin," by which time Laine (who left in 1966, along with original bassist Clint Warwick) had already joined ex-Beatle Paul McCartney in Wings. The Moody Blues, in various configurations anchored by Justin Hayward and John Lodge, the respective replacements for Laine and Warwick, continued on through the start of the twenty-first century.

The Hollies

Two groups took vocal harmony to dizzying heights during this period—the Hollies and the Searchers. The Hollies, formed in Manchester around 1962, created irresistible pop singles with impeccable pitch and arrangements: "Bus Stop," "Look Through Any Window," and "Stop Stop Stop," all released in 1966, sound like the sun breaking through dreary English weather. Besides soaring harmonies and chiming guitars, the Hollies' strongest asset was the songwriting team of singer Allan Clarke with guitarist-vocalist Graham Nash and guitarist Tony Hicks. In the 1960s, only the Beatles had more hits in England than the Hollies, but the latter somehow did not manage to crack the U.S. charts until "Bus Stop" made the Top 10 in 1966. Although Graham Nash quit the group over the usual "creative differences" in 1968 (going on to establish the first 1970s supergroup in Crosby, Stills, and Nash, later joined by Neil Young), he was still fiercely proud of the Hollies' achievements; in December 2004, upon the fortieth anniversary of the group's first record, he told *Rolling Stone*: "The Hollies were a great live band and could really sing . . . people have never really understood how good a rock & roll band [we] were."[16]

The Searchers

The Searchers, a Liverpool quartet that adopted its name from the John Wayne film and started out as a skiffle band, kept to a vocal theme similar to that of the Hollies, since all the members could sing, but they put even more emphasis on guitars. Their distinctive sound came courtesy of the Rickenbacker, a jangly-sounding guitar that would become characteristic of the Byrds (and later of Tom Petty). They were not the first rock band to recognize the power of this particular instrument: John Lennon had been using a 6-string model in the Hamburg and Liverpool days, and he had been influenced by seeing it played by Toots Thielmanns of the jazzy George Shearing Quintet. "We met him in New York," Lennon recalled. "We get the chance to meet a lot of great musicians and talk to them. This guy knocked us out. Yeah, I'd like to play this make of guitar . . . all the time."[17] Referring to the break at the end of

"You Can't Do That," Lennon enthused, "That's George with his 12-string do-ing that bit. Isn't it a great sound? Like a piano. . . . George only got his because he didn't want me to be the only one in the group with a Rickenbacker."[18] (Harrison, who actually received the second of three 12-string prototypes as a gift from the company in February 1964, played that guitar on "Eight Days a Week" and "A Hard Day's Night.")

In the case of the Searchers, the Rickenbacker's ringing tones helped the group achieve hits like 1964's "Don't Throw Your Love Away," "Sugar and Spice," "Needles and Pins" (co-written by Sonny Bono and Jack Nitzsche), and "When You Walk in the Room," (written by Jackie DeShannon), as well as a remake of "Love Potion #9" that charted in 1965. The group formed in 1957 and had its next-to-last Top 100 chart appearance in 1966 ("Take Me for What I'm Worth" came in at a lowly No. 76); however, despite an official break up in 1985, a lineup with one semioriginal member (Frank Allen, who arrived in 1964) has made records and toured, albeit on a spotty basis.

Wayne Fontana and the Mindbenders

The way Fontana tells it, two potential Mindbenders failed to turn up the night of his audition in a Manchester club sometime in 1960, and he cobbled together a new band on the spur of the moment from some other musicians waiting to try out. Luckily, the ad hoc group jelled and was signed. Their first single ("Hello Josephine") made it to No. 46 in the British charts, and the next two flopped. Those were the days when a record label actually stuck by an act it had already put money into, fortunately so, because in 1965 "Game of Love" hit No. 2 in England, No. 1 in America (an unusual feat for a UK group other than the Beatles); the following year, "A Groovy Kind of Love" managed to make it to the second slot in both countries. As rock critic Lester Bangs once noted, "Wayne Fontana and the Mindbenders may have been a one-shot group, but what a shot. . . . ["Game of Love" was] an instant classic, a perfect example of the rock and roll band of no apparent distinction but with a masterpiece in them anyway."[19]

Peter & Gordon

The Beatles' magic touch was bestowed upon Peter & Gordon, who were not managed by Brian Epstein; their connection was Paul McCartney, who had been living in Peter Asher's London home while going out with his younger sis-ter Jane. Asher and Gordon Waller received "A World Without Love" after John Lennon supposedly declared that there was no way he would sing a lyric that began with a request to lock the performer away. In June 1964, Peter & Gordon's version, a softly harmonized ballad, became the first British invasion single to nab a U.S. No. 1 after the Beatles. Their proximity to Lennon and McCartney gave the duo three more hits: "Nobody I Know," "I Don't Want to See You Again," and "Woman," the last song written by McCartney under a pseudonym. But beside that good fortune, Asher and Waller (who had been singing together since they were youngsters at a private school in London) were actually talented, with a sound reminiscent of the Everly Brothers.

Chad & Jeremy

Chad & Jeremy were often confused with Peter & Gordon, since both duos specialized in acoustic-style ballads. Chad Stuart and Jeremy Clyde met, like Asher and Waller, as schoolboys—in their case, at London's Central School of Speech and Drama. Like the former duo, they were well bred and genteel, but with an even more illustrious pedigree: Clyde's maternal grandfather was the duke of Wellington, whose ancestor was a British national hero for his defeat of Napoleon at Waterloo.[20] Chad & Jeremy had been performing since 1963 on the London coffeehouse circuit and had their first single, "Yesterday's Gone," picked up for U.S. distribution after American labels came looking for talent in the wake of the Beatles' success. It made the Top 20 in 1964, followed by "Summer Song" (their biggest hit) and "Willow Weep for Me." Chad and Jeremy were clean-cut by the standards of the time and became more popular in America than at home; accordingly, they relocated to Los Angeles and appeared on any TV shows that would have them, including *Hullaballoo*, *Shindig*, *Hollywood Palace*, *Batman*, *Andy Williams*, *Merv Griffin*, *Danny Kaye*, *Dick Van Dyke*, and *Patty Duke*. In retrospect, grabbing whatever came their way was a wise move, because by 1965, they were finished, although they have since reunited for several oldies tours.

The Swinging Blue Jeans

This Liverpool foursome, which began as a skiffle combo in 1957, played alongside its hometown neighbors, the Beatles, at Hamburg's Star club; although it achieved one American hit, 1964's "Hippy Hippy Shake," it was again overshadowed by that other quartet's BBC-recorded remake of the tune after John Lennon bawled his guts out on the number.

Freddie & the Dreamers

The success of Freddie & the Dreamers was a mystery, unless it could be simply credited to the craze for all things English. Lead singer Freddie Garrity bore something of visual resemblance to the late Buddy Holly, with similar big black eyeglasses and a skinny frame. He hailed from Manchester, England, and started out in skiffle, like the Quarrymen version of the Beatles (his group shared a bill with the latter on at least three occasions in 1962 and 1963 and even supported the Beatles during the band's 1964–1965 Christmas shows). However, Garrity decided that comedy was really his forte, so he accordingly created a dance that any toddler could readily imitate by lifting one arm and leg, then the other. This movement, repeated along with a nonsensical set of lyrics exhorting listeners to follow along, resulted in the 1965 American/UK hit "Do the Freddie." The group capitalized on its success by appearing in four disposable pop flicks: *What A Crazy World* (1963), *Every Day's a Holiday* (1965), *Cuckoo Patrol* (1965), and *Out of Sight* (1966), as well as landing a Coca-Cola commercial.

Ian Whitcomb

Ian Whitcomb was a fan of vaudeville and music-hall material a full half century after its time and well before Paul McCartney reintroduced the genre to a much wider audience with songs like "Your Mother Should Know." He had a massive hit in the summer of 1965 with "You Turn Me On," featuring "questionable" lyrics (basically, the title itself), as well as heavy breathing that bordered on actual panting. After being banned by indignant radio stations, the single took off; this was obviously a much more innocent time. Whitcomb went on to write (among other titles) *Rock Odyssey*, an erudite book about his time as an unlikely teen pop icon. His chosen mode of musical expression did not continue to resonate with the public, although he made several more albums and had a minor hit with "Where Did Robinson Crusoe Go with Friday on Saturday Night?"

FASHION AND STYLE

Mary Quant

At the same time that all this music was making an impact, London was also becoming the world center of fashion, an unexpected status for the country that had previously contributed to the lexicon of style only such sensible goods as tweed, Shetland sweaters, trench coats, and rubber galoshes, all meant to protect against the notoriously inclement British weather. Suddenly, or so it seemed, everything cool emanated from the former British Empire; American teens saw the new clothes in magazine fashion spreads and on their favorite stars, and the "youthquake" demand was such that U.S. companies soon began churning out miniskirts and related accessories.

In those days, music and fashion, film and art, all blended into one another and counted heavily as social signifiers both in the United States and abroad. People declared their allegiance by how they looked: a modest woman wore her skirts below the kneecap, and a company man dressed in a roomy suit that gave no hint of the body beneath. To wear a short skirt or, in the case of a male, tight brocade bell-bottoms was to say that one was young and sexy and did not give a damn about old-fashioned mores—and was, no doubt, into the new rock and roll. Denim was then a fabric employed not for designer jeans worn on the red carpet at high-toned events, but for laborers. Any variation from the norm, including long hair on men and provocative women's wear, could serve

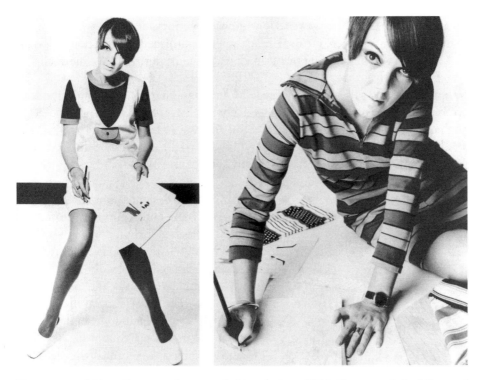

Two images of Mary Quant working on clothing designs, 1966. Courtesy of the Library of Congress.

as justification for being attacked on the street. Those days are long gone, and two major figures in this seismic shift were Mary Quant and Vidal Sassoon.

Quant had been designing her own clothes since childhood, and she had kept a childlike approach to style; in her book, "grownup" was a synonym for "matronly." She blithely described her ideal customer: "I'm very sexy, I enjoy sex. . . . I can't be bought, but if I want you, I'll have you."[21] This was heady talk for the late 1950s and early 1960s. Demand for Quant's clothes quickly outpaced supply; J. C. Penney, an American midpriced department store chain that had been looking for a way to update its stodgy image, soon approached her with an offer to back mass production. Her Ginger Group line began breaking sales records in both the United States and Great Britain.

The "Quant Look" was coltish and required new proportions: all that exposed leg needed to be balanced by low-heeled boots, either ankle height and white (high-end shops carried rip-off versions of the little boot invented by French couturier André Courreges to complement his Mondrian-influenced minis), or high and shiny, sometimes over the knee. Sometimes the wearer played up her youth, creating a Lolita-esque erotic frisson with little-girl shoes called "Mary Janes," which had a strap across the top of the foot and a childlike low heel. The invention of pantyhose inspired a wild rainbow of opaque tights;

although businesswomen wore sheer nylons in various beige tones, the hippest young women's legs were citrus shaded, striped, patterned, and/or polka-dotted.

Other important designers who made their mark during this time included the American Rudi Gernreich (1922–1985), who shocked the world by putting a topless bathing suit on model Peggy Moffitt, invented the "no-bra" brassiere, which was transparent and encouraged a naturally rounded look, as opposed to the pointy style popular in the 1950s; was the first to employ vinyl and cutouts in clothes, and created the body-conscious knitted tube dress. The American Betsey Johnson, who began her career in 1964 at the New York boutique Paraphernalia, is still active in design.

Sixties supermodel Twiggy, 1967, wearing a Native American–inspired miniskirt outfit, with an abbreviated hemline of the type popularized by British fashion designer Mary Quant. Courtesy of Photofest.

The French designer André Courreges employed chain mail (previously used for armor), color blocking, and geometric shapes. In 1964, his famous "Moon Girl" collection featured extremely short skirts in white and silver vinyl and minidresses with transparent plastic portholes (complemented by astronaut-style helmets and white midshin boots) that were knocked off by the thousands—minus the helmets. Barbara Hulanicki was the creative force behind Biba, a London store that opened in 1964 and popularized the instant-gratification mode of fashion. It became a way of life for its dolly-bird clientele: dresses and accessories were inexpensively priced, turned over quickly, and were replaced with new designs, creating a limited-edition rush and necessitating frequent visits.

Vidal Sassoon: Hair Liberation

Meanwhile, there was another element in the female armory yet to be addressed: hair. For years, women had been going to beauty salons (often once a week or even more frequently) for the upkeep of elaborate coiffures that required curling on metal rollers with end papers and setting lotion, then sitting under stationary driers for long periods while the tops of their ears burnt, and then enduring the teasing comb and loads of hairspray for the finishing touches. Ongoing maintenance was necessary, ensuring a constant outlay of money and time spent at the salon. Vidal Sassoon, like the Beatles, altered the meaning of hair as a signifier—what it announced about sexuality, how its owner wanted to appear to the world, how he or she preferred to spend his or her time. It was a radical upending of all that had gone before.

Sassoon literally had a dream ("I dreamt hair in geometry, squares, triangles, oblongs and trapezoids")[22] and a vision: hairstyles that retained their structure through the cut itself, not by artificial means. Thinking like an architect, he came up with an early version of this concept in 1960, which he called the Shape. The women who wore Quant's clothes began flocking to Sassoon, alongside some highly visible male trendsetters. In Sassoon's worldview, one innovation led to another: he got rid of the helmet hairdryer and began using handheld blowdryers instead, which gave hair volume and motion rather than a baked-in set. After he was hired by Clairol to tour the United States demonstrating these new ideas, America took notice.

Fashion all came together in 1963 when Quant sat in Sassoon's chair for a cut and brainstormed about her upcoming show. How would he coif the models? "I'm going to cut the hair like you cut material," he responded. "No fuss . . . just a neat, clean, swinging line."[23] After he came up with the Bob, a geometric style based on the 1920s flapper crop, the new natural look became widely popular both in England and America.

Male Style

Meanwhile, men were unwilling to be left behind in the peacock stakes. England has a long, rich history of men's fashion, from the elaborate outfits worn in olden times to the worldwide acceptance of Savile Row bespoke (made-to-order) suits as the ne plus ultra in business attire, and the 1960s were no exception. Before this particular stylistic explosion, only performers and a few bold homosexuals wore anything that could be considered vain or showy; as Small Faces keyboardist Ian McLagen put it, "Up until the sixties, you couldn't buy clothes other than your parents' clothes."[24] This changed drastically after young Brits noted the sharp, lean-cut suits on the French and Italian émigrés who were crowding Soho coffee bars and riding their Vespa scooters around town.

The Rise of Carnaby Street

When the London-based TV music series *Ready, Steady, Go!* went on the air in England, bands and audience members could be seen wearing the latest styles, which whetted the national appetite. This was unfortunate for the original mods, who prized being original and first with the best; no true mod would divulge where he purchased his clothes

By 1963, Carnaby Street had become the place to see and be seen, with dozens of men's retailers fighting to get in. The original mods were fastidious

WHO WERE THE MODS?

The mods started out as jazz fans, emulating the suits worn by those artists, but the label soon came to encompass young men who positioned themselves as opposites to rockers or "teddy boys." This latter group worshipped the likes of Eddie Cochran and Gene Vincent and wore black leather or "drape" jackets, pegged trousers or denims, and greased ducktail hairstyles à la Elvis Presley, James Dean and Marlon Brando. Mods were just as fetishistic about their appearance as rockers, if not more so, but one major difference was that they were usually (not always) employed, with ready cash. One definition of mod was offered by the subtitle of a 2000 book by author Terry Rawlings, *Mod: Clean Living under Very Difficult Circumstances: A Very British Phenomenon*. Mods were influenced by the Continental look: well-cut clothing and hair, sunglasses, colorful shirts and ties, and imported scooters. They were into soul and R&B music (first from the United States, later homegrown), "leapers" (amphetamines) that allowed them to dance through the night after a full day at work, and posing.

Image was all: the ultimate mod goal was to be a face, a trendsetter, one of the beautiful chosen ones. As one authority, the Who's Pete Townshend, noted: "It was a movement of young people . . . an army, a powerful, aggressive army of teenagers with transport . . . to be a mod, you had to have short hair, money enough to buy a real smart suit, good shoes, good shirts; you had to be able to dance like a madman. You had to be in possession of pills all the time and always be pilled-up. You had to have a scooter [and] you had to have like an army anourak [parka] to wear on the scooter. And that was being a mod, and that was the end of the story."[25] The mod movement still exerts an influence over fashion today, being periodically revived for both men and women.

when it came to their gear, but copycats did not mind a few bloodstains on their stylish threads. A famous 1964 clash put mod on the map: A group of mod wannabes had gone down to Clacton-on-Sea to live it up a little and were joined by more the following day after local papers reported that "youth gangs" were descending on the area. Local rockers took issue with the invaders; when challenged, the mods' superior numbers (and, no doubt, amphetamine-spurred rage) won the day. The London newspapers made a big fuss, so within months, mod versus rocker fisticuffs were occurring in seaside resorts around Great Britain. Eventually the conflict all petered out, but the clashes left a bad taste, and the original mods were all about taste. Those who had been in on the ground floor of the fashion movement were disgusted; they would never have ruined a good outfit by brawling, most certainly not with rockers.

Innovations in male style developed during this time included brightly colored shirts, ties, and suits, and suits in unconventional material such as upholstery fabrics. In the early '60s, fashionable men wore Pierre Cardin's tight-waisted, long-jacketed suits, often in mohair; by the time the Beatles came along in 1964, suits were buttoned up to the chin. "Sharp" (tightly tailored, often in shiny fabrics) suits were favored by Motown's male acts and so were worn by those who appreciated these performers. For more free-spirited types, the Beach Boys inspired a California-casual look that featured Hawaiian-patterned loose shirts, well-worn denims, or baggy surfer-style trousers and moccasin-type loafers.

In 1966, men grew their hair and sideburns in emulation of the Beatles, whose facial hair (the droopy "Fu Manchu" mustache worn by all four on the cover of *Sgt. Pepper*) inspired imitation in the latter half of the decade. In the case of African Americans, Jimi Hendrix's "natural" hair would act as an influence on the Afro, as opposed to the processed style worn by James Brown. The Beatles also spurred male desire for Cuban-heeled, ankle-high leather boots, while John Lennon was personally responsible for starting crazes for wire-framed granny glasses (worn by both genders in a variety of tints) and the flat Greek fisherman's cap, as seen on the cover of his book *In His Own Write.*

More outre youth adopted the louche style seen on the mid-'60s Rolling Stones, characterized by floppy hats—John Kennedy, who rarely wore a hat, had caused the haberdashery industry to despair—long scarves, tight, patterned T-shirts, body-hugging trousers, brocade vests ("waistcoats" in British parlance), and frock coats last seen in the Edwardian era. The most adventurous added lace cuffs and loads of costume jewelry, including military medals prized by previous generations and worn now as an antiwar statement.

NOTES

1. Pete Townshend quoted in Richard Barnes, "Amazing Journey," *The Who—The Inside Story*, special limited edition of *Mojo*, September 2004, p. 9.

2. Ibid., p. 5.

3. Shel Talmy quote, ibid., p. 12.

4. Steve Lowe, "Explosive: Full of Youthful Dysfunction and Sounding Bracingly Macho, 39 Years on the Who's First Album, My Generation, Has Lost None of Its Firepower," *The Who—The Inside Story*, special limited edition of *Mojo*, September 2004, p. 14.

5. John Emery in *Beat Instrumental*, December 1965, available in Lowe, "Explosive," p. 14.

6. "I'm Free," *The Who—The Inside Story*, special limited edition of *Mojo*, September 2004, p. 30.

7. Ibid., p. 29.

8. Jon Savage, *The Kinks—The Official Biography* (London: Faber & Faber, 1984), p. 12.

9. Ibid., p. 71.

10. The characters were named after London's then-reigning "It" couple, actors Terence Stamp (brother of the Who's co-manager) and Julie Christie.

11. Greil Marcus quoted in Savage, *The Kinks*, p. 68; also available in Greil Marcus, *Mystery Train: Images of America in Rock 'n' Roll Music* (New York: Plume, 1997).

12. Ray Davies quoted in Nick Hasted, "Ready Steady Kinks!," *Uncut*, September 2004, pp. 54–55.

13. Ibid., p. 48.

14. Ray Davies quote, ibid., p. 55.

15. Lester Bangs, "The British Invasion," in *The Rolling Stone Illustrated History of Rock & Roll*, ed. Anthony DeCurtis and James Henke with Holly George-Warren (New York: Straight Arrow, 1992), p. 168.

16. Sean Egan, "Hollies Celebrate 'Long Road': Fortieth Anniversary Box Collects

Album Tracks and Rarities," *Rolling Stone*, November 26, 2003, http://www.rollingstone
.com/news/story/_/id/5936653/thehollies?pageid=rs.Artistcage&pageregion=triple3&rn
d=1118712691190&has-player=true.

17. John Lennon quotes from Chris Roberts, "Lennon: If it All Ended Tomorrow
We'd Be Rich and Out of Work," *John Lennon: The Beatles and Beyond*, *NME Originals*
1, no. 10 (2003): 17.

18. Ibid.

19. Bangs, *Rolling Stone Illustrated History of Rock & Roll*, p. 168.

20. According to the biography, "Timeline: Part One (Before 1964),"
chadandjeremynet, http://www.chadandjeremy.net/cj/.

21. Mary Quant quoted in Shawn Levy, *Ready, Steady, Go!* (New York: Doubleday,
2002), pp. 47–48.

22. Vidal Sassoon, ibid., p. 32.

23. Ibid.

24. Ian McLagen, ibid., p. 104.

25. Pete Townshend in *The Rolling Stone Interviews 1967-1980* (New York: Rolling
Stone/Straight Arrow Publishers Inc./St. Martin's Press, 1981), p. 38.

THE REVOLUTION WILL BE TELEVISED AND PUBLICIZED

America used to be the big youth place in everybody's imagination. America had teenagers and everywhere else just had people.

—John Lennon[1]

Although a rudimentary version of television was invented in the late 1920s, and models were available for home use a decade later, the concept really began to take off in the 1950s. In 1951, 5,905,000 sets were sold (15,639,872 had already been sold cumulatively); by 1959, the cumulative total had more than quadrupled, to 67 million. The following year, more than 87 percent of American homes had a television (a total of 45,750,000), and by 1964, the year the Beatles appeared on *Ed Sullivan*, TV had penetrated 92.3 percent of U.S. households (51,600,000). The newfangled color version was reserved for the wealthy when it was introduced in 1964—only 3.1 percent of homes, not even 2 million families, could watch shows in the new format. Six years later, 23,400,000 American homes (39.3 percent) had color.[2]

A quip most often attributed to comedian Ernie Kovacs noted that TV was "a medium in the sense that it's neither rare nor well-done." Nonetheless, the hypnotic box had unprecedented power. Everyone had formerly obtained news and entertainment via the "wireless" (radio), but now the American audience was captivated by flickering images. Citizens who watched John F. Kennedy challenge Vice President Richard M. Nixon in the first televised presidential debate in 1960 were convinced that the former had won, whereas those who listened to the event on the radio (including Kennedy's running mate, Lyndon B. Johnson) perceived the elder politician as the victor. Kennedy appeared handsome and healthy, although his tan was actually the result of drugs taken to combat Addison's disease, a detail not disclosed until decades after his death. Next to the much less attractive Nixon, who was also perspiring heavily under the hot televison lights, Kennedy was a shoo-in. For better or worse, television had an immediate, visceral impact unmatched by any other medium.

TELEVISION PROGRAMMING IN THE 1960s

In the 1960s, there were only three major national television networks. Large markets might have several additional local channels. NET, an educational network that was the forerunner to PBS, began broadcasting in 1952; the only music to be found there was of a symphonic nature. For many people, television provided all the entertainment they were going to get. Movies were not as expensive then as they are now, but still cost considerably more than during the Depression, when dishes had been offered as a lure. It was a rare family that went out en masse to live events, such as concerts or the theater—that usually required planning, considerable cost, and a trip to the nearest urban center. Coming in from the suburbs was difficult enough; for the more isolated rural areas, it was downright prohibitive. The television set was a one-time investment that brought the world into one's living room. It kept the children occupied when their mother was busy, and generally the entire family would gather round the cathode-ray tube in the evenings, when wholesome fare was mandated.

Ed Sullivan

Ed Sullivan pretty much had the entire country to himself Sunday nights at 8 p.m. on CBS. There was something for everyone, and if someone did not like whatever was on the screen at a given moment, in a few minutes it would be replaced. Sullivan booked acts of the widest possible variety, ranging from Russian circus performers to elderly vaudevillians and the principals of currently hot Broadway shows. One of Sullivan's favorites, inexplicably, was Topo Gigio, a mouse puppet with a stereotypically broad Italian accent whose wheedling tagline was "Kees me goo'night, Edd-ee." But there was more to Sullivan—possibly

Ed Sullivan appearing with one of his most popular guests, Topo Gigio. Courtesy of the Library of Congress.

the most stiff, awkward, nonphotogenic man ever to step in front of a TV camera—than a canny understanding of mass taste. As a former newspaperman (he had written a column and wielded a certain power back in the days when papers had more impact), he also had a shrewd eye for anything unusual or newsworthy. Elvis Presley's appearance on his show had galvanized the nation, even though Sullivan had decreed that the singer's erotically charged swiveling be shown only from the waist up. That epochal segment was the highlight of what may have been the first "watercooler" TV show; anyone who had the misfortune to miss it was totally left out of the next morning's workplace conversation.

Sullivan took note of a news package run on his own station that explored the burgeoning Beatlemania in England (see Chapter 4), so Brian Epstein found an unexpectedly receptive audience in the grand pooh-bah of TV variety shows. But the manager's insistence that this unknown quantity of his receive top billing took enormous chutzpah. After four days of discussions and a reduced rate, Sullivan agreed to the manager's demands.

It was a brilliant decision for everyone involved. Decades later, it was still a pivotal moment for many; as Bruce Spizer, the author of *The Beatles Are Coming*, explained: "People put seeing the Beatles on *Ed Sullivan* with memories of where they were when Kennedy was shot, or when man first walked on the moon. It was the first time Americans got to see the Beatles perform live."[3] As British photographer Robert Freeman, who accompanied the group to the Sullivan Theatre, pointed out: "Television was obviously the Beatle launcher."[4]

Sullivan's support of rock music—albeit as just one of many segments on a show that aimed to appeal to everyone—was especially important in light of how often rock performers were ridiculed by other TV hosts. Steve Allen famously intoned gibberish lyrics ("A-wop-bop-a-loo-bomp, a-wop-bam-boom") in a portentous voice, garnering laughs from an audience that enjoyed ridiculing something it could not understand. Those same words issuing from the lungs of a Little Richard were an entirely different story.

Similarly, when the Rolling Stones appeared on *The Hollywood Palace* show in 1964 alongside circus elephants, acrobats, and cowboys, host Dean Martin infuriated the group by insulting them at every possible opportunity. "Their hair isn't that long," Martin proclaimed. "It's just smaller foreheads and higher eyebrows. . . . Now don't go away, everyone," as the show went into a commercial break. "You wouldn't want to leave me alone with these Rolling Stones, would you?" Later, introducing a trampolinist, Martin cracked, "That's the father of the Rolling Stones. He's been trying to kill himself ever since."

In contrast, Sullivan actually singled out controversial rock performers for praise. After first giving Elvis his imprimatur, he did the same for the Beatles in 1964 ("four of the nicest youngsters"). Parents might then reconsider their antipathy; if Ed Sullivan liked and respected these crazy kids, then maybe they were not so bad. However, censorship issues came up when network caution intersected with performers' rebelliousness. (Before appearing on the Sullivan show to promote their hit "Let's Spend the Night Together," the Rolling

Stones were admonished to replace "night" with "time"; in turn, Mick Jagger's lascivious delivery—more of an "mm" than an actual word—left no one in doubt of his intentions.)

Nonetheless, without realizing it, Ed Sullivan became the most subversive missionary of rock and roll simply by giving it an entryway into America's living rooms.

American Bandstand

A TV show that was aimed squarely at teenagers and their music and had been since it had first begun as a local Philadelphia phenomenon in September 1952, *American Bandstand* was an immediate hit after it went national on ABC in 1957 (the hour-long show was cannily scheduled at 3 p.m., when school let out for the day). The show spawned a coterie of fans for the kids who danced on the show; they and their romances were written up in teen magazines, much as reality-show contestants are covered by today's news media. Another noteworthy achievement was host Dick Clark's insistence on racial diversity in

Teenagers dancing on Dick Clark's *American Bandstand*, 1961. Courtesy of the Library of Congress.

both performers and the televised in-studio crowd, thus giving TV an early and much-needed dose of reality.

By 1964, *Bandstand* had relocated to California and was cut back from every afternoon to once a week. Clark diversified his holdings (most notably with *Where the Action Is!*, discussed next), and the show remained popular with teenagers until the late '60s, when many were drawn to a more "underground" style of rock. *Bandstand* was the forerunner of MTV's *Total Request Live* and almost all other subsequent shows that have presented a teencentric point of view.

Where the Action Is!

Having had enormous success with Clark's *Bandstand*, ABC also picked up his next show, *Where the Action Is!*, which began airing in June 1965 on a five-day-a-week schedule. Instead of a cast of real-life teens, *Action* employed a cast of dancers ("the Action Kids") to frug and pony behind acts such as Paul Revere and the Raiders, which Clark had signed as the house band; its first record promptly became gold. Rather than use a studio, the show often went on-location to areas such as the beach in summertime or ski resorts in the winter. *Action* ran for just two years, but the Raiders are still revered by many as one of the most underrated American rock groups of the '60s.

Hullabaloo

Meanwhile, other TV networks had noticed this burgeoning gold mine and were eager to get in on the market, if somewhat clueless about how to do so. One memorable, if short-lived, entry was NBC's *Hullabaloo*, which came on the air in January 1965 and ran until April 1966. This show was hosted by a different star each week, who performed short snippets of top songs with that week's musical guests during a chart rundown. The last song of each show was usually performed on a "mod nightclub" set, with hot-looking go-go girls dancing in cages. During its first hour-long incarnation, *Hullabaloo* gave starved Brit-pop fans segments that were taped in London and hosted by Brian Epstein. By its second season, in a sign of things to come, *Hullabaloo* had been cut down to a mere thirty minutes and soon was no more. In an example of corporate shortsightedness, NBC later destroyed most of the color master videotapes to make room in its libraries, leaving only a few black-and-white kinescopes to hint at former glory.[5]

Shindig!

In contrast, ABC's *Shindig!* began as a half-hour show in September 1964 with a knockout punch, featuring such guests as the Rolling Stones, the Kinks, and the Byrds. It expanded to a full sixty minutes by its second season, although it too fell victim to cancellation in early 1966. The product of a British

TV host/entrepreneur named Jack Good, who had produced the original pilot back in 1962, *Shindig!* had innovations of its own: music came at the audience thick and fast, with only the briefest of introductions, and artists were supposed to be "live," although many, if not all, prerecorded newer versions of their hits and often lip-synched to these instead of the original record. The show also helped introduce the great soul singer Sam Cooke to a wider (i.e., white) audience, as it did with show regular Darlene Love, the powerhouse singer behind Phil Spector's Blossoms and a solo artist in her own right. This was also where audiences saw the Rolling Stones sitting at the feet of one of their idols, Howlin' Wolf, as he performed "The Red Rooster," a song they had covered. Good later went on to write for *The Monkees*.[6]

Other American TV Shows for Teenagers

In 1964, ABC aired one of the most amazing documents of early rock and soul, *The T.A.M.I. Show* (produced by Steve Binder, who would go on to wrest the famous 1968 comeback special out of Elvis Presley). This show featured performances from the Rolling Stones, the Supremes, Chuck Berry, James Brown, Bo Diddley, and the Beach Boys, to name only a few. It later had a theatrical release and is well worth tracking down on video cassette or video disc to see these artists at their peak.

Local stations, too, were vying for a lucrative slice of the teen market. Soupy Sales, a TV host for children in New York, developed a silly dance called the mouse (it had to do with shuffling from side to side while making "mouse ears" on either side of one's head with the first two fingers and overlapping the lower lip with the front teeth) and managed to promote the eponymous single by performing on the *Ed Sullivan Show* in 1965.

A former Los Angeles DJ named Lloyd Thaxton got a show on the air in that area around 1962 that mixed folk, country, and other acts with rock; the show was briefly syndicated starting in 1964, and Thaxton himself became one of the first progenitors of a tie-in marketing plan the following year when the publishers of *Tiger Beat* agreed to put his face on the cover of that music magazine. Unfortunately, Thaxton was neither particularly photogenic nor charismatic, and that idea soon bit the dust, as did his show. Another Angeleno disc jockey, Gene Weed, had better luck with *Shivaree*, which was syndicated nationally for a few years, while on the other coast, a New Yorker named Clay Cole had a brief but influential run on a local station.

Finally, folk music—or its acceptable face, such as the Kingston Trio and Peter, Paul, and Mary—was given a showcase on ABC's *Hootenanny*, which ran for a year (1963–1964). The first regularly scheduled program to feature such musical artists, *Hootenanny* sought to avoid trouble and so hit it headlong from the start when show producers tried to strongarm the left-leaning Pete Seeger and the Weavers into signing a government loyalty oath. Naturally, they refused, and were promptly banned.[7]

INFLUENTIAL BRITISH TV SHOWS

The British were quick to televise shows dedicated strictly to the new music boom. While these programs were chauvinistic enough to focus mostly on homegrown talent, American acts did occasionally appear—Bobby Darin, Ben E. King, Little Richard, the Lovin' Spoonful, Little Eva, the Four Tops, Stevie Wonder, and others all showed up on *Ready, Steady, Go!*, which also devoted an entire episode to Otis Redding. These shows popularized new acts with the English public, which in turn helped the artists' name recognition in the United States.

Juke Box Jury, which ran from 1959 to 1967, featured four panelists predicting whether a new release would be a hit or a miss. Roy Orbison was one of the guests. In July 1964, the Stones followed the Beatles onto the show and voted nearly everything a miss.

Other British TV shows devoted to pop and rock included *Thank Your Lucky Stars* (1961–1966), which was notable primarily for offering both the Beatles and the Rolling Stones their first national television exposure (on January 19, 1963 and July 7, 1963, respectively). In 1964, a short-lived show titled *The Beat Room* on BBC2 was billed as "30 minutes of non-stop beat and shake." Devoted to the R&B so beloved by the Beatles, the Stones, and the Who, it showcased both English and American artists, from Sonny Boy Williamson and Little Walter to Chris Farlowe and Long John Baldry.

However, British TV has the honor of hosting the world's longest-lived music show with *Top of the Pops*, which was first broadcast in 1964 and is still running on the BBC. *Top of the Pops* is just that—a chart-driven show that began by showcasing the Top 20 singles of the current week, growing to cover the Top 40 by 1984. In this way, the show has managed to circumvent fads while simultaneously celebrating and/or promoting them. The structure—starting from the bottom up—also creates dynamic tension by leading viewers to anticipate seeing that week's winner at the end of the show. However, the BBC is primarily a family network, and this is a family-oriented show—it banned the infamous '70s punk band Sex Pistols even when that group's record was actually in the Top 20. In fairness, the show is not called *Top of the Rocks*, and its very conservatism has helped ensure its astonishing longevity.[8]

Shorter-lived, but tremendously influential, *Ready, Steady, Go!*—which began its run in August 1963 and ended in December 1966—was the United Kingdom's biggest exponent of mod music and style, although it did not strictly confine itself to that genre. *Ready, Steady, Go!* was far hipper than the middle-of-the-road *Top of the Pops* and made a star of its attractive female host Cathy McGowan, who had the enviable job of wearing the latest miniskirts while chatting with the hottest pop stars. The "Queen of the Mods," McGowan was a nineteen-year-old former secretary who still lived with her parents and had been chosen from 600 other applicants who answered a newspaper ad; she soon had a clothing line and even her own movable doll. Because it aired on Friday evenings, *Ready, Steady, Go!* had a memorable opening catchphrase, "The weekend starts here!" For the 200 lucky souls in the studio and thousands of young Britons watching intently, that was truth in advertising. The show launched careers, fashion, and dance trends, as well as a spin-off talent competition à la *American Idol* in 1964's *Ready, Steady, Win*, with a panel of guest judges that included Brian Epstein, Mick Jagger, Brian Jones, and Ringo Starr. Still fondly remembered as the ultimate of that era's musical TV programming, *Ready, Steady, Go!* fortunately did not suffer the same mistake that was made with *Hullabaloo* in the '80s, Dave Clark of the Dave Clark Five bought up tapes and the rights to the program and has since made some of the shows commercially available.

THE MONKEES: CREATED FOR TELEVISION

In a cynical effort to capitalize on the Beatles' runaway popularity, television executives came up with the idea of a show about the members of a struggling band. There would be four of them, just like the Beatles; one would be English, like the Beatles; but this group, unlike the Beatles, did not even have to play instruments. Thus "the PreFab Four," as the Monkees later came to be derisively dubbed (as in "prefabricated" or ready-made; the Beatles were often referred to as the Fab Four, a term that may have been coined by *16*'s Gloria Stavers, about whom more later in this chapter).

Oddly enough, the intervening years have created much more respect for the Monkees than they commanded in their heyday. For one thing, their material was impeccable pop crafted by the likes of Neil Diamond, Carole King, and Gerry Goffin, with instrumentation provided by top musicians, including Stephen Stills and Harry Nilsson. The music, quite apart from its nostalgic appeal to those who were around at the time, still sounds fresh, and successive generations have rediscovered the group as if they were "real." In some ways, they were. Whereas Micky Dolenz and Davy Jones had been child actors, Peter Tork and Mike Nesmith were serious musicians.

In fact, the Monkees were far hipper than anyone thought. Almost from the start, the stars made it clear to the audience through ad-libs, a nod, and a wink that they were aware of the ludicrousness of it all. Success emboldened the four to fight for more creative control, and slowly but surely the show reflected more of who they really were. They began playing their own instruments, too. John Lennon himself once praised the show by comparing it to the Marx Brothers. The Monkees employed Jack Nicholson, then a writer, for the psychedelic opus *Head* (he also makes a brief appearance), a bomb at the time and now a historical footnote. Jimi Hendrix once opened for the group on tour, a mismatch of staggering proportion. On the next-to-last episode in early 1968, Nesmith switched identities with the truly out-there Frank Zappa, while the last show was closed by revered cult folk singer Tim Buckley singing one of his own ballads.

The Monkees perform on an episode of their television show, 1966. (Left to right) Davy Jones, Peter Tork, Micky Dolenz, and Mike Nesmith. Courtesy of Photofest.

The story began with an ad placed in the Hollywood trade papers, looking for "four insane boys, ages 17–21," which drew more than 400 hopefuls. The chosen were Davy Jones, an English singer-actor who had appeared with the Broadway cast of *Oliver!* on the same Ed Sullivan show that introduced The Beatles;[9] Micky Dolenz, a Los Angeles–based child actor billed as Micky Braddock on his early TV series *Circus Boy*; former Greenwich Village folksinger Peter Tork, recommended by his friend Steven Stills (of Buffalo Springfield and later Crosby, Stills, Nash, and Young); and Nesmith, a Texan country-folk singer. The show premiered in September 1966, and the following year, the Monkees had a No. 1 album. The hits kept on coming: according to the *Guinness Book of World Records*, as of 2003 three bands remained tied for the highest number of albums ever in the Top 200 simultaneously, with seven each: the Beatles, U2, and the Monkees.

TEEN FAN MAGAZINES

Television was not the only form of entertainment squarely aimed at teenagers. Besides exploitation flicks and the record industry itself, a new mass medium had sprung up to tempt teenagers into spending their allowance (money allotted by parents or, less commonly, earned through part-time work), one that both fed off and tried to instigate trends in pop culture: teen fan magazines.

Fan magazines have been a constant since at least the 1920s, when the newly developed film industry served as an inspiration. There were still periodicals focused on movie stars, which increasingly featured actors popular with the young market such as Sandra Dee and Natalie Wood (who once briefly dated Elvis Presley). But there was still a void in catering to music fans. Britain had the best choice of reading material, including the music-only *New Musical Express* and *Melody Maker*, as well as a smattering of teen-oriented magazines. America took note and began putting out quickie rags devoted to individual acts, as well as monthlies along the lines of *Flip*, *Dig*, *'Teen*, and *Go*. There were also *Hit Parader*, *Song Hits*, and, for the music industry itself, *Billboard* (still being published). But no magazine was the behemoth that *16* became.

16 Magazine and Gloria Stavers

16 magazine began as a quarterly in 1957 and became a monthly six years later under editor Gloria Stavers; it quickly led the teen magazine pack, with more than a million in paid circulation and a pass-along rate that quadrupled its reach. Despite its childish cover illustrations (photos of stars' heads superimposed on cartoon bodies), *16* became the ultimate authority and star-making machinery of its time. Paul McCartney, then a Beatles demigod, recalls: "We were aware of *16* Magazine even before we came to America. We knew it was America's greatest teen magazine. We knew we needed to be in it. . . . I remember Gloria as being very dignified, very professional, totally businesslike. She inspired respect from all of us."[10]

"Gloria was our one, the first person we met when we got off the plane . . . we always gave *16* the first shot at everything, mostly out of loyalty, but partly because we feared her reaction if we didn't," Peter Noone added, many years after his career peak with Herman's Hermits. "Other musicians felt that being in *16* trivialized the music, and I probably should have been concerned about that. But I never was. Herman's Hermits really *was* bubblegum music. . . . The big detriment to being in *16* is that now we're remembered not for our music, but more a creation of *16* and magazines like it. But let me tell you something. In those days we were very happy to be a creation of *16* Magazine. It got bums [behinds] in the seats, as we used to say—people sitting down at the concerts who paid the money and bought the records."[11]

Stavers had created a new medium. As critic and author Dave Marsh puts it: "When you tell people that Gloria Stavers and *16* magazine basically invented rock and pop culture journalism as we know it today, they think you're just talking about the fact that Gloria was close to Jim Morrison of the Doors, or that she ran the early story that kept *Rolling Stone* afloat, or that she was the first person to take good photographs of teen stars, or that you're being charitable because Gloria had the courage to run an obituary in *16* for her great friend Lenny Bruce. Nope. Gloria was the first real pop journalist, no qualification necessary."[12]

A former runway and photographers' model with health problems that forced her to find a less physically taxing job, Stavers began at *16* in 1957 as a clerk earning fifty cents an hour. Her tasks included opening reader mail and collecting subscription fees, quite a comedown from her previous lifestyle and earnings. The plaintive notes that arrived at the office reminded Stavers of what she had cared about as a young girl, so she compiled a list of the most commonly asked questions and set out to have them answered by the stars. She soon became editor in chief of a 250,000-circulation publication, which number she quadrupled in the next five years. Flirty coquette, hard-headed businesswoman, and a steamroller when she felt she had to be, Stavers was the prototype of a career woman decades before the term became common.

The young, almost entirely female readers devoured Stavers's prescient mix of music, TV, and film stars. There were photo portraits to tape to the bedroom wall (she took many of these herself, developing an instantly recognizable style), gossipy but not salacious features, contests ("Win a Dream Date with Bobby!"), and soothing advice columns that claimed that teenage boys and pop stars alike highly prized "personality" and "inner beauty" over more visible assets. Stavers's list format ("what's your favorite color?"), with a few modifications, is still being used today. Other magazines were forced to do "write-around" stories without actual interviews, but stars played along with *16* because of its creampuff approach.

The relentlessly positive formula of *16* is also still employed, with enormous success, by current magazines that offer stars extensive rights of approval, not only of retouched photos but also of copy, something once fiercely guarded in journalistic circles. This naturally makes celebrities likelier to grant access, which in turn brings in readership and advertising dollars. Magazine covers once featured models; now even stalwarts like *Good Housekeeping* and *Reader's Digest* put celebrities on the cover (with a feature interview or "write-around" inside) to maintain visibility. *In Style, People, Us Weekly*, and a slew of imitators have made an extremely lucrative industry catering to stars. This type of coverage was initiated by and perfected in the pages of *16*, where Stavers often changed the wording of interviews to make "her" stars sound better. Dick Clark described the beginnings of show-business synergy, then a still-unnamed concept, in talking about his relationship with Stavers: "Gloria helped *American Bandstand*, and the show helped *16*: it was a two-way street. We kept track of the kids and who was popular. She would publish stories about them; we would have them on as guests. It was a snowball effect, one augmenting the other. The show grew and so did the magazine."[13]

Stavers understood prepubescent desire as it existed during the early '60s: "Girls from 10 to 15 are in a period of development more intense than any other period of their lives," she explained. "They are hungrier than they'll ever be, so they eat more. They see something they want, a skirt or a pair of boots, and they want it more than they'll ever want anything in their lives. By the time a girl actually reaches 16, she's ready to leave the dreamworld; and *16* is way behind her."[14] She knew that her readers wanted to be best friends with a female star and longed to hold hands or obtain a chaste kiss from the male ones. So sex was only hinted at in the publication, while Stavers herself allegedly had affairs with many of the artists she touted (and a confirmed romantic relationship with Jim Morrison). But more often, she acted as career advisor, friend, and confidante, telling stars which records to release or what movies and TV roles to accept. As the *Saturday Evening Post* wrote in 1967: "Stavers's power today is truly awesome. The teenagers she influences pour about nine billion dollars a year into the economy and record companies, cosmetics manufacturers and clothing firms are all scrambling eagerly for a share of the loot. Talent agencies count the number of pages in *16* devoted to their clients as an indication of the act's popularity. Record companies seek Gloria's approval before launching publicity campaigns for their artists."[15] After she left *16* in 1975, Stavers wrote columns and freelance articles and spent time on spiritual pursuits. Diagnosed with lung cancer in the fall of 1982, she died in April 1983 at fifty-seven.

Tiger Beat, established in 1965, was a close runner-up to *16* in the fan magazine stakes. Also headed by a female editor (Anne Moses), *Tiger Beat*, as previously mentioned, tried to develop a synergy with Lloyd Thaxton similar to the teamwork successfully negotiated by Stavers and Dick Clark. *Tiger Beat's* failure only points up Stavers's uniquely intuitive understanding of her market. As the music scene continues to fragment and the Internet takes over as a method of communication, it becomes obvious that never again will another single person be able to dominate the pop-cultural landscape and consolidate power as Gloria Stavers did in her heyday.

NOTES

1. John Lennon quoted in Leonard Gross, "A Shorn Beatles Tries It On His Own," *Look*, December 13, 1966; available at: "The Beatles Ultimate Experience," http://www.geocities.com/~beatleboy1/db121366.int.html.

2. Statistics from Cobbett Steinberg, *TV Facts* (New York: Facts on File Publications, 1985), p. 85.

3. Larry McShane, "Beatlemania Strong 40 Years After Sullivan," Yahoo! Music, February 6, 2004, http://music.yahoo.com/read/news/12174263.

4. Ibid.

5. "Hullabaloo!," TV Tome, http://tvtome.com/tvtome/servlet/ShowMainServlet/showid-1759/.

6. Ibid.

7. "Music on Television," The Museum of Broadcast Communications, http://www.museum.tv/archives/etv/M/htmlM/musicontele/musicontele.htm.

8. "Top of the Pops," The Museum of Broadcast Communications, http://www.museum.tv/archives/etv/T/htmlT/topofthepo/toppfthepo.htm.

9. This show may be seen in its entirety on: *The Four Complete Historic* Ed Sullivan Shows *featuring the Beatles*, set of two DVDs (SOFA Entertainment/Good Times Entertainment, 2003). It also has the show in which Soupy Sales performs the mouse.

10. Randi Reisfeld and Danny Fields, *Who's Your Fave Rave?* (New York: Boulevard/Berkeley, 1997), p. 43.

11. Ibid., pp. 61, 63.

12. Ibid., Preface, p. xii.

13. Ibid., Introduction p. xiv.

14. Ibid., p. xi.

15. Ibid., pp. x, xi.

"FUN, FUN, FUN": THE CALIFORNIA SOUND

Reporter: "John, who is your favorite group in the United States?"
John Lennon: "I've got a few, you know. Byrds, [Lovin'] Spoonful, Mamas and Papas . . ."
Paul McCartney: "[The] Beach Boys."[1]

The West Coast—specifically Southern California—has long exerted a mythic pull on the imagination of Americans as the land of milk and honey. In the second decade of the twentieth century, filmmakers headed west to take advantage of the consistent sunny days; in the '30s, Dust Bowl refugees struggled to get to the farthest edge of the continent, where abundant oranges and avocados simply fell off the trees. California is still associated with the nineteenth-century gold rush and is known worldwide as the cradle of the Hollywood dream factory. So it was only natural that in the heady early days of the 1960s, it once again became the focus of longing and fantasy.

This time, a craze for the little-known sport of surfing helped spark the initial surge of interest. It seemed the most idyllic of lifestyles: bronzed young gods and scantily clad beach bunnies riding to the beach in their wood-paneled station wagons, where they would master the thunderous ocean, flying without wings. Landlocked Americans were suddenly barraged with new phrases like "hanging ten" (every toe over the edge of a surfboard), "shooting the curl" (riding inside a wave), and "wipe-out" (falling off the board into the drink). The music was an essential accompaniment, not just to surfers themselves but to anyone dreaming of the good life.

THE BEGINNINGS OF SURF MUSIC

Dick Dale and the Surf Sound

One of the first proponents of the surf sound, as it came to be known, was guitarist Dick Dale and his group the Del-Tones, out of Newport Beach; their first surf instrumental, "Let's Go Trippin'," came out in the summer of 1961. Dale gave his equipment so much punishment by playing loud and fast that he began working directly on development with Leo Fender of the famed guitar and amplifier firm. Their collaborations resulted in (among other innovations) the JBL speaker, the Fender Showman amplifier, and a portable reverb unit. It was Dale's use of this latter prototype that gave his music the so-called wet echo that helped define the genre. According to one enthusiast, a "true surf tune" is defined by the following guidelines: "1. It must be instrumental! 2. The lead guitar must be playing through a reverb unit, turned up very wet! 3. Band instrumentation must include: Lead guitar; one or two rhythm guitars; bass; sax and even a keyboard (electric piano or organ) and drums. 4. The music must be raw and full of energy."[2]

At the same time, but with less media attention, a group called the Belairs was popular in the Hermosa Beach and Redondo Beach area. Guitarists Paul

Dick Dale during a live performance in 1964. Courtesy of Photofest.

Johnson and Eddie Bertrand were responsible for the unique sound that then had no name, but was driving the local kids wild. They released a single, "Mr. Moto," before Dale came out with "Trippin'," yet it was Dale whose style really took off. Nonetheless, hundreds of "garage" groups began forming in Southern California. They were inspired by the music and undoubtedly fuelled by the fact that there were actually garages available for band practice.

Independent record labels, often started by the musicians themselves or the recording studios where they worked, cranked out hundreds if not thousands of singles, most doomed to obscurity from the start. That did not matter, because it was all about fun, not making money. That was not so for entrepreneurs who noted the burgeoning market and began opening clubs to cater to the surf-music crowd. Still, many groups continued to rent out local halls and auditoriums to promote their own shows, while armories hosted larger "battles of the bands."

The Ventures

Around 1959, a Tacoma, Washington, group called the Impacts decided to discard vocals after a demo tape failed to garner any interest; it changed its name to the Ventures and went into the studio to cut an instrumental track titled "Walk Don't Run," which became a regional hit after it was used as a news lead-in on a local radio station. By the summer of 1960, it was a national smash, kept from the No. 1 slot only by Elvis Presley's "It's Now or Never." The group, centered on Nokie Edwards (first as bassist, later switching to lead guitar), Don Wilson (rhythm guitar), and Bob Bogle (lead guitar, then bass), specialized in covering different genres, everything from country, pop, and psychedelic to garage and TV theme songs. In 1963, the Ventures covered the British Tornadoes' "Telstar," and while the single did not chart, the resulting album made the Top 10 and became the first of several gold records. The group saw more than three dozen albums chart before it quietly slipped into oblivion stateside in the early 1970s. However, the Ventures continue to be enormously popular in Japan, where different configurations have enjoyed great success, and the group picked up more new fans after director Quentin Tarantino featured Bogle's song "Surf Rider" in his 1994 hit film *Pulp Fiction*.

Duane Eddy

Duane Eddy was one of the most successful instrumental rockers and helped popularize the electric guitar through at least fifteen Top 40 hits between 1958 and 1963; he was also one of the first such stars to sell albums, as opposed to singles. His distinctive twangy sound came about through collaborating with Lee Hazlewood, a disc jockey turned producer (also the man behind Nancy Sinatra's classic "These Boots Are Made for Walkin'"). Most of Eddy's hits after 1958's "Rebel Rouser" were variations on a similar theme, although he was a big influence on both Cliff Richard's Shadows and the Beatles' George Harrison; in fact, both Harrison and Paul McCartney, along with Ry Cooder, John Fogerty (of Creedence Clearwater Revival), Steve Cropper (of Booker T. and the MGs), and Jeff Lynne (of ELO), helped Eddy produce an eponymous 1987 "comeback" album. Ironically, it was the British invasion that helped put Eddy out of business: in sticking to his trademark sound, he also became stuck in time. During his heyday, though, Eddy had nearly three dozen singles hit the charts, and he sold more than 100 million records worldwide; in 1994, he was inducted into the Rock and Roll Hall of Fame.

Link Wray

More original, and just as influential, was Link Wray, whose 1958 instrumental "Rumble" contains "the most important D chord in history," one that almost all subsequent rock guitarists have studied—including the Who's Pete Townshend, who declared him "the king; if it hadn't been for Link Wray and 'Rumble,' I would have never picked up a guitar."[3] Wray grew up in poverty and fear, a Shawnee Indian in North Carolina during the reign of the Ku Klux Klan. An early bout with tuberculosis during his army service in the Korean War rendered Wray's voice weak, so he made a virtue out of disability by focusing on guitar rather than vocals. He has been credited with inventing the "power chord," the basis of modern heavy rock, and achieved a special "dirty" sound by piercing the speaker cone of his amplifier with a pencil. The result was so effective that many radio stations refused to play "Rumble," declaring the song too suggestive, even though, as previously noted, it had no lyrics.

Wray was one of the first artists to create his own labels (Rumble and Vermillion), but in 1963, he signed a deal with another independent, Philadelphia's Swan Records (noted for releasing pre-Capitol Beatles singles; see Chapter 4). Swan offered Wray complete artistic control, a rarity at the time, but just a few years later, the label went out of business, and a disillusioned Wray moved to a Maryland farm. He returned to the business in 1971 with an eponymous album that attracted little attention, but a 1977 stint with rockabilly revivalist Robert Gordon drew more fans, and Quentin Tarantino also used his music in the aforementioned *Pulp Fiction*.

Jan and Dean

Dean Torrence and Jan Berry first began harmonizing at University High School in West Los Angeles. For a school talent contest, the pair created a group called the Barons, along with neighbors Bruce Johnston (later to join the Beach Boys) and Sandy Nelson; they did not win, but were bitten by the performing bug. Torrence was preparing for a six-month hitch in the Army Reserves when Berry and a friend, Arnie Ginsberg, wrote a tune called "Jenny Lee," which they took to a Hollywood recording studio to cut a demo. While they were there, a producer overheard the track and offered to add instrumentation in order to make it a "real" record. An excited Berry told Torrence to ditch the army, which he sensibly refused to do, but two months later, while still in the service, he heard "Jenny Lee" on the radio and saw "Jan and Artie" appear on *American Bandstand*. The song peaked at No. 8 in the summer of 1958.

After Torrence finished his hitch, he ran into Berry again, who revealed that his other partner had decided to get out of show business, but he had made some new acquaintances during the "Jenny Lee" period, including Herb Alpert and Lou Adler, who provided the reunited duo with a tune called "Baby Talk."[4] Jan and Dean performed the song not once but twice on *American Bandstand* during the summer of 1959, and it immediately became a Top 10

Jan and Dean, 1965. Courtesy of Photofest.

hit. The pair cut seven more singles and an album over the next three years, but moved on to the then-new Liberty Records around 1963, where they cut a track called "Linda," which made it to No. 28.[5]

That same year, Jan and Dean were booked to play near the beach town of Hawthorne; since they lacked a backup band, the promoter decided to have a local group, the Beach Boys, who had recently released their own single ("Surfin' Safari"), do double duty. They all became friends; Brian Wilson gifted the duo with a composition he originally called "Goody Connie Won't You Come Back Home," which unwieldy title became "Two Girls for Every Boy" and then, in its final, most catchy version, "Surf City." Wilson even sang on the single, and in the summer of 1963, it became the first surf track to hit No. 1 on the *Billboard* charts. The fact that Wilson's harmony was clearly identifiable confused consumers and upset the Beach Boys' label. After a brief tussle, the Beach Boys were allowed off Capitol's premises to record, which would offer Brian Wilson unprecedented freedom; this was not exactly what the label had in mind at the time.

In 1964, Jan and Dean were chosen to star in the classic concert film *The T.A.M.I. Show* and were on a winning streak with "Ride the Wild Surf," the novelty number "Little Old Lady from Pasadena," and "Dead Man's Curve." The latter tune's title was all too prophetic: two years later, while the duo were making another movie titled *Easy Come Easy Go*, Berry hit a parked truck while speeding in his Corvette. He had to be cut out of the car, was in a coma for more than a month, and underwent several risky surgeries; the resultant brain damage left Berry partially paralyzed and unable to talk. Before the accident, he had (by his own declaration) a genius-level IQ and was considered an experimental record producer, along the lines of his friend Brian Wilson, by others. As Berry, with the help of a biographer, told interviewer Larry King in 2003: "I want to be remembered as one of the best record producers of my era. . . . I'm not ashamed to admit that. I want my due, and not one bit more. I was good; and I influenced some close associates who went on to become well-known artists and record producers. I haven't had a public voice for a lot of years, and my professional legacy has become distorted and half-buried."[6]

THE BEACH BOYS

Of all the rampant ironies in this complex era, perhaps the most poignant is that of Brian Wilson, a man who extolled surfing, yet never went into the water (a cringeworthy 1976 *Saturday Night Live* sketch had him being forcibly dragged to the beach). At the time the Beach Boys first came on the scene, the Wilson family—Brian, Carl, and Dennis—looked wholesomely all-American. Time has peeled away that facade to reveal a clan so dysfunctional that it is a wonder anyone survived. The crowning irony is that the sole survivor was the damaged genius Brian. As Wilson would confess years later, "My father used to beat the hell out of us. . . . That is probably why I wrote those happy songs. I try to get as close to paradise as I can. I try to steer clear of heartbreaks. . . . Every now and then I hear voices in my head, but not very clear.

The Beach Boys (left to right) Dennis Wilson, Brian Wilson, Mike Love, Carl Wilson, and Al Jardine, 1965. Courtesy of Photofest.

I can't understand what they are saying. It's a mental illness. I have been diagnosed as a manic depressive."[7]

The Beach Boys formed in Hawthorne, California, a suburb community just a few miles from the edge of the Pacific. Only Dennis was actually interested in surfing; it was he who lent the group its original credibility. Paterfamilias Murry Wilson was a frustrated musician himself and a part-time song plugger who had lost an eye in an industrial accident; one of his favorite methods of torturing his boys, besides actual physical abuse, was to remove the glass replacement, take the child by the back of the neck, and force him to stare into the empty socket. Murry was also not without creativity: discovering that his middle son disliked raw tomatoes, he would force Dennis to eat them at any opportunity, hitting him in the head as he did so. It conditioned the boy so that the very sight of the fruit triggered his gag reflex for years. As Dennis was the most spirited of the clan, he required ever more imagination on his father's part; once he could take a belt whipping in stride, Murry would beat him with a plank or scald him with boiling water in the shower.

But Murry did love music, and he would gather the family around to sing along with him at the piano or Hammond organ as his wife played; since he could not play himself, Wilson paid for lessons and instruments for the children. (Brian's final high-school report card gave him a dreaded C in piano and harmony, along with a much better B rating for "Senior Problems—Personal Psychology.")[8] The Wilsons' cousin Mike Love, the son of Murry's sister, often joined these family songfests. Brian became inspired by Ricky Nelson when the latter sang a cover of Fats Domino's "I'm Walkin'" on his parents' sitcom; the perfect American boy, albeit from a show-business family, gave rock the gloss of middle-class respectability, with which no parent (even one as off-balance as Murry, with his music-business aspirations) could argue.

Brian explored the local music scene, including checking out Dick Dale at the Rendezvous Ballroom; and Dennis, who had discovered the surfing renaissance, with all the freedom and sex it entailed, persuaded him and cousin Mike to write about it. The track "Surfin'" (the boys rented equipment with emergency money left for them by vacationing parents; Murry hurled Brian into a wall when he found out) was released on a local label and credited to the Pendletones (a play on the name of a then-popular shirt manufacturer called Pendleton). The group was given its new name, which Brian always despised, by a label exec and signed by Capitol on July 16, 1962, on the strength of the surf-music craze. Al Jardine, who had joined in 1961, was not entirely convinced of his future in music and was temporarily replaced in the group by David Marks while he attended pharmacy school in Michigan. He returned to the fold in 1963.

Murry established a publishing company, which he called Sea of Tunes, to protect his underage sons; it also meant that he owned all of Brian's work and that of his then collaborator Gary Usher, who was eventually forced out. Brian had been approached by Don Kirshner's Aldon Music, which sent Murry into one of his predictable rages; he insisted that they "keep it in the family," ver-bally assuring Brian that they would be equal partners in the company, but his son would retain the copyrights. However, in November 1969, Murry sold the entire catalogue for a paltry $700,000, from which Brian received nothing. Brian filed suit against the purchaser (the publishing division of A&M Rec-ords) around 1991 and was awarded $10 million for "fraud and malpractice."

In mid-1962, the Beach Boys' debut album *Surfin' Safari* hit the Top 20, and roughly six months later, the sophomore effort *Surfin' U.S.A.* made the Top 10. By the end of 1963, the Beach Boys had put out three full albums, all of which charted, and were constantly on the road to promote them. In 1964, the group scored its first No. 1 single with "I Get Around" and had five records on the charts simultaneously. By this time, the strain of songwriting, producing, and performing had taken a toll on Brian, who quit the road after suffering a public breakdown on an airplane in December 1964. (Wilson's production style had been heavily influenced by Phil Spector, whose motto was "Back to Mono"; Brian could not even hear in stereo, because he is almost totally deaf in his right ear, something he used to attribute to a blow from his father.) Glen Campbell, later to gain fame as a solo artist, was brought in as a replacement; singer-songwriter Bruce Johnston, who stayed on, replaced him.

Even relieved of the pressures of the road, Brian still had to deal with the control freakery of Murry, who had assumed the mantle of manager and pro-ducer, often drunkenly barging into the studio where Brian was working to in-sult, taunt, and tell him how it ought to be done. Murry even tried to re-create the Beach Boys' success with a group he had dubbed the Sunrays and at-tempted to fashion after his sons; the Sunrays made numerous TV appearances and reached No. 41 on the national charts with a single titled "Andrea," but that was as far as they went.

Meanwhile, Brian had heard about the mind-expanding possibilities of a new drug called LSD and took an industrial-strength dose in the spring of 1965. He told his wife that he had seen God and began working on his latest opus, a song cycle he called *Pet Sounds*. Inspired by his ongoing rivalry with the Beatles and that band's *Rubber Soul*, this 1966 record was one of the most influ-ential rock albums ever released. Even at the time, it received a loving recep-tion from critics, although the American audience, which seemed to prefer the earlier records, mostly underrated it. Nonetheless, it scraped the U.S. Top 10 and went to No. 2 in England, where the Beach Boys had hired former Beatles publicist Derek Taylor to launch the record. It also earned the Beach Boys a "best-group" rating in the British *New Musical Express* year-end polls, toppling the homegrown heroes.

Among the '60s groups, the Beach Boys were second only to the Beatles in terms of chart placement and creative ability. In fact, the Beatles admired the Beach Boys so much that they were inspired to create *Sgt. Pepper* after hearing Wilson's masterpiece (after Lennon and McCartney heard *Pet Sounds* at its private London premiere, the pair reportedly went home to begin writing

Revolver's "Here, There, and Everywhere"). In trying to top the Englishmen with *Smile* (originally titled *Dumb Angel*), an ambitious collaboration with Van Dyke Parks, Wilson suffered a complete breakdown. While he was recording the track "Fire," a conflagration erupted across the street from the studio; when brushfires broke out around Los Angeles later, Brian was convinced that his music was responsible and destroyed the tapes of those sessions. When the other Beach Boys returned from tour and heard what Wilson had been doing, they argued incessantly with him over the album's themes and dense, studio-dependent composition.

In late 1966, however, the Beach Boys did release the wildly inventive "Good Vibrations," described by its author as a "pocket symphony." It became the group's biggest-selling No. 1 single, buying Wilson some time to struggle with *Smile* before he abandoned the project in May 1967. He watered down some of the songs for that year's inferior album, *Smiley Smile*. For almost four decades, bootlegged leaks and officially released scraps from the abandoned project helped create a cult of fans who were conversant with the most minute details of this fabled music. Finally, Wilson revisited the vaults with Parks, and the original *Smile*, or as much of it as could be salvaged, was released in 2004.

SONNY AND CHER

Sonny Bono came out of Detroit, a high-school dropout with a gift for songwriting and a hunger for fame. He was not blessed with either height or conventional good looks, but he did have a certain self-deprecating charm and was nothing if not ambitious. Moving to Los Angeles in the late 1950s, Bono found a way into the entertainment industry by becoming a promotions man for a small label called Specialty, where he worked with artists such as Little Richard and Sam Cooke.

By the early '60s, Bono had become something of a fixture at Gold Star Studios, where Phil Spector was creating his "teen symphonies," and during his time there as public relations man, production assistant, and backup singer, he watched and learned how to build a record from scratch. Bono began honing his songwriting skills, most notably in concert with Jack Nitzsche, another of Spector's protégés; the pair wrote

Sonny and Cher. Courtesy of Photofest.

"Needles and Pins," which became a hit for Jackie DeShannon in 1963. Her version was heard by a little-known British band, Cliff Bennett and the Rebel Rousers, which added it to their set in Hamburg. The Searchers, a better-connected group, heard the Rebel Rousers, decided to give the song a complete makeover, and released it as their third single. Their cover of "Needles and Pins," which hit No. 1 in England and the Top 20 in America, had a unique chiming guitar sound that did not go unnoticed by a still-nascent group called the Byrds.

Meanwhile, Bono saw his main chance in a quirkily attractive teenager named Cherilyn Sarkisian, even though her voice was almost as deep as his own. Although Cher (as she would forever after be known) was eleven years Bono's junior, she was just as ambitious. She had been doing some backup singing on Spector records, but soon she and Bono were working together as a duo called Caesar and Cleo. Their early efforts went nowhere, but in 1965 Bono hit the jackpot with the self-penned "I Got You Babe." (His first marriage dissolved after he became involved with Cher.)

Bono understood that image and packaging, as well as the sound itself, would take them a long way. The newly designated Sonny and Cher presented themselves as a married couple (although they would not, in fact, be wed until later on), dressed in matching bell-bottoms and bobcat vests; through Bono's lyrics, they allowed the listener into what he characterized as a misunderstood yet abiding love. Despite the fact that Sonny was considerably past youthful angst, teenagers still related to and adored the pair. Cher, with her flowing black hair and offbeat beauty, became a style icon from the moment she appeared on the scene. Sonny wrote and produced and knew how to promote the songs. They were a terrifically well matched team.

Bono's ear for a good hook led him to pick up on the Byrds's version of Bob Dylan's "All I Really Want to Do" when he heard their performance of the song at a Los Angeles club; he brought the tune to Cher, whose version outsold that of the Byrds and helped push Dylan's name and talent even further into the mainstream. By 1967, Bono was as successful as both his former mentor Phil Spector and another king of Los Angeles, singer, songwriter, and producer John Phillips of the Mamas and the Papas. Perhaps not coincidentally, all three had, and employed, beautiful wives to help them achieve their goals. Harvey Kubernik, a Los Angeles–born-and-bred writer, noted that Sonny also "co-wrote 'She Said Yeah' on [the Stones'] *December's Children* . . . under a pseudonym, 'S. Christy' . . . Christy was the name of his first daughter. Bono had great R 'n' B and bitchin' rock 'n' roll credentials."[9]

But that year, Bono finally overreached by writing the film *Good Times* as a vehicle for Cher; the director was a first-timer named William Friedkin, who would go on to much greater heights with *The French Connection* and *The Exorcist*, among other films. It was thought that the duo's teenage fans would devour them on screen, but *Good Times* was anything but for the executives that gave it the green light: it flopped miserably. Cher would indeed become a fine actress, but her success in that area was far in the future. Furthermore, the new psychedelic rock coming into vogue had pushed Sonny and Cher to the sidelines; suddenly no longer the cutting edge, they seemed rather quaint by comparison. An enormous bill for unpaid taxes helped drive the duo (by now a family, with a small daughter) to appear in Las Vegas by the end of the decade, where they were able to reinvent themselves as family-friendly entertainers.

BUFFALO SPRINGFIELD

Buffalo Springfield contained a full 50 percent of the '70s supergroup Crosby (the Byrds), Stills, Nash (the Hollies), and Young. One day in 1966, while driving on the Sunset Strip, Stephen Stills recognized a hearse with Ontario plates; having previously met Neil Young, he remembered the Canadian's unusual mode of transportation. Stills and fellow folkie Richie Furay had come from New York's Greenwich Village to the Promised Land, and within days they had a band together. They quickly built a reputation with now-legendary stints at the Whisky a Go Go and were soon signed to a division of Atlantic. The group's only pop hit, the prescient "For What It's Worth," was not even on the original 1966 debut album; it was added to a hasty rerelease album after being issued as a stand-alone single and eventually went to No. 7. Stills was inspired to write the tune by culture clashes on the Sunset Strip, where long-haired clubgoers were increasingly engaging in violent battles with the Los Angeles Police Department. The rest of the album blended folk, rock, and country (a hybrid genre later embodied by the Flying Burrito Brothers, Gram Parsons, and the Eagles). The group released three albums before personality struggles between Stills and Young caused the latter to leave; he later joined Crosby, Stills, and Nash after their first album and then slipped in and out of the structure as he saw fit. Of this particular group of artists, Young has since had the most inventive solo career; he is often cited as "the godfather of grunge." Buffalo Springfield was inducted into the Rock and Roll Hall of Fame in 1997.

JINGLE-JANGLE GUITARS: THE BYRDS

The Byrds became the first American group to compete with the Beatles on a visual, as well as a level sonic and popularized not only Bob Dylan's compositions but also the jangly sounds of the 12-string Rickenbacker guitar, also played by John Lennon and George Harrison. Their unmistakable sound influenced, among others to come, Tom Petty and R.E.M.

The core of the group—Jim/Roger McGuinn, David Crosby, and Gene Clark—had all been around the burgeoning acoustic coffeehouse circuit; the lineup was completed with the addition of Chris Hillman, recruited to play electric bass (an instrument on which he had no experience) and drummer

FRANK ZAPPA (1940–1993) AND THE MOTHERS OF INVENTION

A serious student of classical composers such as Igor Stravinsky and Edgard Varèse, Frank Zappa also came to the musical playground equipped with an acidic wit and a formidable work ethic. After scoring several low-budget films and using the wages to buy his own small recording studio, Zappa joined a group called the Soul Giants in 1964 that mutated into the Mothers (the label, correctly understanding Zappa's basic insubordination, insisted on adding "of Invention"). The group's 1966 double-album debut, *Freak Out!*, was arguably the first rock concept album, although the Beatles' *Sgt. Pepper's Lonely Hearts Club Band* would receive that credit the following year. Paul McCartney reportedly acknowledged being inspired by Zappa, as well as the Beach Boys' *Pet Sounds*; Zappa responded to the compliment by issuing *We're Only in It for the Money*, its cover a snide caricature of the one devised for *Sgt. Pepper*.

Michael Clarke, who, lacking a drum kit during rehearsals, improvised on a cardboard box. The group's first hit single, in 1965, was Dylan's "Mr. Tambourine Man," for which they were backed by professional studio musicians; they played most of their own instruments on the subsequent eponymous album and landed another hit in an adaptation of Pete Seeger's "Turn! Turn! Turn!" from the same-titled second album. The Byrds launched electric folk rock in 1966 with "Eight Miles High," which, despite its double-entendre title, lyrics, and psychedelic sound, was actually about an airplane flight. It was banned by many radio stations anyway, stalling the single in the middle of the Top 20; Gene Clark then left the group, reluctant to tour due to his fear of flying. The group continued as a quartet, but by the fifth album, David Crosby was out and Clark was back in. That only lasted a few weeks, at the end of which drummer Clarke (no relation) was also gone. In rebuilding the band, McGuinn and Hillman had the ambitious plan of melding jazz, electronic rock, and country folk, hiring the now-legendary Gram Parsons (and drummer Kevin Kelly) in 1968. The result of that collaboration, *Sweetheart of the Rodeo*, is considered the birth of country rock. The Byrds were inducted into the Rock and Roll Hall of Fame in 1991, a few months before the death of Gene Clark. Michael Clarke died two years later.

HOLLYWOOD AND THE SUNSET STRIP

In 1964, Los Angeles music impresario Lou Adler had seen a need and filled it: he had noticed adults dancing to rock and roll, something of a new phenomenon, along with discovering Johnny Rivers playing at Gazzari's Nightclub on La Cienega Boulevard. Adler introduced Rivers to Elmer Valentine, a former Chicago vice cop then in his mid-thirties who had just opened a club on the Sunset Strip he called the Whisky a Go Go. That summer, Rivers was a smash at the Whisky, and a live album he recorded there put the place on the map.

Meanwhile, other clubgoers were attracted by the sight of Whisky's female DJ gyrating in a cage suspended over the dance floor (this attention-getting tactic was later given widespread exposure when dancing girls in cages became a fixture on the NBC-TV rock variety show *Hullabaloo*). By the end of 1965, Whisky had groups like the Byrds, the Turtles, and the Lovin' Spoonful in residence. The entire Strip was abuzz; new clubs and coffeehouses were opening almost nightly, and Gazzari's relocated there. The cool place to eat was Ben Frank's (where Arthur Lee supposedly formed Love), the streets were packed with gorgeous young things, and it could take up to four hours just to cruise a mile and a half down the Strip in a Volkswagen Beetle. In 1966, Ken Kesey held the first Los Angeles "acid test," and the psychedelic scene took off.

> ### 🎵 JOHNNY RIVERS (B. 1942)
>
> Johnny Rivers was a singer and guitarist whose first successful singles were covers of Chuck Berry's "Maybelline" and "Memphis" in 1964 and a cover of bluesman Willie Dixon's "Seventh Son" the following year. He finally hit real pay dirt with his own "Poor Side of Town"; co-written with Lou Adler, it rose to No. 1 in 1966, followed at No. 3 by a twangy "Secret Agent Man," the theme to a then-current television program. Rivers later reverted to his habit of re-creating songs by others, including a cover of the Beach Boys' "Help Me, Rhonda."

The riots that inspired Buffalo Springfield's "For What It's Worth" were an explosion of pent-up energy vented by teens who felt that they were being singled out for harassment. The police were trying to keep underage clubgoers out of places where alcohol was served and were also responding to the concerns of establishment restaurateurs who were losing business because their older customers did not want to be on the same street with these "new" people. The sheriff's department began arresting the invading teenagers by the hundreds for curfew violations. On November 12, 1966, near a rock club called Pandora's Box at the corner of Sunset and Crescent Heights, a thousand demonstrators protested by throwing rocks, frightening passengers off one bus, and attempting to set fire to another. The city council demanded an investigation into the rebellion, which prompted one county supervisor to declare, "We're not going to surrender that area or any other . . . to beatniks or wild-eyed kids."[10] The council appealed to the Welfare Commission to take away the dance permits of the Strip's most popular rock clubs; that effort failed. Sonny and Cher, who had sided with the teenagers, were tossed off a float in that year's Rose Bowl Parade as punishment, Pandora's Box was demolished, and opportunistic Hollywood moguls rush-released an exploitation flick appropriately titled *Riot on Sunset Strip*.

Love and Arthur Lee

Love, led by Arthur Lee, was the first multiracial rock band of this period, with a psychedelized musical blend of jazz, samba, calypso, folk, pop, and electric blues rock (Robert Plant cited Lee as an influence during Led Zeppelin's 1995 induction into the Rock and Roll Hall of Fame). West Angeleno Lee started the band around 1965; although his early sound had been firmly rooted within the R&B tradition, he became inspired to explore rock after seeing the

Byrds at a club on the Strip. By the end of the following year, Love was the hottest group in the local rock underground, and Lee's out-there persona had people calling him "the first black hippie." This was the first rock act signed by Elektra Records; the Doors were the next, partially on Lee's recommendation. As Doors keyboardist Ray Manzarek put it: "In the summer of 1966, Jim Morrison and I went to the Whisky . . . and saw Arthur Lee and Love. It was packed to the rafters, and the band was just smoking the place. And Morrison turned to me and said, 'You know, Ray, if we could be as big as Love, my life would be complete.' "[11]

Love's first, eponymous album was released in April 1966, announced by an ominously pounding version of the Burt Bacharach and Hal David song "My Little Red Book" (originally done by Manfred Mann for the *What's New, Pussycat?* soundtrack). Love did not peak until 1967's *Forever Changes*, which is considered the group's defining moment; it is still found on most critics' lists of best-ever albums, and *Rolling Stone* calls it "one of the most distinctive masterpieces in that era of masterpieces."[12]

Yet Love was reputedly involved with heroin use, and so associated with what *Rolling Stone* described as a "disquieting clash of sunshine and *noir*" that the group intimidated most of the "flower-power" community.[13] John Phillips of the Mamas and the Papas, no stranger to drugs himself, offered Love a coveted opportunity to perform at the Monterey Pop Festival. Lee refused, which allowed Jimi Hendrix and Otis Redding to seize the moment instead.

Bobby Fuller

A Texan, like his idol Buddy Holly, Bobby Fuller had just put his classic version of "I Fought the Law" (written by the Crickets' Sonny Curtis and later covered by the Clash) into the charts in 1966 when his mysterious death ended his career almost as soon as it began. Although he also wrote and recorded original material, this single, with its ringing guitars and straightforward vocals, assured Fuller's place in the historic rock pantheon.

Fuller moved to California in 1964 with his eponymous Four, briefly flirting with the idea of surf music before settling on what would now be called retro-rockabilly; Fuller's Tex-Mex style would later be emulated by acts such as Los Lobos and the Blasters. Five months after "Law" made the Top 10, Fuller was found dead in his car, reeking of fresh gasoline. The car had not been in the lot a few moments before, and Fuller's body was already in rigor mortis (meaning that he had been dead at least three hours) and appeared battered, with bruises on his chest and shoulders; one finger on his right hand was broken, as if it had been forcibly pushed back. The coroner unaccountably judged Fuller's death a suicide: he had asphyxiated "due to inhalation of gasoline," which was also found in his lungs. As his brother and bandmate Randy asked, "Now how can a man that's dead—in rigor mortis—drive a car and pour gas on himself?"[14] Bobby Fuller was twenty-three years old. Despite the evidence pointing to likely foul play, the case remains closed and sealed under California law. Fuller may have fought the law, but the law won.

PSYCHEDELIA

The West Coast (basically, San Francisco and Los Angeles) was the epicenter of psychedelia around 1965–1966, in no small part due to a talented chemist with the unlikely name of Owsley Stanley, who mass-produced some of the purest LSD (lysergic acid) around, even though it was Dr. Timothy Leary, a former Harvard professor, who became one of the drug's most publicized exponents by urging young people to "turn on, tune in, drop out."

Not everyone's psyche was suited to experimentation: Brian Wilson, for example, was permanently disabled. Less celebrated individuals were also institutionalized, committed suicide, or harbored a popular illusion that they could fly; gravity proved them wrong. Such were the times, and before people saw firsthand what havoc these and other drugs could wreak, the music being produced by psychedelic adventurers was wildly seductive.

The San Francisco Scene

As San Francisco's coffeehouse folk scene became more electrified, the focus moved from the poet stronghold of Sausalito across the Bay and the strip clubs of North Beach to spots around the city, where old movie palaces were renovated and given new life as concert halls: the Matrix, the Avalon, and the Fillmore. In the summer of 1965, the Matrix, in the Marina district, became the first of the venues to open up to music with a performance by the Jefferson Airplane. Less than a month later, the Beatles played the Cow Palace (formerly used for livestock). That October, the Family Dog collective, headed by Texan émigré Chet Helms, promoted a show at Longshoremen's Hall that featured a band called the Great Society; the lead singer, Grace Slick, soon switched her allegiance to the Airplane. In December, the Warlocks (now called the Grateful Dead) appeared at the Fillmore.

Helms, who came to the Bay Area in 1962, had discovered the local folk scene and remembered a girl he knew back home who could really sing the blues. He went back and convinced Janis Joplin to hitchhike to San Francisco with him. Helms was then renting a twenty-five-room mansion in the Haight-Ashbury district, a rundown area where such golden-age properties were cheap, and, hoping to form a band, began holding impromptu jam sessions with the musicians who were constantly flowing in and out of the place. A lineup of sorts eventually fell into place, and Helms decided that his talent was in management, rather than playing; a name was settled upon, Big Brother and the Holding Company. The year was 1966—at the same time, Ken Kesey and the Merry Pranksters attended the Trips Festival parties at Longshoremen's

Hall, where the taking of LSD was encouraged—and Joplin became the lead singer.

Helms promoted the group in the shows he put on at the Avalon (formerly the Edwardian-era Puckett Academy of Dance), which he was renting for $800 a month. For the next two years, Helms and the Avalon featured just about every up-and-coming San Francisco band, such as Quicksilver Messenger Service, the Charlatans, and the Grateful Dead. But unable to compete with Bill Graham's greater firepower and organization (see the next section), the Family Dog moved to Denver around 1968. By that time, the area—for one brief shining moment, a community with laid-back members who shared what they had with one another, whether it be food, drugs, or lovers—had become overrun by would-be hippies who had run away from or been thrown out of thousands of middle-class homes across the nation, and had become a feeding ground for more predatory types.

What attracted all these people to the area in the first place was the freewheeling aura and crazy energy typified by the local musicians, clad in thrift-shop vintage finery accessorized by glowing, acid-pinwheel eyes. The Charlatans were among the first; chased out of the Red Dog Saloon in Virginia City, Nevada, dressed as Edwardian–Wild West freaks, they put on a series of shows at Longshoremen's Hall in 1965 that are now acknowledged as the city's first rock-dance concerts. Member George Hunter was experimenting with creating the first light shows, while guitarist Mike Wilhelm's style had impressed the Grateful Dead's Jerry Garcia. Hunter, an architecture student, created the band as a sort of conceptual outlet for his visual ideas: before it had ever played a note, he had already taken hundreds of publicity photos of the group decked out in its salvaged accoutrements of psychedelic paisley and Art Nouveau–era frippery mixed with gold rush gunslinger imagery. The band's music mattered less than its arresting appearance, which said that all bets were off and one could create of oneself whatever one's imagination decreed.

Meanwhile, the band that would come to typify the era for decades to come, the Grateful Dead, had changed its name from the Warlocks in 1965 and moved into a communal Haight-Ashbury home, paid for by LSD purveyor Owsley Stanley. The group was building its fan base by giving free concerts, and that certainly would not pay the rent. The Dead was signed in 1966 to MGM, which dropped it after hearing the demos; the group's next chance at recording came the following year, just before the fabled "Summer of Love."

Bill Graham

In 1965, Bill Graham, then manager of the San Francisco Mime Troupe, and main concert promoter in San Francisco at the time of psychedelia's rise, put together a pair of rock benefit shows, the second of which was held at the Fillmore Auditorium at Geary and Fillmore Streets, just off the black area of town. The Fillmore had originally opened in 1912, when it was used for socials and masquerade balls; then it became a dance hall until the 1940s, when it was converted into a roller rink. By the early '50s, a local promoter began booking all the top names in black music into the venue, but the place had lain fallow for several years until Graham came along. Graham became the owner of Fillmore West (which later relocated to the old Carousel Ballroom), the East Coast version (in New York's East Village), and Winterland in San Francisco, and one of the most influential rock impresario-promoters of all time.

Graham was born in Berlin to Russian Jews in 1931 and was placed in an orphanage along with his sister, the youngest of five daughters, when his father died two days after his birth and his mother was forced to seek work. Relocated to France on a student exchange program, Graham and sixty-five other children, including his sister, had to outrun invading Nazi troops, fleeing first to Spain, then through northern Africa, Bermuda, and Cuba, and finally to the United States. Only eleven survived; Graham was one of these, but his sister was not. He was raised in a Jewish foster home in the Bronx, became a citizen in 1949, and, after a stint in the army during the Korean War, moved to San Francisco to reunite with two surviving sisters who had emigrated from Israel.

In 1965, he quit a well-paying corporate job to take on the Mime Troupe. He later raised millions for causes in which he believed, such as Amnesty International, the United Farmworkers, and nuclear disarmament. Along the way, he also revolutionized how rock concerts were presented: mixing up the bill to introduce audiences to quality artists they might not have thought to discover, offering value for money by putting several top acts on one show, and catering to the artists as no one before him had thought to do. He also was a tough businessman, often reviled as much as admired (he can be seen doing his famous don't-mess-with-me routine onscreen during the Rolling Stones' documentary *Gimme Shelter*). As Keith Richards recalled: "He was one of those guys that if you didn't know him, he could really get up your nose. But then slowly, as we started to work together more and more, we started to appreciate the man's work . . . you start to appreciate what an extraordinary person he was. . . . He never yelled at me. I've seen him yell at loads of other people . . . 'Bill's having a go at so-and-so! Let's go watch!' But to me, he was always very polite. I think it's because he knew he'd get more out of me that way."[15] The Who's Pete Townshend declared, "Bill changed the way rock evolved. Without him, I would not be here. His Fillmore ballroom promotions provided a model for halls around the world in which audiences would sit, listen and applaud, as well as scream or dance. Rock became music in that process. . . . I once saw Bill take a man who had stolen into our show at the Fillmore East in '69 back to his point of entry, personally escort him out. The man had broken through a roof light on the seventh floor backstage. As he pushed him up through the broken window back onto the roof high above the busy street, he said 'Come to the front door like everybody else and I might let you in for free, you mad motherfucker.' He turned to me and said, 'He's crazy to come over the roof but discriminating—that should be rewarded.'"[16] Even those who had come up against Graham and still bore the scars mourned, along with the rest of the rock world, when he was killed in a 1991 helicopter crash; he was inducted into the Rock and Roll Hall of Fame the following year.

NOTES

1. From the transcript of a Beatles press conference held in Los Angeles, August 28, 1966, available at: "The Beatles Ultimate Experience Database," http://www.geocities.com/~beatleboy1/dbla66.pc.html. (In fact, David Crosby of the Byrds was in attendance, identified as a "mate," or friend, by Lennon. He may be seen behind Paul McCartney in a newsreel of the conference included on *The Beatles Unauthorized*, DVD [New York: Good Times, 2002].)

2. Robert Dalley, *Surfin' Guitars* (Ann Arbor, MI: Popular Culture Ink, 1996); also available at: "Imperials' Surf Band Surf Past," http://members.aol.com/SurfPast/.

3. Cub Koda for All Music Guide, available at: "Biography: Link Wray," AOL Music, http://music.channel.aol.com/artist/artistbio.adp?artistid=5875.

4. As a team, Alpert and Adler wrote several hits for Sam Cooke, including "(What a) Wonderful World." As a trumpeter/arranger/producer, Alpert had many hits with the instrumental group Tijuana Brass (in 1965, "A Taste of Honey" topped the charts). In 1962, he and partner Jerry Moss founded A&M Records, which developed a reputation for nurturing its artists. In 1966, Alpert's "What Now My Love" stayed at No. 1 for nine weeks, and he is still active in the music business.

5. In an interesting sidenote, according to Beach Boys biographer Timothy White (in *The Nearest Faraway Place* [New York: Henry Holt and Co., 1994], p. 174), the song was originally written by Jack Lawrence in 1947 as payment for legal fees owed to East Coast show business attorney Lee Eastman, and named after the lawyer's then five-year-old daughter. She grew up to wed Beatle Paul McCartney.

6. As posted on "Jan and Dean," http://www.jananddean-janberry.com/jan-larry-king.html.

7. Brian Wilson, interview by Deborah Solomon, *The New York Times*, July 6, 2004.

8. Timothy White, *The Nearest Faraway Place: Brian Wilson, the Beach Boys, and the Southern California Experience* (New York: Henry Holt and Co., 1994), p. 2.

9. Harvey Kubernick quoted in Andrew Loog Oldham, *2Stoned* (London: Vintage/Random House, 2003), p. 142.

10. From William Overend, "When The Sun Set on The Strip: Many See Street in Decline; Others Have Hope," *Los Angeles Times*, November 1981; also available at: "Whisky Archives," http://www.whiskyagogo.com/articles/811100.html.

11. From Phil Gallo's liner notes to Love, *Love Story 1966–1972*, Rhino Records 73500, released in July 1985; also available at: "Rhino," http://rhino.com/Features/liners/73500lin.lasso.

12. From Joel Washburn, "Reviews, Love, Forever Changes," RollingStone.com, http://www.rollingstone.com/reviews/album/_/id/232729.

13. Ibid.

14. Randy Fuller quoted in Aaron J. Poehler, "The Strange Case of Bobby Fuller,"

Aaron Poehler Music Journalism, http://www.angelfire.com/in2/aaronmusicarchives/strangecase2.html.

15. Keith Richards quoted in Michael Goldberg, "Remembering Bill," *Rolling Stone*, December 12–26, 1991; also available at: "Interviews," Bill Graham Foundation, http://www.billgrahamfoundation.org/interviews.html.

16. Ibid.

"THE TIMES THEY ARE A-CHANGIN' "

"When I met Dylan I was quite dumbfounded."—John Lennon
"He was our idol."—Paul McCartney
"Bob was our hero."—Ringo Starr[1]

BOB DYLAN AND THE FOLK SCENE

A strong argument could be made that Bob Dylan was the single most influential singer-songwriter of the latter half of the twentieth century. At a time when the entire world looked to the Beatles and the Rolling Stones, they in turn looked up to Dylan, and while these groups were indebted to their respective songwriting teams, Dylan did it all on his own. As Paul McCartney put it: "You've got to remember you were getting the influence of people like Dylan, who was pushing the sort of poetic boundaries. So the minute anyone did something like that, it would make you think 'oh cool, we can go there now,' like the next step. So we were always feeding off these influences, and they were feeding back off us, too. [It was] a rich period."[2] Pete Townshend of the Who also said: "Dylan's thing about writing the lyric and then picking the guitar up and just pumping out the song as it comes out is a direct guide to what will happen in music. People are going to want music to be more realistic, more honest and more of a gift from the heart."[3] Journalist Al Aronowitz noted, "Just as the Beatles had freed the sound of pop music, Bob had liberated its lyrics. . . . No other means of expression could be so searching, so outspoken, so redemptive, so rewarding, so unshackled and so true."[4]

Dylan has been analyzed, ridiculed, revered, harassed, imitated, and investigated almost from the moment he stepped on the scene; perhaps in anticipation or self-protection, he invented himself anew beforehand. Born Robert Allen Zimmerman on May 24, 1941, in Duluth, Minnesota, he was a son of the middle class (his father ran a family-owned furniture and electrical store). Zimmerman admired, among others, James Dean, the folksinger Odetta, and country legend Hank Williams, and absorbed whatever R&B music his radio could pick up from southern stations. In his high-school yearbook, Dylan declared that he wanted to "join Little Richard"; toward that dubious goal, he was already playing piano with regional bands. Around 1959, he began visiting Minneapolis on the weekends; upon graduating from high school, he enrolled in the university there, but spent much of his time hanging around Dinkytown, the local equivalent of Greenwich Village, beginning his apprenticeship as a folksinger. He had already adopted his new surname, reportedly in homage to Welsh poet Dylan Thomas.

Dylan spent some time in Denver in the summer of 1960, where his transformation continued. He had already learned about Woody Guthrie back home, but here he was free to reinvent himself as a boho-hobo, complete with an Okie accent. He had met a bluesman who played guitar while simultaneously blowing harmonica with a harp rack worn around the neck, an innovation he could incorporate. Dylan returned home briefly, just a stopover on his way to New York City. He arrived there in January 1961 and began to play anywhere—"hootenanny" nights at local clubs, even various supporters' living rooms—from Greenwich Village to Saratoga Springs, New York, up to Cambridge and back again. He even managed to land a couple of recording sessions, although not on his own: Dylan played harmonica behind the actor and singer Harry Belafonte on "The Midnight Special" in mid-1961 and did the same for folksinger Carolyn Hester in the autumn.

Dylan had long admired Woody Guthrie—one of his earliest tunes began by addressing Guthrie—and as *Time* magazine wrote of Dylan in 1963, when he was first attracting notice: "The tradition of [Big Bill] Broonzy and Guthrie is being carried on by a large number of disciples, most notably a promising young hobo named Bob Dylan [author's note: Dylan's mythmaking has already begun]. He is 21 and comes from Duluth. He dresses in sheepskin and a black corduroy Huck Finn cap, which covers only a small part of his long, tumbling hair. He makes visits to Woody Guthrie's hospital bed, and he delivers his songs in a studied nasal that has just the right clothespin-on-the-nose honesty to appeal to those who most deeply care."[5] Guthrie was just fifty in 1963 and had already been suffering for eight years from Huntington's chorea, a hereditary neurological disorder for which there is still no cure; he was then confined to Kings County Hospital in Brooklyn, to which Dylan made regular pilgrimages. Dylan was already including Guthrie compositions such as "Pastures of Plenty" and "This Land Is Your Land" in his sets and would later write a long free-association poem called "Last Thoughts on Woody Guthrie." While Dylan was there physically, others were there in spirit: Guthrie's honesty, convictions, and compassion inspired succeeding generations of songwriters to use their own work for social observation or protest.

Greenwich Village

Bob Dylan was naturally drawn to make his home and career in Greenwich Village, the heart of the folk-music scene, with its apex at the crossroads of Bleecker and MacDougal Streets. Because the Village had long welcomed freethinkers, bohemians, and outcasts of all stripes, this was a natural locale for offbeat entertainers to ply their trades. "At the end of the 1950's, Greenwich Village, in downtown Manhattan, probably had the largest number of bars, clubs, coffeehouses and strip joints in North America. . . . Most clubs held a weekly hootenanny night, in which unknown, up and coming musicians and songwriters were given the opportunity to show their stuff onstage. At the basket houses, the 'kitty girls' passed the basket, demanding coins for the folk rookies who were going onstage. [There were at least a dozen clubs that] opened their doors to the new music. It was all happening at once, a magical time and place that would never again be duplicated."[7] In Washington Square Park, musicians gathered for impromptu sing-alongs with anyone who happened by; they passed the hat for spare change, but it was not about the money, just the audience, the experience, and the sheer joy of expressing themselves. In 1961, a police crackdown on this innocent activity led to riots in the park. This creative haven was where Bob Dylan found his voice and made his reputation.

Dylan played the Café Wha? (still in existence; Jimi Hendrix appeared there

WOODY GUTHRIE (1912–1967)

Woody Guthrie was a fierce bantamweight of a man who learned how to play guitar, mandolin, harmonica, and fiddle as a teenager; during the Depression, he hitchhiked and hopped trains. Born in Oklahoma, he arrived in New York in 1941, where he and Pete Seeger formed the Almanac Singers. Guthrie also performed solo, with a guitar famously stickered "This Machine Kills Fascists," and wrote more than 1,000 songs, many of which are indisputable classics ("This Land Is Your Land" is perhaps the most famous) and several books, including the 1943 autobiography *Bound for Glory*. His reputation as a poet of the people was such that he had his own national radio show and made dozens of records before the hereditary illness that had destroyed his mother also laid him waste. The disease also claimed two of his eight children; Guthrie lost another son in a car crash and a young daughter to a fire in an eerie echo of the conflagration that had long ago claimed his sister. Guthrie made it his life's work to stand up for the downtrodden in song and prose, chastising the rich and powerful for their misdeeds while celebrating the ideals that made America the land of hope and freedom—themes that Bob Dylan admired. He was always his own man: he joined the Communist Party at the end of the 1940s, but when a condition of membership involved denouncing God, Guthrie refused. He had no truck with put-downs or empty boasts, writing: "I sing songs about . . . a world where you'll have a good job at union pay, and a right to speak up, to think. . . . I sing the songs of the people who do all of the little jobs and the mean and dirty hard work in the world and of their wants and their hopes and their plans for a decent life. I happen to believe that songs and music can be used to get all of these good things that you want."[6] Woody Guthrie, bedridden for the last decade of his life, was inducted into the Rock and Roll Hall of Fame as an early influence in 1988.

several years later as "Jimmy James and the Blue Flames"), the Fat Black Pussy-cat, the Village Gate, the Gaslight, and Gerde's Folk City, where he made his first professional appearance supporting blues legend John Lee Hooker in March 1961. Now well into his mysterious ramblin'-man persona, Dylan was constantly changing his background and family origins to anything he considered more intriguing or "authentic"; among other tall tales, he told gullible journalists that he was an orphan (his parents, very much alive, were not pleased) and how he had been traveling with a carnival since age thirteen. He was nobody's idea of an actual singer; his vocalizations had a nasal, almost whiny quality, and he later admitted as much: "What voice I have, what little voice I have—I don't really have a good voice. I do most of my stuff with phrasing. I think of myself as just having an edge when it comes to phrasing. I guess my voice sounds pretty close to a coyote or something."[8]

Yet Dylan still seemed to have an unshakable belief in his own destiny, an astounding authority for one so young, and that indefinable essence known as charisma, which was quickly spotted by John Hammond. Hammond was the scion of a wealthy family who tossed away social registry status because of his overwhelming passion for music, particularly of the African American variety. Hammond's financial situation lent him great freedom, while his ability to recognize talent made him a peerless producer and talent scout. He was, therefore, the ideal person to take the risk involved in signing Dylan for Columbia Records, a feat accomplished in the autumn of 1961.

The Role of Robert Shelton

In 1961, a symbiotic stroke of good fortune, critic Robert Shelton anointed Dylan in the *New York Times* after watching him perform at Gerde's in June of that year. Shelton, despite already being in his thirties, was writing about youth culture for the paper and, in 1959, had "discovered" the then eighteen-year-old Joan Baez at the first Newport Folk Festival. Since the *Times* equaled the establishment, its opinion carried enormous clout. During the next decade, Shelton touted other worthy artists such as Phil Ochs, Janis Ian, and Judy Collins and convinced the owner of Gerde's to institute a "hootenanny" night, allowing unsigned talent to take the open mike in hopes of being discovered. At this time, daily papers did not really cover popular music, to say nothing of folk; Dylan had no recording contract, nor was he performing much original material. Shelton's star-making review read, in part:

> Although only 20 years old, Bob Dylan is one of the most distinctive stylists to play in a Manhattan cabaret in months. . . . when he works his guitar, harmonica or piano and composes new songs faster than he can remember them, there is no doubt that he is bursting at the seams with talent.
>
> Mr. Dylan's voice is anything but pretty. . . . All the "husk and bark" are left on his notes, and a searing intensity pervades his songs. . . . [His]

highly personalized approach toward folk song is still evolving . . . if not for every taste, his music-making has the mark of originality and inspiration, all the more noteworthy for his youth. . . . it matters less where he has been than where he is going, and that would seem to be straight up.[9]

Despite the *Times* writeup, most label executives were put off by Dylan's voice and what they considered his mediocre musicianship: "He was known throughout the building as 'Hammond's folly,'" Hammond later recalled. "His genius has been the acuity of his vision of American life, his ability to internalize his observations and experiences, and his artistry in retelling them in a penetrating and dramatic poetry that overwhelms his listeners. . . . He helped shape the attitudes of a generation."[10] When Dylan's first album sold just 8,000 or 9,000 copies, another executive told Hammond that the label planned to cancel the artist's contract because it "didn't see any future for him." The producer's terse response spoke volumes about his discerning taste and loyalty: "You'll drop him over my dead body!"[11]

That first eponymous album, released in March 1962, contained mostly blues and folk chestnuts. During the next few months, Dylan became more influenced by then girlfriend Suze Rotolo to write more original material inspired by and aimed at the growing civil rights movement. "Blowin' in the Wind" was included on his second album, *The Freewheelin' Bob Dylan*, released in May 1963—the cover featured Dylan walking arm-in-arm with Rotolo—and became Dylan's most famous protest song. The same month the album came out, a song that had been left off the record ("Talking John Birch Society Blues") became a flashpoint for controversy when Dylan was banned from singing it on the *Ed Sullivan Show*. His third album, *The Times They Are A-Changin'*, was released in February 1964 and included not only the title track, a warning about the clash of generations then looming, but "The Lonesome Death of Hattie Carroll" and "Only a Pawn in Their Game," both of which addressed civil rights martyrs, and the anti-war classic "With God on Our Side." He was now the official face and voice of the protest movement, whether he liked it or not.

As the year wore on, though, Dylan was clearly feeling reined in by his own image as the folksinging prophet, and began writing more from personal experience. The material that appeared on his fourth album, the aptly entitled *Another Side of Bob Dylan* (released in August 1964), included love songs such as "To Ramona" and "Spanish Harlem Incident," as well as impressionistic excursions like "Chimes of Freedom" and "My Back Pages," both of which were covered and popularized by the Byrds. The fierce tracks "It Ain't Me Babe" and "I Don't Believe You" also had much more of a rock feel than his previous work. It is therefore not surprising that Dylan was interested in checking out the first wave of the British Invasion when it came to town that summer.

Dylan and the Beatles

According to jazz-pop writer Al Aronowitz, Bob Dylan was responsible for turning the Beatles on to marijuana for the first time, during their first meeting. The momentous event took place on August 28, 1964, at the Hotel Delmonico, still in existence, on New York's Park Avenue. Lennon, whom Aronowitz considered Dylan's Beatle counterpart, had already been influenced by the latter's music: "I'll Cry Instead" was a confessional-style song written after listening to Dylan's first album. The Beatles had champagne on hand and offered to send out for cheap wine (Dylan's favorite) and perhaps a few pills, but Aronowitz insisted on smoking some pot he had brought along. He is unsure now if it was he or Dylan who had misinterpreted a line in "I Want to Hold Your Hand" as "I get high," but they thought that the band had previous experience with the drug. Of this meeting of the titans, Aronowitz wrote: "I knew something great would come out of putting Bob and marijuana together with the Beatles. I knew the kind of influence they would exert on one another. The Beatles had become role models for the youth of the entire western world . . . whatever [they] did, the world came to accept. For Bob and the Beatles to meet didn't just change pop music . . . [it] changed the times."[12]

Before consuming this illegal substance (at least twenty uniformed policemen were out in the hallway, guarding the band), the Beatles wanted to know how it would make them feel; when Dylan handed a joint to Lennon, he immediately passed it to Starr, demanding that he try it first—which, Aronowitz noted, signified something about the band's inner pecking order. After Starr began to giggle, the rest joined in. Just as Aronowitz predicted, the Beatles' music changed after they began the regular use of marijuana and psychedelic drugs. Paul McCartney revealed in 2004 that the *Revolver* song "Got to Get You into My Life" was actually about pot: "Just about everyone was doing drugs in one form or another, and we were no different."[13] Also, as Aronowitz foresaw, as the Beatles went, so did many of the world's young—for better or for worse, as someone like Brian Wilson might attest.

More important than the marijuana sharing, though, was the music itself. "Vocally and poetically Dylan was a huge influence," McCartney would admit, and John Lennon concurred: " 'You've Got to Hide Your Love Away' is my Dylan period. . . . I'd started thinking about my own emotions [in songwriting] . . . it was Dylan who helped me realise that—not by any discussion or anything, but by hearing his work."[14]

Dylan Goes Electric

If Dylan had never done anything other than create pungent folk songs that helped spark a singer-songwriter movement, his place in history would be assured, but he had more going on. His powers peaked on all levels during the next two years, as proven by three of the most seminal rock albums of all time: *Bringing It All Back Home* (1965), *Highway 61 Revisited* (1965), and the 1966 double album *Blonde on Blonde*. On the first of this trilogy, Dylan had recently come back from London fired up by the folk rock of the Beatles and, to a lesser extent, the Animals, who had released an incendiary version of "House of the Rising Sun," also included on Dylan's first album. He and producer Tom Wilson rocked up "Subterreanean Homesick Blues" and "Maggie's Farm" before cutting the snarling pièce de résistance "Like a Rolling Stone." Radio, which previously had had an inviolate three-minute rule for singles, had to bow to demand and played this six-minute track in its entirety, rendering the time barrier irrelevant for all that came after. During the summer of 1965, the Byrds' version of Dylan's "Mr. Tambourine Man" and the author's own "Like a Rolling Stone" ruled the airwaves. As the Rolling Stones' manager Andrew Loog Oldham put it, the latter song "wasn't about dancing or driving or teenage love lost and found. . . . [It] erased every rule of pop music. It was the voice, not of a pop star, but the bitter truth. . . . Rock music was capable of far more than almost anyone had imagined."[15]

In late June 1965, appearing at the Newport Folk Festival, Dylan started out playing acoustic guitar, then suddenly switched guitars and plugged into an amplifier. Traditionalist Pete Seeger, who reportedly went berserk backstage, was outvoted when he demanded that the electricity be cut off. After Dylan and his band launched into "Maggie's Farm" and "Like a Rolling Stone," the crowd, according to Newport coordinator Joe Berk, "just erupted. Some people were cheering, some were booing. It was completely schizophrenic."[16] In declaring this one of "Rock's 100 Greatest Moments," *Entertainment Weekly* noted: "Before it, pop and protest were mutually exclu-

Bob Dylan, 1965. Courtesy of Photofest.

sive. In Dylan, they merged. Suddenly, and forever afterward, pop had meaning."[17] As another critic pointed out: "What had been music of comment and protest became songs of unprecedented personal testament, delivered with a literal and savage electricity. Dylan got booed when he showed up with rock musicians behind him, and the booing didn't let up until his great songs like 'Desolation Row' and 'Like a Rolling Stone' pierced the consciousness of a whole new generation, making everyone realize that rock music could be as direct, as personal and as vital as a novel or a poem. . . . Dylan was suddenly a singer no longer. He was a shaman. A lot of people called him a prophet. In a way, it must have been scarier than being booed."[18]

Al Kooper was there that momentous day. He had been part of Dylan's band since he pestered Wilson for a chance to play on a session, although his particular expertise was as a guitarist and songwriter (he had written "This Diamond Ring" and other songs during his Tin Pan Alley/Brill Building days). However, what was needed during this particular session was an organ part, and as Kooper remembers it: "If the other guy hadn't left the damn thing turned on, my career as an organ player would have ended right there. I figured out as best I could how to bluff my way through."[19] The song was "Like a Rolling Stone." Dylan liked what he heard, asking that Kooper's playing be turned up in the mix and also requesting his phone number, "which was like having Brigitte Bardot ask for the key to your hotel room."[20] Kooper went on to a successful career as a musician with the Blues Project and Blood, Sweat, and Tears, as well as playing as a sideman with the Stones, Simon and Garfunkel, and the Who. He also discovered and produced Lynyrd Skynyrd, and was later named to the faculty of the Berklee College of Music. He was fortunate indeed that the organ had been left on.

In 1966, the Los Angeles–based Byrds also helped raise Dylan's profile by covering "Mr. Tambourine Man" before also recording "The Times They Are A-Changin'," "My Back Pages," "All I Really Want to Do," "Chimes of Freedom," and "You Ain't Goin' Nowhere," among other songs. (It was still a few years before Jimi Hendrix's intense take on "All Along the Watchtower," so definitive a version that Dylan himself adopted it.)

Before Dylan decided to scorn almost all media, he allowed filmmaker D. A. Pennebaker to come along in 1965 on his first British tour, from which experience the latter extracted the extraordinary cinema verité titled *Dont Look Back* (without apostrophe; the title was taken from a line in Dylan's "She Belongs to Me"). The star is almost constantly hidden behind large black sunglasses, makes mincemeat out of hapless reporters with surreal chatter when he is not sulking, invents the rock video format during a sequence where he tosses handwritten cue cards as "Subterranean Homesick Blues" plays on the soundtrack and Beat poet Allen Ginsberg lurks in the background, puts down one local admirer, the folksinger Donovan, croons with Joan Baez, and generally displays what we now recognize as the ultimate in rock and roll attitude. Dylan was still just twenty-five years old.

THE BATTLE FOR CIVIL RIGHTS AND FOLK MUSICIANS' RESPONSES

After Rosa Parks, a black seamstress, sat down in and then refused to vacate a bus seat "reserved" for whites in 1955, she was tried and convicted of violating a local ordinance, sparking a yearlong bus boycott by fellow African Americans. In 1960, four black students conducted what came to be known as a "sit-in" at a Woolworth's lunch counter in Greensboro, North Carolina, waiting in vain to be served. In days, others had joined this nonviolent form of protest, including several white students; two weeks later, it had spread to perhaps fifteen other cities (Nashville, Tennessee, was one of the first), involving 500 citizens.

That same year, Muhammad Ali—then known by what he called his "slave name" of Cassius Clay—was in a whites-only Louisville, Kentucky, diner with a friend, waiting to be served. Although he was proudly wearing the gold medal he had just won in the 1960 Olympics for boxing, he was still refused the right to buy food; a group of white bikers reportedly demanded that he surrender his hard-won medal, and a fight ensued. A disgusted Ali later revealed that he had thrown the medal into the Ohio River.

In 1961, 1,000 whites attacked a church where the Reverend Martin Luther King Jr. was preaching, at a time when blacks in Alabama and Mississippi were protesting their ongoing mistreatment. The next year, President Kennedy had to order Alabama governor George Wallace to allow two black students to enroll in the state university; the year after that, black female children were killed in the bombing of a Birmingham church. Kennedy sent in Federal troops to quell race riots, many of which were televised as the nation watched in disbelieving horror.

At this time, whites in the northern states were mostly unaware of what had been going on in the South, whereas southern whites pretty much liked things the way they had always been—with blacks firmly on the bottom rung, knowing their place. (Blacks were called "Negroes" or "colored" in "polite" company then; only other African Americans used the appellation "black.") Those who tried to help literally put their lives on the line. Three civil rights workers— James Chaney, a southern black, and Andrew Goodman and Michael Schwerner, northern whites—went to Mississippi in 1964, hoping to register blacks to vote, and were murdered in the last recorded lynching. The sheriff and members of the local chapter of the Ku Klux Klan, a homegrown terrorist group, were indicted for depriving the three of their civil rights, since a southern jury was unlikely to convict on the basis of murder. It took years to convict several of the attackers and send them to prison for a few years; others were acquitted outright.

During this time frame, protest music—at first, something of a merger of gospel music and folk—began to grow and evolve. "We Shall Overcome," which became the anthem of the civil rights movement, was actually adapted from a nineteenth-century Baptist hymn.[21] But now came newer, ever more topical songs and artists, even those who had come to fame in other genres. Performers such as Harry Belafonte, an actor-pop singer who became known in the late 1950s as the "Calypso King" (although he was American-born), gospel singer Mahalia Jackson and folksinger Odetta—as well as groups such as the Student Nonviolent Coordinating Committee (SNCC) Freedom Singers— brought their personal experiences as black Americans, while folksingers such as Dylan, Joan Baez, Peter, Paul and Mary, and others helped draw the attention of a wider audience to the protest movement.

Baez still cannot quite comprehend that the terror of these early years in the movement has largely been forgotten or never even learned, at least by Caucasians. When she introduced a song to a 2003 audience by talking about a demonstration in Mississippi where police dogs were ordered to attack protesters, "Suddenly I realised I was giving a history class. After the show people came up to me and asked if I was making it up. Setting dogs on black folk wasn't in their history books . . . they didn't believe it could be true. I was shocked by that."[22]

Dylan and Political Songwriting

Dylan was becoming more active in the civil rights movement, appearing at rallies while using his songs to go after racists with a vengeance. He wrote about the murder of civil rights worker Medgar Evers in "Only a Pawn in Their Game," which was debuted at the March on Washington; he described the vicious 1955 slaughter of a fifteen-year-old Mississippi black (who reportedly said, " 'Bye, baby" to a white woman on a dare) in "The Death of Emmett Till"; in the withering "Lonesome Death of Hattie Carroll," he told the story of a servant killed by a wealthy tobacco farmer, who received a mere six months for the crime. Although the last sounded as if it might have happened during the Civil War, the incident actually occurred the very year the song was recorded: Carroll was an African American maid who did not serve a drink fast enough to suit her employer, named in the lyric as "William Zanzinger." When Zantzinger (Dylan spelled his surname without the "t") was tracked down by a writer years later, he retorted that the song was inaccurate and its author "a no-account son of a bitch. . . . I should have sued him and put him in jail."[23]

Pete Seeger performing onstage at Yorktown Heights High School in New York, 1966. Courtesy of the Library of Congress.

Folksinging already had something of a radical element, most notably in Pete Seeger and the Weavers, who at one point were the most popular singing group in America; poet Carl Sandburg proclaimed, "When I hear America singing, the Weavers are there."[24] Formed in 1948, the group performed gentle sing-alongs such as "On Top of Old Smoky," "Goodnight Irene," and "Kisses Sweeter Than Wine," but was blacklisted in the early '50s because of a possible connection with the Communist Party. Seeger, who did have a strong political streak, was briefly sent to jail for asserting his Fifth Amendment rights in front of the House Un-American Activities Committee, but his conviction was overturned on appeal.

Around the same time at which Dylan was making his weekend trips to Minneapolis, the Kingston Trio—the clean-cut, safe face of folk music, with a 1958 hit in the innocuous "Tom Dooley"—was playing San Francisco's Purple Onion, blissfully ignorant of the undercurrents that would soon upend its career. "Politically, we didn't know what was going on," the Trio's Dave Guard would later admit. "We didn't care about McCarthyism . . . we were just starting in the world, full of enthusiasm, in the bloom of our cuteness."[26] Guard left the group in 1961, shortly before it had another hit with—ironically—Seeger's antiwar ballad "Where Have All the Flowers Gone?" The bland was beginning to wear thin, and the antidote was already on his way.

In 1963, a crowd of 200,000 converged on Washington, D.C., in a march for civil rights. Dylan, Seeger, folksinger Joan Baez, and the folksinging group Peter, Paul, and Mary joined Dr. Martin Luther King Jr.—who here gave his immortal speech, "I Have a Dream"—in singing "We Shall Overcome." Peter, Paul, and Mary also sang their hit version of "Blowin' in the Wind," then No. 2 on the pop charts right behind Martha and the Vandellas' "Heat Wave," slightly ironic in light of the racial tone of the times.

PETE SEEGER (B. 1919)

Pete Seeger was the son of a musicologist. He began playing the banjo as a teenager, when he also assisted famed folk archivist Alan Lomax on song-collecting forays into the South. In 1941, he formed the Almanac Singers, a trio specializing in antiwar and pro-union material; World War II and an army stint put an end to that, but then the Weavers were created. After leaving the latter group in 1959 when the others recorded a cigarette commercial over his objections, Seeger went on to record for Columbia (he was signed by his old friend John Hammond) and wrote or co-wrote folk classics such as "If I Had a Hammer," "Where Have All the Flowers Gone?" "Turn! Turn! Turn!" and "The Bells of Rhymney" (the latter two became major hits when they were recorded by the Byrds in the '60s). During the '60s, Seeger was as fiery as ever, attacking Vietnam War policies in "Waist Deep in the Big Muddy" and refusing to be censored or muted. In 1994, he received the nation's highest artistic honor, the Presidential Medal of the Arts, and in 1996, he was inducted into the Rock and Roll Hall of Fame as an early influence. Perhaps more important, generations of children have been introduced to singing and folk music through his work.[25]

Joan Baez

During this period, Dylan and Joan Baez were romantically involved. Accounts differ as to whether the relationship began for reasons of opportunism on his part, but it could just as easily have been physical attraction and/or true love. They had a less-than-amicable parting of the ways after a few years.

Baez (born in 1941) was a superstar at this point, having taken the first Newport Folk Festival by storm in 1959 and becoming "the first post–rock 'n'

Joan Baez and Bob Dylan, 1963. Courtesy of Photofest.

roll youth idol, the patron saint of the new folk music . . . fans would ask for locks of her hair."[27] She had a pure, soaring soprano, the appearance of a Mexican-Scottish Madonna, and the liberal/pacifist political convictions of a Quaker, the faith in which she had been raised. Her first album came out in October 1960, but it was her second, released the following September, that really put Baez on the map; those two and the third (released in September 1962) were all certified gold, and all stayed on the charts for two years; the last, *Joan Baez in Concert*, made it to a rather amazing No. 10 on the pop albums chart. She became the most visible proponent of folk, lending her support, presence, and stirring voice to antiwar and civil rights rallies across the nation.

Baez's career was launched with strictly traditional folksongs, but after meeting Dylan, she moved into covering newer material by him and the emerging breed of socially conscious artists, doing a version of Phil Ochs's "There But For Fortune" on *Joan Baez 5* (released in the autumn of 1964). She also befriended the Beatles, in particular John Lennon, but did not start to write and record her own songs until sometime in the early 1970s (her 1975 autobiographical account of her affair with Dylan, *Diamonds and Rust*, became a best-seller).

MORE FOLK MUSICIANS OF THE '60s

Fred Neil

One major unsung hero of the folk movement was a singer-songwriter named Fred Neil, who knew and was known by everybody who mattered: at some Café Wha? gigs in 1961, Dylan was Neil's backup harmonica player. As Richie Havens wrote in his autobiography, "All somebody had to say was 'Neil and [Dino] Valenti are playing tonight' and the in-crowd would drop everything to be there. . . . The truth is that Fred was a major influence on everybody in the Village music scene and probably would have been among the most recognized singer-songwriters in the world, if two things hadn't happened to him. He got screwed terribly by a lot of people in the music industry. And like so many artists under siege from the insincerity of the business, Fred took a wrong turn to hard drugs out of deep despair and nearly lost his life. . . . While few people in today's music world have any clue what they missed, the music he made is still there."[28]

Neil wrote many songs, including the wistful "Everybody's Talkin'," which became a Top 10 hit when Harry Nilsson recorded it as the theme for the 1969 film *Midnight Cowboy*. As the Lovin' Spoonful's John Sebastian, who also used to accompany Neil on harmonica, put it: "The thing that was so different about Fred was that he . . . was one of the first guys that was crossing racial boundaries in his style. . . . Some of his friends, like [folksingers] Odetta and Len Chandler and some of the black musicians that were our first real close friends, had an affinity with Fred that they didn't have with the New York musicians."[29]

Neil was born in Ohio, but raised in St. Petersburg, Florida. He may have gotten the travel bug from working the road with his father, a jukebox salesman; at twenty-one, he went to New York to land a songwriting deal in the Brill Building, where he composed "Candy Man" (the B side of Roy Orbison's No. 1 hit "Crying") and "Come Back Baby," recorded by Buddy Holly. He did session work on guitar with, among others, Paul Anka and Bobby Darin and recorded a 1960 demo with Doc Pomus for an Elvis Presley soundtrack, which was never used. Neil migrated downtown to the Village, where he became the emcee at Café Wha? (Bill Cosby was one of the club's early comic performers) and began making his own particular brand of music, often on a 12-string guitar. His unusual sound was generally described as an amalgam of folk, blues, jazz, pop, and rock. Jefferson Airplane's Paul Kantner pointed out, "Freddie was very evocative of a certain soulfulness that was generally lacking in the folk movement. His was deeper than most, came from an unexplained source, and therefore was sort of semi-mystical to us sort of whitebread middle-class children. Freddie just led us to places that normal folksingers didn't go."[30] Neil was signed to his own recording contract in 1964, but a growing addiction to heroin made him only erratically employable.

Donovan

Born Donovan Leitch in Scotland in 1946, Donovan began performing at age eighteen and made his first Newport Folk Festival appearance the following year (1965); he was quickly dubbed the "British Bob Dylan," although he possessed none of Dylan's nasty streak, nor, as it turned out, his eloquence or staying power. As Donovan later told the BBC, "For me [Dylan] was a spearhead into protest, and we all had a go at his style. I sounded like him for five minutes; others made a career of his sound."[31]

Donovan was soon experimenting with psychedelia ("Mellow Yellow" was supposedly about smoking banana peels, a short-lived and ineffective fad, and featured Paul McCartney on uncredited background vocals) and spending time with the Beatles. He contributed a line to "Yellow Submarine" and also traveled with them to India in 1967 on their Maharishi sojourn, during which time Brian Epstein died and much of the so-called *White Album* was written. "While we were out there," Donovan recalled, "I taught John the folk finger-picking style that I had learned, and he then taught it to George. You can hear John use it on the *White Album* . . . he used it when he was writing 'Dear Prudence.'"[32] Donovan maintained a core fan base for decades, which allowed him to put out a steady stream of albums and frequently perform live. He retired from music for a while in the '80s, but made a minor comeback in the mid-'90s; he now often appears at various Beatlefests to discuss his association with the Fab Four.

Judy Collins

Joan Baez was not the only folk goddess on the scene; Judy Collins (born in 1939) was another important figure, something of a den mother to the many artists and wannabes drifting around the Village. She had released her first album in 1961, while still in her early twenties. "Her apartment was the social hub of folk music on the east coast," Al Kooper recalls. "She was *always* helping somebody out . . . if you were an up-and-coming writer, she would always be one of the first to showcase your material."[33] Collins was equally generous to females whom she might well have considered competitors. After Al Kooper met Joni Mitchell and recognized her talent, he introduced her to Collins, who recorded Mitchell's "Both Sides Now" on her breakthrough album *Wildflowers* (1967). With impeccable taste, Collins covered songs by Dylan, Lennon, Ochs, and Leonard Cohen and also popularized the song "Thirsty Boots," written by Eric Andersen, a singer-songwriter out of Pittsburgh via San Francisco.

Eric Andersen

During his early education in Buffalo, New York, Eric Andersen (born in 1943) taught himself piano and guitar while devouring the writings of Rimbaud, Kerouac, Baudelaire, and Allen Ginsberg; he was also knocked out by the Everly Brothers when they played at his high-school gym and by seeing Elvis Presley (wearing his famous gold lamé suit) at a local auditorium. After two years of premed studies, Andersen hitchhiked westward to try his folksinging chances in the coffeehouses of North Beach. He met the Beat Generation poets he adored, including Lawrence Ferlinghetti, Kerouac sidekick Neal Cassady, and Ginsberg. After one of Andersen's North Beach sets in the fall of 1963, Tom Paxton, who was in the audience, invited him to New York. Andersen readily slipped into the group of promising performers who orbited around Dylan; after his first city gig opening at Gerde's, Robert Shelton wrote that he had "that magical element called star quality,"[34] and he was on his way. Al Kooper and the Blues Project covered his "Violets of Dawn"; he was invited onstage by Phil Ochs at the Philadelphia Folk Festival, where the two harmonized on "Thirsty Boots" (inspired by the Freedom Riders); he went to England and was being eyed as a possible acquisition by Beatles manager Brian Epstein before the latter's untimely death. Andersen even appeared in an Andy Warhol film (*Space*, 1966). Unlike some of his contemporaries, Andersen made it through the vagaries of his early career and has continued writing, recording, and performing.

Buffy Sainte-Marie

Buffy Sainte-Marie, adopted soon after her birth in 1941, was a Canadian Cree Indian with a doctorate in fine art from the University of Massachusetts to go with her degrees in teaching and Oriental philosophy. At a time when Caucasians were still largely under the impression that Indians were blood-thirsty savages who had been justly eliminated to create the "real" America, Sainte-Marie was a wake-up call. After graduating in 1962, she began touring all over the globe and was voted "Best New Artist" by music trade magazine *Billboard* upon the release of her first album. Elvis Presley, Cher, and Barbra Streisand all covered Sainte-Marie's love ballad "Until It's Time for You to Go," and her "Universal Soldier" became an anthem of the antiwar movement. Later, during the Lyndon Johnson years, she was on a blacklist of artists (such as the outspoken Eartha Kitt) whose music "deserved to be suppressed."[35] Sainte-Marie and her son Dakota Starblanket Wolfchild appeared on the children's TV series *Sesame Street* for five years. In 1982, she won an Academy Award for her song "Up Where We Belong." She still lectures, teaches, performs, and creates digital art and music.

Ian and Sylvia

Two other Canadian natives who came on the Village scene were Ian Tyson (born in 1933) and Sylvia Fricker Tyson (born in 1940), who began performing as a team in 1960; soon after they came to New York, they were snapped up by manager Albert Grossman, who also helmed the careers of Dylan, Odetta, and Peter, Paul, and Mary. They had been performing traditional folk songs, but Ian began writing original material with an eye toward Dylan's success; he was good enough at it that royalties from "Four Strong Winds" allowed him to buy a ranch and get out of the music business (he returned to performing years later). Sylvia also did well in that area; her yearning "You Were on My Mind" became a No. 3 hit in 1965 for We Five. The pair, wed in 1964, split up personally and professionally in 1975; their relationship, along with much of the early '60s folk scene, was satirized in the 2003 Christopher Guest film *A Mighty Wind* (actress Catherine O'Hara, who played "Mickey" to Eugene Levy's "Mitch," reportedly consulted Sylvia before filming began).[36]

Simon and Garfunkel

Art Garfunkel (vocals) and Paul Simon (singer, songwriter, and guitarist) were both born in 1941 and were childhood friends from Forest Hills, a middle-class part of the New York suburb of Queens; they had scored a minor late '50s hit as Tom and Jerry with an Everlys-style track called "Hey Schoolgirl." The pair broke up, but reconvened as a folk duo around 1963, flopping with their first album, *Wednesday Morning 3 a.m.*, in 1964. However, after producer Tom Wilson (who had been instrumental in Dylan's early career) added electric guitars, bass, and drums to the single "Sounds of Silence," it became a No. 1 hit in early 1966. Simon and Garfunkel's collegiate angst and sweet harmonies were the antidote for those who found Dylan's nasality off-putting; their album *Parsley Sage Rosemary and Thyme*, released later the same year, was a critical and commercial success and placed them firmly atop the folk-pop pantheon.

Tom Paxton

Tom Paxton, whose main stock-in-trade was topical humor, was one of a handful of folkies who both succeeded in music and managed to survive the '60s intact. Born in 1937 in Chicago and raised in Oklahoma, Paxton came to New York courtesy of the U.S. Army, where he played Village clubs like the Gaslight and the Bitter End to build an audience before releasing his first album in 1965. In the four decades since, he has continued to write (not only songs, but also books for children), record, tour, and inspire other generations. As riot-grrl artist and Righteous Babe label founder Ani DeFranco noted, he "embodies the spirit of folk music in the most beautiful sense. Not just in his song crafting, his work ethic, his politics and his dedication to people's music, but also in his kind and generous heart. When I first started playing folk festivals, I was all of eighteen, shaved-headed and politically outspoken. Many people in the folk community at that time seemed defensive and threatened by me, but I remember Tom was a notable exception. He was nothing but warm, welcoming and supportive to me from the git-go. He's the coolest."[37]

The Lost Ones: Tim Buckley, Phil Ochs, and Tim Hardin

Less heralded by the mainstream, but fiercely adored by the cognoscenti, were three doomed singer-songwriters: Tim Buckley, Phil Ochs, and Tim Hardin. Although Buckley was signed out of Los Angeles and originally hailed from Orange County, California, he had knocked around the Village for a while and had a New York kind of sensibility. His debut album was released in 1966, and for a while he was hailed as one of the best new voices of his generation. But whether the cause was his uncompromising personality, his love of jazz, or his heavy drinking, somewhere down the line Buckley and his career went off the rails. (The British band Starsailor took its name from one of his best-realized albums, released in 1970.) Buckley died at twenty-eight of an accidental heroin overdose.[38]

The tale of Phil Ochs also began with great promise and ended in tragedy. A native Ohioan, he moved to New York in 1960 and landed his first paying gig opening for John ("Jeep") Hammond at Gerde's Folk City, the same club where Dylan got his start. His topical, well-written songs were published in the tiny but influential folk magazine *Broadside* and led to an invitation to perform at the 1963 Newport Folk Festival alongside Dylan, Baez, and Seeger. From there, he won a recording contract. Like Dylan, Ochs wrote a song about Medgar Evers, included on his first album (1964's *All the News That's Fit to Sing*), and he too was down South on a concert tour and voter registration drive the same summer the three civil rights workers were slain. By his second album, *I Ain't Marching Anymore* (1965), Ochs was staking out his personal protest territory in the Vietnam War with the title track and the sarcastic "Draft Dodger Rag." As the decade wore on, Ochs's political involvement grew deeper, and his music continued to explore social issues on a more personal scale: "There But For Fortune" pointed out that it only takes a bad turn of luck to end up on the street, while "Outside of a Small Circle of Friends" was inspired by the 1964 stabbing death of Kitty Genovese in Queens, New York, as thirty-eight of her neighbors watched from windows but chose not to intervene.

Yet Ochs's gift for irony (one of his earliest songs was titled "Love Me, I'm a Liberal") was sadly lost on the folk crowd, which was bewildered when he turned up at Carnegie Hall in a gold lamé suit by famed cowboy tailor Nudie. His pop-art concept/commentary was meant to evoke Elvis as Che Guevara—music fomenting a revolution—but the audience failed to catch on to that idea and his later work, as well. Disillusioned and discouraged by the waning trajectory of his career, constant comparisons to Dylan (where, like everyone else, he was found wanting), and ongoing political turmoil, Ochs soon devolved into drinking, watching TV, and traveling. On a trip to South Africa, his vocal chords were ruptured during a robbery, destroying his top register, which caused him to sink into a deeper depression. At thirty-five, Ochs hanged himself.

Tim Hardin was a singer-songwriter whose first album came out in 1966 after he was "discovered" by Lovin' Spoonful producer Erik Jacobsen. In fact, Hardin, then twenty-four, had already been knocking around the Village for a while, performing blues covers. Born in Oregon, he had moved to the East Coast after a stint in the U.S. Marines; his early recordings were not released until after that first album made some impression, particularly with the poignant "Reason to Believe" (later covered by Rod Stewart). Hardin also wrote and recorded "If I Were a Carpenter," which went into the Top 10 in 1966 when it was covered by Bobby Darin, but, to paraphrase Ochs, Hardin remained relatively unknown outside of a small circle of fans. Embittered by what he perceived as a lack of success, Hardin was experiencing problems with drink and drugs as early as 1970. Ten years later, after releasing several more albums to increasing public disinterest, Hardin died of a heroin overdose just a few days after his thirty-ninth birthday.[39]

The Lovin' Spoonful (left to right) John Sebastian, Joe Butler, Zalman Yanovsky, and Steve Boone, 1966. Courtesy of Photofest.

 JUG-BAND MUSIC

Skiffle was the British version of jug-band music; both may be played on noninstruments such as washboards, tubs, combs, and jugs. Jug-band music originated with black vaudevillians unemployed after that form of entertainment fell out of favor; they would play on street corners for tips, improvising instrumentation in a musical format based on blues, ragtime, and Appalachian folk. The Rooftop Singers had a hit in 1963 with "Walk Right In," a song written in 1929 by Gus Cannon, who died in poverty at 104. Other '60s proponents of the sound included the Jim Kweskin Jug Band and the Even Dozen Jug Band, both of which included Maria Muldaur. John Fogerty and Creedence Clearwater Revival paid tribute to the style in the song "Willie and the Poor Boys."[41]

The Lovin' Spoonful

On Hardin's first album, he was backed on harmonica by Lovin' Spoonful leader John Sebastian. The Spoonful was working the sunnier side of the street; one grumpy critic called them "a crafty combination of infernal affability, cartoon costumes, rock and roll and jug-band music."[40] The foursome (singer-songwriter John Sebastian, born in 1944; guitarist Zal Yanovsky, born in Toronto, Canada, the same year; bassist Steve Boone, born in 1943; and drummer Joe Butler, born the same year) did wear tie-dye and striped shirts, but between 1965 and 1967 their cheery, sometimes wistful music was a much-needed antidote to gloomier prognostications. "Do You Believe in Magic?," "Daydream," "Darling Be Home Soon," and especially "Summer in the City" still hold up as shimmering slices of a

particular place and time. Sebastian went on to a moderately successful solo career (including writing the theme song for the TV series *Welcome Back, Kotter*),
and the Lovin' Spoonful was inducted into the Rock and Roll Hall of Fame in
2000, in time for Yanovsky to enjoy the accolade before his death from a heart
attack in December 2002.

The Mamas and the Papas

Sebastian and Yanovsky were the link between the Lovin' Spoonful and the
Mamas and the Papas; both men had been in the latter's previous incarnation,
known as the Mugwumps before a fortunate name change. (The autobiographical Mamas and Papas song "Creeque Alley" is a neat synopsis of these
interwoven relationships.) In the early part of the '60s, "Papa" John Phillips
(1935–2001) formed a folk trio called the Journeymen with Scott McKenzie
(born in 1944), who would later have a hit with the pair's sentimental paean to
hippiedom, "If You're Going to San Francisco (Be Sure to Wear Some Flowers
in Your Hair)." When the Journeymen's album flopped, Phillips disbanded the
group and formed the New Journeymen, which included model-singer Michelle
Gilliam (born in 1944). After Phillips's first marriage foundered, he wed
Gilliam.

Cass Elliot (1941–1974) had already tasted a bit of success with some off-
Broadway musical work and, as a member of the Big Three, had done rather
well at the Village's Bitter End, leading to a few albums, singles, and commer-
cials. The Big Three later took on, among others, Sebastian, Yanovsky, and a
singer named Denny Doherty (born in 1941), whose voice Phillips would later
describe as "an instrument of breathtaking delicacy and precision."[42] The
group had a nice brew of electric/folk starting to jell, but it fell apart after no
contracts were forthcoming. Elliot had moved on to singing jazz when Doherty
brought the Phillipses to see her perform at a gig in Washington, D.C., and despite John's initial reservations over her outsize shape and voice, she was in. In
late 1965, they finally got their act together and headed west, only to be shot
down by a likely manager, whose group the We Five had a similar-sounding hit
with "You Were on My Mind." But an old friend of Phillips (Barry McGuire,
who scored with "Eve of Destruction" in 1965; see Chapter 9) put the group in
touch with impresario Lou Adler, the head of We Five's label. He signed them
right away, and by early 1966, "California Dreamin'" was climbing the charts,
with the debut album *If You Can Believe Your Eyes and Ears* soaring right behind.

Internal conflicts soon began to tear the group apart; the twin demons of
love and jealousy were exacerbated by drugs and success. Elliot was crazy about
Doherty, who loved her platonically but was sleeping with Michelle Phillips,
which did not endear either party to John Phillips (although he did generously
credit Doherty as co-author of "I Saw Her Again Last Night" for inspiring him
to write it in the voice of the Other Man). Soon after "Monday, Monday"
came out and almost instantly lodged at No. 1, Michelle started seeing Gene

Clark of the Byrds, making both Phillips and Doherty fairly unhappy. John's solution was to take LSD every time he heard Michelle's name, and he then took a vote on whether to throw her out of the group. The other two agreed (Elliot was still bitter about the affair with Doherty). That summer of 1966, while the group was riding high on the charts, Michelle was no longer a Mama. She did, however, rejoin the group in time to close 1967's Monterey International Pop Festival, the watershed event organized by John Phillips and Lou Adler and immortalized in the 1968 D. A. Pennebaker time-capsule film *Monterey Pop*. The Mamas and the Papas were inducted into the Rock and Roll Hall of Fame in 1998.

As singer-songwriters, inspired by Bob Dylan and his acolytes, moved further away from the "moon-June-spoon" type of innocent love songs towards more candid personal expression, it was inevitable, but shocking nonetheless, when some artists began to push previously acceptable boundaries by using words and ideas formerly forbidden within the context of popular music. Besides politically charged rhetoric, they also made explicit reference to illegal drugs and sex, refusing to self-censor even the most extreme of human experience. Given the climate of the time, it is rather remarkable that these artists recorded any material at all, because they could not realistically expect to land a label contract with this sort of music, never mind be heard on the radio. Therefore stardom, as it was understood then, was not their primary goal; rather, they were defiantly making a statement for themselves, friends and self-selecting audiences. Yet, much as Dylan had found freedom and recognition using Greenwich Village—that historic hotbed of radicalism—as a home-base and springboard, so did cutting-edge bands like the Fugs and the Velvet Underground.

The Fugs

In the East Village during the mid-'60s, a curious group called the Fugs was creating all kinds of havoc. That these "beatnik-turning-hippie poet-politicos . . . were hardly musicians at all was definitely kind of punk, and crucial to their sound and achievement," as rock critic Robert Christgau says, adding: "The thing you have to accept about the Fugs is that they'll never sound as good as you hope. . . . However obscure the Fugs' corner of rock history may seem,

---

LOU ADLER (B. 1933)

Lou Adler deserves a chapter to himself as an all-around mover and shaker. He collaborated with Sam Cooke and artist/label mogul Herb Alpert (with whom Adler also co-managed Jan and Dean) on "(What a) Wonderful World," a No. 12 pop hit in 1960, and co-wrote "Poor Side of Town" with Johnny Rivers, a No. 1 hit in 1966. Adler (married to Shelley Fabares, who starred on TV's *The Donna Reed Show* and had a No. 1 hit with "Johnny Angel" in 1962) founded two record labels and co-produced the 1967 Monterey Pop Festival, as well as the film of that epochal event. Adler also produced the 1971 Carole King album *Tapestry*, which became one of the most critically and commercially successful albums ever released, and executive-produced 1975's *The Rocky Horror Picture Show*, which became a popular "midnight movie," and the Cheech and Chong film *Up in Smoke* (1978).

Ed Sanders and Tuli Kupferberg are bigger than that. We're lucky they passed through."[43] The Fugs were indeed almost unlistenable in a musical sense, but they were certainly inspirational in terms of sheer funky freedom—the spiritual fathers of the Mothers of Invention, as well as the Dead Kennedys and any number of other political/sexual musical outlaws.

The Fugs were led, if that is the correct word for such an anarchic group, by Sanders (born in 1939) and Kupferberg (born in 1923), later aided and abetted by banjo and fiddle player Peter Stampfel, guitarist Steve Weber, and drummer Ken Weaver. In Sanders's words, inspiration came "from a long and varied tradition, going all the way back to the dances of Dionysus in the ancient Greek plays and . . . the famous premier performance of Alfred Jarry's *Ubu Roi* in 1896, to the *poèmes simultanés* of the Dadaists in Zurich's Cabaret Voltaire in 1916, to the jazz-poetry of the Beats, to Charlie Parker's seething sax, to the silence of John Cage, to the calm pushiness of the Happening movement, the songs of the Civil Rights movement, and to our concept that there was oodles of freedom guaranteed by the United States Constitution that was not being used."[44]

The group's first album, *The Village Fugs*, was released in mid-1965 on a small folk label; it featured tunes like "I Couldn't Get High," "Boobs a Lot," and "Slum Goddess (of the Lower East Side)." The second album, recorded for a different independent label in 1966, included the classic Vietnam War satire "Kill for Peace." The group was then signed by Atlantic, which refused to release the resulting record; it went on to Warner Brothers and was unceremoniously fobbed off onto a subsidiary, where four more albums were recorded. The group as an entity was finished by 1970. Kupferberg summed up the group's attitude: "We were poets. Poets can say whatever they want about anything. So we felt that we did that with music. Pop music from the '20s to the '60s was mostly courtship music. In pop music, the Beatles sang about everything in life and so did everyone else, including us."[45]

The Velvet Underground

The Beatles, the Rolling Stones and Bob Dylan may be the holy trinity of '60s rock, but . . . seminal New York outfit the Velvet Underground can claim to have shaped the future of music almost as significantly as their more successful contemporaries . . . creating urban street tableaux mired in the dark appeal of hard drugs, sadomasochism, prostitution and gender-bending. The Velvets released only four albums during their short lifespan (1966–71), radio ignored them, and not many people bought them. But, with their Warhol-endorsed chic, poisonous attitude, atonal vocals, shuddering rhythms and thrashy distorting guitars, they became [the] godfathers of art-rock, punk, indie and goth. . . . the Velvet template can be detected in every band who have favoured noise, attitude, experimentalism (and perhaps the vampiric appeal of wearing sunglasses at night). . . . It is probably fair to say that no other band ever achieved so little success in their time and yet exerted such a vast influence on those who followed.[46]

At the Café Bizarre on Bleecker Street in 1966, pop artist Andy Warhol (1928–1987) was watching a group that called itself the Velvet Underground, after the title of a book about sexual fetishes. The band had been formed the previous year on the Lower East Side by Lou Reed (born in 1942), employed as a teen-pop songwriter while working on more personal material such as "Heroin"; John Cale (born the same year), a bassist and viola player who had been classically trained; guitarist Sterling Morrison (1942–1995); and drummer Angus MacLise (born in 1938). Writer Al Aronowitz was then, in a conflict of interest, managing a folk-rock band called the Myddle Class; he booked the Velvets as a support act for a high-school gig in Summit, New Jersey. It paid $75, took place on November 11, 1965, and marked one of the first appearances anywhere by a female rock instrumentalist: MacLise had gone to India and was replaced by Maureen "Moe" Tucker (born in 1945), who had first been asked to loan her equipment and then to join the band.

Warhol, intrigued by the group's heady subject matter and experimental improvisations, allowed the band to rehearse at his studio space, the Factory. He also built a multimedia fantasia around them, "The Exploding Plastic Inevitable," showing slides and film clips as his anointed "superstars" wielded whips and props and/or danced seminaked during the band's sets. Rolling Stone Brian Jones came by the Factory with a Teutonic goddess who called herself Nico; Warhol made her the Face of "his" band. The Exploding Plastic Inevitable undertook a six-month stint at the Dom on St. Mark's Place in the East Village in 1966, turning what had previously been a quiet Polish-Ukrainian neighborhood into the epicenter of the hippie-freak movement.

Warhol's influence over the scene can hardly be overstated: wherever he went and whatever he did were scrutinized and aped by those who aspired to hipness, so when he began holding court in the infamous restaurant/nightclub max's Kansas City on Park Avenue South, movie and rock stars followed. Inevitably, the Velvet Underground became the focal point of attention in the back room, where only the brave, famous, or truly out-there dared venture. (One of Lou Reed's most famous songs, "Walk on the Wild Side," is an accurate description of what went on in max's back room during the heyday of the Velvet Underground.) Sterling Morrison later alleged that the entire group attended a Warhol party featured in the 1969 film *Midnight Cowboy*.

The Velvets' first album was released in 1967, financed by $18,000 the group earned during its first week at the Dom (it featured a Warhol-designed cover of a plastic banana sticker that could be peeled off to reveal a phallic pink fruit); it barely charted, struggling to No. 171 in *Billboard*'s Top 200. It received some airplay on the West Coast, but was banned by nearly every radio station in New York, their home base: "They wouldn't even accept advertising for the album, because it was about drugs and sex and perversion," as Morrison later recalled.[47] Yet the influence of *The Velvet Underground and Nico* is inestimable: this debauched confessional and its exploration of the dark side sounded like nothing that had come before, with its classicism clashing against rock, violence juxtaposed with gentleness, and poetry risen from the gutter. As one oft-cited quote (attributed to Brian Eno, co-founder of the British band Roxy Music, later producer of U2 and other artists) noted, while the album did not sell many copies, everyone who heard it went on to form a band.[48]

In an odd twist, the Velvets once almost became stablemates with their polar opposites. Morrison claims that the group "had a lot of dealings with Brian Epstein. He loved the first album, and it was his favourite record for a long time . . . he wanted to sign us and have us be his only American group." Realizing that the Beatles would always come first, the band refused. Then the members considered merging their publishing company with Epstein's, but could not see who else might ever want to record their material. "But then the third offer Epstein made was to put together a big European tour. And we said that was fine. And then, on the eve of the final signing, Epstein died."[49]

The Velvets made only four "official" records (previously unreleased material surfaced in the mid-'80s); when Patti Smith inducted the group into the Rock and Roll Hall of Fame in 1996, she noted that these "brilliant albums . . . formed a blueprint for the next three decades of rock and roll."[50] Naturally, there were the usual "creative differences" and disputes, and by the third album, Cale was ousted after squabbling with Reed over everything from direction to credit, and was replaced by Doug Yule. By 1970, Morrison and Reed were the only original members.

Members of the Velvet Underground

In many rock critics' opinion, Lou Reed is as much a visionary as Bob Dylan for the way he expanded rock's vocabulary by writing about decadence and depression, heroin and transvestites, and sexual sadism and masochism. Yet his career path started as a straightforward pop writer in the Pickwick Records "stable." In 1962, under his given name, Lewis Reed, he cut the self-penned "Your Love" and "Merry Go Round"; in 1964, he was the lead vocal, and cowriter, for a group called the Primitives, which recorded "The Ostrich."

Born the son of a Welsh coal miner, John Cale was something of a child prodigy, performing an original composition on the BBC before entering his teen years. In the early '60s, he was assisted by classical luminaries Aaron Copland and Leonard Bernstein in obtaining a scholarship to study music in America; moving to New York in 1963, Cale participated in an eighteen-hour piano recital alongside the avant-garde John Cage and later joined the Dream Syndicate, a minimalist ensemble that employed repetitive droning—a tactic he would use with the Velvets, helping to bring out the group's morbid side.

Sterling Morrison actually wrote more of the band's material than anyone realized: "Lou really did want to have a whole lot of credit for the songs, so on nearly all of the albums we gave it to him. It kept him happy . . . now he's credited for being the absolute and singular genius of the Underground, which is not true. There are a lot of songs I should have coauthorship on, and the same holds true for John Cale."[51]

Maureen "Moe" Tucker brought a minimalist aesthetic to the group, including a disdain for the use of cymbals. Tucker was a strictly self-taught drummer, drawing on what she called "her Bo Diddley and African Olatunji influences to create primal, mesmerizing backbeats," adding, not without justifiable pride, that she "inaugurated the very idea of the female-as-instrumentalist into the collective rock n' roll consciousness."[52]

Warhol chose the icily beautiful blonde Nico (1938–1988) to front the Velvet Underground for her astonishing appearance and disaffected aura, not her vocal abilities. Born Christa Päffgen in Germany, Nico was six feet tall by her teens, which led to a European modeling career and bit parts in film, including Fellini's landmark *La Dolce Vita*. She abandoned her small son by French film star Alain Delon in 1964 and relocated to New York, hoping to rekindle an affair begun with Bob Dylan during his British tour. Warhol, who always had a keen eye for the unusual, put her in front of the camera (in 1966's *The Velvet Underground and Nico* and then *Chelsea Girls* the following year) and then inserted her into the Velvets. The 1995 documentary *Nico: Icon* offers a closer look at an intriguing woman who had affairs with (and/or had songs written for or about her) by Dylan, Lou Reed, Jackson Browne, Iggy Pop, Jim Morrison, Brian Jones, Leonard Cohen, and Jimmy Page.[53]

NOTES

1. Beatles quotes from the Beatles, *The Beatles Anthology* (San Francisco: Chronicle Books LLC, 2000), p. 158.

2. Paul McCartney interviewed by AOL Sessions for the "Driving USA" tour, 2002, http://mp.aol.com/dalaillama/video.index.asp?mxia=ti,1103028et_AOLFORM=w656.h395.p7.R10.

3. Pete Townshend, interviewed by Jann Wenner in 1968, *The Rolling Stone Interviews 1967–1980* (New York: Rolling Stone/Straight Arrow Publishers Inc./St. Martin's Press, 1981), p. 42.

4. Al Aronowitz, *Bob Dylan and the Beatles: Volume One of the Best of the Blacklisted Journalist*, vol. 1, (Bloomington, IN: 1st Books Library, 2003), p. 254.

5. "Woody Guthrie," http://www.bobdylanroots.com/guthrie.html.

6. Woody Guthrie, "W N E W," in *Born to Win* (New York: Macmillan, 1966), p. 223.

7. Toni Ruiz and Henry Llach, "The Other Side of Greenwich Village 60's Folk Scene," Perfect Sound Forever, http://www.furious.com/perfect/folkniks.html.

8. Quoted in Jay Cocks, "Hellhound on the Loose: Bob Dylan Releases A Historic Five-record Album," *Time Magazine Archive Article* 126, no. 21, November 25, 1985, http://www.time.com/time/archive/preview/0,10987,1050610,00.html.

9. Robert Shelton, "Dylan Bibliography: Shelton—Times Review," *The New York Times*, September 29, 1961, http://www.taxhelp.com/shelton-61times.html.

10. John Hammond, *John Hammond on Record: An Autobiography* (New York: Summit Books, 1977), p. 353.

11. Ibid.

12. Aronowitz, *Best of the Blacklisted Journalist*, p. 232.

13. Paul McCartney quoted on "Sir Paul Reveals Drug Use," *BBC News/Entertainment/Music*, June 2, 2004, http://news.bbc.co.uk/1/hi/entertainment/music/3769511.stm.

14. Paul McCartney and John Lennon quotes from the Beatles, *Anthology*, p. 158.

15. Andrew Loog Oldham, *2Stoned* (London: Vintage/Random House, 2003), p. 216.

16. "#4: Dylan Goes Electric," *Entertainment Weekly's 100 Greatest Moments in Rock Music*, July 25, 1965, http://www.ew.com/ew/fab400/music100/3-4.html.

17. Ibid.

18. From Jay Cocks, "Bob Dylan: Master Poet, Caustic Social Critic and Intrepid, Guiding Spirit of the Counterculture Generation," *Time*, November 25, 1985, http://www.time.com/time/time100/artists/profile/dylan1.html.

19. Al Kooper with Ben Edmonds, *Backstage Passes: Rock 'n' Roll Life in the Sixties* (New York: Stein and Day, 1977), p. 55.

20. Ibid.

21. The hymn from which "We Shall Overcome" was adapted is credited to Charles Tindley, "Independent Lens, Strange Fruit: War, Labor and Race," http://www.pbs.org/independentlens/strangefruit/war.html.

22. Joan Baez quoted in Nigel Williamson, "It Ain't Me, Babe—It's Madame Zinzanni!," *London Guardian*, August 27, 2003, http://www.guardian.co.uk/arts/features/story/0,11710,1029819,00.html.

23. Howard Sounes, *Down The Highway: The Life of Bob Dylan* (New York: Doubleday, 2001), quoted by Bob Egginton, "Dylanology Lives On," by *BBC News/Reviews*, http://news.bbc.co.uk/1/hi/entertainment/reviews/1285169.stm.

24. Carl Sandburg quote, "The Weavers," Folk Music Archives, http://folkmusicarchives.org/weavers.htm, and Donald Clarke, "Weavers, The," *MusicWeb*, http://www.musicweb-international.com/encyclopaedia/w/W39.HTM.

25. "Pete Seeger, Performer," Rock and Roll Hall of Fame and Museum, http://www.rockhall.com/hof/inductee.asp?id=185.

26. Kingston Trio's Dave Guard quoted in Bruce Pollock, "When Rock Was Young," Rock's Backpages, http://www.rocksbackpages.com/article.html?ArticleID=3566.

27. Joan Baez quoted in Mary Harron, "Joan Baez: The Folk Heroine Mellows With Age," *London Guardian*, June 22, 1984.

28. Excerpt from Richie Havens and Steve Davidowitz, *They Can't Hide Us Anymore* (New York: William Morrow and Co., 1999), pp. 45–49, as reprinted on "Fred Neil," http://www.fredneil.com/rhavens.html.

29. Richie Unterberger, *Urban Spacemen and Wayfaring Strangers: Overlooked Innovators and Eccentric Visionaries of '60s Rock* (San Francisco: Backbeat Books, 2000), available at: http://www.richieunterberger.com/urbhome.html.

30. Ibid.

31. Donovan quoted in Alex Webb, "Donovan Remembers Dylan," BBC News/Music, May 23, 2001, http://news.bbc.co.uk/2/hi/entertainment/1347199.stm.

32. *Q Magazine* (United Kingdom), no. 111, December 1995, p. 70.

33. Kooper with Edmunds, *Backstage Passes*, pp. 242–243.

34. From "Biography," Eric Andersen's official Web site, http://www.ericandersen.com/bio.htm.

35. "Buffy Saint-Marie Biography," http://www.creative-native.com/biograp.htm.

36. From John Robinson, "Near as Folk," *London Guardian*, January 17, 2004, http://film.guardian.co.uk/features/featurepages/0,4120,1124740,00.html.

37. Ani DiFranco quoted on Tom Paxton's official Web site, http://www.tompaxton.com/about.html.

38. His son Jeff, from an early broken marriage, never really knew Tim, yet his own career had eerie similarities: acclaimed as a singular, sensitive singer-songwriter, he managed to put out one extended-play minialbum and one full-length album before his 1994 drowning at thirty in a freak swimming accident in the Mississippi River. Other examples of his work, including demos for what would have been his sophomore album, have been posthumously released.

39. From "Tim Hardin: Biography," VHI, http://www.vh1.com/artists/az/hardin_tim/bio.jhtml.

40. Paul Nelson, *The Rolling Stone Illustrated History of Rock & Roll* (New York: Rolling Stone/Straight Arrow Publishers Inc./St. Martin's Press, 1981), p. 217.

41. Wikipedia, http://en.wikipedia.org/wiki/Jug_band, and *The Jug Band Rag* Web site, http://home.earthlink.net/~jugband/.

42. John Phillips with Jim Jerome, *Papa John: An Autobiography* (New York: Dell, 1986), p. 158.

43. Bob Christgau, "Teach Yourself Fugging," *Village Voice*, February 15, 2002, http://www.villagevoice.com/music/0208,christgau,32449,22.html.

44. "The Fugs," http://www.thefugs.com/history2.html.

45. Tuli Kupferberg quoted in Theresa Stern, "The Fugs: Tuli Kupferberg," Perfect Sound Forever, http://www.furious.com/perfect/tuli.html.

46. From Neil McCormick, "Lou Reed: The Rave Makeover," *London Telegraph*, July 29, 2004, http://www.telegraph.co.uk/arts/main.jhtml?xml=/arts/2004/07/29/bmlou29.xml.

47. Sterling Morrison quoted in Mary Harron, "The Lost History of the Velvet Underground: An Interview with Sterling Morrison," *New Musical Express*, April 25, 1981.

48. Velvet Underground quote attributed to Brian Eno is cited in the Velvet Underground biographies on: Wikipedia, http://en.wikipedia.org/wiki/The_Velvet_Underground, and Yahoo! Music, http://music.yahoo.com/ar-268056-bio-The-Velvet-Underground, as well as Tim de Lisle, "Roxy Is The Drug," *London Guardian*, May 20, 2005, http://www.guardian.co.uk/arts/fridayreview/story/0,12102,1487397,00.html.

49. Ibid.

50. From "The Velvet Underground," Rock and Roll Hall of Fame, http://www.rockhall.com/hof/inductee.asp?id=204.

51. Sterling Morrison talking to Velvet Underground biographer Victor Bockris, All Music Guide, http://www.allmusic.com/cg/amg.dll.

52. From "Moe's Bio," Maureen Tucker's Web site, http://www.spearedpeanut
.com/tajmoehal/bio/moebio.html.

53. Information from Chris Strodder, "Girls Girls Girls," Swingin' Chicks of the
'60s, http://www.swinginchicks.com/workinitfordaddy.htm.

ONE- OR TWO-HIT WONDERS AND LASTING LEGACIES

In every era there are artists or records that somehow unexpectedly seize the zeitgeist, only to disappear whence they came. They are mysterious and random occurrences, akin to lightning but harder to explain. Some tunes or particular riffs prove intriguing or exciting at just the right moment and become so wildly popular that the phenomenon can never quite be duplicated, although that does not stop anyone from trying. Sometimes, a talented performer connects with a wider audience than he or she had ever dreamed of, then goes right back to a cult following (if he or she is fortunate). As for other hits, sometimes there is no accounting for taste.

In the following chapter, there are hits that may be grouped together or for some reason stand on their own. This chapter is by no means intended to be an exhaustive survey, because the very nature of one-hit wonders is so enormous in scope that entire books have been written about them. Rather, it is a sampling of songs or artists emblematic of the era or noteworthy because their influence has endured. In several cases, the artist(s) went on recording and/or performing, but never again reached equivalent popularity; in others, they managed to eke out two or even three hits before fading away. Or the artist may have been a brief flash in the pan, but the song itself had an ongoing life in future incarnations or derivations. In other words, these are mostly the novelties, or distinctive popular music, of which compilation albums are made.

THE TWIST AND OTHER DANCE CRAZES

The romantic style of dancing that involved close physical contact, as seen in Fred Astaire and Ginger Rogers films, went by the wayside around 1960 with

Chubby Checker in *Twist Around the Clock*, 1961. Courtesy of Photofest.

the arrival of Chubby Checker and the twist. Hank Ballard and the Mid-nighters originally recorded "The Twist" in 1958 as the B side of a single that made the R&B charts. Dick Clark actually booked them for *American Band-stand*, but when they inexplicably failed to show up, the track was shopped around for a more cooperative artist and finally given to Checker (born Ernest Evans). The twist caught on because just about everyone could do it, even the most rhythmically challenged. The hips moved from side to side as hands or fists, held at midchest or hip level, went to the opposite side, or, as one instruc-tion booklet helpfully noted: "Pretend you're stubbing out a cigarette with both feet while drying your back with a towel."[1] The Twist begat variations, most notably "The Peppermint Twist" by Joey Dee and the Starliters, who were appearing at New York's Peppermint Lounge, and "Twist and Shout" by the Isley Brothers (later covered by the Beatles). The dances themselves were not any different; they were just another way to sell the same fad. Twist competi-tions began springing up, echoing the marathon dances of the Depression era.

Checker belabored the point by recording "Let's Twist Again," "Twist It Up," and other twist songs. He landed deals for clothing, chewing gum, and other merchandise, and also appeared in two quickie exploitation flicks, *Twist Around the Clock* (1961) and *Don't Knock the Twist* (1962). Checker himself had absolutely no reason to knock the twist, instead thanking his lucky stars that he was in the right place at the right time: his original "Twist" record sold 3 million copies, and he has been making "oldies" appearances throughout the decades since.

After the twist came the pony, and then a slew of other dance crazes, all short-lived: the hully gully, the jerk, the fly, the swim, the mashed potato, the Watusi, the hitch hike, the Philly dog, and the loco-motion (the eponymous single was written by Carole King and recorded by Little Eva, her former baby-sitter). Even more simpleminded than the twist was the Freddie, by British proto-geeks Freddie and the Dreamers: the "dancer" lifted each arm and leg in tandem. That was all there was to it, but it became a hit record.

NOVELTIES

"Telstar" and Other Tunes

Joe Meek was a small-time English record producer in 1962 when he was inspired by the American launch of a small communications satellite to write this sonic reverie. Awed by Telstar's transmission of the first picture from outer space (an American flag), Meek called songwriting partner Dave Adams in the middle of the night, demanding that he come over to help him write what became a soaring electronic instrumental. Meek then rang a local group known for its instrumental prowess and brought it into his studio to cut the basic track. While the Tornadoes went back out on the road for their regular gig as Billy Fury's backup band, Meek tinkered with his baby, overdubbing a Clavioline, a primitive electric valve-driven organ that could only play one note at a time and produced a thin,

Joe Meek in his apartment/studio, 1963. © John Pratt/Keystone Features/Getty Images.

otherworldly wail. Then he added more sound effects, including the simulation of a rocket taking off (supposedly, a tape of a toilet flush played backwards). Decca picked up the single, and it immediately went to No. 1, becoming the best-selling instrumental record in British history. "Telstar" repeated the feat in America, making the Tornadoes the first English group to top the U.S. charts, a full year before the Beatles.

A French composer named Jean Ledrut, who had written the theme for an obscure film called *The Battle of Austerlitz*, sued Meek, claiming that he had lifted "Telstar" from Ledrut's score. All royalties were frozen as soon as the writ was issued, and Meek had to spend much money and time defending himself in a French court. Meek was again sued for alleged plagiarism by British musician Geoff Goddard, who settled before the case ever got to court; this time, it was over "Have I The Right," a hit for the Honeycombs, a group produced by Meek. But a few singles later, the Honeycombs were finished and their producer was once more out of a job. He also now had a different kind of record: a 1963 arrest for soliciting an undercover police agent for homosexual activity—against the law in England at that time and something of a social stigma.

Nonetheless, around 1966 the chairman of EMI, Sir Joseph Lockwood, offered Meek the position of chief recording manager and producer of the Abbey Road studios when it was rumored that George Martin was leaving to open a studio of his own. Presumably, since the Beatles were still under contract to EMI, Meek would have effectively become their producer, but Martin stayed on. Meek was still recording artists and reportedly suffering from depression in February 1967 when he got into some kind of altercation with Violet Shenton, his landlady. Shenton sustained a shotgun wound in the back and died en route to hospital; Meek, with a single shot to the head, was dead on the spot. An inquest determined that it was a murder-suicide, but the motive remains inexplicable.

Several weeks later, the French legal system found that Meek had, in fact, not plagiarized Ledrut. Because he died without a will, all of "Telstar"'s frozen royalties were seized by the British Internal Revenue and various attorneys, accountants, and creditors. Co-writer Dave Adams and the Tornadoes never saw another dime. Meanwhile, the Telstar satellite itself fell silent after radiation from Earth interfered with its circuitry, turning the miraculous little machine into no more than a piece of very expensive space junk.[2]

Metaphorically out of this world was the bizarre single "They're Coming to Take Me Away, Ha-Ha"; Napoleon XIV's ode to mental illness went to No. 3 on the U.S. national charts in 1966. Chanted—not sung—against a backdrop of tambourine, drums, and thigh slaps, the song also features ambulance sirens wailing away as the protagonist aurally falls apart. It sold a million copies and stayed in the Top 20 for five weeks before being banned by nervous radio stations responding to angry calls from parents and equally offended mental health professionals.

"Napoleon" was actually a twenty-eight-year-old recording engineer named Jerry Samuels, who had previously had his songs cut by Sammy Davis Jr. and Johnny Ray. In what was an innovation for the time, Samuels used his knowledge of studio technology to "loop" a ten-second bit of tape, creating the annoyingly monotonous drum pattern, and sped up his own vocals at the end to convincingly create the sound of a man going mad. The flip side was the same song played backwards.

Once the single became an unlikely smash, Samuels hired a composer and a comedy writer to craft his follow-up album, which included similar songs such as "Bats in My Belfry." The novelty, however, had worn extremely thin, and while Samuels made a few more records, none of them were successful. For a while, he made a living selling "roach clips" to head shops, and later worked as an entertainer in piano bars and senior facilities.

Bobby "Boris" Pickett's "The Monster Mash" is now a Halloween perennial, but first became a smash in 1962, when it went to No. 1 on October 20, eight weeks after its release. It has been reissued two times, reentering the charts in August 1970 (when it peaked at No. 91) and again in May 1972, when it reached No. 10. One of a mere handful of singles that have achieved such status, "Mash" has sold some 4 million copies during the ensuing decades.

As a child, Bobby Pickett loved horror movies, so he was fortunate that his father managed a theater; at age nine, he was already imitating his favorite actor, Boris Karloff. After a stint in the army, Pickett moved to Los Angeles and joined a vocal group, where he cracked up the audience with impressions of the dour Karloff singing love ballads. Novelty songs were popular at the time, so Pickett co-wrote the tune as a variant on the "mashed potatoes" dance craze with bandmate Lenny Capizi at the latter's suggestion; they completed it within approximately ninety minutes. Pickett cut the track in one take and later added inexpensive sound effects, such as rattling some chains and using a claw hammer to pull a nail out of a hunk of wood to simulate the sound of an opening coffin; the "boiling cauldron" is actually Pickett blowing bubbles into water with a straw. In terms of profit margin, there may not be a better example in all of show business. Pickett still makes a living out of this song and also maintains a good sense of humor: on his official Web site, he notes that he "is available year round and can be dug up to appear and sing a medley of his hit."[3]

The more wholesome Brian Hyland was a sixteen-year-old high-school sophomore when he recorded the catchy "Itsy Bitsy Teeny Weeny Yellow Polka Dot Bikini" (written by Paul Vance and Lee Pockriss). After being picked up by a minor label, it became a No. 1 hit in the summer of 1960. An attempt to repeat the trick (with the unfortunately titled "Lopsided, Overloaded, and It Wiggled When I Rode It") flopped. However, Hyland had another big

Brian Hyland performs at an EMI House reception thrown in his honor, 1963. © Hulton-Deutsch Collection/Corbis.

hit with 1962's "Sealed With a Kiss," which became a Top 10 hit all over again in England when it was reissued in 1975. Hyland was later produced by Del Shannon, who helped the singer achieve his last Top 40 record with a 1970 cover of Curtis Mayfield's "Gypsy Woman."

"Little" Peggy March (a child prodigy on TV at age five) had her moment in the sun with "I Will Follow Him." She was fifteen when she recorded this song in 1963 and was then the youngest person ever to hit No. 1. That was pretty much her career, at least in America. March enjoyed some success in Germany during the following decades and later performed her sole smash in the 1987 film *Hairspray*, director John Waters's parodic homage to pre-Beatles pop, which itself served as the basis for a hugely successful Broadway musical.

Of more topical interest was Barry McGuire's doleful protest song "Eve of Destruction," which topped out at No. 1 in 1965. A veteran of the folk-based New Christy Minstrels, McGuire had hooked up with singer-songwriter P. F.

Sloan and label head Lou Adler to record his debut album two years earlier. McGuire was friendly with other pop-rock artists such as the Mamas and the Papas, but turned away from secular music to become a Christian gospel artist in the early '70s. He later moved to New Zealand to work with a poverty organization, and upon his 1990 return to the United States began recording more albums with titles like *Journey to Bible Times*.

Sgt. Barry Sadler's "The Ballad of the Green Berets" was certainly not a rock record, yet it became the biggest hit single of 1966 by tapping into the backlash against Vietnam protestors. Sadler was the perfect man for the job: an actual Green Beret, trained as a medic in Special Forces, and a wounded Vietnam vet. During the time he spent recuperating from a leg injury sustained near Saigon, Sadler, who had been interested in music as a young boy, created and sang songs to boost the spirits of his fellow patients. A TV crew visited and taped Sadler singing this number about bravery in the face of adversity, and RCA came calling after the show was aired back in the United States. Sadler cut a full album, and when the single was released, it sold more than 2 million copies in its first

Sgt. Barry Sadler sings "The Ballad of the Green Berets," on the *Ed Sullivan Show*, 1966. © Ted Russell/Time Life Pictures/Getty Images.

five weeks and lodged at No. 1 for an equal length of time; the album also hit No. 1.

Perhaps it was the looming specter of the Vietnam War, or maybe it was just youthful morbid fascination, that led to the genre that came to be known as "death rock." Teenagers, while considering themselves invulnerable, are also drawn to demise; this fascination is now often expressed through Goth music and the so-called slasher genre of horror film, in which young people (usually exploring their sexuality) meet gory, often inventive ends. But in the early and mid-'60s, there was for some reason a brief flurry of this so-called death rock, even though its elements were actually more pop in spirit. This short-lived specialty was occasionally banned from radio before it died of natural causes by itself. The components are basically the same: Teen meets mate; romance blossoms; the Grim Reaper intervenes. The theme is at least as old as Romeo and Juliet, but it puts a different spin on the concept of losing love than is usual in pop songs; in this case, once the loved one is gone, he or she is never coming back.

The first of the death-rock series, Mark Dinning's "Teen Angel," topped the charts in 1960. The title essentially says it all: the singer loses his girl when she inexplicably runs back to the car stalled on the railroad tracks; wanting to retrieve his high-school ring costs her sixteen-year-old life. Ray Peterson's "Tell Laura I Love Her" also made the 1960 Top 10; it concerned a car crash. The singer wants to make sure that the girlfriend he is leaving behind in this vale of tears knows how much he cares, or rather cared. Dickey Lee's "Patches" was a variation on the theme, with not just one, but two suicides. Lee is in love with a girl from the wrong side of the tracks, but breaks their engagement for fear of parental disapproval. When he hears that she has been found face down in the river, his guilt causes him to swear that he will join her that very evening. Brill Building songwriter Barry Mann was one of the authors of this track, which sold a million copies and entered the Top 10 in 1962. Lee later had a comeback with "Laurie"—no relation to Laura, since this "angel" of a girl whom he meets at a 1965 dance and drives home is really a ghost. He discovers this important fact after he attempts to retrieve a sweater he had loaned the girl, and the man who answers the door says that his daughter died a year ago that very day—her birthday, no less. Lee is irresistibly drawn to the cemetery and somehow (with only a first name to go on) finds the sweater draped over her grave.

J. Frank Wilson and the Cavaliers' "Last Kiss," a cover version of a song by Wayne Cochran, hit No. 2 in 1964 (and, for some reason, charted again ten years later). In the song, J. Frank promises to be good in this world so he can see his "baby" again in the next; all he remembers of the car crash that took her life is sharing that final tender kiss. As the single was climbing the charts, Wilson was actually involved in a car crash with Sonley Roush, who had been obsessed with the song, brought it to the group's attention, and produced the single. Roush was killed, and Wilson was badly injured. He never managed another hit. However, when Pearl Jam covered the song again in 1999, perhaps with postmodern irony, it reached No. 1.

The Shangri-Las did notch up several other hits, as discussed in Chapter 3, but their famous "Leader of the Pack" (1964) belongs squarely in the death-rock genre. In call-and-response style, the singer wails to her friends that she met her new boyfriend at the candy store, but since he comes from the wrong part of town, her parents disapprove and have forced the young lovers to break up. As he drives away in the rain, presumably blinded by tears, he becomes yet another rock road casualty.

WORLD MUSIC

The concept of "world" music, drawing from different nations or ethnicities, has by now thoroughly infiltrated pop. Western ears became accustomed to the sound of the East Indian sitar through first the Beatles' George Harrison, then the Rolling Stones (on the single "Paint It, Black"); through Harrison's efforts, master player Ravi Shankar was introduced to a new audience. Bob Marley and the Wailers made reggae famous around the globe, and the Stones later signed alumnus Peter Tosh to their own label. Paul Simon's *Graceland* album, featuring the spectacular Ladysmith Black Mambazo, helped popularize South African "township" music. British artist Peter Gabriel, formerly of Genesis, created the WOMAD world music tours; Bjork and the Sugarcubes put Iceland on the pop map; East Indian bhangra has become accepted in clubs; and the ethnic clothing chain Putamayo even began releasing compilation CDs. But this period marked the first time that an unprecedented number of nonhomegrown songs made chart appearances; some of them were not even performed in English, which is still a rarity for a hit record.

Kyu Sakamoto

The lilting, wistful melody of "Sukiyaki," which was sung entirely in Japanese, had nothing whatever to do with sukiyaki (a stir-fry dish that usually incorporates meat); Western DJs could not pronounce its real title, "Ue o Muite Aruko," which meant "I Look Up When I Walk," so the label gave them something they could work with. The lyrics had to do with loneliness and a broken heart, a common theme in pop music, and despite the fact that no one in America of non-Japanese descent understood them, the song became No. 1 in June 1963. Although Sakamoto was tragically killed in a plane crash, he has achieved immortality of a sort: "Sukiyaki" has since been covered by PM Dawn and other artists and remains the biggest international hit ever by a Japanese performer.[4]

Los Bravos

Originally formed as Mike and the Runaways, after the group was renamed Los Sonor, it became the most popular rock band in Spain. Several of its singles found their way to a British producer, who was intrigued enough to fly to Madrid to check the group out. Taken to London and renamed once again, this time as Los Bravos, the band recorded the pounding "Black Is Black," which eventually reached No. 4 in 1966. Although sung in English, this marked the first appearance of a Spanish group on the American charts and the international pop scene. It was undoubtedly helpful that lead singer, Mike Kogel (who was born in Berlin), had a voice somewhat reminiscent of Gene Pitney and he delivered the material without any discernible accent; in fact, rather than having any Latino influence, Los Bravos was a new hybrid that could be called garage-pop.

The Tokens

Neil Sedaka was in the forerunner to the Tokens, a Brooklyn high-school vocal quartet called the Linc-Tones. After Sedaka left the group, a different lineup of what was now being called the Tokens had a No. 15 record in 1960 with "Tonight I Fell in Love." But it was a rewritten Zulu hunting song, "The Lion Sleeps Tonight," that would give the group its greatest success.

The original version (titled "Mbube," which means "lion") was popularized in South Africa in 1939 by Solomon Linda and his Evening Birds, whose label sent it to the United States almost a decade later in hopes of a release. Instead, Pete Seeger of the Weavers heard it and began working up an English version he called "Wimoweh," his aural take on the lyric; in fact, the singers were chanting "Uyimbube," a nonsense word in any language.[5] The Weavers had a No. 15 hit with "Wimoweh" in 1952 and included it on a popular 1957 live album, *The Weavers at Carnegie Hall*. Miriam Makeba recorded her version (in the original language) at around the same time.

The Tokens auditioned for producers Hugo Peretti and Luigi Creatore with "Wimoweh"; liking the sound of the tune, the producers drafted writer George Weiss to rewrite the number. "Lion" was originally the flip side of a Portuguese song titled "Tina"; after a DJ turned it over, this catchy chant reached the top of the charts during the 1961–1962 Christmas holidays and stayed there for three weeks. The Tokens put nine more songs in the Top 100 from 1962 to 1970; various members went on to pursue careers in music production, most notably with the Chiffons, and have since reunited for oldies tours. A singer named Robert John recorded another version of "Lion" in 1972, which reached No. 3, while the original song picked up a whole new legion of fans in the 1990s when it was featured on the TV series *Friends* as the favorite tune of Ross Geller's pet monkey Marcel.

The Singing Nun

There has never been a single quite like "Dominique," recorded by a Dominican nun based at the Fichermont convent in Belgium; born Jeanine Deckers (1933–1985), she became known as Sister Luc-Gabrielle and was stage-named

Soeur Sourire ("Sister Smile"). She wrote this pretty, catchy tune as a tribute to the founder of her Dominican order and paid to have a recording cut so she could hand it out as gifts. Word of this got back to a local label, which grasped the marketing potential in a singing nun and promptly signed her. Uncomfortable with performing, Sister Luc-Gabrielle bowed to pressure and pretaped the song for broadcast on the *Ed Sullivan Show*; initially, her mother superior objected to this early example of "rock" video being shown, and the affair required intervention by the archdiocese. "Dominique" went on to win a 1963 Grammy Award for Best Gospel or Other Religious Recording, Musical.

In 1965, Sister Luc-Gabrielle left the convent to resume her singing career just as Debbie Reynolds was starring in an MGM musical called *The Singing Nun*. As Luc Dominique, she recorded "I Am Not a Star" in 1967 and went on to criticize the church in her music, even admitting to a woman's magazine that she used tranquilizers in order to sleep. She also reportedly agreed with John Lennon's statement that the Beatles were more popular in the modern world than Jesus: "I may not feel this is right," she said, "but it is certainly undeniable."[6]

This unique pop star has inspired several books (*Soeur Sourire: A Faceless Voice: Passions and Death of the Fichermont Singing Nun* by Henry Evearet, and *Soeur Sourire* by Florence Delaporte) and at least one more film (*Sister Smile*, directed by Roger Deutsch in Italian).[7]

Stan Getz with João and Astrud Gilberto

Something of a bossa nova craze took hold in 1964 after jazz saxophonist Stan Getz collaborated with guitarist João Gilberto and his sweet-voiced wife, Astrud, on "The Girl from Ipanema." The samba-swaying melody was lazily seductive, and although the lyrics were in Portuguese, Astrud (who had no previous professional musical experience) sang the second verse in English, making the tune much more accessible. "Girl" rose to the middle of the Top 10 and gave Astrud—uncredited on the original release—a long-running career with the easy-listening audience. Although she vanished from American radar shortly afterwards, she was cherished in Brazil through the '70s, and in 1984, the song made it back onto the British charts in the wake of a revived bossa nova fad.

Millie Small

Millie Small was born in Jamaica and was discovered by Chris Blackwell, an Englishman living on the island; "My Boy Lollipop," with more than 7 million in sales, gave him the industry credibility to later launch Bob Marley and the Wailers, financially back the making of the classic reggae-outlaw-music film *The Harder They Come*, and sign U2 to his Island label. Blackwell brought Small, the daughter of an overseer on a sugar plantation, to England in late 1963. This was her fourth recording, backed by a group of session musicians that allegedly included Rod Stewart on harmonica. The bouncy tune, which in late 1964 hit No. 1 in the United Kingdom and No. 2 in America, was based on ska or "blue beat," a form of Jamaican R&B popularized many years later by the Specials and UB40 in England and No Doubt in America. Blackwell later mused that the single "worked well for radio, but partly because it was a minute and 51 seconds. That was important for . . . putting playlists together. Also, Millie's voice was irresistible—for a certain length of time, anyway. So a short record worked well for her."[8] Indeed, this was her only U.S. hit.

ROMANCE, '60s-STYLE

The Left Banke

Sixteen-year-old Mike Brown (né Lookofsky) helped out around his violinist dad's small storefront recording studio in New York City, occasionally sitting in as a session pianist. Once he got a set of keys to the studio, Brown and his friends began messing around, and in 1965 the group (Steve Martin on vocals, Tom Finn on bass, Rick Brand on lead guitar, and drummer George Cameron) decided to call themselves the Left Banke.

One fateful day, so the story goes, Finn brought his blonde girlfriend, an aspiring ballerina named Renee Fladen, to band practice. Brown fell instantly in love and funneled his fantasy crush into the song "Walk Away Renee." Unusual for the time in that it incorporated strings, "Renee" was a forerunner of the "baroque-rock" school later explored further in such songs as Procul Harum's "Whiter Shade of Pale." But the Left Banke did it first.

Almost a dozen labels turned down the single before it was picked up by Smash; it entered the charts in the autumn of 1966 and stayed there for several months, topping out at No. 5. The next year, Brown wrote "Pretty Ballerina," undoubtedly with the same inspiration, and that too made its mark, going to No. 15 nationally. (Steven Van Zandt, Springsteen guitarist, Sopranos star and producer, and a music archivist with his own syndicated radio show, has gone on record with his belief that the Left Banke should be in the Rock and Roll Hall of Fame for this single alone.) The group tried for a third grab at the brass ring, to no avail; after Brown's departure, it was finished. Brown stayed in the business for a while, forming another band called Stories, but never again enjoyed the success he achieved at the tender age of sixteen. The Four Tops had a No. 14 hit with "Renee" in 1968. The young lady herself reportedly moved to Boston with her family shortly after the hit(s) she inspired, and no one in the band ever saw her again.[9]

Dino, Desi, and Billy

When it came to pedigree and privilege, the Beverly Hills–based Dino, Desi, and Billy had it all. Dino was the son of singer-entertainer Dean Martin; Desi was the child of sitcom superstars Lucille Ball and Desi Arnaz; classmate Billy Hinsche's father was a wealthy real estate developer. These connections landed the fledgling group an audition with Dean Martin's good friend Frank Sinatra, whose label (Reprise) released the first single in 1964. The boys did not play their own instruments in the studio; that precision task was handled by session pros like Hal Blaine, Carol Kaye, and James Burton. The group's singles also received kid-glove treatment from top producers and arrangers such as Lee Hazlewood, Billy Strange, and Jimmy Bowen (who had also all contributed, in one way or another, to Nancy Sinatra's smash hit "These Boots Are Made for Walkin' ").

"I'm a Fool" made the Top 20 in 1965, while the follow-up "Not the Loving Kind" reached the Top 30 several months later. The band, blessed with photogenic good looks (and the distinction of being the only group to present a Filipino American boy, Billy, as a heartthrob), attracted a teenybopper following and appeared on *Ed Sullivan* and the covers of numerous fan magazines. They landed a 1965 tour supporting the Beach Boys and cut four albums without equivalent success. They disbanded in 1970 after recording a Brian Wilson–Billy Hinsche composition titled "Lady Love" (Hinsche's sister had wed Brian's brother Carl, who later married Dino's sister Gina).

Gary Lewis and the Playboys

In another conspicuous example of Hollywood nepotism, the son of Dean Martin's former comedy partner Jerry Lewis had seven songs that made the Top 10 during the years 1965–1966. In Lewis's defense, it should be noted that he had been playing drums since 1960 and also had good taste in musicians, collaborating on songs with his arranger Leon Russell, who eventually recruited several group members for his own band.

Lewis's group was playing at the original Disneyland when it was spotted and signed by producer Snuff Garrett, who suggested that Lewis's father pull some strings to get them on the *Ed Sullivan Show*. After their appearance in January 1965, demand for "This Diamond Ring" (written by Al Kooper) was so intense that pressing plants were reportedly working around the clock to meet it, and the record went to No. 1. A string of highly polished pop hits followed, including "Everybody Loves a Clown" (No. 4) and "She's Just My Style" (No. 3), and that year, Lewis was named *Cashbox* magazine's "Male Vocalist of the Year," which was rather astonishing considering that other nominees were surnamed Presley and Sinatra. However, Lewis's career was derailed at the start of 1967 when he was drafted into the army. When Lewis returned to recording two years later, the prevailing trend toward psychedelia made his style sound outdated. Nonetheless, Lewis, with a changing lineup of Playboys, continued playing music, and as of 1999 was still making appearances on the oldies circuit.

GARAGE ROCK

Garage rock began enjoying a renaissance in the late 1990s, but the fact is that this charmingly Neanderthal art form never really went away, although its peak years were the early and mid-'60s. Based on simple chords that a novice could emulate, often filigreed by a Farfisa organ, garage rock got its name from the many would-be artists who took over the family's car port for band rehearsal, sometimes lining the walls with sound-insulating material (such as egg crates or foam) to prevent neighbors from calling the police.

Paul Revere and the Raiders

Much more polished than the average group in this sector, Paul Revere and the Raiders had a surprisingly grunge feel for such a mainstream act. Singer Mark Lindsay's gritty vocals and the stomping band behind him made for a string of perfectly realized protogarage singles. The campily attired group (they dressed like Revolutionary War soldiers, although it is doubtful that anyone of that era wore trousers as tight and spotlessly white as did the ponytailed Lindsay) had massive hits from 1966 to 1969, including—all in 1966—"Hungry," "Just like Me," and "Kicks" (the last an antidrug song, a fairly bold move for the time).

Founder Paul Revere (his real name) was raised in Idaho, where he fell for the music of Jerry Lee Lewis. At seventeen, he joined a local band called the Downbeats, followed by sixteen-year-old Mark Lindsay. As one of the few resident rock bands in the area, the Downbeats enjoyed local popularity. After a demo they took to Los Angeles caught the attention of a label executive, who urged Revere to take advantage of his birth name, the rechristened Raiders cut several singles before an instrumental, "Like Long Hair," got some airplay in 1961.

Revere was drafted, but was granted conscientious objector status as the son of pacifist Mennonites, and served out his hitch as a cook in an Oregon mental hospital. In late 1962, Lindsay once more joined Revere in a new lineup of the group, now based out of Portland. At this point, the Pacific Northwest was host to a league of hot bands, including the Kingsmen and the Wailers (no relation to the reggae group fronted by Bob Marley), but Revere and the Raiders managed to set themselves apart with an acrobatic, comedy-inspired stage act. Their manager suggested that they cut a single of "Louie Louie" (on which Lindsay played tenor sax), which had been going over well for them live; they had learned it from the Kingsmen's version. The track was sent to Columbia in New York, which promptly signed the group and assigned it to producer Terry Melcher, the son of singer-actress Doris Day and a former member of surf-rock duo Bruce and Terry (with songwriter-producer Bruce Johnston, later of the Beach Boys). Under the guidance of Melcher and Johnston, the Raiders finally hit upon a winning combination of fast, Beach Boys–style guitar and vocals with a Stones-esque R&B feel. "Steppin' Out," written by Revere and Lindsay, hit the national charts in 1965.

The previous year, the Raiders had been touring with the Stones when Dick Clark spotted them and decided that they would be a good house band on his new afternoon TV show, *Where the Action Is!* The group spent the next two years getting daily national exposure; the only other artists that ever came close to receiving such massive free promotion were Ricky Nelson and the Monkees, and they were on only once a week.

While it was a given that the Raiders would take off, given such circumstances —to fail, they would have had to be truly awful—they actually were a terrific rock band. As one writer pointed out, the Raiders had "impressive instrumentation . . . superb singing (Lindsay at times approached the status of an American Jagger) and enthralling precise harmonies—in short, [the group made] some of the best American rock and roll of the sixties."[10] When *Action* went off the air in 1967 and the Raiders lost their showcase after more than 500 shows, the group never again enjoyed quite the same success. Lindsay and Revere have kept on with their careers, however, and both continue performing. Rock critic Chuck Eddy, who ranked the Raiders' *Greatest Hits* album No. 33 on his list of the "500 Best Heavy Metal Albums in the Universe," declared, "Ages before Subpop Records made the Great Northwest famous again, this Portland bunch rocked with more guts and gusto than Soundgarden and Mudhoney ever would."[11]

The Kingsmen

Entire books have been written about the seminal "Louie Louie," a tune that still enjoys enormous popularity on jukeboxes, in karaoke bars, and with garage bands around the world. No one could understand what the singer (Jack Ely) was really saying, but his slurred delivery insinuated that it was dirty; a Senate subcommittee actually held hearings about just how dirty. In fact, the lyrics are not dirty at all, but it took the Federal Bureau of Investigation two full years to determine that the song was "unintelligible at any speed."[12]

Songwriter Richard Berry, a habitué of the Los Angeles doo-wop music scene, had provided uncredited lead vocals on the original version of Lieber and Stoller's "Riot in Cell Block #9," cut by the Robins (who later evolved into the Drifters). His was the male response voice on Etta James's salacious "Roll with Me Henry." Offered a contract with a local label, Berry was thinking of combining cha-cha with an R&B feel when, in 1956, he wrote "Louie Louie" down on a napkin backstage between sets with a local group. Inspired by calypso rhythms, Berry imagined a Jamaican sailor (hence the "unintelligible" patois) telling a bartender named Louie that he had to leave to meet his girl-friend. His version was a local success; thinking the song had run its course, Berry then sold the publishing rights for $750.

In Tacoma, Washington, a group called the Wailers had picked up a copy of Berry's single and decided to redo it in their own, more rock-oriented style.

Released on a regional label, it became something of a Pacific Northwest anthem. There is some dispute about who covered the song first: various sources attribute the honor to Little Bill and the Blue Notes, Ron Holden of the Playboys, or the Frantics and the Dave Lewis Combo. In any case, it was the Wailers' version that originally took hold.

In nearby Portland, Oregon, the song reached the ears of two local bands: Paul Revere and the Raiders, and the Kingsmen. Both recorded versions at the same studio within a week of each other in 1963. After the Kingsmen's cover became a hit, it helped launch the Raiders' career when Columbia Records realized that that group might have had the same success. The Raiders did become much more visible as a result, but it is the Kingmen's version that has gone down in history as the "original." Ely, who had left the group to attend college, tried to get back in after the song became a hit, but was turned down; he began touring with a backup band, calling it Jack Ely and the Kingsmen, while his former group was lip-synching to the smash on national television. Multiple lawsuits ensued.

Springsteen biographer and rock critic Dave Marsh believes that the Kingsmen's sloppy "protopunk" rendition was "the most profound and sublime expression of rock 'n' roll's ability to create something from nothing," and views the investigation into the so-called vulgar lyrics as a forerunner of the Parental Music Resource Center and other forms of music censorship. Marsh, who wrote a book about the song, sees its cultural history—the selling of the rights dirt-cheap, the lawsuits, the grabbing for credit, the controversy over its smutty sound—as "the story of rock 'n' roll in a nutshell."[13]

"Louie Louie" inspired similar tracks by the Kinks, the Who, and Jimi Hendrix (who had been a fan of the Wailers) and was remade by the Beach Boys, Jan and Dean, Otis Redding, the Raiders, and Barry White. There have been instrumental covers, jazz-fusion remakes, punk tributes, and at least one rap rendition. A California radio station held an event called "Maximum Louie Louie" in August 1983, playing every known version of the song while encouraging listeners to drop off their own takes; the marathon consumed sixty-three hours of airtime. At that point, there were more than 800 documented covers, and since then, according to the Web site LouieLouie.Net, the number has doubled, hovering in the range of 1,600. With the exception of the Beatles' "Yesterday," that makes "Louie Louie" the most covered song in pop history.

In 2003, the British music magazine *Mojo* asked a group of writers and musicians to compile a "ultimate jukebox," a list of 100 singles that every music fan should own, and "Louie Louie" came in at No. 1.[14] Somewhere, Richard Berry has been kicking himself for decades.

The Standells

"Dirty Water," a stone-cold classic that made it to No. 11 in 1966, was written by producer Ed Cobb, who had once been in the clean-cut vocal group the

Four Preps. The Standells did not even like the track upon first hearing. This Los Angeles–based group (although the song's lyrics are about the Charles River in Boston) had something of a Hollywood pedigree: Dick Dodd, the drummer and eventual lead singer, had been a Mouseketeer on the *Mickey Mouse Club,* and organ player Larry Tamblyn was the brother of actor Russ Tamblyn, who had starred in *West Side Story.* The group had been playing clubs since the early '60s, mostly doing covers of pre-Beatles pop songs, when they somehow lucked into a few show–business breaks: appearing in the film *Get Yourself a College Girl* and several TV appearances, including performing what was reportedly a terrible version of the Beatles' "I Want to Hold Your Hand" on the popular show *The Munsters.* The Standells eventually hooked up with Cobb and recorded "Dirty Water," but it was six months before the song became a hit.

After that, the group churned out four albums during 1966 and 1967 and wrote the theme song to the psychedelic-exploitation flick *Riot on Sunset Strip,* as well as appearing in the film. Dick Dodd went solo in 1968, the year the group released its last single, but never again enjoyed a similar level of success. The Standells struggled on the oldies circuit until they called it quits in the early '70s. Thanks to a resurgence of interest due to champions of the genre like Steve Van Zandt, a few members did reform for a 1999 appearance at his "Cavestomp" series of shows, which was subsequently released as an album called *Ban This!*

The Shadows of Knight

In March 1966, the Shadows of Knight's cover of "Gloria," a Van Morrison and Them song, infiltrated the airwaves and became a No. 10 smash. In an interesting inversion, the Chicago-based group took inspiration from the British interpretation of Chicago electric blues. The original "Gloria" album was rereleased by Sundazed Records in 1997 to capitalize on the garage-rock revival.

The Sir Douglas Quintet

Only in America could a psychedelic Tex-Mex garage group try to fool rock fans into thinking it was part of the British Invasion by calling its lead singer "Sir." Vocalist/songwriter Doug Sahm, born in San Antonio, Texas, was considered something of a child prodigy in country music, and had turned down a spot on the Grand Old Opry in order to finish junior high school. Meanwhile, a Houston producer of Sahm's acquaintance who had studied the Beatles' records and thought that the beat owed something to a dance move called the Cajun two-step, set about convincing Doug to grow his hair long and write a song blending the two disparate styles. The group that Sahm formed with some local friends was promptly dubbed the Sir Douglas Quintet, and cut a debut single that went nowhere. But the followup, "She's About A Mover" (which owed more than a small debt to the Beatles' "She's a Woman"), which hit the U.S. pop charts at No. 13 in 1965, is still considered a garage-rock classic.

The Troggs

"Wild Thing," which was just about as nasty-sounding as "Louie Louie," went to No. 1 in 1966. After the Troggs and their manager/producer discovered a demo of the song by songwriter Chip Taylor, they put their own grungy spin on it, initiating the short-lived "caveman-rock" genre. The unusual, ear-grabbing melody in the bridge was played on the ocarina, a small wind instrument similar to the kazoo. The rest is history: Jimi Hendrix famously made the tune his own when closing his incendiary set at the Monterey Pop Festival in 1967. A legal dispute prevented the Troggs from touring the United States to capitalize on the single for several years, an eternity in rock time, which also damped the American success of the other 1966 singles, "I Can't Control Myself " and "With a Girl like You." The group had one last hit in 1968 with "Love Is All Around," which entered the U.S. Top 10.

The notorious "Troggs Tapes," a widely bootlegged, secretly taped in-studio diatribe among group members that was unintentionally hilarious in its stupidity, allegedly inspired the rock-movie classic *Spinal Tap*. The band was belatedly recognized as being an influence on groups as disparate as the MC5 and the Ramones, and in 1992 was joined by members of R.E.M. for a "comeback" album titled *Athens Andover* (the former is R.E.M.'s home base, while the latter is the British town from which the Troggs originally hailed). However, the comeback never came.

? and the Mysterians

The Farfisa organ–fueled riff that drives "96 Tears" is insanely memorable; once heard, it is never forgotten. Lead singer ? (he chose to legally change his name to a question mark, thereby becoming the first artist to use a symbol, long before Prince thought of the idea) was plain Rudy Martinez when he was born in Texas, although he later reportedly claimed to originate from the planet Mars. Martinez and his brother Robert were raised in Saginaw, Michigan, and formed the group around 1964 along with several others (most notably Frank Rodriguez Jr. on keyboards). The song was first called "69 Tears," but the group changed the number after considering whether the original title's double entendre might cost them airplay. Their manager had a few hundred copies pressed, and in 1966 sent the single to regional radio stations such as WTAC in Flint and Detroit's CKLW. Then the requests began to flood in. A savvy record mogul named Neil Bogart (who later ran the Casablanca label) spotted its potential and struck a deal for distribution rights, and the single went to No. 1, with a million copies sold. The group promptly recorded an album under the same title, and its second single ("I Need Somebody") reached No. 2 in late

1966. "?" has since tried to recapture that early success, to no avail; however, singer-songwriter Garland Jeffreys did have a minor hit with his 1980 cover of the tune.[15]

The Count Five

The Count Five originated in San Jose, California, around 1964; its grunge classic "Psychotic Reaction" (written by Irish-born guitarist, singer, and songwriter Sean Byrne), caught the attention of a local DJ, who managed to get the single placed with a small Los Angeles label. It eventually hit No. 5 nationally in 1966, but the group was never able to follow it up with anything remotely as successful, and broke up soon afterwards. The track attained renewed popularity after guitarist and rock historian Lenny Kaye included it on *Nuggets*, his first collection of influential garage and psychedelic nonhits.

The McCoys

The McCoys, an Indiana-reared group, had a 1965 No. 1 hit while still in high school with the catchily chorused "Hang On Sloopy," followed by "Fever" that same year, its only other Top 10 entry. In the late '60s, the group moved to a more progressive record label in an effort to shake its pop image, turning to psychedelic rock without attracting much notice. However, the band's "Sorrow" did become a UK hit in a cover version by the Merseys, and was also cut by David Bowie for his *Pin Ups* album. Lead singer and guitarist Rick Derringer went on to join Edgar Winter's band and later enjoyed a moderately successful solo career of his own.

The Beau Brummels

The first American band to respond to the British invasion with a similar sound, San Francisco's Beau Brummels were frequently mistaken for Brits. The core of the group was comprised of guitarist and songwriter Ron Elliot, who wrote most of the material, and singer Sal Valentino; they were signed to a small label owned by local DJ Tom Donahue in 1964 and were produced by Sylvester Stewart, who later became widely renowned as Sly Stone of the Family Stone. The first single, "Laugh Laugh," was a No. 15 hit out of the box in 1965, while the follow-up, "Just a Little," made the national Top 10. The group's mournful-sounding folk-rock sound predated the Byrds, but its ongoing success was hampered by the label's lack of promotional clout and because Elliot's diabetes kept the group off the road. When Donahue's label was sold in 1966 to Warner Brothers, the new bosses insisted that the Beau Brummels record an album of Top 40 covers, effectively stifling its original voice. The band made a few more records, none of which did well, although the Beau Brummels were among the first artists (along with Bob Dylan and the Byrds) to work in the country-rock genre with its 1968 *Bradley's Barn* album.

Sam the Sham and the Pharaohs

In show business, it does not hurt to have a gimmick, and Sam (aka Domingo Samudio, born in 1937) did: he and his band "thought Ramses [in the movie version of *The Ten Commandments*] looked pretty cool,"[16] so they all dressed up in head towels and pseudo-Arab costumes to become the Pharaohs. Their 1965 hit "Wooly Bully" (No. 2) had nonsense lyrics, but Sam's growl and the insistent keyboard riff he laid down made the tune intriguing enough to sell more than 3 million copies. A new lineup of Pharaohs backed him on the follow-up single, "Li'l Red Riding Hood" (No. 2, 1966), but by then Sam had tired of the game: "The company still wouldn't let us record what we wanted, so I decided to hang it up. When you're not happy, you can't do it right."[17] Sam later tried to revive his career, but outside of contributing several songs to Ry Cooder's soundtrack for *The Border*, nothing quite clicked. He now reportedly works with transients and inmates as a lay preacher in Memphis.

Unit 4 + 2

The British group responsible for "Concrete and Clay" was originally an instrumental quartet (Unit 4) with guitarist Brian Parker, who had once played in Adam Faith's backing band, joined by Tommy Moeller and David Meikle, also on guitar, and singer Brian Moules. Parker left the band, although he continued to write with Moeller, and was replaced by Howard Lubin before the group signed with British Decca in 1964. After the Beatles hit, the group added a drummer, Hugh Halliday, and a bassist, Ron Garwood, hence the mysteriously simplistic name. "Concrete and Clay," the group's third single, came out in 1965 and quickly rose to the top chart position in England and No. 35 in America. Unfortunately, the band never managed to bottle lightning again; when it strayed too far from this particular sound, no one bought, and when it tried to duplicate it, it sounded like the retread it was. Perhaps not coincidentally, this single was the first time the core of the band had been joined by two of Parker's former bandmates, guitarist Russ Ballard and drummer Bob Henrit (which, it could be argued, really made it Unit 4 + 2 + 2). Ballard and Henrit later went on to work with former Zombie Rod Argent in his eponymous protoarena rock band ("Hold Your Head Up" and other songs).

THE ADVENT OF BLUE-EYED SOUL

The term "blue-eyed soul" has nothing to do with the actual color of a person's eyes; it refers to the concept of a white person emoting with passion normally attributed to individuals of African descent. This supposedly radical concept was swiftly accepted by the mainstream, in no small part because of Elvis Presley and the following artists.

The Righteous Brothers (left to right) Bill Medley and Bobby Hatfield, 1966. Courtesy of Photofest.

The Righteous Brothers

According to their official biography, Bobby Hatfield and Bill Medley adopted the name the Righteous Brothers in 1963 after a black marine in the audience shouted out, "That's righteous, brothers!" during their performance as part of a five-piece vocal group called the Paramours. Under their new title, the duo enjoyed a Top 50 hit in 1963 with "Little Latin Lupe Lu," but it was not until Phil Spector took them under his wing that they became really successful. In late 1964, Spector and the duo entered Gold Star Studios with a song by Brill Building composers Barry Mann and Cynthia Weill, "You've Lost That Lovin' Feeling," custom-crafted to capitalize on Hatfield's high falsetto and Medley's deep bass. "We had no idea if it would be a hit," Medley mused. "It was too slow, too long and right in the middle of the Beatles and the British Invasion."[18] The single did run almost four minutes, about sixty to ninety seconds longer than most, but Spector used the ploy of listing its length as "3:05" on the label, and once it was played, it was a knockout. The song debuted at No. 72 in December 1964, rose to No. 1 six weeks later, and reportedly still holds the record as the most played song in the history of American radio, at 8 million spins and counting.[19]

Although the Righteous Brothers went on to create other hits with Spector ("Just Once in My Life," "Unchained Melody," and "Ebb Tide," all Top 5 in 1965), the duo left the producer for a new label in 1966, where Medley took on Spector's role, reproducing Spector's "Wall of Sound" well enough to achieve another No. 1 with "(You're My) Soul and Inspiration." Hatfield suddenly died in his hotel room shortly before going onstage in November 2003, the same year the duo was inducted into the Rock and Roll Hall of Fame.

The Walker Brothers

Los Angeles natives John Maus, Scott Engel, and Gary Leeds grew their hair long and relocated to London in 1964, where they all adopted the surname "Walker" (much like the Ramones two decades later; in fact, the punk pioneers took their *nom de rock* from a pseudonym once used by Beatle Paul McCartney, "Paul Ramon"). Now rechristened the Walker Brothers and passing themselves off as part of the British invasion, the trio also made a conscious effort to emulate the Righteous Brothers by recording melodramatically orchestrated, over-the-top ballads. The ploy struck gold, first in England and then in America, with "Make It Easy on Yourself" (No. 16 in 1965) and "The Sun Ain't Gonna Shine Anymore" (No. 13 in 1966), but by the following year frontman Scott Walker had departed for a solo career, and the group was no more.

Mitch Ryder and the Detroit Wheels

Mitch Ryder and the Detroit Wheels were a demolition derby on record, pounding out viscerally exciting hits such as 1965's "Jenny Take a Ride/C. C. Rider," its follow-up "Little Latin Lupe Lu," and a Top 5 medley of "Devil with a Blue Dress On/Good Golly Miss Molly" (both in 1966) that can still induce heart palpitations. Ryder, born William Levise Jr., grew up in Detroit and was singing in a black quartet at just seventeen. Reverse racial harassment induced him to create an all-white band, which was picked up by manager-producer Bob Crewe. The name "Mitch Ryder" was allegedly chosen at random out of a phone directory. "Jenny" was actually a medley of a '50s Chuck Willis number, "See See Rider," and "Jenny Jenny," a Top 10 hit for Little Richard; Ryder's fiery delivery took the songs to a whole new level.

The (Young) Rascals

Although the Rascals had only two hits within the time frame of this volume (1965's "I Ain't Gonna Eat Out My Heart Anymore," followed by "Good Lovin'," a No. 1 smash in 1966), they went on to create enduring classics with "Groovin'," "It's a Beautiful Morning," "A Girl like You," and "People Got to Be Free." As guitarist, journalist, and rock historian Lenny Kaye once put it, "I know this may sound a little overboard, but there once was a time when the Young Rascals were the greatest rock & roll band in the world . . . in terms of stage presence, dynamics, and a flair for the most unique and ground-breaking style this side of Liverpool, I can't think of any other group that could have cut the Young Rascals in their prime."[20]

Led by Felix Cavaliere on organ and vocals, the Rascals were a three-quarters Italian American quartet out of New York; bassist Gene Cornish was the sole blue-eyed member. When the group was formed in 1964, all except drummer Dino Danielli had been performing with Joey Dee and the Starlighters ("Peppermint Twist"). All of the members had honed their chops during many hours spent live onstage and in the studio as session players, but still managed a raw soulful sound. Manager Sid Bernstein (the promoter of the Beatles' first shows in America) chose their name from a TV comedy, and the group originally dressed in hokey knickerbocker trousers with round-collared shirts; "Young" was dropped from the band's name in 1967. Unusually for the time, the group performed mostly all-original material composed by Cavaliere and singer Eddie Brigati (except for "Good Lovin'," a cover of an R&B tune by the Olympics), and flat-out refused to play on segregated bills.

As commonly happens, there was considerable acrimony after the group dissolved in 1971 (including lawsuits over the use of the name), although reunions without one or more original members have since taken place. The Rascals were inducted into the Rock and Roll Hall of Fame in 1997, and Cavaliere continues to pursue a solo career.

LENNY BRUCE: A SATIRIST WITH A LASTING LEGACY

Lenny Bruce in New York, 1964. Courtesy of the Library of Congress.

Lenny Bruce (1925–1966) was a social satirist so important to artistic freedom that Bob Dylan paid tribute to him in a song on 1981's *Shot of Love*. Bruce tore through mid-'60s hypocrisy by talking about sex, religion, race, censorship, and politics in the type of language that anyone might use on the street, but was not then supposed to be heard from a stage. By breaking the rules with routines such as "How to Relax Your Colored Friends at Parties," Bruce became not only the father of modern comedy, but a martyr for free speech. His "concert" performances in halls, a first for the era, were a direct result of being banned from working in clubs and cabarets. Even after his first acquittal on obscenity charges, Bruce was imprisoned for his "bad speech" in 1961; he was barred from performing in Great Britain or Australia, and was continually arrested for obscenity or narcotics abuse in major cities across the United States. He was found guilty of narcotics possession in 1963, and between 1961 and 1964 (the year he had to declare bankruptcy), Bruce was arrested four times for obscenity. The final such bust, which took place onstage at New York's Café au Go Go, resulted in a lengthy trial and conviction, despite the fact that Norman Mailer, James Jones, and other acclaimed individuals defended him as a social satirist "in the tradition of Swift, Rabelais and Twain," and Bruce begged the judge: "Please don't lock up these words." Even though the conviction was overturned two years after his death, Bruce's career was all but finished by it. Bill Graham was one of the few brave enough to book him: Bruce appeared on a Fillmore bill with the Mothers of Invention in San Francisco just two months before he died.

Lenny Bruce paid for his outspokenness with constant legal harassment, drug addiction and an early demise at forty, presumably of a heroin overdose; he was found sprawled on the floor of his bathroom, pants pulled down, with a needle in his arm. In the end, Bruce's last true friend and benefactor was Phil Spector, who recorded him when no one else would (the 1965 *Lenny Bruce Is Out Again* album), and paid for his funeral; the producer later wryly commented that Bruce had died from "an overdose of police."[21]

Lenny, an account of Bruce's life, was mounted as a Broadway play in 1971 and became a 1974 film starring Dustin Hoffman, directed by Bob Fosse. In 2003, after a campaign led by Robin Williams, Steve Martin, and other performers, New York governor George Pataki made the symbolic gesture of granting Bruce a posthumous pardon on his 1964 conviction. Bruce was the last American performer to be tried for obscene language, although in the 1990s an attempt was made to nail rappers 2 Live Crew.

NOTES

1. From "Dance Crazes and Sixties Youth Culture," Sixties City, http://www.sixtiescity.com/Culture/dance.htm.

2. Information on Joe Meek and "Telstar" from Eric Lefcowitz, "Welcome to the Retro Future," http://www.retrofuture.com/telstar.html. The biography of Meek from "Meeksville," http://www.meeksville.com/bio/1967.htm. The unedited version of a piece on Meek (originally ran in *Mojo* magazine), from John McCready, "Joe Meek," http://www.mccready.cwc.net/meek.html.

3. From "Monster Mash," http://www.themonstermash.com/mmdex.html.

4. Information obtained from "Kyu Sakamoto Profile," Japanorama, http://www.japanorama.com/kyuchan.html, and "Sakamoto," The Covers Project, http://www.coversproject.com/artist/Kyu+Sakamoto.

5. According to "Lion Sleeps Tonight," SongFacts, http://songfacts.com/detail.lasso?id=1841.

6. Singing Nun quote from her profile on Chris Stoddard, "Swingin' Chicks of the Sixties," http://www.swinginchicks.com/singing_nun.htm.

7. Information from Stoddard, "Swingin' Chicks of the Sixties," http://www.swinginchicks.com/.

8. From Dan Daley, "Chris Blackwell: From LP to DVD, Living The Island Life," *Mix*, December 1, 1999, http://mixonline.com/ar/audio_chris_blackwell_lp/.

9. Information from Tom Simon, "Walk Away Renee," http://www.tsimon.com/renee.htm.

10. Ken Barnes, in *Phonograph Record Magazine*, March 1973, available at: Mark Lindsay, "History," http://www.marklindsay.com/history.htm.

11. Ibid.

12. From "The F.B.I. Investigation of the Song 'Louie Louie,'" LouieLouie.net, http://www.louielouie.net/11-fbi.htm; also quoted by Associated Press, "'Louie Louie,' You Gotta Go," *CBS News*, May 5, 2005, http://www.freep.com/news/statewire/sw115360_20050505.htm.

13. From Kirkus Reviews, review of *Louie Louie: The History and Mythology of the World's Most Famous Rock 'n' Roll Song*, by Dave Marsh, available at: http://www.amazon.com/exec/obidos/ASIN/0786880287/ref=ase_thebompbookstore/102-5577531-3969737.

14. From "Mojo's Ultimate Jukebox—The 100 Singles You Must Own," giveaway booklet, *Mojo*, no. 113 (April 2003).

15. "Band Biography and History," 96 Tears, http://www.pharaohweb.com/Qmark/bio.html.

16. Wayne Jancik and Tad Lathrop, *Cult Rockers* (New York: Fireside/Simon & Schuster, 1995), p. 255.

17. Ibid.

18. Jim Irwin for the Associated Press, "Righteous Brothers' Bobby Hatfield Mourned," *Newsday*, http://www.newsday.com/entertainment/news/wire/sns-ap-obit-hatfield,0,3002582,print.story?coll=sns-ap-entertainment-headlines.

19. Ibid.

20. Lenny Kaye, "The Rascals: Five Years of the Rascals," *Rolling Stone*, June 10, 1971, available at: http://www.rocksbackpages.com/writers/kaye.html.

21. As quoted by Caroline Frost, "Lenny Bruce: Profile," BBC Four Documentaries, http://www.bbc.co.uk/bbcfour/documentaries/features/lenny-bruce-profile.shtml; also quoted in Mick Brown, "Pop's Lost Genius," *London Telegraph*, February 4, 2003, http://www.telegraph.co.uk/arts/main.jhtml?xml=/arts/2003/02/04/bmspec01.xml; and Ralph J. Gleason, "An Obituary," http://members.aol.com/dcspohr/lenny/obgleas.htm.

A-TO-Z OF ROCK, 1960–1966

Bold-faced terms refer to other entries in this A-to-Z chapter.

Every effort has been made to ensure the accuracy of birth and/or death dates (marked by an asterisk if unknown), as well as the duration of each artist or group's career; however, due to shifting personnel and other circumstances, line-ups given relate solely to the period covered within this volume. Additionally, some time spans are approximate and/or denote years during which bands fell inactive, then reunited.

Adler, Lou (b. 1933). Adler began his music career as co-manager of **Jan and Dean** (with Herb Alpert, later co-founder of A&M Records). Adler and Alpert also wrote "Only Sixteen," a 1959 hit for **Sam Cooke**. Adler formed Dunhill Records in 1964, signed and produced the **Mamas and the Papas**, and then co-produced the Monterey Pop Festival with John Phillips. See also Chapter 8.

Andersen, Eric (b. 1943). This **Greenwich Village**–based **folk**singer and songwriter, although well respected, never reached widespread fame; his best-known song remains 1965's **civil rights** Freedom Rider–inspired "Thirsty Boots," which was covered by **Judy Collins**. See also Chapter 8.

The Animals (1962–1966). Eric Burdon (b. 1941), vocals; Alan Price (b. 1942), piano; Chas Chandler (1938–1996), bass; Hilton Valentine (b. 1943), guitar; John Steel (b. 1941), drums. One of the most important **R&B**-based bands to come out of the British invasion, the Animals had an impressively deep-voiced frontman in Eric Burdon, who (along with **Van Morrison** and Stevie Winwood of the **Spencer Davis Group**) typified the best of British **blue-eyed soul**. The group's major hits—classics all—included 1964's

"House of the Rising Sun," "Don't Let Me Be Misunderstood," and "We Gotta Get out of This Place" in 1965, and "It's My Life" and "Don't Bring Me Down" (1966). Bassist Chas Chandler later co-managed and produced the Jimi Hendrix Experience. The group was inducted into the Rock and Roll Hall of Fame in 1994. See also Chapter 5.

Antiwar. A **folk**-based music genre, expressing sorrow and/or rage over the **Vietnam War**. See also **Protest**.

Aronowitz, Al (1928–2005). A journalist who covered jazz, pop, and rock for the *New York Post*, *Saturday Evening Post*, and other outlets, Aronowitz also at one point road-managed **Bob Dylan** and introduced him to the **Beatles**. He is the author of *Bob Dylan and the Beatles, Volume 1 of The Best of the Blacklisted Journalist*. See also Chapter 8.

Atco. Record label, division of **Atlantic**.

Atlantic. New York–based record label that originally focused on **R&B/soul** and later moved into **rock**. See also **Ertegun, Ahmet**.

Avalon, Frankie (Francis Avallone, b. 1939). This Italian American **pop** teen idol began his career as a child-prodigy trumpet player, but became best known for his chart-topping 1959 hit "Venus" and for costarring with Annette Funicello in a series of early and mid-'60s "beach-party" movies. See also Chapter 1.

Bacharach, Burt (b. 1928) and Hal David (b. 1921). Brill Building songwriting team best known for chart-topping '60s work with **Dionne Warwick**—"Don't Make Me Over," "Anyone Who Had a Heart," "Walk On By," "You'll Never Get to Heaven (If You Break My Heart)," "I Say a Little Prayer," "A House Is Not a Home," "I'll Never Fall in Love Again," "Trains and Boats and Planes" (also a hit in the United Kingdom for **Billy J. Kramer** and the Dakotas)—and the film theme songs "Alfie" and "What's New Pussycat?" among others. Bacharach, who began his career playing piano behind Marlene Dietrich, enjoyed renewed appreciation in the 1990s via the release of a boxed set of his work, a writing collaboration with Elvis Costello, and appearances as himself in two *Austin Powers* movies. See also Chapter 3.

Baez, Joan (b. 1941). This singer-songwriter was considered the Madonna of the **folk** world after her 1959 triumph at the first Newport Folk Festival for her purity of voice and attractive au naturel appearance. Her romance with **Bob Dylan** raised both parties' public profiles; Baez is prominently featured in the 1966 Dylan documentary ***Dont Look Back***. Her first three albums (1960–1962) were all awarded gold records and stayed in the charts for two years; a 1964 cover of **Phil Ochs**'s "There but for Fortune" made the Top 10 in England. Baez also befriended the **Beatles**, in particular John Lennon, and stayed active in the **civil rights** and **antiwar** movements, as well as continuing with her career to the present. See also Chapter 8.

The Beach Boys (1961–present). Brian Wilson (b. 1942), songwriting/vocals/keyboards/arrangements/production; Carl Wilson (1946–1998), vocals/guitar; Dennis Wilson (1944–1983), drums; Alan Jardine (b. 1942), vocals/guitar; Mike Love (b. 1941), lead vocals. One of the most popular groups of the era and beyond, the Beach Boys were initially dismissed as simply a surfing-oriented band, but had a secret weapon in eldest Wilson brother Brian, whose songwriting and gift for arrangements were unsurpassed. Wilson considered his group's only real competition to be the **Beatles**, and in fact, Paul McCartney has long admitted that the fabled 1966 *Pet Sounds* album helped inspire *Sgt. Pepper*. Wilson became increasingly psychologically fragile (possibly due to an abusive upbringing, coupled with the use of **psychedelic** drugs) and stopped touring early on. The group's best-known songs of this period include "Surfin' Safari" and "Surfin'" (1962), "In My Room," "Little Deuce Coupe," "Surfer Girl," and "Surfin' U.S.A." (1963), "Don't Worry Baby," "Wendy," "Fun, Fun, Fun," and "I Get Around" (1964), "California Girls," "Barbara Ann," and "Help Me, Rhonda" (1965), and "God Only Knows," "Good Vibrations," and "Sloop John B" (1966). The group was inducted into the Rock and Roll Hall of Fame in 1988. See also Chapter 7.

The Beatles (1960–1970). John Lennon (1940–1980), songwriting/guitar/vocals; (Sir) Paul McCartney (b. 1942), songwriting/bass/vocals; George Harrison (1943–2001), songwriting/lead guitar/vocals; Ringo Starr (Richard Starkey, b. 1940), drums/vocals. Generally acknowledged to be the most popular rock and roll band of all time, with at least a billion albums sold (more than 163 million by 2001 in America alone), the Beatles hold several world records: the most No. 1 U.S. albums, with nineteen (more than twice those of the nearest competitors, **Elvis Presley** and the **Rolling Stones**), as well as the greatest number of No. 1 U.S. singles (twenty between 1964 and 1970). During the period covered in this volume, the band formed in the tough British port city of Liverpool from the remnants of a **skiffle** group called the Quarrymen led by John Lennon, honed its performing abilities with a grueling apprenticeship in the red-light Reeperbahn district of Hamburg, Germany, and came to worldwide prominence as managed by **Brian Epstein**. The Beatles rapidly conquered the planet with energy, charm, and music via recordings, live performance, and mass media, including *Ed Sullivan Show* performances seen by millions and two films (1965's **A Hard Day's Night** and **Help!** the following year). The Beatles blazed many new paths: first rock band to sell millions of dollars in merchandise (much of it unauthorized), first to play a concert in a stadium, and first to gain serious critical respect. The young female desire sparked by Frank Sinatra and Elvis Presley was now writ much larger, times four, creating hysterical pandemonium on such a huge scale that a new word ("Beatlemania") was coined to describe it. The group set trends in everything it did or wore, from clothing and hairstyles to music, attitudes, and even the drugs used in later years. Between 1963 and 1966, the Beatles released eight full albums (and nonalbum singles, including Christmas records for its fan club), each a creative leap beyond the previous release, most notably with **Rubber Soul** in 1965 and **Revolver** the following year, both of which demonstrated the effect of **psychedelics** on the group's composing and studio experimentation. Although the Beatles gave their final live performance in 1966, the group continued to create innovative music, inspired innumerable other musicians, and remain beloved by fans to this day, including many who were not born until decades after the group hung up its performing spurs. The group was inducted into the Rock and Roll Hall of Fame in 1988. See also Chapter 4.

The Beau Brummels (1964–1968). Sal Valentino (Spampinato, b. 1942), lead vocals; Ron Elliot (b. 1943), songwriting/guitar/vocals; Declan Mulligan (b. 1938), guitar/vocals/songwriting; Ron Meagher (b. 1941), bass; John Peterson (b. 1942), drums. This American group was originally mistaken for a British invasion band with its brooding 1965 hit "Laugh Laugh," produced by Sly Stewart (later known as Sly of the Family Stone), followed by "Just a Little" the same year. See also Chapter 9.

Bernstein, Sid (b. 1918). Ambitious talent agent and promoter who booked **the Beatles**, sight unseen, for Carnegie Hall in 1964 and Shea Stadium in 1965; he later managed the **Rascals** and participated with a writer for the autobiographical *It's Sid Bernstein Calling*. See also Chapter 4.

Best, Peter (b. 1941). The original drummer for the **Beatles**, Best joined the group in 1960 and was replaced by Ringo Starr in 1962. He later formed the Pete Best Four and is the author of *Beatle! The Pete Best Story*. See also Chapter 4.

Big Brother and the Holding Company (1965–1972). Janis Joplin (1943–1970), vocals; Sam Andrew (b. 1941), guitar/vocals; James Gurley (b. 1941), guitar; Peter Albin (b. 1944), bass; David Getz (b. 1938), drums. Singer Janis Joplin moved to San Francisco from Texas, joining the band in mid-1966; she quickly became a star attraction with her powerful voice and presence. The group itself had a reputation for sloppy musicianship, but still managed to crystallize the reckless, high-energy **psychedelic** blues emanating from the city during this period.

Blonde on Blonde, 1966. Groundbreaking double album by **Bob Dylan** that ushered in the **folk-rock** era with its electrified, sometimes raucous instrumentation; it was chosen as No. 9 for the *Rolling Stone* list of the greatest albums of all time. Key tracks include "Rainy Day Women #12 & 35" (better known by its chorus, "Everybody Must Get Stoned"), "Just Like a Woman," and "Visions of Johanna." See also Chapter 8.

Bloomfield, Michael (1943–1981). A white American **blues** guitarist who became infatuated with Chicago-style electric blues early on, Bloomfield boldly sought out his heroes (and jumped onstage to jam with the likes of

Muddy Waters and **Howlin' Wolf**) while still a young teenager. He was re-cruited to play in **Paul Butterfield**'s band and also backed **Bob Dylan** on *Highway 61 Revisited*, as well as on the 1965 Newport Folk Festival date when **folk** became electrified. Bloomfield went on to form the Electric Flag and work with Stephen Stills of **Buffalo Springfield** and **Al Kooper** on the *Super Session* album. He played with Dylan one last time (in 1980) before dying of a drug overdose. See also Chapter 4.

Blue-Eyed Soul. Musical genre of white musicians and/or singers work-ing within a **blues**-based context usually associated with African Americans. There is also a subdivision for Latino artists known as "brown-eyed soul." See also **Soul**.

Blues/R&B. Genres of music ("R&B," a term coined by producer **Jerry Wexler**, stands for "rhythm and blues") that may also include **soul** and splinter off into certain varieties of **pop** (e.g., **Sam Cooke** and **Motown**); these vivid means of self-expression were once thought to be confined purely to African American practitioners, but during the period covered in this volume were adopted by many white musicians. The blues that inspired the British invasion was of the electrified variety, created in Chicago in the '40s and '50s after a mi-gration of southern blacks; it amplified the acoustic school of Delta blues (from southern Mississippi, comprised of vocals, guitar, and harmonica) into a small-band context, adding drums, wind instruments, and keyboards.

The Bobby Fuller Four (1964–1966). Bobby Fuller (1942–1966), vocals/guitar/songwriting; Randy Fuller*, bass/harmony vocals/songwriting; Jim Reese*, guitar; DeWayne Quirico*, drums. Although Bobby Fuller is renowned for a single song (1966's "I Fought the Law"), it was an influential one; the Clash covered it years later, and in the words of one rock critic, Fuller was the "missing link between Buddy Holly and . . . Creedence Clearwater Re-vival."[1] He died in a highly suspicious manner soon after his one hit. See also Chapter 7.

Booker T. and the MGs (1962–1971). Booker T. Jones (b. 1944), organ; Steve Cropper (b. 1941), guitar; Donald "Duck" Dunn (b. 1941), bass; Al Jack-son Jr. (1935–1975), drums. One of the first racially integrated **rock-soul** groups (two white members, two black), Booker T. and the MGs were the stu-dio band for **Stax-Volt Records**, helping to create the "Memphis Sound" be-hind artists like **Otis Redding**, **Wilson Pickett**, and **Sam and Dave**. The group—which, early on, could not play publicly in its segregated hometown—also had hits of its own like the instrumental "Green Onions," which reached No. 3 on the national charts in 1962. The group was inducted into the Rock and Roll Hall of Fame in 1992. See also Chapter 2.

Boyce, Tommy (1939–1994) and Bobby Hart (b. 1939). The songwrit-ing team responsible for 1964's "Come a Little Bit Closer" by **Jay and the**

Americans is perhaps best known for the **Monkees'** hits "Last Train to Clarksville" (No. 1, 1966) and "(I'm Not Your) Stepping Stone" (1967). See also Chapter 3.

Los Bravos. Mike Kogel (b. 1945), lead vocals; Antonio Martinez (b. 1945), guitar; Miguel Vicens Danus (b. 1944) bass; Manuel (Manolo) Fernandez (b. 1943), organ; Pablo Samllehi (b. 1943), drums. The 1966 Top 5 hit "Black Is Black" marked the first appearance by a Spanish group on the international pop scene, although it was sung in English by Kogel, who was born in Germany. See also Chapter 9.

Brill Building. The Brill Building at 1619 Broadway in New York City (formerly the site of the Brill Brothers' ground-level clothing shop) held a multitude of then-inexpensive offices; when Tin Pan Alley, the center of the city's songwriting industry, moved northwards around the mid-twentieth century, this building housed many composers and other music-related businesses. The music referred to as "Brill Building" was an amalgam of **rock, pop**, and **R&B**, usually producer driven, that often utilized sophisticated arrangements with orchestras and strings; it was dependent on artists such as **girl groups** who, in turn, required outside material. The Brill Building fell out of favor after the **Beatles** and **Bob Dylan** helped create a demand for singer-songwriters who performed self-penned material (before hooking up with Dylan, **Al Kooper** was a teenaged songwriter here). See also **Bacharach, Burt, and Hal David; King, Carole, and Gerry Goffin; Lieber, Jerry, and Mike Stoller; Mann, Barry, and Cynthia Weil; Pomus, Doc, and Mort Shuman; Spector, Phil**; Chapter 3.

Brown, James (b. 1928). It would be impossible to overstate the importance of James Brown, who awed the **Rolling Stones** and helped give African Americans a sense of pride. He transformed **R&B** into **soul**, supplied the very definition of funk, and—through sampling of his work—provided the basis for hip-hop. He was born dirt-poor in the segregated South. His landmark 1963 *Live at the Apollo* album (for which he put up his own money) reached No. 2 on the *Billboard* albums chart. He captured a wide white audience with the 1965 hit "Papa's Got a Brand New Bag," followed by "I Got You (I Feel Good)." Brown's much-imitated stage performances, which often climaxed in his throwing off a protective cape and coming back for just one more number, led to the nicknames that say it all: he is the "Godfather of Soul," "Soul Brother No. 1," and "the Hardest-Working Man in Show Business." He was inducted into the Rock and Roll Hall of Fame in 1986. See also Chapter 2.

Bruce, Lenny (Leonard Alfred Schneider, 1925–1966). The "Charlie Parker of comedy," as he was once called, became a martyr for free speech when he was put on trial and banned from his satirist livelihood for using "obscene" language from the stage and on albums; he was recorded by his friend **Phil Spector**, who also paid for his funeral. See also Chapter 9.

Buckley, Tim (1947–1975). Buckley was a singer-songwriter from Southern California who started out in **folk** but later ventured into edgier, **psychedelic**-jazz territory; although he never reached more than a relatively small, underground audience during his brief lifetime, he continues to be rediscovered by successive generations for his lyrical and vocal talents. Buckley died of a heroin overdose (his son, Jeff, also had an all-too-short life and career as a singer-songwriter in the 1990s). See also Chapter 8.

Buffalo Springfield (1966–1968). Stephen Stills (b. 1945), guitar/-vocals/songwriting; Richie Furay (b. 1944), guitar/vocals; Neil Young (b. 1945), guitar/vocals; Bruce Palmer (b. 1946), bass; Dewey Martin (b. 1942), drums. Buffalo Springfield was one of the earliest **folk-rock** groups (along with another Los Angeles–based band, the **Byrds**). The Springfield's only hit—its debut single, 1966's "For What It's Worth"—addressed youth riots on the Sunset Strip, but has retained a contemporary relevance during succeeding decades. Stills and Young teamed up again in the '70s supergroup Crosby, Stills, Nash, and Young, which included former members of the Byrds and the **Hollies**. The group was inducted into the Rock and Roll Hall of Fame in 1997. See also Chapter 7.

Burke, Solomon (b. 1936). Burke, whose roots were in a Philadelphia ministry (he was preaching and hosting a gospel radio show even before adolescence), brought a countrified **soul** feel to the songs "Cry to Me" (1962) and "Everybody Needs Somebody to Love" (1964), both of which were covered by the **Rolling Stones**. Burke was inducted into the Rock and Roll Hall of Fame in 2001. See also Chapter 2.

Butterfield, Paul (1942–1987). Chicago-born Paul Butterfield was greatly influential as the first white **blues** harmonica player who had strong enough chops to stand alongside the African American masters of that city's electric blues genre. Like the **Rolling Stones**, he helped popularize citified blues (as opposed to the acoustic Delta version). Butterfield's band backed **Bob Dylan** at the famous 1965 Newport Folk Festival when **folk** became **folk rock**. When he became interested in Indian music, as many did at the time, Butterfield created a wholly original fusion of raga-influenced, jazzy blues/**rock** on his second album, *East-West* (1966), and later worked with his idol **Muddy Waters**. See also Chapter 4.

The Byrds (1964–1973). Jim, aka Roger, McGuinn (b. 1942), guitar; Gene Clark (1944–1991), guitar; Chris Hillman (b. 1944), bass; David Crosby (b. 1941), guitar; Michael Clarke (1946–1993), drums. The Byrds' first chart single was the **Bob Dylan** song "All I Really Want to Do" (1965); the following year, the band's cover of his "Mr. Tambourine Man" soared to No. 1, followed by the No. 1 "Turn! Turn! Turn" (written by **Pete Seeger**). Other 1966 chart hits included "Eight Miles High" and "Mr. Spaceman." The Byrds pioneered the **folk-rock** genre and the Rickenbacker guitar (noted for its distinctive "chiming" tone, it was also favored by John Lennon); Tom Petty is a direct acolyte. Chris Hillman later formed the Flying Burrito Brothers, an important country-rock group, while David Crosby went on to become part of Crosby, Stills, and Nash (sometimes joined by **Buffalo Springfield** alumnus Neil Young), the first "supergroup" of the early 1970s. Stephen Stills also came out of the Springfield, while Graham Nash had been a member of the **Hollies**. The Byrds were inducted into the Rock and Roll Hall of Fame in 1991. See also Chapter 7.

Capitol. A bicoastal record label, home to the **Beach Boys** and the **Beatles'** American label.

Carnaby Street. A London thoroughfare lined with boutiques that came to be recognized as the center of all things fashionable in the mid-to-late 1960s. See also Chapter 5.

The Charlatans (1964–1970). Michael Wilhelm (b. 1942), guitar/vocals; Richard Olsen*, bass/vocals/woodwinds; Michael Ferguson*, (d. 1975), keyboards/poster art; Daniel Hicks (b. 1941), drums/vocals; George Hunter*, "style." Possibly the first group created as an artistic concept (or conceit), the Charlatans were at the forefront of the early San Francisco hippie/acid-rock scene in their Edwardian Wild West gear. See also Chapter 7.

Charles, Ray (1930–2004). Georgia-born Ray Charles, who lost his sight as a child and was orphaned by age fifteen, learned to play piano and wind instruments, as well as reading and writing music in Braille, at a school for the deaf and blind. He created a furor—and a new musical genre called **soul**—as one of the first performers to fuse gospel stylings (such as call-and-response vocals) with secular, **blues**-based lyrics and melodies, as in his 1954 hit "I Got a Woman." He continued creating music for the next half century; some of the smashes released during the time frame of this volume include "Georgia on My Mind" (1960), "Hit the Road Jack" (No. 1 in 1961), "I Can't Stop Loving You" (No. 1 in 1962), "Unchain My Heart" (1962), "Take These Chains from My Heart" (1963), and "Crying Time" (No. 1 on the *Billboard* Adult Contemporary chart in 1966). Charles's revolutionary 1962 album *Modern Sounds in Country and Western Music* marked the first time an **R&B** artist had ventured into previously all-white territory; his well-earned nickname, "the Genius," was bestowed upon him by Frank Sinatra. He was inducted into the Rock and Roll Hall of Fame in 1986. See also Chapter 2.

Checker, Chubby (Ernest Evans, b. 1941). Chubby Checker will forever be associated with the early '60s **dance** craze "the twist," which he popularized through an eponymous 1960 single (and its 1961 follow-up, neatly titled "Let's Twist Again"), although he also promoted lesser gyrations like the pony and the fly. Checker had three Top 10 hits in 1962 with "Slow Twistin'," "Limbo Rock," and "Popeye the Hitchhiker" and also starred in two twist-related exploitation flicks. See also Chapter 5.

The Chiffons (1960–1972). Judy Craig (b. 1946), lead vocals; Sylvia Peterson (b. 1946), vocals; Barbara Lee (b. 1947), vocals; Patricia Bennett (b. 1947), vocals. The **Tokens** wrote and produced "He's So Fine" (No. 1, 1963) for this New York–based group; "One Fine Day," written by **Carole King and Gerry Goffin**, rose to No. 5 the same year, while "Sweet Talkin' Guy" made the Top 10 in 1966. The Chiffons were among the opening acts at the **Beatles' first** U,S. concert at Washington Memorial Coliseum in 1964, and in June of that year they also opened for the **Rolling Stones** on their first American tour. See also Chapter 3.

A Christmas Gift for You From Phil Spector **(1963).** Although it barely scraped into the Top 15 upon release, this album is a timeless showcase for **Phil Spector**'s fabled "Wall of Sound" and his stable of artists (the **Ronettes**, the **Crystals**, **Darlene Love**, and Bob B. Soxx and the Blue Jeans). See also Chapter 3.

Civil Rights Movement. A mid-1960s effort to attain equality for African American citizens whose key figures included the assassinated leaders Malcolm X and the Reverend Martin Luther King Jr., and that helped spur the **protest** genre of music. See also Chapter 8.

Clark, Dick (b. 1929). Clark was the producer and host of *American Bandstand*, the first network TV show dedicated to **rock** and **pop** music, as well as the longest-running music show in television history (1957–1989). He also created *Where the Action Is!*, which introduced **Paul Revere and the Raiders**. Clark was let off relatively unscathed in the **"payola"** scandal of the early 1960s, which nailed **Alan Freed**, and is also founder of the American Music Awards and still a popular television personality, particularly for his New Year's Eve programming. He was inducted into the Rock and Roll Hall of Fame in 1993. See also Chapters 1, 6.

Clark, Petula (b. 1932). The most commercially successful female British singer, this former child star had her own radio show at eleven and made more than two dozen films before becoming the first British woman to top the American charts with 1964's Grammy-winning "Downtown," followed by hits "I Know a Place" (which sounded suspiciously like the Cavern Club) the next year and 1966's "I Couldn't Live without Your Love." See also Chapter 3.

Cochran, Eddie (1938–1960). This rockabilly star was revered in England, where a young Paul McCartney gained membership in what later evolved into the **Beatles** by impressing John Lennon with his knowledge of Cochran's "Twenty Flight Rock," a hit in 1956. His 1958 "Summertime Blues" charted both black and **pop**, a rare feat for such an artist, and became a live staple for the **Who**; "C'mon Everybody" charted in 1959, a year before Cochran died in a car crash while touring the United Kingdom. He was inducted into the Rock and Roll Hall of Fame in 1987. See also Chapter 1.

Collins, Judy (b. 1939). A singer-songwriter beloved in the **Greenwich Village folk** scene for her support of other artists, Collins became a popular recording artist as an interpreter of others' material. For *Judy Collins #3*, Roger McGuinn of the **Byrds** worked out arrangements of "The Bells of Rhymney" and **Pete Seeger**'s "Turn! Turn! Turn!" before covering them with his own band. Collins is still active in her career. See also Chapter 8.

Columbia. New York–based record label, home to **Bob Dylan**; it employed **John Hammond** as a producer, talent scout, and A&R man.

Cooke, Sam (1931–1964). Cooke is considered the inventor of modern **soul**, an innovative songwriter and performer who also possessed impressive business sense. He founded a record label and publishing company and took creative control of his music in the early 1960s, when such ventures were unheard of for any artist, never mind an African American. Cooke's charm, good looks, and smooth voice made him popular with white fans of all ages, yet he never alienated his core black audience, although he did enrage the world of gospel music after he left the Soul Stirrers to "go secular" with his self-penned "You Send Me," which hit No. 1 on both the **pop** and **R&B** charts in 1957. Cooke kicked off the '60s with the uncharacteristically gritty "Chain Gang," reverted to form with "(What a) Wonderful World" (both in 1960), scored another crossover hit the following year with "Cupid," and had three smashes in 1962 with "Bring It on Home to Me," "Havin' a Party," and "Twistin' the Night Away." His 1964 engagement at the Copa was a triumph, resulting in a 1965 live album, the year Cooke had hits with two very different songs: "Shake" and the **civil rights**–inspired "A Change Is Gonna Come," which pointed to the evolution his music might have had. Unfortunately, this towering figure did not live to enjoy his success: Sam Cooke was shot and killed under mysterious circumstances in the last month of 1964, a passing that came too soon and went strangely uninvestigated. See also Chapter 2.

The Count Five (1965–1967). Kenn Ellner (b. 1948), lead vocals; John "Mouse" Michalski (b. 1949), guitar; Sean Byrne (b. 1947), guitar/vocals/songwriting; Roy Chaney (b.1948), bass; Craig "Butch" Atkinson (b. 1947), drums. These **garage-rock** pioneers had one Top 10 single in 1966 with "Psychotic Reaction," a feat the group could never duplicate. See also Chapter 9.

The Crystals (1961–1966). Barbara Alston (b. 1945), vocals; Dolores "LaLa" Brooks (b. 1946), vocals; Dee Dee Kennibrew (b. 1945), vocals; Mary Thomas (b. 1946), vocals; Patricia Wright*, vocals. Discovered by **Phil Spector** while they were cutting demo records at the **Brill Building**, the Crystals ushered in a new era of social semirealism with 1962's "Uptown" (written by **Barry Mann and Cynthia Weil**), where class issues impact a romantic relationship. That same year, Spector almost torpedoed the group's career when he recorded "He Hit Me (and It Felt like a Kiss)," from the **King and Goffin** team;

the group hated it, and so did DJs. Spector then bypassed the group entirely to use **Darlene Love** as the voice of the next "Crystals" singles, "He's a Rebel," which went to No. 1 in 1962, and "He's Sure the Boy I Love." He reverted to the original lineup for 1963's "Da Doo Ron Ron (When He Walked Me Home)" and "Then He Kissed Me," both of which went to the Top 5. But by now Spector had discovered the **Ronettes** and lost interest in the Crystals, putting the final nail in the group's coffin by making it record "(Let's Dance) the Screw," a 1964 contractual obligation and flip of the bird to his former partner. See also Chapter 3.

Dale, Dick (Richard Monsour, b. 1937). Dale, the son of a Lebanese father and a Polish mother, learned in childhood about both cultures' folk music and string instruments and later employed the resultant melodic mashup via self-taught ukelele and guitar; he played so fiercely in a style that would later become known as "shredding" that he often broke even the heaviest-gauge strings. Dale developed new guitar and amplifier technology in concert with Leo Fender, including a portable reverb unit, and his speedy playing and showy performances influenced later artists such as Jimi Hendrix. Crowned "King of the Surf Guitar" for classics like 1961's "Let's Go Trippin'," the first recorded surf instrumental, in some quarters Dale is also considered the father of heavy-metal music. See also Chapter 7.

Dance. The 1960s craze for fast, noncontact dancing replaced 1950s jitter-bugging with such popular forms of physical expression as the twist, the swim, the pony, the hitchhike, the loco-motion, the Watusi, the frug, the jerk, and the mashed potato, almost all of which inspired at least one single. See also Chapter 9.

Darin, Bobby (Walden Robert Cassotto, 1936–1973). Darin was already a teen idol, albeit a more mature one than, say, Fabian, when his 1960 song "Beyond the Sea" made the Top 10. Darin had something of a junior-league Rat Pack image, yet there was a certain **R&B** feel to some of his vocals, and he tended to bounce between genres, working in **pop**, semi**rock**, country, and even **folk rock**: he employed a pre-**Byrds** Roger (then Jim) McGuinn as a backup musician in 1963, and two years later, the **Searchers** had a hit with the Darin-written "When I Get Home," the same year he was involved in a **civil rights** march in Alabama. Darin was inducted into the Rock and Roll Hall of Fame in 1990. See also Chapter 1.

The Dave Clark Five (1961–1970). Dave Clark (b. 1942), drums/vocals/songwriting; Mike Smith (b. 1943), lead vocals/keyboards/ songwriting; Denis Payton (b. 1943), saxophone/harmonica/acoustic guitar/vocals; Rick Huxley (b. 1944), bass/acoustic guitar/vocals; Lenny Davidson (b. 1944), lead/acoustic guitar/vocals. This London-based group was touted as a threat to the **Beatles** for a short period, thanks to pounding hits like "Glad All Over," "Bits and Pieces," the uncharacteristically soft ballad "Because" (all in 1964), and, in 1965, "Catch Us If You Can" and the group's only No. 1, "Over and Over." However, more authentic challengers supplanted the band within a year or two, and its 1965 film *Having a Wild Weekend* came and went. Clark, though, was a savvy businessman as well as a clever songwriter; he managed and produced the band, a rarity in that era, and later bought up the rights to the British TV series *Ready, Steady, Go!* for licensing purposes. See also Chapter 4.

DeShannon, Jackie (Sharon Lee Myers, b. 1944). A folk-rock-oriented singer-songwriter who toured with the **Beatles** and the **Dave Clark Five**, De-Shannon wrote "When You Walk in the Room," a 1964 hit for herself and the **Searchers**, and her "Don't Doubt Yourself Babe" was covered by the **Byrds** on their debut album. Her sole Top 10 hit during this period, however, was the **Bacharach and David** song "What the World Needs Now Is Love" (1965). See also Chapter 3.

Dinning, Mark (1933–1986). Dinning inaugurated the "death-rock" genre with his 1960 hit "Teen Angel." See also Chapter 9.

Dino, Desi, and Billy (1964–1970). Dean Martin Jr. (1953–1987), bass/vocals; Desiderio Arnaz IV (b. 1953), drums; Billy Hinsche (b. 1951), lead guitar. These teen idols were blessed with Hollywood pedigrees (Dino was the son of singer Dean Martin; Desi, the progeny of Lucille Ball and Desi Arnaz; and Billy was a local Beverly Hills boy); their connections guaranteed top studio production with real musicians and a record company that would push their singles. In 1965, the trio had a Top 20 hit with "I'm a Fool" and placed "Not the Lovin' Kind" into the Top 30 months later; that year, the band, none of whom was yet fifteen, also toured with the **Beach Boys**. See also Chapter 9.

Dion (Dion DiMucci, b. 1939). Dion left his popular doo-wop group, the Belmonts, to go solo in 1960 and promptly notched hits like 1961's "Runaround Sue," "The Wanderer" in 1962, and "Donna the Prima Donna" and "Ruby Baby," both in 1963. An addiction to heroin preoccupied Dion until he got clean around 1968 and returned to music as a reinvented **folk rock**er with his lament for fallen leaders, "Abraham, Martin, and John." He was inducted into the Rock and Roll Hall of Fame in 1989. See also Chapter 1.

The Dixie Cups (1963–1966). Barbara Ann Hawkins (b. 1943), vocals; Rosa Lee Hawkins (b. 1946), vocals; Joan Marie Johnson (b. 1945), vocals. 1964's No. 1 "Chapel of Love," written by **Phil Spector** and **Ellie Greenwich and Jeff Barry**, had originally been intended for the **Ronettes** or the **Crystals** but instead was recorded by this trio of two sisters and their cousin. The group also charted with "People Say" that same year and "Iko Iko" in 1965. See also Chapter 3.

Donegan, Lonnie (Anthony) (1931–2002). This Scottish-born singer and self-taught guitarist began his career by working in London jazz bands, although his first interest was in American **blues**, **folk**, and country-and-western music; he would play these songs on breaks from Dixieland performances, on either guitar or banjo, backed by an upright bass and drums; sometimes a thimble and washboard served for percussion. To describe this amalgam, Donegan decided upon the word "**skiffle**" (reportedly after a 1930s Chicago group). His 1956 single "Rock Island Line" sold 3 million copies, extraordinary in those days, and also made the American Top 10; but more important, it inspired the pre-**Beatles** Quarrymen, among other would-be musicians, with its rhythm and easily duplicated, often homemade instrumentation. Donegan had one more American hit single, the 1964 novelty number "Does Your Chewing Gum Lose Its Flavor (on the Bedpost Overnight)?" but by then those he had inspired had taken over the charts. (Ringo Starr, along with other superstars, did return the favor by backing Donegan on a 1978 comeback album, *Putting On the Style*.) See also Chapter 4.

Donovan (Donovan Leitch, b. 1946). This Scottish-born singer-songwriter served as a gentle-troubadour counterpart to **Bob Dylan**'s more acid-tongued **folk-rock** prophet; he may have been mocked by Dylan in the film *Dont Look Back*, but he was a close friend of the **Beatles**. During the time frame of this volume, his hits were 1965's "Catch the Wind" and the following year's "Mellow Yellow" and "Sunshine Superman," which hit No. 1. See also Chapter 8.

***Dont Look Back*, 1966.** This *cinema verité*, directed by D. A. Pennebaker, of **Bob Dylan** during a British tour on his initial rise to fame is a fly-on-the-wall look at this enigmatic figure and a valuable document in its own right; there is some debate whether music video was invented with the **Beatles**' *Hard Day's Night* or here, with a surreal setup of a deadpan Dylan holding, then tossing, cue cards with handwritten lyrics to "Subterranean Homesick Blues" while Beat poet Allen Ginsberg lurks in the background. The film also features **Joan Baez** and **Donovan**. See also Chapter 8.

Dunhill. Los Angeles–based record label founded in 1965 by **Lou Adler**. It was home to the **Mamas and the Papas** and **Barry McGuire** before Adler sold it in 1966 to start another label called Ode.

Dylan, Bob (Robert Zimmerman, b. 1941). Arguably the most influential singer-songwriter of the latter half of the twentieth century, Bob Dylan began his career as a **folk** admirer of **Woody Guthrie**, but soon moved beyond accompanying himself on a single acoustic guitar to a full electrified band, creating the hybrid known as **folk rock**. Dylan was enormously important in both the **civil rights** and the **antiwar** movements of the 1960s, writing anthems such as "Blowin' in the Wind" (popularized by **Peter, Paul, and Mary**) and "The Times They Are A-Changin'"; his vitriolic six-minute single "Like a Rolling Stone" shattered radio time barriers and restrictions on the types of topics that could be addressed in popular song. Dylan was inducted into the Rock and Roll Hall of Fame in 1988. See also Chapter 8.

Eddy, Duane (b. 1938). Eddy, along with Chuck Berry, was one of the most important 1950s proponents of the electric guitar, and his patented "twangy" sound helped him become one of the first **rock** artists to sell albums, as opposed to singles. While "Rebel Rouser," released in 1958, remains the tune with which he is most identified, Eddy's biggest hit actually came in 1960 with "Because They're Young." His music influenced, among others, the **Beatles'** George Harrison; Harrison and Paul McCartney were guest stars on a 1987 eponymous Eddy album. He was inducted into the Rock and Roll Hall of Fame in 1994. See also Chapter 7.

Elektra. This Los Angeles–based record label was formed in 1950, and was home to Arthur Lee and **Love, Tom Paxton,** and **Judy Collins.**

EMI (Electric and Music Industries Ltd). This British-based record label was formed in 1931 and was home to the **Beatles,** among others. **Capitol** was its U.S. subsidiary.

Epstein, Brian (1934–1967). An urbane former drama student put in charge of one of his father's North England Music Stores, Epstein was a record buyer for the shop and a music columnist for *Mersey Beat* when he saw the **Beatles** perform at the Cavern Club in 1961. He became the group's first real manager, although, as an old-school gentleman whose word was his bond, Epstein purposely did not sign his February 1962 contract with the band until nine months later, which allowed the band a temporary escape clause. Although he made several costly mistakes along the way due to the unprecedented nature of the Beatles' success (and, possibly, problems of a personal nature), Epstein polished the group's image, was relentless in pursuit of a recording contract, and proved himself both fiercely loyal to and protective of his charges. He later added **Gerry and the Pacemakers, Billy J. Kramer** and the Dakotas, and Cilla Black to his stable of artists. Epstein was the credited author of the 1964 autobiography *A Cellarful of Noise,* although the book is generally thought to be the work of public relations man Derek Taylor. After he died of an overdose of pills, ruled as accidental, the Beatles began to fragment as an entity; as Paul McCartney acknowledged in 1997, "If anyone was the fifth Beatle, it was Brian."[2] See also Chapter 4.

Ertegun, Ahmet (b. 1923). A music fan since childhood, the Turkish-born Ertegun co-founded **Atlantic** Records in 1947 with Herb Abramson; **Jerry Wexler** became a partner in 1953, and Ahmet's brother Nesuhi joined in 1956. Atlantic/Atco became the country's top **R&B** label with a top-notch roster of **soul** and **rock** greats in the '60s and beyond, including **Otis**

Redding, **Aretha Franklin**, **Ray Charles**, **Buffalo Springfield**, the Young **Rascals**, and in 1966, Cream, Eric Clapton's first band after leaving **John Mayall**'s Bluesbreakers. Ertegun was inducted into the Rock and Roll Hall of Fame in 1987.

Fabian (Forte, b. 1943). Fabian was a teen idol around 1959–1961, mostly due to pretty looks, songs provided by the songwriting team of Doc Pomus and Mort Shuman, and repeated exposure on **Dick Clark**'s televised *American Bandstand*, then broadcast out of his Philadelphia hometown. See also Chapter 1.

Faithfull, Marianne (b. 1946). This ethereal-looking **pop** princess had only one real hit, "As Tears Go By," provided for her in 1964 by the **Rolling Stones'** songwriting team of Mick Jagger (as whose consort she became better known) and Keith Richards. Faithfull proved more resilient than she appeared when, after a long heroin addiction, she resurrected her career in 1979 with the savage *Broken English* album. She is now considered one of the ultimate '60s survivors. See also Chapter 3.

Fame, Georgie (Clive Powell, b. 1943). This British **blues**-jazz pianist and vocalist led an **R&B** band that was highly popular in London around 1962; his sound also incorporated the then-novel Jamaican ska or bluebeat. Fame hit No. 1 in England with his 1965 "Yeh Yeh," which also skimmed the American Top 20. See also Chapter 1.

Folk. A musical genre played on acoustic instruments, primarily guitar (sometimes by a single person); if it is performed by a group, vocal harmonies are a primary component. During the time frame of this volume, folk topics usually addressed personal or political issues. See also **Eric Andersen**; **Antiwar**; **Joan Baez**; **Tim Buckley**; **Judy Collins**; **Folk Rock**; **Woody Guthrie**; **Phil Ochs**; **Tom Paxton**; **Peter, Paul, and Mary**; **Protest**; **Pete Seeger**; Chapter 8.

Folk Rock. A musical genre pioneered by **Bob Dylan** (credited with creating this hybrid when he "went electric"), the **Byrds**, **Donovan**, the **Lovin' Spoonful**, and others. Often generated and performed by singer-songwriters, folk rock was characterized by prominent vocal harmonies and "chiming" or "ringing" guitar sounds. See also **Antiwar**; **Protest**; Chapters 7, 8.

Wayne Fontana and the Mindbenders (1963–1968). Wayne Fontana (Glyn Geoffrey Ellis, b. 1945), vocals; Eric Stewart (b. 1945), guitar/vocals; Bob Lang (b. 1946), bass; Ric Rothwell (b. 1944), drums. In 1965, Fontana's "Game of Love" reached No. 2 in England, No. 1 in America, which was an unusual feat at the time for a British group other than the **Beatles**. The following year "A Groovy Kind of Love" was No. 2 in both countries. See also Chapter 5.

The Four Seasons (1961–present). Frankie Valli (Francis Castelluccio, b. 1937), lead vocals; Bob Gaudio (b. 1942), vocals/keyboards/songwriting/arrangements/production; Tommy DeVito (b. 1946), guitar; Nick Massi (Nicholas Macioci, 1935–2000), bass/arrangements. This doo-wop descendant group had massive hits like "Sherry," "Big Girls Don't Cry" (both No. 1 in 1962), and "Walk like a Man" (No. 1 in 1963), featuring Valli's instantly identifiable falsetto. One of the few Italian American acts to survive the British invasion, the Four Seasons had no fewer than six Top 20 hits in 1964, including "Stay," "Dawn (Go Away)," and "Rag Doll," which made it to No. 1. The group was inducted into the Rock and Roll Hall of Fame in 1990. See also Chapter 1.

The Four Tops (1963–1997). Levi Stubbs (b. 1936), lead vocals; Abdul "Duke" Fakir (b. 1935), first tenor; Lawrence Payton (1938–1997), second tenor; Renaldo "Obie" Benson (1937–2005), baritone. **Motown** act known for smooth choreography, longevity (the group formed in high school and stayed together for forty years without a single change in personnel), and **Holland-Dozier-Holland** hits such as "Baby I Need Your Loving" (1964), "I Can't Help Myself (Sugar Pie Honey Bunch)" (No. 1 **pop** in 1965), "Reach Out, I'll Be There" (No. 1 in pop, 1966), and 1966's "Shake Me, Wake Me (When It's Over)." The group was inducted into the Rock and Roll Hall of Fame in 1990. See also Chapter 2.

Francis, Connie (Concetta Franconero, b. 1938). Italian American female **pop** singer whose heyday was the early 1960s; by 1967, she had sold 35 million records worldwide, with thirty-five Top 40 hits, including No. 1s "Everybody's Somebody's Fool" and "My Heart Has a Mind of Its Own" (1960), "Together" (1961), and "Don't Break the Heart That Loves You" (1962). See also Chapter 3.

Franklin, Aretha (b. 1942). The "Queen of Soul" was discovered by **John Hammond** and recorded for **Columbia** during her early career before switching to **Atlantic** and finding success in the latter half of the '60s as produced by **Jerry Wexler**. She was inducted into the Rock and Roll Hall of Fame in 1987. See also Chapter 3.

Freed, Alan (1921–1965). A pioneering disc jockey and concert promoter, Freed was enormously popular (and given credit for coining the term "rock and roll") before being taken down in the **"payola"** scandal of the early 1960s; he died soon after pleading guilty to various charges. He was inducted into the Rock and Roll Hall of Fame in 1986. See also **Dick Clark**; Chapter 1.

The Fugs (1964–1970). Tuli Kupferberg (b. 1923), songwriter/vocals; Ed Sanders (b. 1939), songwriter/lead vocals/arrangements. Possibly the first underground **rock** band, the Fugs were an East Village collective formed around the nucleus of Beat poets Kupferberg and Sanders, who shattered lyrical taboos with their satirical, sometimes profane wordplay. See also Chapter 8.

Fuller, Bobby. See Bobby Fuller Four.

The Funk Brothers (1959–1972). James Jamerson (1936–1983), bass; William "Benny" Benjamin (1925–1968), drums; Robert White (1936–1994), guitar; Earl Van Dyke (1930–1992), piano/bandleader. Also, Eddie Willis (b. 1936), guitar; Joe Messina (b. 1928), guitar; Jack Ashford (b. 1934), vibes/percussion; Johnny Griffiths, keyboards (1936–2002). This group of highly accomplished studio musicians was an essential component of the **Motown** hit machine, playing uncredited on many singles by the **Supremes, Mary Wells, Marvin Gaye, Smokey Robinson** and the **Miracles**, the **Four Tops**, and the **Temptations**. They were responsible for creating the unique blend of **soul**, **R&B**, and **pop** that gave Motown's records their inimitable sound. Jamerson was inducted into the Rock and Roll Hall of Fame in a newly created "Sidemen" category in 2000; Benjamin, in 2002. See also Chapter 2.

Garage Rock. Musical genre known for its guitar- and/or organ-heavy sound and often indecipherable lyrics. It was popularized via ease of replication by amateur musicians practicing in carports, hence "garage." It was best exemplified by the **Kingsmen** ("Louie Louie"), the **Standells** ("Dirty Water"), the **Seeds** ("Pushin' Too Hard"), and the Shadows of Knight ("Gloria"). It enjoyed a revival in the late '90s and early 2000s through a *Nuggets* boxed set and proponent "Little" Steven Van Zandt's syndicated radio show; it was the antecedent of mid-'90s Seattle grunge. See also Chapter 9.

Gaye, Marvin (Marvin Gay Jr., 1939–1984). This inventive **soul, pop,** and **R&B** singer-songwriter began singing in church at age three and was signed by **Motown** in 1961. His fourth single, 1962's "Stubborn Kind of Fellow," became a minor hit, followed by major ones in "Hitchhike" and "Can I Get a Witness" in 1963. That same year, Gaye reached the Top 10 with "Pride and Joy," a feat he repeated three times in 1965 with "Ain't That Peculiar," "I'll Be Doggone," and "How Sweet It Is to Be Loved by You." His career total for Motown included more than three dozen Top 40 singles, many of which he also wrote and arranged. He was inducted into the Rock and Roll Hall of Fame in 1987. See also Chapter 2.

Getz, Stan (1927–1991). This renowned jazz saxophonist had an unexpected pop hit and helped spark a craze for the bossa nova when he recorded "The Girl from Ipanema" in 1964 with guitarist João Gilberto (b. 1931) and his wife Astrud (b. 1940), who delivered some of the vocals in Portuguese. See also Chapter 9.

Girl Groups. A genre of music most popular from approximately 1962 to 1965, typified by groups of young females dependent upon producers and/or outside songwriting teams, which included the **Chiffons**, the **Crystals**, **Martha and the Vandellas**, the **Ronettes**, the **Shangri-Las**, the **Shirelles**, and the **Supremes**. See also Chapter 3.

Goldie and the Gingerbreads (1963–1965). Goldie Zelkowitz (aka Genya Ravan); (b. 1945), vocals; Carol MacDonald, guitar; Margo Crocitto (aka Lewis)*, keyboards; Ginger Bianco*, drums. The first all-female instrumentalist **rock** and roll band, discovered in New York City by **Animals** lead singer Eric Burdon and brought to England by manager **Mike Jeffries**; Keith Richards personally chose the band to open for a 1965 **Rolling Stones** tour of the United Kingdom. The Gingerbreads also toured with the **Kinks**, the **Yardbirds** in the Jeff Beck period, and the **Hollies**. Animal Alan Price produced the Gingerbreads' 1965 single "Can't You Hear My Heart Beat," a hit in England, but not in America (it was a No. 2 smash in the United States when it was covered by **Herman's Hermits** that same year). See also Chapter 3.

Gomelsky, Giorgio (b. 1934). R&B promoter and unofficial first manager of the **Rolling Stones** (replaced by **Andrew Loog Oldham**); having befriended the **Beatles** in 1963, Gomelsky invited the Liverpudlians to see the Stones at the Crawdaddy Club, which he operated, during the latter band's residency. He went on to manage and produce the **Yardbirds**. See also Chapter 4.

Gordy, Berry, Jr. (b. 1929). This multitalented songwriter, producer, talent scout, and entrepreneur was the original founder of **Motown** Records and, as such, the first true African American music mogul. He called his label "the Sound of Young America," without regard to skin color, and it became true; Motown helped break down the barriers to racial integration through the music made by talented artists such as the **Supremes**, the **Four Tops**, the **Temptations**, **Smokey Robinson** and the **Miracles**, and many more (all of whom were greatly admired by the **Beatles**). Berry is also a film producer, the father of Diana Ross's eldest daughter, and the author of the autobiography *To Be Loved*. He was inducted into the Rock and Roll Hall of Fame in 1990. See also Chapter 2.

Gore, Lesley (b. 1946). Teen **pop** idol identified with the **girl-group** sound, best known for hits such as 1963's "It's My Party" (produced by Quincy Jones), "Judy's Turn to Cry" (1963), "That's the Way Boys Are" (1964), and 1964's protofeminist "You Don't Own Me." Gore also appeared in *The T.A.M.I. Show* alongside the **Rolling Stones**, **James Brown**, **Smokey Robinson** and the **Miracles**, and other stars of the era. See also Chapter 3.

Graham, Bill (Wolfgang Granjonca, 1931–1991). This San Francisco–based promoter and impresario created the noted **rock** venues Fillmores West and East, which helped popularize the **psychedelic** sounds that made the northern California city the focus of 1967's "Summer of Love." He was inducted into the Rock and Roll Hall of Fame in 1992. See also Chapter 7.

The Great Society (1964–1966). Grace (Barnett Wing) Slick (b. 1939), vocals; Darby Slick*, guitar/songwriting; David Minor*, guitar; Bard DuPont*, bass; Gerald "Jerry" Slick*, drums. The forerunner to **Jefferson**

Airplane; Darby, the author of "Somebody to Love," was Grace Slick's brother-in-law (her husband, Jerry, played drums). See also **Jefferson Airplane**, Chapter 7.

Greenwich, Ellie (b. 1940) and Jeff Barry (b. 1938). Brill Building songwriting team (and married couple), responsible for many mid-'60s hits recorded by **Phil Spector**'s acts, such as "Baby I Love You" and "Be My Baby" for the **Ronettes**, "Da Doo Ron Ron" and "Then He Kissed Me" for the **Crystals**, and "**River Deep, Mountain High**" by Ike and Tina Turner. See also Chapter 3.

Greenwich Village. A section of downtown New York City anchored by Washington Square Park that became a focal point of the early and mid-1960s **folk** and **folk-rock** scene. See also Chapter 8.

Grossman, Albert (1926–1986). Grossman, who held a degree in economics, opened Chicago's foremost **folk** music club, the Gate of Horn, in the mid-1950s; he later moved to **Greenwich Village**, where he began his management career with Odetta and also co-founded the Newport Folk Festival. After adding **Bob Dylan** to his résumé, Grossman, a tough negotiator who always got the best possible deals and treatment for his artists, also managed **Peter, Paul, and Mary**, **Ian and Sylvia**, Richie Havens, **Paul Butterfield**, **Michael Bloomfield**, and Janis Joplin and later opened the famed Bearsville recording facilities in that upstate New York town near Woodstock. Grossman may be seen in action in the 1966 Dylan tour film *Dont Look Back*. See also Chapter 8.

Guthrie, Woody (1912–1967). The godfather of **folk** and an early harbinger of **protest** music, Guthrie put a sticker on his guitar that proclaimed, "This Machine Kills Fascists." The idol of **Bob Dylan** and an inspiration to countless others (including Bruce Springsteen), Guthrie authored several books, as well as classic songs such as "This Land Is Your Land" and "Pastures of Plenty," among many others. He was inducted into the Rock and Roll Hall of Fame as an early influence in 1988. See also **Pete Seeger**; Chapter 8.

Hammond, John (1910–1987). This born-wealthy scion of the Vanderbilt family early turned his back on the social register, although privilege allowed him to champion the causes dearest to his heart, **civil rights** and music, which he combined as the promoter of the first racially integrated concert on a major American stage with the 1938 "Spirituals to Swing" shows at Carnegie Hall. As a talent scout and/or producer, Hammond discovered and signed giants including **Bob Dylan** and **Aretha Franklin**; his son, John Paul Hammond, became a **blues** singer-songwriter. Hammond received a Lifetime Achievement Award at the first Rock and Roll Hall of Fame induction ceremonies in 1986. See also Chapter 8.

***A Hard Day's Night*, 1964.** The **Beatles**' first film (accompanied by a corresponding soundtrack album) was directed by Richard Lester on a shoestring budget and at a breakneck pace because the band was then considered a flash-in-the-pan phenomenon; the charm of its principals and Lester's innovative camerawork created a classic. See also Chapter 4.

Helms, Chet (b. 1942). Helms, an émigré from Austin, Texas, created the Family Dog, a "safe house" for the then-burgeoning San Francisco counterculture, and became the chief competition for **Bill Graham** as a concert promoter, booking and operating the Avalon Ballroom from 1966 to 1968. Helms also managed **Big Brother and the Holding Company** (he hitchhiked to California with his friend Janis Joplin in 1963). See also Chapter 7.

Help!, **1965.** The **Beatles'** second film, generally considered inferior to *A Hard Day's Night*; however, the soundtrack album contains many gems, including the title track, the smash hit "Ticket to Ride," and Paul McCartney's much-covered experiment with strings, "Yesterday." See also Chapter 4.

Herman's Hermits (1964–1970). Peter Noone (b. 1947), vocals; Keith Hopwood (b. 1946), vocals/guitar; Derek Leckenby (1945–1994), vocals/guitar; Karl Green (b. 1947), vocals/bass; Barry Whitwam (b. 1946), drums. This Manchester group's music was aimed at the younger end of the teen market, which almost guaranteed that it would receive no respect, although in retrospect its carefully crafted records have come to be appreciated as excellent examples of **pop**; in fact, the band's 1964 hit "I'm into Something Good" was penned by the team of **Carole King** and **Gerry Goffin**, and several of its records—produced by **Animals** studio master **Mickie Most**—actually featured the work of future Led Zeppelin members Jimmy Page (guitar) and John Paul Jones (bass). The Hermits went on to have hits in 1965 with "Can't You Hear My Heartbeat," "Silhouettes," a cover of **Sam Cooke**'s "(What a) Wonderful World," "Mrs. Brown, You've Got a Lovely Daughter"—a music-hall-style number that sold an astounding 14 million copies worldwide—and the similar "I'm Henry the Eighth, I Am." The following year, the group placed no fewer than six singles in the Top 20, including "Dandy" and "This Door Swings Both Ways." All told, the Hermits charted twenty singles between 1964 and 1970, most of which made the Top 10. See also Chapters 5, 6.

Highway 61 Revisited, **1965.** One of **Bob Dylan**'s early crowning achievements, when he "plugged in" and electrified folk, this album was also named as No. 4 on the *Rolling Stone* list of the greatest albums of all time. Key tracks include "Like a Rolling Stone" and "Desolation Row." See also Chapter 8.

Holland-Dozier-Holland. Brian Holland (b. 1941); Lamont Dozier (b. 1941); Eddie Holland (b. 1939). The **Motown** songwriting team responsible for dozens of hits, including **Marvin Gaye**'s 1963 "Can I Get a Witness" and "Little Darling I Need You" (1966); **Martha and the Vandellas'** "Heat Wave," "Come and Get These Memories" (1963), and "I'm Ready for Love" (1966); the **Four Tops'** "I Can't Help Myself (Sugar Pie Honey Bunch)" (1963), "Baby

I Need Your Loving" (1964), and "It's the Same Old Song" (1965); the **Supremes'** "Come See about Me" (1963), "Baby Love" and "Where Did Our Love Go?" (1964), and "Love Is Like an Itching in My Heart" (1966). They were inducted into the Rock and Roll Hall of Fame in 1990. See also Chapter 2.

The Hollies (1962, continuing, minus original members, into the 1990s). Allan Clarke (b. 1942), lead vocals; Graham Nash (b. 1942), vocals/guitar; Tony Hicks (b. 1945), guitar; Bobby Elliot (b. 1941), drums. One of the most melodic **pop-rock** groups of the British invasion, noted for soaring three-part harmonies by Clarke, Nash, and Hicks, who also proved to be a formidable songwriting team. The group charted repeatedly in England before its first U.S. hit with 1965's "Bus Stop," followed by "Look Through Any Window" that same year. See also Chapter 5.

Howlin' Wolf (Chester Arthur Burnett, 1910–1976). Out of the Deep South and strongly influenced by Delta-style **blues**, the physically imposing Wolf (partnered with guitarist Hubert Sumlin) was an extraordinary harmonica player and delivered material in a growly manner that gave his stage name credence. His "Smokestack Lightnin'," recorded in 1958, became a huge hit in England six years after its original release and won him acolytes like the **Rolling Stones**, who covered Wolf's "The Red Rooster" in 1965; as a condition of appearing on the TV series *Shindig!* later that year, the group demanded that Wolf also be booked, and it sat at his feet to pay public homage. Wolf was inducted into the Rock and Roll Hall of Fame as an early influence in 1991. See also Chapter 4.

Hyland, Brian (b. 1943). Hyland hit No. 1 in 1962 with the novelty number "Itsy Bitsy Teeny Weeny Yellow Polka Dot Bikini"; his "Sealed with a Kiss" reached the Top 10 in America upon its original release in 1962 and went into the Top 10 in England after a 1975 reissue. See also Chapter 9.

Ian and Sylvia (1960–1975). Ian Tyson (b. 1933), vocals, guitar; Sylvia Fricker Tyson (b. 1940), vocals. A married couple that performed in **Greenwich Village** and were managed by **Albert Grossman**. Sylvia wrote "You Were on My Mind," which became a No. 3 **pop** hit for the group We Five in 1965. The couple was considered the inspiration for the fictional duo "Mitch and Mickey" in the film *A Mighty Wind* (2003), a satire of the **folk** music scene. See also Chapter 8.

Jack, Wolfman (Robert Weston Smith, 1938–1995). An influential disc jockey with a wild-man persona, Wolfman Jack hosted a widely broadcast Mexican radio show that began airing in 1965. Jack went on to host the TV music show *Midnight Special* (1973–1981), appeared as himself in the 1973 film *American Graffiti*, and inspired songs by artists such as Todd Rundgren. See also Chapter 1.

Jackson, Mahalia (1911–1972). Gospel music's first superstar, Jackson made her singing debut in her local Baptist church choir at age four. She rose to fame in the 1940s, hosted her own radio show in the 1950s, and sang at the inauguration of John F. Kennedy in 1960. As an active supporter of the civil rights movement in the 1960s, she appeared at various benefits and events. See also Chapter 8.

Jackson, Wanda (b. 1937). Singer-songwriter-guitarist Jackson, who started her career in country and moved towards rock and rockabilly (a country-rock fusion) at the suggestion of Elvis Presley, an early tourmate and friend. Her version of "Let's Have a Party," previously recorded by Elvis, grazed the Top 40 in 1960. See also Chapter 3.

Jan and Dean (1958–1966). Jan Berry (1941–2004); Dean Torrence (b. 1940). These Southern California former high-school classmates helped create the two-girls-for-every-guy, sun-drenched surfer mythology with the composition "Surf City," begun by Brian Wilson and completed by Berry, which reached No. 1 in 1963; "Little Old Lady from Pasadena" entered the Top 20 the following year, when Jan and Dean were chosen to host the seminal *T.A.M.I. Show*. Berry was a close friend of Wilson and, like the **Beach Boys** mastermind, was also something of a studio innovator before his near-fatal car crash in 1966. It took him years just to relearn how to walk and talk, and although the duo did tour the oldies circuit, its moment in the sun was by then over. See also Chapter 7.

Jay (Black) and the Americans (1961–1971). "Jay" Black (David Blatt, b. 1941), lead vocals; Kenny Vance (Rosenberg, b. 1943), vocals; Sandy Deane (Yaguda, b. 1940), vocals; Howie Kane (Kerschenbaum, b. 1940), vocals; Marty Sanders (Kupersmith, b. 1940), guitar. After being signed to a recording contract by **Jerry Lieber** and **Mike Stoller**, the Americans—something of a throwback to 1950s doo-wop vocal groups, akin to the **Four Seasons**—scored major hits with 1963's "Only in America," "Come a Little Bit Closer" and "Let's Lock the Door (and Throw Away the Key)" (both in 1964), and the semioperatic "Cara Mia" in 1965. See also Chapter 1.

Jefferson Airplane (1965–1973). Signe (Toly) Anderson (b. 1941), vocals, replaced by Grace Slick (b. 1939); Marty Balin (b. 1942), vocals; Paul Kantner (b. 1941), guitar/vocals; Jorma Kaukonen (b. 1940), guitar; Jack Casady (b. 1944), bass; Skip Spence (1946–1999), drums, replaced by Spencer Dryden (1938–2005). This San Francisco group, formed by Balin and Kantner, was the first from that area to gain national recognition, with double lead vocalists and **psychedelic**-influenced lyrics and sound. Its debut album was released in 1966, but the band took off only after Slick replaced Anderson that year. See also **Great Society**; Chapter 7.

Jeffries, Mike (aka Jeffreys). Very little public information is available about the mysterious manager of the **Animals** and **Goldie and the Gingerbreads**, who also co-managed Jimi Hendrix with the Animals' Chas Chandler. See also Chapter 5.

Kaufman, Murray, "Murray the K" (1922–1982). Murray the K was one of New York's most popular and influential disc jockeys from the late 1950s through the late 1960s; the multiartist shows he promoted at Brooklyn's Fox Theatre have become the stuff of legend. He brought many new artists to audiences' attention, including **Bobby Darin**, and was one of the first to latch on to the **Beatles**, dubbing himself the "fifth" member of the band (he even became George Harrison's hotel roommate for a while). Murray can be seen taking the group to the Peppermint Lounge in the Albert Maysles film of *The First U.S. Visit*. See also Chapter 1.

King, Carole (b. 1942) and Gerry Goffin (b. 1939). This **Brill Building** songwriting team (and then-married couple) was responsible for many mid-'60s hits, such as the **Shirelles**' "Will You Still Love Me Tomorrow," "Chains" (originally cut by the Cookies, then covered by the **Beatles**), "The Loco-Motion" (**Little Eva**), "Up on the Roof" (the Drifters), "One Fine Day" (the **Chiffons**), "I'm into Something Good" (**Herman's Hermits**), and "Don't Bring Me Down" (the **Animals**). See also Chapter 3.

The Kingsmen (1957–1968). Jack Ely*, lead vocals/guitar; Mike Mitchell*, lead guitar; Bob Nordby*, bass; Don Gallucci*, piano; Lynn Easton*, drums. This Portland, Oregon, band defined **garage rock** with its 1963 version of "Louie Louie," written by Richard Berry (1935–1994). After the single went to No. 2, government hearings were held to determine if the song (delivered in a slurred style, with mock-patois lyrics) was obscene. See also Chapter 9.

The Kinks (1963–1990s). Ray Davies (b. 1944), vocals/guitar/songwriting; Dave Davies (b. 1947), lead guitar; Peter Quaife (b. 1943), bass; Mick Avory (b. 1944), drums. Formed by the Davies brothers, the Kinks began as just another **R&B**-based group but soon defined their turf as the most British of invasion bands, focusing on their own London roots. Dave's guitar playing on songs such as "You Really Got Me" (the third single, released in 1964, made the Top 10 in America) and "All Day and All of the Night" (the same year, also Top 10) is considered highly influential, even protometal. The group's profile in America took a nosedive after it was banned by the Musicians' Union following a 1965 tour. The group was inducted into the Rock and Roll Hall of Fame in 1990. See also Chapter 5.

Kirshner, Don (b. 1934). Brill Building (actually, across the street at 1650 Broadway) impresario who formed Aldon Music in 1958 with partner Al Nevins. He was an early manager of **Bobby Darin** and **Connie Francis**, signed Neil Sedaka as a songwriter in the dawn of his career, and created a hit-song factory by hiring teams like **Barry Mann and Cynthia Weil**, and **Carole King and Gerry Goffin**, who worked in tiny cubicles. Kirshner hired **Lou Adler** to run his Los Angeles office and later had a hand in creating the **Monkees**; he also hosted a TV show, *Don Kirshner's Rock Concert* (1973–1981), in a famously personality-free manner. See also Chapter 3.

Kooper, Al (b. 1944). A one-time teenage songwriter from the **Brill Building** era ("This Diamond Ring" for **Gary Lewis and the Playboys**), this keyboard player and sideman is noted for his contributions to **Bob Dylan**'s **folk-rock** sound ("Like a Rolling Stone"), as well as being a founding member of the Blues Project and Blood, Sweat, and Tears. Kooper is also the author of *Backstage Passes*. See also Chapter 8.

Korner, Alexis (1928–1984). The entire early British **R&B** scene rotated around Korner, a guitarist who opened a London blues club in the mid-1950s and formed Blues Incorporated in 1962 (the sometime drummer was Charlie Watts, later of the **Rolling Stones**; the bassist was often Jack Bruce, who would join former **Yardbird** Eric Clapton in Cream). At one time or another, Korner employed, inspired, or encouraged artists like the Rolling Stones, the **Animals**, **John Mayall**, and **Manfred Mann**, although his own career was eclipsed by these illustrious protégés. See also Chapter 4.

Kramer, Billy J. (b. 1943). As lead singer for the Dakotas, Liverpudlian Kramer was part of **Brian Epstein**'s "stable" and benefited from several songs written by the **Beatles** team of John Lennon and Paul McCartney, such as "Do You Want to Know a Secret" and "Bad to Me" (in 1963). His 1964 hit "Little Children," however, was not written by them, and although Kramer appeared that year in the seminal *T.A.M.I. Show* alongside other stars of the day, his career was already faltering. See also Chapter 4.

Lambert, Kit (1935–1981) and Chris Stamp (b. 1942). Both men were assistant film directors (Stamp was the brother of '60s actor Terence Stamp) who were looking for a band to star in a film about fashion and music when they discovered the High Numbers, which became the **Who**; Lambert and Stamp took over the group's management. In 1966, the pair launched Track Records, signing, among others, the Jimi Hendrix Experience, Thunderclap Newman, and the Crazy World of Arthur Brown. See also Chapter 5.

Leary, Dr. Timothy (1920–1996). Leary had been a Harvard psychology lecturer, researcher, and author before being fired by the university in 1963 after giving graduate students lysergic acid (LSD). He became an advocate for this powerful synthesized hallucinogen that, when taken by popular musicians (including the **Beatles**), gave rise to the **psychedelic** era. See also Chapter 7.

Lee, Dickey (Lipscomb, b. 1936). Dickey Lee had not one but two "death-rock" hits: "Patches," written by **Barry Mann**, Top 10 in 1962, and 1965's "Laura" (about a ghost). See also Chapter 9.

The Left Banke (1965–1969). Michael Brown (Lookofsky, b. 1949), songwriter/keyboards; Steve Martin*, vocals; Rick Brand*, guitar; George Cameron*, drums; Tom Finn, bass. Originators of the "baroque" school of rock in its use of strings, this New York combo scored with two romantic hits, "Walk Away Renee" and "Pretty Ballerina," both released in 1965 and reportedly written about the same young woman. See also Chapter 9.

Gary Lewis and the Playboys. Gary Lewis (Gary Levitch, b. 1945), vocals/drums; David Costell (b. 1944), lead guitar; David Walker*, rhythm guitar; Allan Ramsay (b. 1943–1985), bass; John West (b. 1939), keyboards/electric accordion. The son of comedian Jerry Lewis, drummer Gary seized his birthright opportunity in 1965 with the highly polished "This Diamond Ring" (written by **Al Kooper**), a No. 1 single; two years later, his career was derailed by induction into the army. See also Chapter 9.

Lieber, Jerry (b. 1933) and Mike Stoller (b. 1933). Brill Building songwriters ("Kansas City," "Hound Dog," "Love Potion #9," "Poison Ivy," "Stand by Me," "On Broadway"), mentors to **Phil Spector** and **Ellie Greenwich** and **Jeff Barry**, and founders of the Red Bird record label, home to many '60s **girl groups**. The team was inducted into the Rock and Roll Hall of Fame in 1987. See also Chapter 3.

Little Eva (Eva Narcissus Boyd, 1943–2003). Eva was sixteen and working as a baby-sitter for songwriters **Carole King** and **Gerry Goffin** for $35 a week in 1962 when they asked her to record their song "The Loco-Motion"; her royalties from the hit totaled approximately $30,000. Eva's only other success was 1962's "Keep Your Hands off My Baby." See also **Dance**; Chapter 3.

Love (1965–1974). Arthur Lee (Arthur Taylor Porter, b. 1945), vocals/guitar/songwriting; Bryan MacLean (1947–1988), vocals/guitar/songwriting; John Echols (b. 1945), guitar; Ken Forssi (b. 1943), bass; Alban "Snoopy" Pfisterer (b. 1947), drums. There is no question that Arthur Lee, as a black hippie with a slightly sinister aura, was one of **rock**'s first African American front men, paving the path for the likes of Jimi Hendrix (with whom he once recorded). The group was also a revelation with its early melange of **garage**, **folk**, and **psychedelia**; its 1967 *Forever Changes* is considered one of the most significant of the era. After being signed, Lee recommended that fellow Sunset Strip habitués the Doors also receive a recording contract, and while the latter group achieved far greater success, Lee ran into trouble with drugs and the law. See also Chapter 7.

Love, Darlene (Darlene Wright, b. 1938). A member of the '50s **girl group** the Blossoms, Love became a favored lead singer for producer **Phil Spector**, fronting the **Crystals** for the No. 1 single "He's a Rebel" (1962) and Bob B. Soxx and the Blue Jeans, as well as recording 1963's "Wait Till My Bobby Gets Home" and "Christmas (Baby Please Come Home)" under her own name. Love later sued Spector for back royalties (she was awarded more than $263,000 in 1997) and appeared as Danny Glover's wife in all four *Lethal Weapon* films and as herself in the Broadway musical *Leader of the Pack*, based upon the songs of **Ellie Greenwich**. She is also the author of the autobiography *My Name Is Love*. See also Chapter 3.

The Lovin' Spoonful (1965–1968). John Sebastian (b. 1944), vocals/guitar/autoharp/harmonica/songwriting; Zal Yanovsky (1944–2002), guitar/vocals; Steve Boone (b. 1943), bass; Joe Butler (b. 1943), drums. This **Greenwich Village**–based quartet specialized in gentle **folk rock** such as "Do You Believe in Magic?" "You Didn't Have to Be So Nice" (both Top 10 hits in 1965), 1966's "Daydream," and, with a slightly harder edge, "Summer in the City," which hit No. 1 that same year. The band was close to the **Mamas and the Papas** before the latter group moved to Los Angeles. It was inducted into the Rock and Roll Hall of Fame in 2000. See also Chapter 8.

The Mamas and the Papas (1965–1972). John Phillips (1935–2001), Michelle Phillips (b. 1944), Cass Elliot (1941–1974), Denny Doherty (b. 1941). It was a good thing that this **Greenwich Village**–formed quintet changed its name from the Mugwumps and switched coasts; the results were three massive Top 10 hits in 1966: "California Dreamin'," "I Saw Her Again," and "Monday, Monday" (No. 1), all featuring the group's exquisitely arranged vocal harmonies. The group was inducted into the Rock and Roll Hall of Fame in 1998. See also Chapter 8.

Manfred Mann (1962–1971). Manfred Mann (Lubowitz, b. 1940), keyboards/vocals; Paul Jones (Pond, b. 1942), lead vocals/harmonica/ songwriting; Mike Vickers (b. 1941), guitar/sax/flute; Tom McGuinness (b. 1941), bass; Mike Hugg (b. 1942), percussion. A London-based **blues** group that became more of a **pop** band, Manfred Mann had two memorable hits with "Doo Wah Diddy" (1964) and "Pretty Flamingo" in 1966. See also Chapter 5.

Mann, Barry (b. 1939) and Cynthia Weil (b. 1937). Brill Building husband-and-wife songwriting team that was responsible for innumerable mid-'60s hits, including the **Crystals'** "Uptown," **Paul Revere and the Raiders'** "Kicks," "We Gotta Get out of This Place" for the **Animals**, and "You've Lost That Lovin' Feelin'" for the **Righteous Brothers**. See also Chapter 3.

March, Peggy (Margaret Battavio, b. 1948). Peggy March was a child star who became, at age fifteen, the youngest person to ever have a No. 1 record with 1963's "I Will Follow Him." See also Chapter 9.

Martha and the Vandellas (1963–1972). Martha Reeves (b. 1941), lead vocals; Annette Sterling Beard*, vocals (replaced by Betty Kelly, b. 1944); Rosalind (aka Rosalyn) Ashford (b. 1943), vocals. This acclaimed **Motown girl group**, which backed **Marvin Gaye** on his 1962 "Stubborn Kind of Fellow," became a harder-edged alternative to the **Supremes** with its own feverish-sounding hits like "Heat Wave" (1963), "Dancing in the Street" (1964), "Nowhere to Run" (1965), and "I'm Ready for Love" (1966). Martha Reeves began a solo career in 1972. The group was inducted into the Rock and Roll Hall of Fame in 1995. See also Chapter 3.

Martin (Sir), George (b. 1926). While there are many competitors for the coveted title of "fifth **Beatle**" (from actual band members like **Pete Best** and **Stuart Sutcliffe** to manager **Brian Epstein**), perhaps the title rightfully belongs to Martin, the visionary producer who signed the group to a recording contract in 1962 and helped it recognize increasingly ambitious aims in the recording studio. Martin was inducted into the Rock and Roll Hall of Fame in 1999. See also Chapter 4.

Mayall, John (b. 1933). John Mayall's London-based **R&B** group the Bluesbreakers, with its rotating cast of members—at least fifteen different line-ups between 1963 and 1970—served as a launching pad for a number of stars, including guitar gods Eric Clapton (who joined after leaving the **Yardbirds** and left in mid-1966 to form Cream) and Mick Taylor (who replaced Brian Jones in the **Rolling Stones**). Mayall himself, though, never attained the lofty heights reached by his protégés. See also Chapter 4.

The McCoys (1962–1969). Rick Derringer (Zehringer, b. 1947), lead vocals/guitar; Randy Jo Hobbs (b. 1948), bass; Randy Zehringer (b. 1949), drums; Bobby Peterson*, keyboards. The McCoys hit No. 1 in 1965 with "Hang On Sloopy" while still in high school and followed up with a Top 10 cover of the standard "Fever." The group's "Sorrow" later became a hit for David Bowie, and Rick Derringer went on to a solo career that included a stint with Johnny Winter. See also Chapter 9.

McGuire, Barry (b. 1935). McGuire, whose singing career began in the clean-cut folk group the New Christy Minstrels, took a radical left turn with his apocalyptic 1965 hit "Eve of Destruction," which made it to No. 1; he became a Christian recording artist in the 1970s. See also Chapter 9.

Meek, Joe (1929–1967). The producer of the Tornadoes' 1962 "Telstar" (the first single by a British group to achieve a U.S. No. 1) and 1964's "Have I the Right" for the Honeycombs, Joe Meek shot his landlady before killing himself. See also Chapter 9.

MGM. Los Angeles–based record label (a division of film studio Metro-Goldwyn-Mayer), home to **Herman's Hermits** and other performers.

The Miracles (1955–1990) with Smokey Robinson (b. 1940). This group put **Motown** on the map with its 1961 smash, "Shop Around," which sold more than a million copies. The Miracles had twenty-seven Top 40 hits, mostly due to Robinson, who was not just an extraordinary singer but also a highly prolific songwriter/producer, penning such smashes as "Mickey's Monkey" and "You've Really Got a Hold on Me" (1962), "Ooh Baby Baby" and "The Tracks of My Tears" (1965), and "Choosey Beggar," "(Come 'Round Here) I'm the One That You Need," and "Going to a Go-Go" (1966). See also Chapter 2.

Modern. The record label of Elmore James, John Lee Hooker, and **Howlin' Wolf.**

Mods and Rockers. Fashion was lifestyle to these youthful British subsets. The former, often gainfully employed with cash to spend, patterned themselves after Continental sharpies who frequented the Soho coffeehouse scene, wearing tailored suits (often in unconventional fabrics or colors), riding Vespa motorscooters, and consuming pep pills, the better to dance all night to music that included that of the **Who.** The latter group adhered to the **Gene Vincent/Eddie Cochran** aesthetic, loyal to old-school rock and roll, with slicked-back ducktail hairdos, leather jackets, and pointed boots. When the two factions came together, as occurred in English seaside resorts in the mid-'60s, violence accompanied the culture clash. See also Chapter 5.

The Monkees (1965–1971). Michael Nesmith (b. 1942), guitar/vocals; Micky Dolenz (b. 1945), drums/vocals; David "Davy" Jones (b. 1945), vocals; Peter Tork (b. 1944), bass/vocals. The first manufactured-for-television **pop/rock** band was comprised of two serious musicians (singer-songwriter Nesmith and Tork, a former **Greenwich Village folk** singer) and two former child stars (Dolenz, who had starred in the 1950s TV series *Circus Boy*, and Jones, who had appeared in the London and Broadway stage productions of *Oliver!*). "I'm a Believer" went to No. 1 in 1966, as did "Last Train to Clarksville." See also Chapter 6.

The Monkees (1966). The debut album of this manufactured pop group cynically dubbed "the Prefab Four" yielded several No. 1 hits, including 1966's "Last Train to Clarksville" (written by **Tommy Boyce and Bobby Hart**). The **psychedelic**-slapstick TV show designed to promote the group's music (with instrumentation often provided by studio musicians) to the subteen set was a hit and ran for several years, while the group became a touring/performing entity. One notable mismatch had the Jimi Hendrix Experience as an opening act. See also Chapter 6.

The Moody Blues (1964–present). Ray Thomas (b. 1941), harmonica/flute/vocals; Denny Laine (b. 1944), vocals/guitar, replaced by Justin Hayward (b. 1946) in 1966; Mike Pinder (b. 1941), keyboards/vocals; Clint Warwick (Albert Eccles, 1941–2004), bass/vocals, replaced by John Lodge (b. 1945) in 1966; Graeme Edge (b. 1941), drums. This Birmingham band had one Top 10 hit, 1964's memorable "Go Now," sung by Denny Laine. Laine and bassist Warwick left the group in 1966, replaced, respectively, by Justin Hayward and John Lodge, who anchored the band for the next several decades; its next chart showing ("Nights in White Satin") came in 1972, by which time Laine had already joined Paul McCartney in Wings. See also Chapter 5.

Morrison, Van (b. 1945) and Them (1963–1966). Them originated in Belfast, Ireland; Morrison was (and is) a remarkable **soul** shouter who evolved into a more spiritual, jazz-inflected singer-songwriter after he quit the group in 1966. The group's hits included "Mystic Eyes," written by Morrison, and "Here Comes the Night" (both in 1965) and 1966's "Gloria," also by Morrison (which was a bigger hit for the Shadows of Knight the previous year and was later covered by artists such as the Doors and Patti Smith). Morrison was inducted into the Rock and Roll Hall of Fame in 1993. See also Chapter 5.

Morton, "Shadow" (George) (b. 1944). Morton, who earned the nickname "Shadow" for his elusive qualities, hooked up with acquaintance **Ellie Greenwich** during her **Brill Building** days and went on to write 1964's "Walking in the Sand," a monster hit that he produced for the **Shangri-Las**, followed by "Leader of the Pack," a No. 1 smash that same year. Morton was briefly employed by **Jerry Lieber and Mike Stoller** as a staff producer and later produced artists as diverse as Janis Ian, Vanilla Fudge, and the New York Dolls.

Most, Mickie (Michael Hayes, 1938–2003). Most had been the front man for a covers band before he discovered the **Animals**; his 1964 production of "House of the Rising Sun" shot the group to stardom. That same year, Most also produced "I'm into Something Good" for **Herman's Hermits** and did the same for **Donovan**'s 1966 hit "Sunshine Superman."

The Mothers of Invention (1964–1969). Frank Zappa (1940–1993) joined the Soul Giants in 1964, which had mutated into the Mothers two years later when the group was signed and released the first double concept album, titled *Freak Out!* The material was all written by Zappa, a serious student of classical composers possessed of a sardonic wit; his liner notes pointed out, "Note the obvious lack of commercial potential." Zappa was posthumously inducted into the Rock and Roll Hall of Fame in 1995.

Motown. This Detroit-based record label started by **Berry Gordy Jr.** was home to the **Supremes**, the **Four Tops**, the **Temptations**, **Smokey Robinson** and the **Miracles**, **Stevie Wonder**, and many others and was the first major African American–owned label. See also Chapter 2.

***Mr. Tambourine Man* (1965).** The **Byrds'** debut album was driven by this hit single of the same title, which reached No. 6, and featured **folk-rock** renditions of songs by **Bob Dylan** and **Pete Seeger**. See also Chapter 8.

Napoleon XIV (Jerry Samuels, b. 1938). Napoleon XIV hit No. 3 on the national charts in 1966 with his loopy ode to mental illness, "They're Coming to Take Me Away, Ha-Ha," before the song was banned due to complaints from mental health professionals. See also Chapter 9.

Neil, Fred (1936–2001). Singer-songwriter Fred Neil, best known for "Everybody's Talkin'" (recorded by Harry Nilsson as the theme song for the

1969 film *Midnight Cowboy*), was a hub of the **Greenwich Village folk** scene and a friend or inspiration to many, including the **Jefferson Airplane**'s Paul Kantner, Richie Havens, and the **Lovin' Spoonful**. Neil's tune "Other Side of This Life" was covered by the Jefferson Airplane, the Youngbloods, and **Peter, Paul, and Mary**, among others. See also Chapter 8.

Nelson, Rick(y) (1940–1985). Both music and stardom were Nelson's birthright: his father Ozzie, who had been a 1940s bandleader, and his mother Harriet, a singer, had parlayed their popularity into a radio show and then a television series that became the longest-running sitcom in American TV history (1952–1966). Since it was supposedly based on the family's home life, Ricky and older brother David were conscripted to play "themselves." Ricky (who dropped the "y" from his name once he got older) had already racked up an impressive number of hits before 1961's "Hello Mary Lou" and "Travelin' Man" (No. 1); even at the height of the British invasion, his "For You" could still make the Top 10 (1964). Nelson was inducted into the Rock and Roll Hall of Fame in 1987. See also Chapter 1.

Nicol, Jimmy (b. 1940). Nicol replaced Ringo Starr for approximately two weeks in June 1964 while the **Beatles**' drummer recovered from illness; he appeared with the band at concerts in Scandinavia, Holland, the Far East, and Australia and then promptly sank back into obscurity, except as a curious historical footnote. See also Chapter 4.

Ochs, Phil (1940–1976). Ochs considered himself something of a musical journalist, hence the title of his 1964 debut, *All the News That's Fit to Sing*. His next album the following year, which included the title song "I Ain't Marchin' Any More" and the satirical "Draft Dodger Rag," boosted the **antiwar** movement. Ochs continued to address **civil rights** and social justice issues in his songs, including the devastating indictment "Outside of a Small Circle of Friends" and "There but for Fortune," but his albums never rose higher than No. 149 (with 1966's *Phil Ochs in Concert*), and he later developed severe psychological problems. See also Chapter 8.

Oldham, Andrew Loog (b. 1944). Oldham was nineteen when he discovered the **Rolling Stones** playing in a London suburb. He subsequently managed the band from 1963 through 1967. He obtained the group's first hit, 1963's "I Wanna Be Your Man," from the **Beatles**' John Lennon and Paul McCartney (Oldham had once worked with **Mary Quant** and **Brian Epstein**) and then promptly positioned the band as the anti-Beatles, famously planting the headline "Would You Let Your Daughter Marry a Rolling Stone?" in the British tabloid press. He encouraged Mick Jagger and Keith Richards to write their own material for the band, discovered and produced **Marianne Faithfull**, and founded the Immediate record label, which recorded Rod Stewart, the Small Faces, Eric Clapton, and Jimmy Page. Oldham is the author of memoirs *Stoned* and *2Stoned*. See also Chapter 4.

Parker, "Colonel" Tom (Andreas van Kujik, 1909–1997). The colorful, controversial manager of **Elvis Presley** from the start of his career until well after his death, Parker was an illegal immigrant who may or may not have committed a murder in his Dutch homeland, and therefore, he ensured that Presley never toured overseas where he could not follow without a passport. However, even the iron-fisted Parker had no control over the U.S. Army, which stationed Presley in Germany from 1958 to 1960. A former carnival worker and dogcatcher, Parker arranged for Presley to churn out a stream of highly lucrative and artistically bankrupt films in the early 1960s, accompanied by mostly substandard soundtracks, despite the star's early demonstration of promise as a serious dramatic actor. Some see Parker as Machiavellian (after Presley's death, he was quoted as saying "This changes nothing"); others argue that it was his guidance that steered a young, unschooled truckdriver to unrivalled fame and fortune. See also Chapter 1.

Parlophone. British record label, a division of **EMI**.

Paxton, Tom (b. 1937). An old-school **folk** singer-songwriter, Paxton was an integral part of the '60s **Greenwich Village** music scene and something of a mentor to younger artists like **Bob Dylan** and **Phil Ochs**, as well as an associate of stalwarts such as **Pete Seeger**. Paxton was given to writing topical **protest** (and children's) songs with a humorous bent, although his biggest success came with the wistful romantic ballad "The Last Thing on My Mind," covered in 1965 by artists as diverse as **Peter, Paul, and Mary** and **Marianne Faithfull**. See also Chapter 8.

"Payola." A slang word coined to describe the practice of bribing or similarly coercing media (radio, TV) to play records or feature artists. In 1959, the Senate opened an investigation. **Dick Clark** testified and was forced to divest himself of publishing and recording companies considered a conflict of interest with his position as host of *American Bandstand*. DJ **Alan Freed** was not as fortunate. After claiming that any monies received were for "consultation," Freed pled guilty in 1962 to twenty-six counts of commercial bribery; although he was fined only $300 and given a suspended sentence, his career was over, and he died a few years later. See also Chapter 1.

Peter & Gordon (1963–1968). Peter Asher (b. 1944) and Gordon Waller (b. 1945). Asher was fortunate to have **Paul McCartney** hanging around the house, living with his family as the boyfriend of his younger sister Jane. After McCartney gave the **folk-pop** duo his composition "A World without Love" (reportedly because **John Lennon** refused to sing a song that began with a request to lock the performer away), it became their first hit (No. 1, 1964). Asher went on to produce and/or manage stars such as Linda Ronstadt and James Taylor. See also Chapter 5.

Peter, Paul, and Mary (1961–1970). Peter Yarrow (b. 1938); Paul (aka Noel) Stookey (b. 1937); Mary Travers (b. 1936). A clean-cut **Greenwich**

Village folk vocal and acoustic guitar trio extremely popular in middle America, Peter, Paul, and Mary helped popularize **Bob Dylan** songs such as "Blowin' in the Wind" (No. 1 in 1963) and "Don't Think Twice," which made the Top 10 that same year. The group also appeared with Dylan and Odetta at the 1963 **civil rights** March on Washington. See also **Antiwar**; **Protest**; Chapter 8.

Peterson, Ray (b. 1939). Peterson had a death-rock hit in 1960 with the mournful "Tell Laura I Love Her." See also Chapter 9.

***Pet Sounds*, 1966.** Brian Wilson's masterpiece inspired the **Beatles** to write *Sgt. Pepper* and is No. 2 on the *Rolling Stone* list of the greatest albums of all time. Key tracks include "Wouldn't It Be Nice," "Sloop John B," and "God Only Knows." See also **Beach Boys**; Chapter 7.

Philles. The record label started by **Phil Spector** and partner Lester Sill; home of the girl-group sound personified by the **Ronettes**, the **Crystals**, and Bob B. Soxx and the Blue Jeans (the latter two groups were often fronted by **Darlene Love**). See also Chapter 3.

Pickett, Bobby "Boris" (b. 1940). Pickett charted three times with his "Monster Mash," starting in late October 1962 when the song, now a Halloween perennial, went to No. 1. See also Chapter 9.

Pickett, Wilson (b. 1941). One of the foremost proponents of southern **soul**, the "Wicked" Pickett signed to **Atlantic** Records in 1964 and was teamed with producer **Jerry Wexler** and backing band **Booker T. and the MGs** at the Fame Studios in Muscle Shoals, Alabama to record for **Stax**; they came up with 1965's "In the Midnight Hour," a raw number that topped the **R&B** charts and also had a respectable **pop** showing. The next year, Pickett followed up with hits like "634-5789," "Mustang Sally," and "Land of 1,000 Dances" (a roll call of then-popular **dance** moves). Pickett was inducted into the Rock and Roll Hall of Fame in 1991. See also Chapter 2.

Pitney, Gene (b. 1941). Often dismissed as a melodramatic interpreter of teen angst because of hits such as "Town without Pity" (1961) and "It Hurts to Be in Love" (1964), Pitney was also in fact a talented songwriter, penning such classics as 1961's "Hello Mary Lou" (for **Rick Nelson**) and, in 1962, "He's a Rebel," a smash for the **Crystals**. Pitney was the first American to cover an original **Rolling Stones** composition ("That Girl Belongs to Yesterday") and also one of the first to record Randy Newman, with the 1966 "Nobody Needs Your Love." Pitney was inducted into the Rock and Roll Hall of Fame in 2002. See also Chapter 1.

Pomus, Doc (1925–1991) and Mort Shuman (1936–1991). Brill **Building** songwriters whose most famous compositions included "Little Sister" and "Viva Las Vegas" for **Elvis Presley**, as well as many hits for the Coasters, the Drifters, and Ben E. King. Pomus was inducted into the Rock and Roll Hall of Fame in 1992. See also Chapter 3.

Pop. Genre of music, derived from the word "popular"; catchall term, usually employed to describe lighter fare (as opposed to **rock**).

Presley, Elvis (1935–1977). Elvis Presley was the "King of Rock and Roll," at least until his induction into the U.S. Army; after his 1960 discharge, Presley's persona was considerably tamer, although it is unclear whether this was due to the death of his mother during that period or his fully grasping the fact that he would forever remain under the thumb of his Machiavellian manager, **"Colonel" Tom Parker**. During this period, Presley began performing in a series of films with increasingly preposterous plots and insipid soundtracks, almost all of which grossed enormous amounts of money from his devoted fan base. Presley was inducted into the Rock and Roll Hall of Fame in 1986. See also Chapter 1.

Protest. A genre of music, usually **folk** influenced, that expressed anger, mostly over the failures of the **civil rights** movement and the ongoing **Vietnam War**. See also **Antiwar**; Chapter 8.

Psychedelic/psychedelia. A musical genre influenced by and evocative of psychoactive drugs (marijuana, hashish, LSD) that became popular in the mid- and late 1960s; it often incorporated free-form stylings reminiscent of jazz, Eastern instruments such as sitar, and vocal/instrumental distortion or experimentation, such as utilizing feedback or guitar "fuzz" effects. Examples include music by the **Beatles** ("Tomorrow Never Knows," "Strawberry Fields"), the **Rolling Stones** ("Paint It, Black"), the **Byrds** ("Eight Miles High"), the **Yardbirds** ("Over Under Sideways Down"), the **Beach Boys** ("Good Vibrations"), and groups such as the **Grateful Dead** and **Jefferson Airplane**.

Quant, Mary (b. 1934). This British fashion designer was credited with inventing, or at least popularizing, the miniskirt. The giant American retailer J. C. Penney eventually brought Quant's stylistic revolution, launched from her London boutique, to the masses. As she put it, "I think that I broke the couture stranglehold . . . on fashion, when I created styles at the working-girl level. It [was] a democratization of fashion and entertainment."[3] See also Chapter 5.

? and the Mysterians (1962–1999). "?" aka Question Mark (Rudy Martinez, b. 1945), vocals; Bobby Balderrama (Lee, b. 1950), guitar; Frank Rodriguez Jr. (b. 1951), organ; Frank Lugo (b. 1947), bass; Eduardo Delgardo "Eddie" Serrato (b. 1945), drums. Garage rock began evolving into early punk with this Latino group's organ-driven "96 Tears," a No. 1 smash in 1966. The band's mystique was further enhanced by the singer's legally changing his name to the question-mark symbol (decades before Prince came on the scene), his wraparound black shades, and his insistence that he was born on Mars. While the group never had another hit, this single assures its place in **rock** history. See also Chapter 9.

R&B. A musical genre whose initials stand for "rhythm and blues" (the phrase was coined by **Jerry Wexler** during his time at the music trade magazine *Billboard*). It was considered a forerunner to **rock** and roll for its **blues**-style chord patterns and strong backbeat; the lines are often blurred between R&B and **soul**.

The Rascals (1964–1972). Felix Cavaliere (b. 1944), vocals/organ/songwriting; Eddie Brigati (b. 1946), vocals/songwriting; Gene Cornish (b. 1945), bass; Dino Danielli (b. 1944), drums. This New York–based **blue-eyed soul** group, which was initially managed by Beatles promoter **Sid Bernstein**, racked up self-penned hits like "I Ain't Gonna Eat Out My Heart Any More" in 1965 and the following year's No. 1 "Good Lovin'." The group was inducted into the Rock and Roll Hall of Fame in 1997. See also Chapter 9.

RCA Victor. American record label, home to **Elvis Presley**.

Redding, Otis (1941–1967). The exemplar of southern deep **soul** vocals, Otis Redding was poised for a major **pop** crossover at the time of his death, partially thanks to **Rolling Stones'** manager **Andrew Loog Oldham**, who arranged for Redding's invitation to appear at the Monterey Pop Festival (the Stones had covered his 1961 "Pain in My Heart" and "That's How Strong My Love Is"; Redding covered their smash "Satisfaction"). Redding, who wrote most of his own material, first hit the **R&B** charts in 1962 with "These Arms of Mine"; his biggest pop outing of this period came with "I've Been Loving You Too Long," which grazed the Top 20 in 1965. Shortly after he died, his "(Sitting on) The Dock of the Bay" went to No. 1. Redding was inducted into the Rock and Roll Hall of Fame in 1989. See also Chapter 2.

Reed, Jimmy (1925–1976). Jimmy Reed was born on a Mississippi plantation. His guitar and harmonica vocal **blues** were constructed with a deceptive simplicity that invited imitation. He recorded his first sides for **Vee-Jay**, eventually besting even the enormously popular B. B. King with a total of eleven singles that made the **pop** charts, fourteen on the **R&B** side. Unfortunately, Reed was saddled with severe alcoholism, coupled with epilepsy that went undiagnosed for some time. Still, his records were (and remain) highly influential, not least for British artists such as the **Rolling Stones**. Reed was inducted into the Rock and Roll Hall of Fame in 1991. See also Chapter 4.

Paul Revere and the Raiders (1960–1967). Paul Revere (b. 1938), vocals/keyboards; Mark Lindsay (b. 1942), vocals; Drake Levin (Drake Maxwell Levinshefski)*, guitar; Phil "Fang" Volk*, bass; Mike Smith*, drums. This polished **garage** band—an oxymoron—had a 1965 hit with "Steppin' Out" before nabbing the rare advantage of becoming the "house band" on Dick Clark's nationally syndicated mid-'60s TV show *Where the Action Is!*, which helped promote the songs "Just like Me," "Kicks," and "Hungry" (all in 1966). See also Chapters 6, 9.

***Revolver*, 1966.** This, the seventh album in three years for the **Beatles**, was named the No. 1 greatest record by VH-1 in 2003 and is No. 3 on the *Rolling Stone* list of the greatest albums of all time. Among other landmarks, it contains three songs written by George Harrison and one of the first examples of **psychedelia** in John Lennon's "Tomorrow Never Knows," and it introduced the use of the now-standard automatic double tracking, a technique that allowed vocals to be doubled without having to be sung twice. (The stark cover, a black-and-white illustration/photo collage, was created by Klaus Voorman, a bassist and friend from Hamburg days, who later went on to form the group Trio, which had an '80s hit with "Da-Da-Da"). See also Chapter 4.

Richard, (Sir) Cliff (Harry Webb, b. 1940). This British singer started in **rock**, drifted into **pop**, and later moved into religious music; nonetheless, the early Richard, backed by the Shadows, was an inspiration to the first English bands with hits like 1958's "Move It." His only U.S. chart appearance during this volume's time frame was a Top 40 showing with 1963's "It's All in the Game." See also Chapter 4.

The Righteous Brothers (1962–2003). Bobby Hatfield (1940–2003) and Bill Medley (b. 1940). This nonrelated **blue-eyed soul** Caucasian duo reportedly got its name from a black enthusiast and had already scored a Top 50 hit in 1963 with "Little Latin Lupe Lu" before hooking up with **Phil Spector**, who steered it to the **Barry Mann and Cynthia Weil** "You've Lost That Lovin' Feelin'," a smash No. 1 single in early 1965. It was followed that same year by "Just Once in My Life," "Unchained Melody," and "Ebb Tide," all Top 5, before the pair left Spector to strike out on its own, scoring one last No. 1 in 1966 with the Medley-produced "(You're My) Soul and Inspiration." See also Chapter 9.

"River Deep, Mountain High" (1966). This single, produced by **Phil Spector** and written by Spector with **Ellie Greenwich** and **Jeff Barry**, made it to No. 3 in England but only No. 88 in America; although it is now acknowledged as a classic, its failure at the time badly shook Spector, who took a four-year hiatus from producing. The single was attributed to Ike and Tina Turner, but Ike was kept out of the studio during recording. See also Chapter 3.

Rivers, Johnny (b. 1942). This singer and guitarist was discovered in 1964 by **Lou Adler** while playing the Sunset Strip; he had hits in 1964 and 1965 with covers of Chuck Berry's "Memphis" and "Maybelline" and Willie Dixon's "Seventh Son," respectively, and hit No. 1 in 1966 with "Poor Side of Town," then had a No. 3 single with the theme to TV's "Secret Agent Man." See also Chapter 7.

Robinson, William "Smokey" (b. 1940). This multitalented singer-songwriter was one of **Motown's** first signings and also produced artists such as **Mary Wells** and **Marvin Gaye**, as well as the group he fronted, the **Miracles**. Robinson's smooth **pop-soul** style was a forerunner to the radio format known as "Quiet Storm." Robinson (who met **Berry Gordy Jr.** around 1958) also wrote and/or produced for **Marvin Gaye** (1965's "Ain't That Peculiar" and "I'll Be Doggone"), **Mary Wells** ("You Beat Me to the Punch" in 1962 and "My Guy" in 1964), and the **Temptations** ("The Way You Do the Things You Do" in 1964, "My Girl" in 1965, and 1966's "Get Ready"), among other artists. Robinson, whom **Bob Dylan** once called "America's greatest living poet," left the Miracles in 1972 for a successful solo career. He was inducted into the Rock and Roll Hall of Fame in 1987. See also Chapter 2.

Rock/Rock and Roll. A musical genre considered more reality based and "heavier" than **pop**; however, many styles fall under this umbrella term, since rock reinvents itself on a continual basis. It is generally considered that rock began when **Elvis Presley** wed **R&B** to country, although many historians—including Sun Records' Sam Phillips, who recorded Presley—consider 1951's "Rocket 88" the first real rock single. Credited to Jackie Brenston and his Delta Cats, a group that did not exist, it was in fact written by Ike Turner and recorded by his band, the Kings of Rhythm. Rock music is usually played on amplified electric instruments, often with the guitar as a major focus.

The Rolling Stones (1963–present). Mick Jagger (b. 1943); Keith Richards (b. 1943); Brian Jones (1942–1969); Bill Wyman (b. 1936); Charlie Watts (b. 1941). The self-proclaimed "World's Greatest Rock Band" is certainly one of the most durable and influential: Mick Jagger all but created the role of sexually charged frontman, while Keith Richards's guitar lines wrote the book on hard rock. The London-based group's career began as **R&B**/Chuck Berry enthusiasts, although it took the gift of a John Lennon and Paul McCartney song ("I Wanna Be Your Man") to give the band a jump-start British hit in late 1963. Its first American chart appearance, in 1964, came with a cover of Buddy Holly's "Not Fade Away." Manager **Andrew Loog Oldham** promoted the group as a sexy, uncontrollable antidote to the **Beatles**, and he insisted that the singer and guitarist begin writing their own material. The team duly provided such hits as the classic No. 1 "(I Can't Get No) Satisfaction" (1965), "Get Off of My Cloud" (No. 1, 1965), "The Last Time" (No. 9, 1965), and, all in 1966, "19th Nervous Breakdown," "As Tears Go By," "Have You Seen Your Mother, Baby, Standing in the Shadows?," "Lady Jane," "Mother's Little Helper," and "Paint It, Black" (No. 1). To this day, the Rolling Stones continue to tower over all competition from the British invasion except the Beatles. The group was inducted into the Rock and Roll Hall of Fame in 1989. See also Chapter 4.

The Ronettes (1959–1966). Veronica "Ronnie" Bennett (b. 1943), lead vocals; Estelle Bennett (b. 1944), vocals; Nedra Talley (b. 1947), vocals. Ronnie and younger sister Estelle teamed up with cousin Nedra to begin their career singing at places like New York's Peppermint Lounge before being discovered by **Phil Spector**, who wed Ronnie and produced many hits for the group, including 1963's No. 2 smash "Be My Baby" (written by Spector with **Ellie Greenwich** and **Jeff Barry**), "Baby, I Love You," No. 24 in 1963, and "Walking in the Rain" (written by Spector with **Cynthia Weil and Barry Mann**, it hit No. 23 in 1964 and garnered Spector his only Grammy, for best sound effects). The group toured England with the **Rolling Stones** in 1964 and also became friendly with the **Beatles**. See also Chapter 3.

Rubber Soul, **1965.** The **Beatles'** first foray into a different sound, with exotic instrumentation such as sitar, was recorded in seven weeks to be released in time for the holiday season. It marked a new maturity in songwriting direction, inspired by **Bob Dylan**, with such Lennon numbers such as "Norwegian Wood" and "In My Life," along with McCartney's string-embellished "Michelle" (partially sung in French); Harrison contributed two original compositions, "Think for Yourself" and "If I Needed Someone." Brian Wilson noted that this was the first **rock** album "without filler," and despite its varying themes, it does feel thoroughly organic and consistent. This is *Rolling Stone*'s No. 5 pick on its list of the greatest albums of all time. See also Chapter 4.

Rydell, Bobby (Robert Ridarelli, b. 1940). Rydell became a teen **pop** idol in 1959 with the hit "Kissin' Time" and later starred in the 1963 **Elvis Presley**–spoofing musical *Bye Bye Birdie*. See also Chapter 1.

Ryder, Mitch (William Levise Jr., b. 1945) and the Detroit Wheels. James "Jim" McCarty (b. 1945), guitar; Joseph Cubert (b. 1947), guitar; Earl Eliot (b. 1947), bass; Johnny "Bee" Badanjek (b. 1948), drums. Ryder helped create the genre known as **blue-eyed soul** around 1966 with his gritty vocals and energetic performances of songs such as "Jenny Take a Ride," "Little Latin Lupe Lu," and "Devil with a Blue Dress On/Good Golly Miss Molly." See also Chapter 9.

Sadler, Sgt. Barry (1940–1989). Sadler became the voice of patriotic America during the **Vietnam War** era with his 1966 No. 1 hit "Ballad of the Green Berets." See also **Protest**; Chapter 9.

Sainte-Marie, Buffy (b. 1941). This Canadian Cree Indian singer-songwriter-activist became prominent during the **protest** movement with songs like "My Country 'Tis of Thy People You're Dying," "Now That the Buffalo's Gone," and "Universal Soldier" (a hit for **Donovan** in 1965). But Sainte-Marie's laments could also be more specifically romantic, as evidenced by "Until It's Time for You to Go," which was covered by artists including **Elvis Presley**, Cher (see **Sonny and Cher**) and Barbra Streisand. See also Chapter 8.

Sakamoto, Kyu (1941–1985). Kyu Sakamoto had a No. 1 hit in 1963 with the wistful "Sukiyaki," sung entirely in Japanese. Its real title was "Ue o Muite Aruko" (which meant "I Look Up When I Walk"), but the record label was convinced that no DJ could pronounce it, so it changed the title to "Sukiyaki," a stir-fry dish familiar to Americans. See also Chapter 9.

Sam and Dave (1961–1971). Sam Moore (b. 1935), vocals; Dave Prater (1937–1988), vocals. This high-energy **R&B** duo, produced for **Stax** by **Jerry Wexler**, broke onto the national scene in 1965 with "You Don't Know Like I Know" (No. 7, R&B), followed by 1966's "Hold On! I'm a Comin'" (No. 21, **pop**). They were inducted into the Rock and Roll Hall of Fame in 1992. See also Chapter 2.

Sam the Sham and the Pharaohs (1964–1967). Domingo Samudio (b. 1940), vocals/songwriting; Ray Stinnet*, guitar; David Martin (d. 1987), bass; Jerry Patterson*, drums; Butch Gibson*, sax. This group's gimmicky appearance (turbans and beards) may have drawn attention, but it was the insistently pounding sound of hits such as "Wooly Bully" (No. 2, 1965) and "Li'l Red Riding Hood" (also No. 2 in 1965) that put it on the **pop-rock** map. See also Chapter 9.

Sassoon, Vidal (b. 1928). This British hairstylist revolutionized female hairstyles in the mid-1960s by developing geometric, natural, "swingy" cuts that were blown or air dried, rather than set on rollers, teased, and sprayed into shape. See also Chapter 5.

The Searchers (1957–1985). Tony Jackson (b. 1940), lead vocals; John McNally (b. 1941), guitar/vocals; Michael Pender (Prendergast, b. 1942), guitar/vocals; Frank Allen (b. 1943), bass; Chris Curtis (Crummy, b. 1941), drums. A Liverpool group that began in **skiffle**, the Searchers helped popularize the use of the Rickenbacker guitar also favored by the **Beatles** and the **Byrds** while recording beautifully harmonized songs such as "Needles and Pins," "Don't Throw Your Love Away," "Sugar and Spice," and "When You Walk in the Room" (all 1964) and "What Have They Done to the Rain" and "Love Potion #9" the following year. See also Chapter 5.

Seeger, Pete (b. 1919). A member of the **Weavers** and a close friend of **Woody Guthrie** (both were in the Almanac Singers), this longtime **antiwar** and environmental activist is considered a grandfather figure in modern **folk** music, having introduced **Bob Dylan** to a mainstream audience. However, an infuriated Seeger had to be physically prevented from pulling the plug on the advent of **folk rock** when his protégé "went electric" at the 1965 Newport Folk Festival. Seeger's 1962 song "Turn! Turn! Turn!" with lyrics adapted from the Book of Ecclesiastes, was covered by the **Byrds** on that group's debut album. Seeger was inducted into the Rock and Roll Hall of Fame as an early influence in 1996. See also Chapter 8.

The Shadows of Knight (1964–1969). Jim Sohns (b. 1946), lead vocals; Jerry McGeorge*, rhythm guitar; Joe Kelley*, guitar; Warren Rogers*, bass/guitar; Tom Schiffour*, drums. A group out of Chicago with a raw blues-punk sound reminiscent of the early **Rolling Stones**, The Shadows of Knight hit No. 1 in April 1966 with a cover of **Van Morrison** and **Them's**

"Gloria." The band is considered a progenitor of **garage rock**. See also Chapter 9.

The Shangri-Las (1963–1969). Betty Weiss*, vocals; Mary Weiss*, vocals; Marge Ganser (1947–1996), vocals; Mary-Ann Ganser (1947–1970), vocals. This bad-girl quartet was comprised of the Ganser twins and the Weiss sisters; with the help of producer **Shadow Morton**, it had a No. 5 hit in 1964 with "Remember (Walking in the Sand)"; the follow-up "Leader of the Pack" went to No. 1 that same year, while "Give Him a Great Big Kiss" landed at No. 18 in 1965. See also Chapter 3.

Shannon, Del (Charles Westover, 1934–1990). A singer, songwriter, and guitarist who was the first to cover a Beatles song in America ("From Me to You," which reached No. 77 in 1963), Shannon is best known for self-penned hits such as 1961's "Hats Off to Larry" and "Runaway," along with "Little Town Flirt" (1963) and "Keep Searchin' (We'll Follow the Sun)" in 1965. Shannon was inducted into the Rock and Roll Hall of Fame in 1999. See also Chapter 1.

Sheridan, Tony (Anthony Sheridan McGinnity, b. 1940). Sheridan achieved his place in **rock** history by recording the traditional folksong "My Bonnie" in 1961, backed by several members of the original **Beatles** lineup. See also Chapter 4.

The Shirelles (1958–1982). Shirley Alston Reeves (b. 1941), vocals; Beverley Lee (b. 1941), vocals; Addie Harris (b. 1940), vocals; Doris Kenner-Jackson (1941–2000), vocals. One of the first **girl groups**, the Shirelles had a No. 1 pop smash in 1961 with the **Carole King** and **Gerry Goffin** composition "Will You Love Me Tomorrow," followed by a rerelease of "Dedicated to the One I Love" (originally recorded in 1959 and later a hit for the **Mamas and the Papas**) and "Mama Said" in 1961, both of which entered the Top 5. 1962's "Soldier Boy" was the group's second No. 1 single; "Baby, It's You" (1962) and 1963's "Foolish Little Girl" entered the Top 10. The **Beatles** covered the Shirelles' "Boys," while **Manfred Mann** remade "Sha La La." The group was inducted into the Rock and Roll Hall of Fame in 1996. See also Chapter 3.

Simon and Garfunkel (1964–1970). Paul Simon (b. 1941), songwriting/vocals/guitar; Art Garfunkel (b. 1941), vocals. These school friends originally cracked the Top 50 in 1957 as "Tom and Jerry" with "Hey Little Schoolgirl," then temporarily disbanded. Their acoustic 1964 debut album *Wednesday Morning 3 a.m.* went nowhere, but in 1966 they achieved their first No. 1, "The Sounds of Silence." The duo was inducted into the Rock and Roll Hall of Fame in 1990. See also **Folk**; **Folk Rock**; **Protest**; Chapter 8.

Sinatra, Nancy (b. 1940). Frank Sinatra's daughter became a **mod** icon for her dress style and the No. 1 protofeminist single "These Boots Are Made for Walkin'" (1966). See also Chapter 3.

The "Singing Nun" (Jeanine Deckers, 1933–1985). A Dominican nun, whose convent-given name was Sister Luc-Gabrielle, the "Singing Nun" was stage-named Soeur Sourire ("Sister Smile") and had an unlikely hit record with the lilting "Dominique," which she wrote as a tribute to the founder of her order. She appeared on the *Ed Sullivan Show* in a pretaped segment and won a 1963 Grammy Award for Best Gospel or Other Religious Recording, Musical. See also Chapter 9.

The Sir Douglas Quintet (1964–1972). Douglas Sahm (1941–1999), vocals, guitar, songwriting; Augie Meyers (b. 1940), organ; Jack Barber*, bass; Frank Morin*, saxophone; Johnny Perez (b. 1942), drums. Doug Sahm, dubbed "Sir" to fool American rock fans into thinking the band was British, led this influential Tex-Mex **garage-rock** group of No. 13 in 1965 with "She's About A Mover," a song that made a conscious effort to combine the **Beatles'** beat with that of Cajun dance music. See also Chapter 9.

Skiffle. A genre of music popular in England in the early 1960s, its most visible proponent was **Lonnie Donegan** ("Rock Island Line"). Skiffle was played on makeshift instruments such as tea chests and broomstick bass, often by amateur musicians; it inspired John Lennon's first group, the Quarrymen. With its skill-does-not-matter ethos, skiffle could be considered both a primitive version of **folk** music and a forerunner to punk. See also Chapter 4.

Small, Millie (b. 1946). Millie Small hit No. 1 in the United Kingdom and No. 2 in America in 1964 with the bouncy "My Boy Lollipop," the first mainstream appearance of ska (aka "blue beat"), a form of Jamaican **R&B** later popularized by the Specials and UB40 in England and No Doubt in the United States. Small's producer, Chris Blackwell, later founded Island Records (home to Bob Marley and U2). See also Chapter 9.

SNCC (Student Nonviolent Coordinating Committee) Freedom Singers (1962–1964). Rutha Mae Harris*, soprano; Bertha Gober*, soprano; Charles Neblett*, baritone; Cordell Hull Reagon, tenor (1943–1996); Bernice Johnson (Reagon) (b. 1942), alto. These African American a capella (unaccompanied by musical instruments) singers were organized to raise public awareness about racial injustice in the southern states, and performed in concert venues as well as churches, clubs, and schools to garner support and funds for the committee's activities. The Freedom Singers performed "We Shall Not Be Moved" at the August 1963 March on Washington, just before the legendary "I Have a Dream" speech by Dr. Martin Luther King Jr. Bernice Johnson Reagon later formed the all-female a capella group Sweet Honey in the Rock. See also **civil rights movement,** Chapter 8.

Sonny and Cher. Sonny Bono (1935–1998) and Cherilyn Sarkisian Bono (b. 1946). A married couple, Sonny and Cher were known for setting unisex fashion trends—wearing matching bell-bottomed trousers, fur vests, and long hair—as well as **pop-rock** songs such as "Baby Don't Go," "I Got You, Babe" (No. 1), and Sonny's stab at **protest**, "Laugh at Me," all in 1965. However, contrary to his ordinary-guy-got-lucky persona, Bono had been in A&R and record promotion (and had worked in the studio with **Phil Spector**) before he created the duo. See also Chapter 7.

Soul. This musical genre was associated with African Americans and could be characterized as gritty (**Stax-Volt**), gospel influenced (**Atlantic**), southern (as in the case of **Otis Redding**), or **pop** oriented (**Motown**). Soul often crosses boundaries with **R&B**. "Blue-eyed soul" was the term given to similar music created and/or sung by white artists, regardless of their actual eye color (e.g., the **Righteous Brothers, Mitch Ryder**, the **Spencer Davis Group**, and **Van Morrison and Them**); a Latino branch of the genre has been referred to as "brown-eyed soul," which would almost seem to defeat the entire purpose of such categories. See also Chapters 2, 5, 9.

Specialty. Los Angeles–based record label started in 1944, home to Little Richard, who in 1964 recommended signing the **Beatles** (label owner Art Rupe passed). Specialty also once employed Sonny Bono (of **Sonny and Cher**) in A&R; the label signed **Sam Cooke**, but lost him when it refused to allow him to move to **pop** from gospel.

Spector, Phil (Harvey Philip, b. 1940). A troubled genius whose first hit was the 1958 "To Know Him Is to Love Him" by his group the Teddy Bears, Spector was mentored by the **Brill Building** team of **Jerry Lieber and Mike Stoller** before he began writing his own songs and developed the highly orchestrated recording technique known as the "Wall of Sound." Spector became the Svengali-esque producer of various artists, notably the **Ronettes**, the **Righteous Brothers**, and the **Crystals**, and also co-founded his own label, **Philles** Records. Spector was inducted into the Rock and Roll Hall of Fame in 1989. See also Chapter 3.

Spencer Davis Group featuring Stevie Winwood (1963–1967). Spencer Davis (b. 1941), guitar/harmonica/vocals; Stevie Winwood (b. 1948), vocals/keyboards/organ; Muff Winwood (b. 1943), bass; Peter York (b. 1942), drums. British invasion group fronted by the then fifteen-year-old Stevie Winwood, known for bluesy hits like "I'm a Man" and "Gimme Some Lovin'" (both released in 1967). See also Chapter 5.

Springfield, Dusty (Mary Isabel Catherine Bernadette O'Brien, 1939–1999). The most soulful British diva of all, Springfield had already achieved **folk** success singing with the Springfields, whose 1962 release "Silver Threads and Golden Needles" had gone into the U.S. Top 20. The next year, she began a solo career after becoming infatuated with **Motown** and American **soul** and immediately entered the Top 10 with her debut single, "I Only Want to Be With You," followed by "All Cried Out," "Stay Awhile," and the

Burt Bacharach and Hal David composition "Wishin' and Hopin'." In 1965, Springfield hosted a British TV show devoted to Motown, introducing the artists she loved to a mass English audience. Her signature hit, "You Don't Have to Say You Love Me," made the U.S. Top 5 the following year. Springfield was inducted into the Rock and Roll Hall of Fame in 1999. See also Chapter 3.

The Standells (1962–1983). Dick Dodd (b. 1943), drums/vocals; Larry Tamblyn (b. 1943), organ; Tony Valentino (b. 1941), guitar; John Fleck*, bass. One-hit-wonder **garage-rock** band famed for "Dirty Water" (1966). See also Chapter 9.

Stanley, Owsley (b. 1935). Augustus Owsley Stanley III, known as "Bear" to the denizens of San Francisco's Haight-Ashbury district, became the first underground chemist to supply high-quality LSD to the public. Stanley created up to 10 million doses of LSD, some of which went to the Merry Pranksters for their 1966 "Acid Tests"; he bankrolled the fledgling Grateful Dead and also worked as the group's soundman, a position he took again after being released from prison on a 1967 drug conviction.

Stavers, Gloria (1926–1983). The editor and photographer for *16* magazine was the first woman in charge of a **rock/pop** magazine and became the most powerful image maker for the 1960s pubescent set. See also Chapter 6.

Stax-Volt Records. A soul/R&B record label and studio located in Memphis, Tennessee, where **Booker T. and the MGs** were the house band. **Otis Redding** recorded here, as did **Sam and Dave** and other artists overseen by Atlantic's **Jerry Wexler**. See also Chapter 2.

Stewart, Ian "Stu" (1938–1985). The "sixth" **Rolling Stone**, Stewart was booted out of the official lineup by **Andrew Loog Oldham** because his looks did not fit the band's guitar-based, youthfully scruffy image. Stewart still stayed on for decades with the band as pianist, road manager, and overall grounding influence. When the Stones were inducted into the Rock and Roll Hall of Fame in January 1989, Mick Jagger's acceptance speech paid tribute to Stewart, as well as co-founder Brian Jones. See also Chapter 4.

Strong, Barrett (b. 1941). Strong's 1960 hit "Money (That's What I Want)," co-written with **Motown** founder **Berry Gordy Jr.**, provided much of the capital that got the fledgling label off the ground. The song hit No. 2 on the **R&B** charts and just missed making the **pop** Top 20, but was covered by the **Beatles** on their debut album. Strong later co-wrote hits such as **Marvin Gaye's** "I Heard It through the Grapevine," "Papa Was a Rolling Stone" for the **Temptations**, and "War" (Edwin Starr). See also Chapter 2.

Sullivan, Ed (1902–1974). This former newspaper columnist and host of an eponymous Sunday-evening variety show on CBS-TV (1948–1971) provided mainstream mass-media exposure to **Elvis Presley**, the **Beatles**, and many other musical artists. See also Chapter 6.

The Supremes (1961–1977). Diana Ross (Diane Ross, b. 1944); Florence Ballard (1943-1976); Mary Wilson (b. 1944). "Where Did Our Love Go?" (1964) was just the first No. 1 hit for this **Motown** act, the top female African American group of the 1960s; they notched up another four consecutive No. 1 singles during 1964 and 1965 ("Baby Love," "Stop! In the Name of Love," "Come See about Me," and "Back in My Arms Again"), all written and produced by the team of **Holland-Dozier-Holland**. The group was inducted into the Rock and Roll Hall of Fame in 1988. See also Chapter 2.

Surf. A genre of music created by and for those interested in the sport of surfing that was characterized by Fender guitars and "wet" reverb, and centered in Southern California. Its best-known proponents include **Dick Dale**, **Jan and Dean**, and the **Beach Boys**. See also Chapter 7.

Sutcliffe, Stuart (1940–1962). Sutcliffe was a talented painter, the original bass player for the **Beatles**, and a close friend of **John Lennon**; he died tragically young in Hamburg, where he had moved after falling in love with a photographer during the Beatles' first tours there. See also Chapter 4.

Swan. A small Philadelphia-based **R&B** record label founded in 1957, Swan is noted for its early distribution of the first **Beatles** singles before **Capitol** exercised its option, among them "She Loves You," backed with "I'll Get You" (Swan 4152), which came out in September 1963 and hit No. 1 in January 1964. See also **Vee-Jay**; Chapter 4.

The Swinging Blue Jeans (1959–1968). Ray Ennis (b. 1942), guitar; Les Braid (b. 1941), bass; Norman Kuhkle (b. 1942), drums; Ralph Ellis (b. 1942), banjo. Liverpool-based **skiffle** unit best known for the 1964 hit "Hippy Hippy Shake" (No. 24), which was covered to better effect by the **Beatles**. See also Chapter 4.

Talmy, Shel*. An American producer of British invasion acts such as the **Who**, the **Kinks**, the Small Faces, **Manfred Mann**, the Easybeats, **Chad & Jeremy**, Davy Jones (David Bowie, not the **Monkee**), and the Mannish Boys.

Tamla. A record label division of **Motown**. See also Chapter 2.

The Temptations (1961–1990s). Eddie Kendricks (1939–1992), tenor vocals; Otis Williams (b. 1941), tenor vocals; Paul Williams (1939–1971), baritone; Melvin Franklin (1942–1995), bass vocals; David Ruffin (1941–1991), tenor vocals. One of **Motown**'s most valuable assets, the Temptations (along with the **Miracles** and the **Four Tops**) all but defined male **R&B** vocal groups in the early and mid-'60s with smooth choreography and tight harmonies on hits like "The Way You Do the Things You Do" (1964), "My Girl" (1965), and "Get Ready," "Ain't Too Proud to Beg," and "(I Know) I'm Losing You" (all in

1966). The group was inducted into the Rock and Roll Hall of Fame in 1989. See also Chapter 2.

Thomas, Carla (b. 1942). This **Stax** artist, daughter of Rufus "Walking the Dog" Thomas, began her career by singing with her father; she also cut "Tramp" on a duet album with **Otis Redding** and had solo hits with 1961's "Gee Whiz (Look at His Eyes)" and "B-A-B-Y" in 1966. Her last album was released in 1971. See also Chapter 3.

The Tokens (1960–1971). Mitch Margo (b. 1947); Phil Margo (b. 1942); Hank Medress (b. 1938); Jay Siegel (b. 1939). Known for their 1960 No. 1 smash "The Lion Sleeps Tonight" (a remake of the **Weavers'** "Wimoweh," which itself was a rewritten traditional Zulu song), the Tokens also wrote and produced the hit "He's So Fine" for the **Chiffons**. See also Chapter 9.

The Troggs (1964–1990s). Reg Presley (Reginald Ball) (b. 1943), vocals/songwriting; Chris Britton (b. 1945), lead guitar; Peter Staples (b. 1944), bass; Ronnie Bond (1943–1992), drums. This group was generally more popular in its native England than in America, except for its 1966 No. 1 hit, the nasty-sounding "Wild Thing," a **garage-rock** classic memorably covered by Jimi Hendrix during his Monterey Pop Festival performance the following year. See also Chapter 9.

The Twist. See **Chubby Checker**; **Dance**; Chapter 9.

Unit 4+2 (1963–1967). Pete Moules (b. 1944), lead vocals; Tommy Moeller (b. 1945), songwriting/vocals/guitar; David Meikle (b. 1942), guitar; Russ Ballard (b. 1947), guitar; Rod Garwood (b. 1944), bass; Bob Henrit (b. 1944), drums. This group had a No. 28 hit with 1965's "Concrete and Clay" and never duplicated the feat. See also Chapter 9.

Vee, Bobby (Robert Thomas Velline, b. 1943). The **pop**-oriented Vee was originally part of a combo called the Shadows, which was called to fill in for his idol Buddy Holly "the day the music died" (i.e., after the plane crash that killed Holly, Ritchie Valens, and the Big Bopper). Although his first solo recording session was a few months later, Vee did not have a chart hit until 1960, with "Devil or Angel," followed by "Rubber Ball." His biggest hit, "Take Good Care of My Baby," spent three weeks in the top slot in 1961, and its follow-up ("Run to Him") barely missed making No. 1, but after his last Top 10 record ("The Night Has a Thousand Eyes" in 1962), his career faltered in the wake of the British invasion. See also Chapter 1.

Vee-Jay. An independent Chicago-based **R&B** record label, launched in 1953 by James and Vivian Carter Bracken, Vee-Jay was the most successful black-owned record company before **Motown**, mostly on the strength of its doo-wop groups, and was one of the first distributors of **Beatles** singles before **Capitol** exercised its option. "Please Please Me," backed with "Ask Me Why," was released in February 1963, making it the first Beatles record issued in America; "From Me to You," backed with "Thank You Girl," came out in May 1963, but **Del Shannon**'s cover caused confusion, and his was the version that initially made the Top 20. Other artists on Vee-Jay at different times included the **Four Seasons**, **Jimmy Reed**, and John Lee Hooker. See also **Swan**; Chapter 4.

The Velvet Underground (1965–1970). Nico (1938–1988), vocals; Lou Reed (b. 1942), vocals/guitar/songwriting; John Cale (b. 1942), bass/viola; Sterling Morrison (1942–1995), guitar; Maureen "Mo" or "Moe" Tucker (b. 1945), drums. As Roxy Music co-founder Brian Eno once noted, while this group's debut album (*The Velvet Underground and Nico*, aka "the banana cover") did not sell many copies, everyone who heard it went on to form a band. Its best-known songs include "Heroin" and "I'm Waiting for My Man." Maureen Tucker helped revolutionize the role of female musicians in rock music by her mere presence; the minimalist style of the White Stripes' Meg White is a direct descendant of Tucker's own. The group was inducted into the Rock and Roll Hall of Fame in 1996. See also Chapter 8.

The Ventures (1959–present). Don Wilson (b. 1933), guitar; Nokie Edwards (b. 1939), lead guitar; Bob Bogle (b. 1937), bass; Howie Johnson (b. 1937), drums (replaced in 1963 by Mel Taylor, 1933–1996). This Seattle instrumental group got a break when a local DJ played its **surf**-styled "Walk Don't Run" after each news bulletin; upon national release in 1960, it became a million-selling No. 2 single. Three years later, the album *The Ventures Play Telstar/The Lonely Bull* hit No. 3, while a reworked "Walk" also charted. The band made the U.S. Top 10 just once more (in 1969, with the theme to TV's *Hawaii 5–0*); however, it did become successful in Japan, where it continues to enjoy great popularity. See also Chapter 7.

Vietnam War. This conflict in Southeast Asia, whose heaviest U.S. engagement took place from 1961 to 1975, eventually cost almost 60,000 American and countless Vietnamese lives. Anger and sorrow over the war helped create the **antiwar** and **protest** genres of music.

Vincent, Gene (1935–1971). This rockabilly pioneer, whose biggest hit was 1956's "Be-Bop-A-Lula," was idolized by rockers including the **Beatles**. He was seriously injured in the 1960 car crash in England that killed **Eddie Cochran**. Vincent was inducted into the Rock and Roll Hall of Fame in 1998. See also Chapter 1.

Vinton, Bobby (Stanley Robert Vintulla, b. 1935). Basically a middle-of-the-road **pop** crooner, Vinton enjoyed a brief surge of popularity with teenage record buyers in the early 1960s. His best-known tunes include 1962's "Roses Are Red (My Love)," 1963's "Blue Velvet," later used as the theme song in a film by director David Lynch, and "Mr. Lonely" (1964). See also Chapter 1.

The Walker Brothers (1964–1967). John Maus (b. 1943); Scott Engel (b. 1944); Gary Leeds (b. 1944). They were not brothers, and their name was not Walker, but this vocal trio passed as British during the invasion with two Top 20 hits: a melodramatic ballad, "The Sun Ain't Gonna Shine Anymore" (1965), and the similarly brooding "Make It Easy on Yourself" (1966). Maus originally came from New York, Engel from Ohio, and Leeds from California, where the group originally formed before it moved to England. See also Chapter 9.

Warwick, Dionne (b. 1940). This **pop-soul** singer had a string of hits with tunes by **Burt Bacharach** and **Hal David**, such as "Don't Make Me Over" (1963) and "Anyone Who Had a Heart" and "Walk On By" (both 1964); her career continued through the late 1980s. She is also the aunt of '80s superstar Whitney Houston. See also Chapter 3.

Waters, Muddy (McKinley Morganfield, 1915–1983). A key figure in the musical education of such artists as the **Rolling Stones** and the **Yardbirds**, Waters grew up picking cotton on a Mississippi plantation. He learned harmonica as a child and guitar as a teenager and moved to Chicago in the early '40s, where he became a pioneer on electric guitar. His recordings from 1951 to 1960 virtually defined Chicago **blues**: "Got My Mojo Working," "Hoochie Coochi Man," "I Just Want to Make Love to You," "Mannish Boy," and "Rollin' Stone" (from which the British group borrowed its name). After Waters appeared at the 1960 Newport Folk Festival, his fame and acolytes increased exponentially. He was inducted into the Rock and Roll Hall of Fame in 1987. See also Chapter 4.

The Weavers (1948–1952). A traditional **folk** quartet that included **Pete Seeger**; its song "Wimoweh" later became a 1962 **pop** hit for the Tokens under the title "The Lion Sleeps Tonight." Additionally, Weaver Lee Hays (1914–1981) wrote a song with poet Carl Sandburg called "Wreck of the John B," later revised by the **Beach Boys** into the 1966 hit "Sloop John B," which was included on the seminal *Pet Sounds* album. See also **Antiwar**; **Folk**; **Protest**.

Wells, Mary (1943–1992). An R&B/pop singer best known for her sweet, sultry voice and songs like "The One Who Really Loves You" and "You Beat Me to the Punch" (both 1962), "Two Lovers" (1963), and "My Guy" (No. 1 in 1964), Wells was one of the original artists signed by **Motown** and was the most important female at the label until Diana Ross and the **Supremes** arrived. See also Chapter 3.

Wexler, Jerry (b. 1918). This **Atlantic** Records executive produced **Ray Charles**, **Sam and Dave**, Percy Sledge, **Wilson Pickett**, **Aretha Franklin**, and many other **soul/R&B** artists. He was inducted into the Rock and Roll Hall of Fame in 1987. See also Chapter 2.

Whitcomb, Ian (b. 1941). This eccentric performer (ukelele/vocals), a fan of English music-hall/vaudeville numbers, reached the Top 10 in 1965 with his heavy-breathing hit "You Turn Me On." See also Chapter 5.

The Who (1964–present). Pete Townshend (b. 1945) songwriting, guitar, vocals; Roger Daltrey (b. 1944), vocals; Keith Moon (1947–1978), drums; John Entwistle (1944–2002), bass. Although this **mod**-inspired **R&B/rock** band had only two singles reach the Top 100 during this volume's time frame ("Can't Explain" in 1965 and "My Generation" the following year), its ongoing influence is inestimable, particularly in regard to the instrumentalists, and it must be considered one of history's most passionate, visionary rock groups. The Who was inducted into the Rock and Roll Hall of Fame in 1990. See also Chapter 5.

Williams, Allan (b. 1930). Early manager of the **Beatles** and the author of *The Man Who Gave the Beatles Away*. See also Chapter 4.

Wilson, Brian. See the **Beach Boys**.

J. Frank Wilson and the Cavaliers (1955–1964). J. Frank Wilson (1941–1991), vocals/keyboards; Sid Holmes*, guitar; Lewis Elliott*, bass; Rob Zeller*, saxophone; Ray Smith*, drums. This group had a No. 2 "death-rock" hit in 1962 with a cover of Wayne Cochran's "Last Kiss." See also Chapter 9.

Wonder, Stevie (Steveland Judkins), b. 1950. Wonder, a blind singer, songwriter, and pianist, was only twelve when he cut his first record for **Motown**; in 1963, that record, "Fingertips, Part 2," became the first live recording to hit No. 1, on both the **pop** and **R&B** charts. He went on to a highly successful career and was inducted into the Rock and Roll Hall of Fame in 1989. See also Chapter 2.

Wray, Link (b. 1929). Eddie Cochran looked like the all-American boy next to the black-leather-jacketed Wray, whose stinging licks on the 1958 instrumental "Rumble" (he had given up singing after losing a lung to tuberculosis) influenced guitarists around the world, including the Who's Pete Townshend: "He is the king; if it hadn't been for Link Wray and 'Rumble,' I would have never picked up a guitar."[4] Wray's sole charting single in the time frame of this volume was "Jack the Ripper," recorded for **Swan** in 1963. See also Chapter 7.

The Yardbirds (1963–1968). Keith Relf (1943–1976), vocals; Jim McCarty (b. 1943), drums; Paul Samwell-Smith (b. 1943), bass, replaced by Jimmy Page (b. 1944) in mid-1966; Chris Dreja (b. 1945), rhythm guitar; Jeff Beck (b. 1944), guitar, until 1966; Eric Clapton (b. Eric Patrick Clapp, b. 1945), guitar, until 1965. Known primarily for its revolving, stunning array of superstar guitarists (Beck, Page, and Clapton), the Yardbirds were also highly important for their early fusion of **R&B** with **psychedelic rock**. The band was featured in the "Swinging London" film *Blow-Up* (1966). Its best-known songs include "For Your Love" and "Heart Full of Soul" (both Top 10 in 1965) and "Over Under Sideways Down" in 1966. The group was inducted into the Rock and Roll Hall of Fame in 1992. See also Chapter 5.

The Young Rascals. See the **Rascals.**

The Zombies (1962–1967). Colin Blunstone (b. 1945), vocals; Rod Argent (b. 1945), keyboards/songwriting; Chris White (b. 1943), bass/songwriting; Paul Atkinson (1946–2004), guitar; Hugh Grundy (b. 1945), drums. This British invasion band specialized in atmospheric songs like "She's Not There" (No. 2 in 1964) and "Tell Her No" (Top 10 in 1965). See also Chapter 5.

NOTES

1. Bill Holdship, "The Bobby Fuller Four," Rockabilly Hall of Fame, http://www .rockabillyhall.com/BobbyFuller.html.

2. Paul McCartney quoted in Brian Epstein, "A Cellarful of Noise," http://www .brianepstein.com/cellarful .html; also quoted by McCartney's spokesperson Geoff Baker in Kevin Core, "Jude Law to Play Beatles Manager," *Daily Post*, March 17, 2003, http://icliverpool.icnetwork.co.uk/0300whatson/newandreviews/page.cfm?objectid=12743 902&method=full&siteid=50061.

3. Quote attributed to Quant in Specialist Schools Trust (United Kingdom), "Design and Market Influences, Advanced Level Product Design: Textiles, Fashion Design Classics, Fashion Timeline & Fashion Designers," http://www.schoolsnetwork.org.uk/ content/articles/4521/designclassics.pdf.

4. Cub Koda, "Link Wray, Biography," AllMusicGuide, http://www.allmusic.com/cg/ amg.dll?p=amg&sql=11:58q8g4kttv6z~T1; also quoted on "Link Wray," Rockabilly Hall of Fame, http://www.rockabillyhall.com/LinkWray.html, and L. Kent Wolgamott, "Zoo Bar Ready to Rumble," *Lincoln* [Nebraska] *Journal Star*, August 7, 2005, http://www.journalstar.com/articles/2005/05/20/gz/doc428ce167c7cc6952132473.txt.

APPENDICES

List of Top-Selling Recordings, 1960–1966

These are the top-selling hits of the era from *Cash Box* magazine's year-end charts. The number before each title indicates its status; in some cases, lower-ranking records have been chosen to demonstrate where they ranked in the marketplace during the given time frame. Until 1963, there were separate charts for single-channel monaural (known as "mono") and stereo recordings; afterwards, all long-playing albums were released in the latter format. Mono albums are indicated by the symbol (M) and until 1963, stereo indicated by (S).

1960

1. *The Sound of Music*, Original Cast (Columbia) (M)
3. *Sold Out*, The Kingston Trio (Capitol) (M)
4. *Heavenly*, Johnny Mathis (Columbia) (M)
6. *Encore of Golden Hits*, The Platters (Mercury) (M)
8. *Elvis Is Back!*, Elvis Presley (RCA Victor) (M)

8. *Nice 'n' Easy*, Frank Sinatra (Capitol) (S)
9. *String Along*, The Kingston Trio (Capitol) (S)
12. *Here We Go Again!*, The Kingston Trio (Capitol) (S)
18. *Elvis Is Back!*, Elvis Presley (RCA Victor) (S)
20. *The Lord's Prayer*, The Mormon Tabernacle Choir (Columbia) (S)

1961

1. *Camelot*, Original Cast (Columbia) (M), and *Exodus*, Original Soundtrack (RCA Victor) (tie) (M)
4. *G.I. Blues*, Original Soundtrack/Elvis Presley (RCA Victor) (M)
10. *Encore of Golden Hits*, The Platters (Mercury) (M)
16. *Something for Everybody*, Elvis Presley (RCA Victor) (M)
21. *Genius + Soul = Jazz*, Ray Charles (Impulse) (M)

1. *The Sound of Music*, Original Cast (Columbia) (S)
2. *Exodus*, Original Soundtrack (RCA Victor) (S)
8. *G.I. Blues*, Original Soundtrack/Elvis Presley (RCA Victor) (S)
19. *Happy Times! Sing Along with Mitch*, Mitch Miller and the Gang (Columbia) (S)
21. *Last Date*, Lawrence Welk (Dot) (S)

1962

1. *West Side Story*, Original Soundtrack (Columbia) (M)
3. *Blue Hawaii*, Original Soundtrack/Elvis Presley (RCA Victor) (M)
4. *Joan Baez, Vol. 2*, Joan Baez (Vanguard) (M)
5. *Modern Sounds in Country and Western Music*, Ray Charles (ABC-Paramount) (M)
6. *Peter, Paul, and Mary*, Peter, Paul, and Mary (Warner Bros.) (M)

1. *West Side Story*, Original Soundtrack (Columbia) (S)
5. *Blue Hawaii*, Original Soundtrack/Elvis Presley (RCA Victor) (S)
8. *Modern Sounds in Country and Western Music*, Ray Charles (ABC-Paramount) (S)
11. *Peter, Paul, and Mary*, Peter, Paul, and Mary (Warner Bros.) (S)
20. *College Concert*, The Kingston Trio (Capitol) (S)

1963

1. *West Side Story*, Original Soundtrack (Columbia)
2. *Peter, Paul, and Mary*, Peter, Paul, and Mary (Warner Bros.)
3. *Movin'*, Peter, Paul, and Mary (Warner Bros.)
4. *Joan Baez in Concert*, Joan Baez (Vanguard)
8. *Pot Luck*, Original Soundtrack/Elvis Presley (RCA Victor)
11. *Bye Bye Birdie*, Original Soundtrack (RCA Victor)
15. *Roy Orbison's Greatest Hits*, Roy Orbison (Monument)
16. *Surfin' U.S.A.*, The Beach Boys (Capitol)
18. *#16*, The Kingston Trio (Capitol)
25. *James Brown Live at the Apollo*, James Brown (King)

1964

1. *Meet the Beatles*, The Beatles (Capitol)
5. *In the Wind*, Peter, Paul, and Mary (Warner Bros.)

8. *Peter, Paul, and Mary*, Peter, Paul, and Mary (Warner Bros.)
11. *Moving*, Peter, Paul, and Mary (Warner Bros.)
16. *Introducing . . . the Beatles*, The Beatles (Vee-Jay)
19. *Shut Down, Volume 2*, The Beach Boys (Capitol)
22. *Joan Baez in Concert*, Joan Baez (Vanguard)
23. *The Beatles' Second Album*, The Beatles (Capitol)
24. *Getz/Gilberto*, Stan Getz and Joao Gilberto (Verve)
25. *The Singing Nun*, Soeur Sourire (Philips)

1965

1. *Mary Poppins*, Original Soundtrack (Buena Vista)
4. *Where Did Our Love Go?*, The Supremes (Motown)
8. *Beatles '65*, The Beatles (Capitol)
9. *The Beach Boys in Concert*, The Beach Boys (Capitol)
12. *Bringing It All Back Home*, Bob Dylan (Columbia)
15. *The Rolling Stones Now!*, The Rolling Stones (London)
22. *On Tour*, Herman's Hermits (MGM)
23. *The Kingsmen in Person*, The Kingsmen (Wand)
24. *Beatles VI*, The Beatles (Capitol)
25. *Roustabout*, Original Soundtrack/Elvis Presley (RCA Victor)

1966

1. *The Sound of Music*, Original Soundtrack (RCA Victor)
6. *The Best of Herman's Hermits*, Herman's Hermits (MGM)
7. *The Best of the Animals*, The Animals (MGM)
8. *What Now My Love*, Herb Alpert and The Tijuana Brass (A&M)
12. *If You Can Believe Your Eyes and Ears*, The Mamas and the Papas (Dunhill)
13. *Big Hits (High Tide and Green Grass)*, The Rolling Stones (London)
16. *Rubber Soul*, The Beatles (Capitol)
18. *Greatest Hits*, The Dave Clark Five (Epic)
22. *Aftermath*, The Rolling Stones (London)
25. *Just Like Us!*, Paul Revere and the Raiders (Columbia)

List of Most Significant Rock Albums, 1960–1966

James Brown
Live at the Apollo
January 1963

Bob Dylan
The Freewheelin' Bob Dylan
May 1963

The Beach Boys
Surfer Girl
September 1963

The Beatles
With the Beatles
November 1963

Phil Spector and various artists
A Christmas Gift for You From Phil Spector
December 1963

The Rolling Stones
England's Newest Hitmakers
May 1964

The Beatles
A Hard Day's Night
July 1964

The Supremes
Where Did Our Love Go?
August 1964

The Rolling Stones
12×5
October 1964

The Beatles
Beatles for Sale
December 1964

The Kinks
Kinda Kinks
February 1965

Bob Dylan
Bringing It All Back Home
March 1965

The Byrds
Mr. Tambourine Man
June 1965

The Beatles
Help!
August 1965

Bob Dylan
Highway 61 Revisited
August 1965

The Rolling Stones
Out of Our Heads
August 1965

The Yardbirds
Having a Rave-up
November 1965

The Beatles
Rubber Soul
December 1965

The Who
My Generation
December 1965

The Beach Boys
Pet Sounds
May 1966

Bob Dylan
Blonde on Blonde
May 1966

The Rolling Stones
Aftermath
June 1966

The Byrds
Fifth Dimension
July 1966

The Beatles
Revolver
August 1966

REFERENCE GUIDE

PRINT

Aronowitz, Al. *Bob Dylan and the Beatles: Volume One of the Best of the Blacklisted Journalist.* New York: 1st Books Library, 2003.

Baird, Julia, with Geoffrey Guiliano. *John Lennon, My Brother: Memories of Growing Up Together* (paperback edition). New York: Jove Books, 1989.

Barnes, Richard. *The Who: Maximum R&B.* London: Plexus Publishing, 1996.

The Beatles. *The Beatles Anthology.* San Francisco: Chronicle Books, 2000.

"The Beatles: 40th Anniversary Collectors Edition." AMI Specials, 2004.

Bernstein, Sid (as told to Arthur Aaron). *It's Sid Bernstein Calling. . . .* Middle Village, NY: Jonathan David Publishers, 2002.

Best, Pete, and Patrick Doncaster. *Beatle! The Pete Best Story.* London: Plexus Publishing, 1985.

Bockris, Victor, and Gerard Malanga. *Uptight: The Velvet Underground Story.* New York: Omnibus Press, 1983.

Booth, Stanley. *Rythm [sic] Oil: A Journey through the Music of the American South.* New York: Vintage Books, 1991.

Braun, Michael. *Love Me Do! The Beatles' Progress.* London: Penguin, 1964.

Brown, James, with Bruce Tucker. *James Brown: The Godfather of Soul, an Autobiography.* New York: Thunder's Mouth Press, 1990.

Brown, Peter, and Steven Gaines. *The Love You Make: An Insider's Story of the Beatles.* New York: New American Library, 2002.

Bruce, Lenny. *How to Talk Dirty and Influence People: An Autobiography.* New York: Fireside Books, 1992.

Buskin, Richard. *Inside Tracks: A First-hand History of Popular Music from the World's Greatest Record Producers and Engineers.* New York: Spike/Avon, 1999.

Butler, Dougal, with Chris Trengove and Peter Lawrence. *Full Moon: The Amazing Rock and Roll Life of the Late Keith Moon*. New York: Morrow Quill Paperbacks, 1981.

Chapple, Steve, and Reebee Garafalo. *Rock 'n' Roll is Here to Pay: The History and Politics of the Music Industry*. Chicago: Nelson-Hall, 1977.

Charles, Ray, with David Ritz. *Brother Ray: Ray Charles' Own Story*. New York: Da Capo Press/Perseus, 2003.

Coleman, Ray. *The Man Who Made the Beatles: An Intimate Biography of Brian Epstein*. New York: McGraw-Hill, 1989.

Cooper, Michael (photographs), and Terry Southern (text). *The Early Stones: Legendary Photographs of a Band in the Making, 1963–1973*. New York: Hyperion, 1992.

Dalley, Robert. *Surfin' Guitars*. Ann Arbor, MI: Popular Culture Ink, 1996.

Dalton, David, ed. *The Rolling Stones: An Unauthorized Biography in Words, Photographs, and Music*. New York: Amsco Music Publishing Co., 1972.

Dannen, Fredric. *Hit Men*. New York: Vintage/Random House, 1991.

Davies, Hunter. *The Beatles: The Authorized Biography*. New York: McGraw-Hill, 1968.

———. *The Quarrymen*. New York: Omnibus Press, 2001.

Davis, Andy. *The Beatles Files*. London: Metro/Salamander Books, 2000.

DeCurtis, Anthony, and James Henke with Holly George-Warren, eds. *The Rolling Stone Illustrated History of Rock & Roll*, 3rd ed. New York: Rolling Stone Press/Random House, 1992.

Des Barres, Pamela. *Rock Bottom: Dark Moments in Music Babylon*. New York: St. Martin's Press, 1996.

Dylan, Bob. *Chronicles*. Vol. 1. New York: Simon & Schuster, 2004.

Dyson, Michael Eric. *Mercy, Mercy Me: The Arts, Loves, and Demons of Marvin Gaye*. Philadelphia: Basic Civitas Books/Perseus Books, 2004.

Faithfull, Marianne, with David Dalton. *Faithfull: An Autobiography*. New York: Little, Brown, 1994.

Fletcher, Tony. *Moon: The Life and Death of a Rock Legend*. New York: Spike/Avon, 1999.

Flippo, Chet. *Yesterday: The Unauthorized Biography of Paul McCartney*. New York: Doubleday, 1988.

Fong-Torres, Ben, Elvis Mitchell, Dave Marsh, and Berry Gordy. *The Motown Album: The Sound of Young America*. New York: St. Martin's Press, 1990.

Friedan, Betty. *The Feminine Mystique*. New York: W. W. Norton & Co., 1963.

Gaines, Steven. *Heroes and Villains: The True Story of the Beach Boys*. New York: New American Library, 1986.

George-Warren, Holly, ed. *Zagat Survey Music Guide: 1,000 Top Albums of All Time*. New York: Zagat Survey, 2003.

Giuliano, Geoffrey. *The Lost Beatles Interviews*. New York: Dutton, 1994.

Gordy, Berry. *To Be Loved: The Music, the Magic, the Memories of Motown: An Autobiography*. New York: Warner Books, 1995.

Guralnick, Peter. *Sweet Soul Music: Rhythm and Blues and the Southern Dream of Freedom*. New York: HarperCollins, 1986.

Guthrie, Woody, edited by Robert Shelton. *Born to Win*. New York: Macmillan Publishing Co., 1966.

Hammond, John, with Irving Townsend. *On Record: An Autobiography*. New York: Summit Books, 1977.

Harry, Bill. *The Encyclopedia of Beatles People*. London, England: Blandford Books, 1997.

———. *The Ultimate Beatles Encyclopedia*. New York: Hyperion, 1992.

Havens, Richie, with Fred Davidowitz. *They Can't Hide Us Anymore*. New York: William Morrow and Co., 1999.

Hertsgaard, Mark. *A Day in the Life: The Music and Artistry of the Beatles*. New York: Delta, 1995.

"Immortals: The Fifty Greatest Artists of All Time." *Rolling Stone*, no. 946 (April 15, 2004): cover.

"Inside the Beatles 1964 U.S. Tour." *Mojo*, September 2004.

"It Was 40 Years Ago Today!" *Rolling Stone*, no. 942 (February 19, 2004): cover.

Jancik, Wayne, and Tad Lathrop. *Cult Rockers*. New York: Fireside/Simon & Schuster, 1995.

"John Lennon: The Beatles and Beyond." *NME Originals* 1, no. 10 (2003).

Jones, Dylan, ed. *Meaty Beaty Big & Bouncy! Classic Rock & Pop Writing from Elvis to Oasis*. London: Hodder & Staughton, 1996.

Kane, Larry. *Ticket to Ride: Inside the Beatles' 1964 Tour that Changed the World*. Philadelphia: Running Press/Perseus, 2003.

"The Kinks." *Uncut*, September 2004.

Kooper, Al, with Ben Edmonds. *Backstage Passes: Rock 'n' Roll Life in the Sixties*. New York: Stein and Day, 1977.

Lennon, John. *John Lennon in his Own Write*. New York: Simon & Schuster, 2000.

Levy, Shawn. *Ready, Steady, Go! The Smashing Rise and Giddy Fall of Swinging London*. New York: Doubleday, 2002.

Lewisohn, Mark, and George Martin. *The Complete Beatles Chronicle*. New York: Harmony Books, 1992.

Life, editors of. *From Yesterday to Today: The Beatles*. Boston: Bulfinch Press, 1996.

May, Chris, and Tim Phillips. *British Beat*. London: Socion/Sociopack Publications, 1974.

McCartney, Peter Michael. *The Macs: Mike McCartney's Family Album*. New York: Delilah Books, 1981.

Miles, Barry. *Many Years from Now*. New York: Henry Holt and Company, 1997.

Miller, Jim, ed. *The Rolling Stone Illustrated History of Rock and Roll*. New York: Rolling Stone Press/Random House, 1976.

"MOD." *Uncut presents NME Originals* 2, no. 2 (2005).

Nash, Alanna. *The Colonel: The Extraordinary Story of Colonel Tom Parker and Elvis Presley*. New York: Simon & Schuster, 2003.

Norman, Philip. *Shout! The Beatles in Their Generation*. New York: Simon & Schuster, 1981.

Oldham, Andrew Loog. *Stoned: A Memoir of London in the 1960s*. New York: St. Martin's Press, 2000.

———. *2Stoned*. London: Vintage/Random House, 2003.

"1000 Days of Beatlemania." *Mojo*, 2004.

Pareles, Jon, and Patricia Romanowski, eds. *The Rolling Stone Encyclopedia of Rock and Roll*. New York: Summit/Simon & Schuster, 1983.

Pawlowski, Gareth L. *How They Became the Beatles: A Definitive History of the Early Years, 1960–1964*. New York: E. P. Dutton, 1989.

Philips, John, with Jim Jerome. *Papa John: An Autobiography*. New York: Dell, 1986.

Pritchard, David, and Alan Lysaght. *The Beatles, An Oral History*. New York: Hyperion, 1998.

Ravan, Genya. *Lollipop Lounge: Memoirs of a Rock and Roll Refugee*. New York: Billboard Books, 2004.

Rees, Dafydd, and Luke Crampton. *Rock Stars Encyclopedia*. New York: DK Publishing, 1999.

Reisfeld, Randi, and Danny Fields. *Who's Your Fave Rave?* New York: Boulevard/ Berkley, 1997.

Riley, Tim. *Tell Me Why: The Beatles: Album by Album, Song by Song, the Sixties and After*. New York: Da Capo Press/Perseus, 2002.

Ritz, David. *Divided Soul: The Life of Marvin Gaye*. New York: Da Capo Press/Perseus, 2003.

Rolling Stone, editors of. *The Rolling Stone Interviews: Talking with the Legends of Rock and Roll, 1967–1980*. New York: Rolling Stone/Straight Arrow Publishers/ St. Martin's Press, 1981.

"Rolling Stones, 40th Anniversary Collectors' Edition." *Mojo*, 2004.

Ryan, Thomas. *American Hit Radio: A History of Popular Singles from 1995 to the Present*. New York: Prima Publishing/Random House, 1996.

Salewicz, Chris. *Mick and Keith*. London: Orion, 2001.

Savage, Jon. *The Kinks: The Official Biography*. London: Faber & Faber, 1984.

Shapiro, Harry. *Alexis Korner: The Biography*. London: Bloomsbury Publishing PLC, 1996.

Shotton, Pete, and Nicholas Schaffner. *The Beatles, Lennon, and Me*. New York: Stein and Day, 1984.

Somach, Denny, Kathleen Somach, and Kevin Gunn. *Ticket to Ride (A Celebration of the Beatles, Based on the Hit Radio Show)*. New York: William Morrow, 1989.

Sounes, Howard. *Down The Highway: The Life of Bob Dylan*. New York: Doubleday, 2001.

Spector, Ronnie, with Vince Waldron. *Be My Baby: How I Survived Mascara, Miniskirts, and Madness or My Life as a Fabulous Ronette*. New York: Harmony Books, 1990.

Steinberg, Cobbett. *TV Facts*. New York: Facts on File Publications, 1985.

Stewart, Tony, ed. *Cool Cats: 25 Years of Rock 'n' Roll Style*. New York: Delilah Books, 1982.

Strodder, Chris. *Swingin' Chicks of the '60s*. San Rafael, CA: Cedco Publishing, 2000.

Taylor, Alistair. *With the Beatles*. London: John Blake Publishing, 2003.

"20 LPs That Shook The World." *Record Collector*, February 2004.

Unterberger, Richie. *Urban Spacemen and Wayfaring Strangers: Overlooked Innovators and Eccentric Visionaries of '60s Rock*. San Francisco: Backbeat Books, 2000.

Weinberg, Max, with Robert Santelli. *The Big Beat: Conversations with Rock's Great Drummers*. New York: Contemporary Books/McGraw-Hill, 1984.

Whitburn, Joel, ed. *The Billboard Book of Top 40 Albums: The Complete Chart Guide to Every Album in the Top 40 since 1955*. 3rd ed. New York: BPI Communications, 1995.

White, Timothy. *The Nearest Faraway Place: Brian Wilson, the Beach Boys, and the Southern California Experience*. New York: Henry Holt, 1994.

"The Who: The Inside Story." *Mojo*, special limited edition, 2004.

Williams, Allan, and William Marshall. *The Man Who Gave the Beatles Away*. New York: Ballantine Books/Random House, 1975.

Wooldridge, Max. *Rock 'n' Roll London*. London: New Holland Publishers, 2002.

Wyman, Bill. *Rolling with the Stones*. New York: DK Publishing, 2002.
Wyman, Bill, with Ray Coleman. *Bill Wyman, Stone Alone: The Story of a Rock 'n' Roll Band*. London: Viking, 1990.

Any given issue of *Mojo* magazine usually has a wealth of material regarding music from this era.

WEB SITES

AMG/All Music Guide. http://www.allmusic.com/.
    From All Media Guide, part of Alliance Entertainment Corporation, with biographies of various artists by different writers.

Beatles-discography-com. http://www.beatles-discography.com/.
    List of recordings, by author Craig Cross.

Beatles Fandom Directory. http://www.beatlefan.com/directory.html.
    With links to Beatles sites, regularly scheduled radio shows, memorabilia dealers, conventions, tours, fan magazine subscriptions, etc.

Beatles Internet Resource Guide. http://www.beatlelinks.net/links/.
    Including links to reference material, sheet music, memorabilia dealers, and fan sites.

Beatles Ultimate Database. http://www.geocities.com/SunsetStrip/Frontrow/4853/main menu.html.
    With links to many interviews and photos of the band.

The Bill Graham Foundation: Biography. http://www.billgrahamfoundation.org/about.html.

Bob Dylan.com. http://www.bobdylan.com/index.html.

Booker T. Jones.com. http://www.bookert.com/main/.
    The official site of Booker T. Jones (Booker T. and the MGs).

British Beat Boom 1963–1966. http://www.lights.com/publisher/bi/.
    Including British record charts, articles from *Mersey Beat* and other periodicals of the day.

British Invasion. http://encyclopedia.thefreedictionary.com/British%20Invasion.
    A free encyclopedia with links to biographical material.

Britmania. http://www.geocities.com/fabgear5/britmania.html.
    Featuring "the best British bands of the Sixties."

Cash Box Top Singles. http://members.aol.com/_ht_a/randypny/cashbox/60s.html.
    Charts from 1950–1996.

Dick Dale's Official World Wide Web Site. www.dickdale.com.

Dusty Springfield: Woman of Repute. http://www.isd.net/mbayly/intro.htm.

The Fugs. http://www.thefugs.com/home.html.

Gene Pitney.com. http://www.gene-pitney.com/.

George Harrison.com. http://www.georgeharrison.com/.

Georgemartinmusic. http://www.georgemartinmusic.com/. The Beatles' producer.

Girl Groups. http://www.girl-groups.com/history.htm.

Hippies on the Web. http://www.rockument.com/links.html.
    A page of links to various psychedelic/Haight-Ashbury pages.

James Brown, the Godfather of Soul. http://www.godfatherofsoul.com/.

John Lennon. http://www.johnlennon.com

The Kinks Preservation Society. http://www.kinks.org/home.htm.

Lemelson Center Invention Features: From Frying Pan to Flying V: The Rise of the
    Electric Guitar. http://invention.smithsonian.org/centerpieces/guitars/.
    A "virtual exhibition" by the Smithsonian Museum.

Lovin' Spoonful. http://www.lovinspoonful.com/.

Martin Lewis Columns. http://www.martinlewis.com/column.pl?cat=beatles.
    A collection of various articles on the Beatles written by group historian Mar-
    tin Lewis.

MBE: The Official Brian Epstein Web Site. http://www.brianepstein.com/.

Museum of Music. http://www.museumofmusic.org/index.html.

My Generation. http://www.my-generation.org.uk/.
    "Unashamedly promoting the best of the UK's 60s music today."

National Academy of Recording Arts & Sciences (Grammys). http://www.grammy
    .com/.

New Music Express (British music weekly). http://www.nme.com/index.htm.

The Official Barry Mann and Cynthia Weil Web Site. http://www.mann-weil.com.

The Official Mike Bloomfield Web Site. http://www.mikebloomfield.com/.

The Official Web site of Billy J. Kramer. http://www.billyjkramer.com/.

One Hit Wonder Central. http://www.onehitwondercentral.com/60s.cfm.

Paul McCartney Site. http://www.paulmccartney.com/main.html.

Pete Best, Beatle. http://www.petebest.com/.
    Former Beatle.

Premature Deaths of Rock Stars. http://www.av1611.org/rockdead.html.

Ray Charles.com, The Official Site. http://www.raycharles.com/.

The Recording Industry Association of America. http://www.riaa.org/.
    The RIAA awards gold/platinum records and keep track of sales.

Ringo Starr.com. http://www.ringostarr.com/.

The Rock and Roll Hall of Fame. http://rockhall.com/.

Rock & Roll Library. http://www.rocklibrary.com/.

Rockmine. http://www.rockmine.music.co.uk/Rockmn.html.
  "Europe's largest independent rock music archive," with articles, artwork, audio interviews, and links.

Rock's Backpages. http://www.rocksbackpages.com.
  Subscription site containing library archives of previously-published articles.

Rolling Stone Magazine. http://www.rollingstone.com.

Rolling Stones Newsletter Online. http://www.beggarsbanquetonline.com/.

Sixties Pop. http://www.sixtiespop.com/.
  Includes current interviews with stars from this volume's timeframe.

Sixties Rock. http://www.sixtiesrock.com/index.html.
  An affliate of Amazon Books with a list of books and articles relating to the era.

Sixties Timeline. http://www.gfsnet.org/msweb/sixties/sixtiestimeline/sixtiestimeline.htm.

Surf-O-Rama. http://www.penetrators.com/surf.html.
  Links to sites about surfing and the related music genre.

Swingin' Chicks of the Sixties. http://www.swinginchicks.com/.
  Also available as a book.

Tim Buckley. http://www.timbuckley.com/.

Top 100 Songs, 1960–1969. http://top40.about.com/cs/60shits/.

VH-1. http://www.vh1.com.

MUSEUMS OR SPECIAL COLLECTIONS

Archives of African American Music and Culture (at Indiana University)
Smith Research Center, Suites 180–181
2805 East Tenth Street
Bloomington, IN 47408-2601
Phone: (812) 855-8547
Fax: (812) 855-8545
E-mail: afamarch@indiana.edu
http://www.indiana.edu/~aaamc/index2.html

Beatles Story Exhibition
Britannia Vaults, Albert Dock
Liverpool L3 4AD, England
Phone: 0151 709 1963 (if calling from overseas, add prefix: 440)
E-mail: info@beatlesstory.com
http://www.beatlesstory.com/

Blues & Legends Hall of Fame and Museum
1021 Casino Center Drive

Robinsonville, MS 38664
Curator's Office:
107 South Front Street, Suite 43
Memphis, TN 38103
Phone: (901) 521-0086, (866) 618-0088
Fax: (901) 521-0087
http://www.bluesmuseum.org/

The Boston Rock & Roll Museum/New England Music Hall of Fame
1684 Commonwealth Avenue
Newton, MA 02465
http://www.dirtywater.com/

Experience Music Project (on the Seattle Center Campus)
325 Fifth Avenue North
Seattle, WA 98109
Mailing address:
EMP Headquarters
330 Sixth Avenue North, Suite 100
Seattle, WA 98109
Phone: (206) 367-5483, (877) 367-5483
Fax: (206) 770-2727
http://www.emplive.com/

Fender Museum of Music and the Arts (Fender guitars)
365 North Main Street
Corona, CA 92880
Phone: (951) 735-2440
Fax: (951) 735-2576
http://www.fendermuseum.com/

Govinda Gallery (rock photography)
1227 34th Street NW
Washington, D.C. 20007
Phone: (202) 333-1180
Fax: (202) 625-0440
http://www.govindagallery.com/

Graceland
Elvis Presley Enterprises
P.O. Box 16508
3734 Elvis Presley Boulevard
Memphis, TN 38186-0508
Phone: (901) 332-3322, (800) 238-2000
TTY: (901) 344-3146
E-mail (for tours): http://www.elvis.com/contact/graceland_tour_form.asp
http://www.elvis.com/graceland/default.asp

Memphis Rock & Soul Museum (inside the Gibson Guitar Factory)
145 Lt. George W. Lee Avenue
Memphis, TN 38103

Phone: (901) 543-0800
http://www.memphisrocknsoul.org

Motown Historical Museum
2648 W. Grand Boulevard
Detroit, MI 48208
Phone: (313) 875-2264
Fax: (313) 875-2267
E-mail: info@motownmuseum.com
http://www.motownmuseum.com/

Museum of Television and Radio
25 West 52nd Street
New York, NY 10019
Phone: (212) 621-6800
Also:
Museum of Television and Radio
465 North Beverly Drive
Beverly Hills, CA 90210
http://www.mtr.org/

Rock and Roll Hall of Fame and Museum
One Key Plaza
Cleveland, OH 44114
http://rockhall.com

Rock-a-billy Hall of Fame and Museum
105 North Church Street
Jackson, TN 38301
Phone: (731) 427-6262
E-mail: rock@rockabillyhall.org

Stax Museum of American Soul Music
926 East McLemore Avenue
Memphis, TN 38106
Phone: (901) 942-7685, (888) 942-7685
Fax: (901) 507-1463
http://www.soulsvilleusa.com/

Tours of Liverpool by bus or taxi (sometimes guided by a person who once knew or worked with the Beatles) as well as links to hotels and other information, may be found at http://www.liveapool.com/ and http://www.cavern-liverpool.co.uk/mmt/contentoftours.htm, among other sites.

FILMS

In chronological order:

The T.A.M.I. Show. Directed by Steve Binder. Electronovision, 1965. Time capsule of some of the era's most popular artists, including the Beach Boys, Jan and Dean, James Brown, and the Rolling Stones.

Beach Boys: An American Band. Directed by Malcolm Leo. 1985.

John Hammond: From Bessie Smith to Bruce Springsteen. Directed by Hart Perry. CMV Home Video, 1990.
> This tribute to the revolutionary talent scout features some of the artists he worked with, including Bob Dylan.

Shindig Presents: British Invasion, Vols. 1 and 2 (1964); Groovy Gals (1964); Sixties Superstars; Motor City Magic; The Kinks. WEA/Rhino, 1991–1993. VHS cassettes.
> Episodes of the TV series, edited to specific artists or categories.

Brian Wilson: I Just Wasn't Made for These Times. Directed by Don Was. 1995. DVD set, Lionsgate/Fox, 2002.
> The first disc is an overview of the group made during the 1980s, although it does cover previous history and includes studio outtakes, an unreleased 1967 concert in Hawaii; TV appearances, and interview footage from the mid-1970s. The latter film focuses on Wilson as the troubled artist continues his ongoing struggle to maintain a semblance of productivity and sanity.

The Beatles, The First U.S. Visit. Directed by Kathy Dougherty and Albert Maysles. MPI Home Video, 1998.
> This documentary, shot by the Maysles brothers (Albert and David) during the Fab Four's first visit to the United States in 1964 for appearances on the *Ed Sullivan Show*, offers the only glimpse inside the maelstrom of Beatlemania in its infancy. The DVD includes previously unseen footage, and commentary from director Albert Maysles.

Dont [sic] Look Back. Directed by D. A. Pennebaker. New Video, 1999.
> This 1964 documentary is what it was like to be a fly on the wall during Bob Dylan's epochal tour of England just as his career was taking off. (DVD, collector's edition, with commentary from Pennebaker and Dylan tour manager, Bob Neuwirth.)

Hullabaloo, Vols. 1–4 (1964), Vols. 5–8 (1965), and Vols. 9–12 (1965). MPI Home Video, 2001–2002. DVD.
> Episodes of the two primetime U.S. TV series dedicated to rock and pop in the mid-1960s.

Ed Sullivan's Rock 'n' Roll Classics. Rhino Home Video, 2002. Boxed set of DVDs.
> A plethora of artists from the era, edited into specific categories.

Standing in the Shadows of Motown. Directed by Paul Justman. Artisan Home Entertainment, 2002.
> The story of Motown's inhouse studio band, the Funk Brothers, and the creation of those memorable hits.

Ray. Directed by Taylor Hackford. Universal Studios, 2003.
> This Hollywood biopic about the late Ray Charles features an Oscar-winning titular performance by Jamie Foxx.

Bob Dylan—No Direction Home. Directed by Martin Scorsese. Paramount Home Video, 2005.
> Including the following Bob Dylan performances: "Blowin' in the Wind," "Girl of the North Country," "Man of Constant Sorrow," "Mr. Tambourine

Man," "Love Minus Zero/No Limit," "Like a Rolling Stone," "One Too Many Mornings." Other features include an unused promotion spot for "Positively 4th Street" and "I Can't Leave Her Behind."

Fictionalized Films

The films listed here may or may not currently be available on video cassette or DVD.

Expresso Bongo. Directed by Val Guest. Kino Video, 1960.
> Evocative black-and-white look at early starmaking machinery and subsequent exploitation set in London's Soho coffeebar scene, starring Sir Cliff Richard.

Good Times. Directed by William Friedkin. American Broadcasting Companies Inc./Anchor Bay Entertainment, 1967.
> The only film starring Sonny and Cher together.

Stardust. Directed by Michael Apted. 1974.
> A sequel of sorts to *That'll Be the Day*, this film again starrs real-life musicians, including Adam Faith, Dave Edmunds, and Keith Moon.

American Hot Wax. Directed by Floyd Mutrux. Paramount, 1978.
> The fictionalized rise and fall of the "payola" scandal deejay Alan Freed, with musical appearances by the real Chuck Berry, Jerry Lee Lewis, and Screamin' Jay Hawkins.

Absolute Beginners. Directed by Julian Temple. MGM DVD, 1986.
> A fanciful, somewhat surreal musical adaptation of Colin MacInnes' novel about life in late 1950s London as a young photographer becomes involved with a pop promoter. Director Julian Temple cast David Bowie and Ray Davies of the Kinks in minor roles.

The Hours and Times. Directed by Christopher Münch. Artistic License Films, Fox Lorber Home Video, 1991.
> A little-seen black-and-white speculation about what really happened during a famous 1963 Spanish holiday taken by John Lennon and Brian Epstein. Ian Hart, as Lennon, is so eerily evocative of the young Beatle that he reprised the role in *Backbeat*.

Backbeat. Directed by Iain Softley. Focus Films, Universal DVD, 1994.
> A dramatized account of the Beatles' days in Hamburg and Stu Sutcliffe's doomed romance with photographer Astrid Kirchherr, who documented the group's formative era. (The collector's edition has an interview with Kirchherr.)

Head. Directed by Bob Rafelson. Rhino Home Video, 1994.
> A 1968 semipsychedelic mishmash starring the Monkees, with bizarre cameos from Frank Zappa, Annette Funicello, boxer Sonny Liston, Rita Hayworth, Dennis Hopper, and Jack Nicholson (who wrote the script); the music is by Carole King and Harry Nilsson.

Help! Directed by Richard Lester. MPI Home Video, 1997.
> Nowhere near as inventive or as influential as *A Hard Day's Night*, this 1965 film is necessary nonetheless, because it stars the Beatles.

Grace of My Heart. Directed by Allison Anders. Universal DVD, 1999.

Set during the days of the Brill Building, this film dramatizes the story of a female singer-songwriter who may or may not have been inspired by a real-life individual (Carole King).

The Idolmaker. Directed by Taylor Hackford. DVD MGM Home Entertainment, 2000.

1980 film based on the life of manager-promoter Bob Marucci, who discovered Frankie Avalon and Fabian, among others, this film is a harshly realistic look at what it took, or takes, to create a teen sensation.

That'll Be the Day. Directed by Claude Whatham. Anchor Bay, 2000.

A 1973 grittily downbeat look at mid-1960s rock wannabes with the genius casting of real life rockers in dramatic roles, including Ringo Starr, Billy Fury, and the Who's Keith Moon.

A Hard Day's Night. Directed by Richard Lester. Miramax/Buena Vista Home Entertainment, 2002.

Supposedly a day in the life of the Beatles, this 1964 classic was made on a shoestring to squeeze cash out of what executives thought was a short-lived pop phenomenon. Instead, the black-and-white romp perfectly showcases the group's wit, charm, and exuberance. It is a toss-up as to whether this film or the Bob Dylan and D. A. Pennebaker collaboration *Dont Look Back*, was the forerunner of rock video: the Beatles' musical numbers here could be clipped, shown outside of context, and still work as performance pieces. In the latter film, Dylan performs "Subterranean Homesick Blues" in a stand-alone, somewhat surreal segment.

That Thing You Do! Directed by Tom Hanks. 20th Century Fox Home Entertainment, 2002.

This charming 1996 evocation of pop dreams lived out by a small-town band in 1964 captures the feel of the era.

A Mighty Wind. Directed by Christopher Guest. Warner Home Video DVD, 2003.

Clever spoof of the mid-'60s folk-singing craze.

Tom Dowd and the Language of Music. Directed by Mark Moorman. 2003.

Dowd was still a teenager when he worked on the Manhattan Project (the creation of the atomic bomb); he became Atlantic Records' top engineer and producer, working with almost every artist on the label, including Ray Charles, Aretha Franklin, and the Young Rascals. Features appearances by Charles, Franklin, and Otis Redding. This film is a capsule history of recorded music since Edison first captured sound.

I Wanna Hold Your Hand. Directed by Robert Zemeckis. DVD Universal, 2004.

1978 film in which four young girls who are obsessed with the Beatles try to crash the Ed Sullivan Theatre to attend the band's first appearance.

Beatles historian Martin Lewis holds an annual Mods and Rockers Film Festival, featuring films of and about the '60s era and special guests, in the Los Angeles area. For more information, see the Web site, http://www.modsandrockers.com/main.html.

INDEX

About the Author

RHONDA MARKOWITZ is a rock journalist, freelance author, editor, and producer, and has writtten for VH-1, *Spin Magazine*, and People.com.